LANGUAGE AND SOCIETY IN
ANGLO-IRISH LITERATURE

Language and Society in Anglo-Irish Literature

A. C. Partridge

GILL AND MACMILLAN

BARNES & NOBLE BOOKS
Totowa, New Jersey

First published in Ireland 1984 by
Gill and Macmillan Ltd
Goldenbridge
Dublin 8
with associated companies in
Auckland, Dallas, Delhi, Hong Kong,
Johannesburg, Lagos, London, Manzini,
Melbourne, Nairobi, New York, Singapore,
Tokyo, Washington
© A. C. Partridge, 1984

7171 1360 4
First published in the USA 1984 by
Barnes & Noble Books
81 Adams Drive
Totowa, New Jersey, 07512
ISBN: 0-389-20494-3

Library of Congress Cataloging in Publication Data

Partridge, A. C. (Astley Cooper)
    Language and Society in Anglo-Irish Literature.

    Bibliography: p. 360
    1. English Literature — Irish Authors — History and Criticism.   2. Ireland in
Literature.   3. Ireland — Civilization.   4. English Language — Ireland.   5. Irish
Philology.   6. Celts — Ireland.   I. Title.
PR8718 1984.   820'.9'9415   84-11122
ISBN 0-389-20494-3

Print origination in Ireland by Galaxy Reproductions Ltd.
Printed and bound in Great Britain by
Biddles Ltd, Guildford and King's Lynn

To my wife

Acknowledgments

Author and publishers express their thanks for permission to use copyright material as follows: Selections from 'Respectable People' and 'A Jocular Retort' from *The Collected Poems* of Austin Clarke, Dolmen Press © 1974. Oliver St John Gogarty, 'To the Liffey with the Swans', by permission of Oliver D. Gogarty, and of Devin Adair Publishers of Greenwich, C.T.; copyright © by Oliver St John Gogarty 1954, renewed 1982. An extract from Douglas Hyde, 'The Lament of Queen Maev', by permission of D. H. Sealy. An extract from AE (George Russell), 'On behalf of some Irishmen not followers of tradition' by permission of A. M. Heath & Co. An extract from Seán O'Faoláin, 'At St Patrick's Purgatory' by permission of Seán O'Faoláin, and taken from *The Silver Branch* by Seán O'Faoláin; copyright 1938, renewed copyright © 1965 by Seán O'Faoláin. Reprinted by permission of Viking Penguin Inc. Selections from W. B. Yeats's 'To Ireland in the coming times' and 'September 1913' by permission of Michael Yeats and Macmillan London Ltd; reprinted with permission of Macmillan Publishing Company from W. B. Yeats, *The Poems*, edited by Richard J. Finneran; copyright 1916 by Macmillan Publishing Co., Inc., renewed 1944 by Bertha Georgie Yeats. An extract from James Stephens, 'The Centaur' by permission of the Society of Authors on behalf of the copyright owner, Mrs Iris Wise; reprinted with permission of Macmillan Publishing Company from *Collected Poems* by James Stephens; copyright 1915 by Macmillan Publishing Co., Inc., renewed 1943 by James Stephens. Selections from Frank O'Connor, 'The Reverie', 'I shall not die' and 'On the death of his wife' reprinted by permission of A. D. Peters & Co. Ltd; reprinted also by permission of Joan Daves, copyright © 1959. An extract from Padraic Colum, 'The Drover' in *The Poets' Circuits* (1981). Due acknowledgement is made to the Estate of Padraic Colum and The Dolmen Press, Portlaoise, Ireland.

The publishers have made every effort to trace copyright holders, but if they have inadvertently overlooked any, they will be pleased to make the necessary arrangements at the first opportunity.

Contents

The Celt has at last reached his horizon.
There is no shore beyond. He knows it.
This has been the burden of his song since
Malvina led the blind Oisín to his grave
by the sea. . . . The Celt falls, but his
spirit rises in the heart and the brain
of the Anglo-Celtic peoples.

E. Renan

The Irish had the choice between imagination
and intellect, and they chose imagination.

Frank O'Connor

Preface

The Celtic substratum to British and Irish culture presents the political observer with two imponderables which ought to be reconcilable — the ill-defined nature of the Celtic spirit and the periodic resurgence of Celtic nationalism.

In the sixteenth and seventeenth centuries writers as enlightened as Camden seem to have regarded the Celts as bare-footed savages; and the English handling of the Irish peasantry, from Henry II to Oliver Cromwell, can be explained only by the credence given to such generalisations. Edmund Spenser, who lived and worked among the Irish from 1580 until his death in 1599, spoke of their brutishness, unclean-liness and 'rebellious disposition'. Dr Johnson, refuting the authenticity of Macpherson's *Ossian* in *A Journey to the Western Islands* (1775), described the Erse language (meaning Scots Gaelic) as 'the rude speech of a barbarous people, who had few thoughts to express'; though he recanted later by conceding that 'Welsh and Irish are cultivated tongues'.

Renaissance writers were apparently ignorant of the tradition that Celtic speakers had been in touch with Medi-terranean culture for several thousand years, during the early part of which nature-worship had been their universal religion. Under Christianity, *Ge*, the earth-mother, was, according to J. M. Bailey, supplanted by the Virgin Mary. In *The God Kings and the Titans* (Hodder and Stoughton, 1973) he suggests that 'the Irish cross was a sun-symbol preceding Christianity', and that the Celtic god *Lug* of so many place-names was none other than Apollo of the Greek and eastern mythologies. The Irish legendary hero, Cú Chulainn, whose ultimate triumph was to conquer the Atlantic, could not have accomplished his destiny had he been other than of super-natural origin.

The romantic movement in England was due in part to the influence of Celtic literature, and to the interest aroused by

Bishop Percy's translation of P. H. Mallet's *Northern Anti-quities* (1770). This work was the principal source of Blake's ideas in the Prophetic Books, begun in 1804, another being Edward Davies's *Celtic Researches* published in the same year. Blake's Celto-Biblical symbolism in turn stimulated W. B. Yeats, who knew no Gaelic, but who perceived the essence of the Celtic spirit in Irish literature. In *Ideas of Good and Evil* ('The Celtic Element in Literature') Yeats appraised Malory's *Morte d'Arthur*, the *Mabinogion*, even the works of Wagner and William Morris, as genuine expressions of that Celtic spirit, created from the indigenous ingredients of Gaelic legends. He characterised this spirit as the love of nature for its own sake, a feeling for magic, and a melancholy 'mistaking of dreams for realities', notions he seems to have borrowed from Ernest Renan's *Poetry of the Celtic Races*.

Celtic *nationalism*, on the other hand, was founded on political realities which do not suggest brooding imagination or vague melancholy. In *John Bull's Other Island* Shaw, in fact, demonstrated that the Gaelic mentality, after the Great Famine of the mid-nineteenth century, became coldly logical and devoid of purposeless sentiment. The Irish temperament (he argued) had by the twentieth century acquired the merit of 'freedom from illusion, the power of facing facts, the nervous industry, the sharpened wits, the sensitive pride of the imaginative man who has fought his way up through social persecution and poverty' (*Prefaces*, 1934, p. 440). Shaw's encomium saw the modern Irishman as a dissenter — the product of Danish, Norman, Cromwellian and Scottish invasions, and essentially a republican. But nationalism, Shaw finally decided, was a curse, poised between patriotism and political enlightenment. He said, with Shavian assurance, that 'A healthy nation is as unconscious of its nationality as a healthy man of his bones' (p. 455).

Consciousness of nationality is thought to have arisen during the Crusades, when rival armies, speaking different languages, were gathered in the Holy Land under their respective rulers. Panegyrics of the bards, using vernacular languages, stimulated local pride; and the spirit of nation-hood acquired official status when writers of standing began to produce sagas, epics and ballads, such as the *Chanson de Roland, Le Cid, Nebelungenlied, Mabinogion* and *Edda*.

There is nothing in the history of the Middle Ages to suggest, however, that rulers thought of granting rights to nationalities, as such. Celtic peoples usually respected most the genealogies of ruling families, who were vassals of the king. In England families were especially powerful in the Marches of the Welsh frontier and on the Scottish border. Feudalism took shape among such families in order to suppress any popular or nationalistic movements. Rulers were proud of their ability to govern different national elements in the same state. For peaceful co-existence was a cardinal principle of freedom in the Middle Ages, a condition under which civilisation ought to advance the welfare of inferior races. To fertilise unity of ideas among peoples of differing origin was the exacting discipline of the Roman and Christian worlds and the principal instrument of racial tolerance.

Modern ideas regarding the self-determination of nations were indubitably the product of nineteenth-century liberalism. A passage in W. B. Yeats's 'J. M. Synge and the Ireland of his Time' (1910), published in *The Cutting of an Agate*, expresses the changed situation admirably:

> A zealous Irishman, especially if he lives much out of Ireland, spends his time in a never-ending argument about Oliver Cromwell, the Danes, the penal laws, the Rebellion of 1798, the famine, the Irish peasant, and ends by substituting a traditional casuistry for the country . . .

The idea of this study came to me on literary tours of Ireland undertaken in the late sixties and early seventies, and was renewed when I attended the PEN Jubilee Congress at Dún Laoghaire in 1971. A shadowy figure in our family history had been an Irishman, named John McIlwain Moore, who became godfather to my uncle, and furnished our book shelves with three of the popular novels of Charles Lever. Interest in Irish literature was further aroused when the late Thomas Rice Henn of Sligo became my supervisor at Cambridge University in 1933-34, and urged me to enjoy the plays of Yeats and Synge. When I taught at the University of Alberta in the Summer School of 1971, Ronald Ayling presented me with a collection of essays he had compiled from the writings of Sean O'Casey; and my pleasure in Irish fiction was finally increased by the writings of my friend, Professor John Cronin, of Queen's University, Belfast.

My purpose has been, not to attempt a literary history of Ireland, for which several volumes would be desirable, but to examine the kind of thinking and writing that makes the Irish way of life memorable. Any judgement unrelated to the country's troubled history would, I fear, miss that quality of 'Irishness' which undoubtedly exists. There are many facets to this, other than the religious, fabulous, tragic and comic, that need to be noticed in order to reach a better understanding of the Gael and his aspirations.

If several admirable writers, such as Goldsmith, Sheridan and Wilde, have received merely passing mention, this is not because they spent most of their working life in London; a better reason is that they contributed less to the image of the Celt that gives to Irish literature its unique flavour.

Ireland of the last three centuries justly occupies a major part of this survey, whose concern is to evaluate propensities, rather than discuss works of art. From the evidence presented, much of value, besides realism and romance, was contributed to English literature from Anglo-Irish sources. Poetry and fiction were deeply enriched by the cultural and psychological impact of Yeats, Joyce and Beckett. To the rebirth of the Celtic spirit through fable and the stage we owe the many new forms of expression that it has been the object of this essay to explore.

Thanks are due to the Librarian of the University of the Witwatersrand, Professor Reuben Musiker, and to his staff, especially Mesdames Bronstein, Cowley and Moss. Without the courteous services of Inter-library Loans and of Mr James Winter of the Johannesburg City Library, in obtaining primary and secondary sources, this study would hardly have been feasible. But my deepest debt is to my wife, who typed the manuscript and helped with the indexing. Her assistance is gratefully acknowledged in the dedication.

Johannesburg, September, 1983   A. C. Partridge

I

Celts in Ireland

As early as the Bronze Age, Ireland was known to possess deposits of copper in Munster and gold in the region of the Liffey. It was a country of craftsmen, in which the bronze sword was in use by the seventh century BC. Irish designers, working under the La Tène influence, were responsible for some of the finest Celtic decorative art. Though inspired by Etruscan and Greek technologists, this art achieved an aesthetic value essentially Irish. It was aristocratic in taste, and reached a peak in book illustration during the early Christian era, which began in the fifth century AD.

Archaeologists hold that the integration of peoples in Ireland occupied the greater part of a millennium, and that the earlier neolithic successions were not very different from those that occurred in Britain. But it is important to know why Irish Bronze-Age culture was more active in the northeast than the south; Ulster has always had the more vigorous industries. One reason is that Ulster has better harbours, as well as fertile and arable soil in the hinterland. Bronze-Age pottery of this area was of a food-vessel, lowland type, indicating relationship with a similar culture in England; for the shortest and most convenient sea-crossings to Ulster are from England and Scotland.

The Iberian traders in metals, however, sailed from northwestern Spain or France, and landed in the Irish river-estuaries of the south, bringing their megalithic culture, which spread throughout the country. Ogham stone inscriptions are confined to Munster in southern Ireland; but no memorials record immigrations during the Iron Age, which in Ireland date from 300 BC to AD 450. Elsewhere such migrations were the result of Roman expansion in the Continental Celtic areas. The evidence of Celtic incursions rests on material culture and the composition of different population elements, noticeable by the first century AD.

Pytheas in 325 BC was the first to give Ireland its name; five centuries later Ptolemy called the people *Iverni*. Unfortunately, the latter's account of Ireland was based on the (now lost) work of Marinus of Tyre, who wrote in the early part of the second century BC; is was therefore three hundred years out of date.

Since Ireland was a swampy country, many groups of Iron-Age inhabitants sought security by living on *crannogs*, which were artificial islands created in the shallow water of lakes. Their thatched, timber houses were circular, and erected on stone foundations. The Celts were largely cattle-farmers, freemen in a stratified society, with a pagan religion highly conscious of genealogy and magic. They invented legendary ancestors, some of whom lived two thousand years before their own time. The ritual was elaborate, sacrifices being offered to persuade the magic powers to respond with good fortune, while myths served to placate the tribal gods; many of these were associated with Indo-Germanic forebears.

Some pagan feasts of the Irish druids survived into Christian times. The seasonal festivals celebrated the turning points of the lunar year in a pastoral community. First came *Samain*, New Year's day, which fell on the first of November, when the grazing season ended. The cattle were then herded together for breeding or for slaughter. To ensure fertility and renewal of the tribe's prosperity, this feast began on the previous evening, in the belief that the supernatural forces of the world were liberated on Old Year's night. The god propitiated was Dagdá ('guardian' and 'doer of good'), whose consort was *Morrigain*, goddess of nature, identified with the demon-queen, Morgan la Fey. Deities had different names among different tribes, *Maeve* being the commonest for Morrígain, whose symbol was a mare.

The winter festival *Imbolc* (which became the Christian feast of St Brigit) was celebrated on 1 February; *Beltine* was on 1 May, and *Lugnasad* on 1 August. The last was devoted to the rites of Lug, a god introduced by Gaulish tribesmen in the first century AD, whose office was to safeguard the maturing of the harvest. Among Celtic peoples the calendar was reckoned in nights, not days, a relic of the system surviving in the Anglo-Saxon term, 'fortnight'. The *filid*, Ireland's 'learned men' or 'seers', did not belong solely to the druid class. Knowledge was regarded as inspiration from visionary powers, induced by a state of trance; the idea appears in mythological tales and throughout Irish literature, as late as W. B. Yeats.

Irish tradition acknowledged that there were several waves of Celtic immigration, but all were Goidels, who sprang from an ancient ancestor. Yet by the first century AD there was clear evidence of two dialects, Brittonic and Goidelic. The older settlers gave the name *Goidels* to the newcomers, whose language was regarded as an archaic form of their own. The Celts of Ulster must have emanated from northern Britain, which included the lowlands of Scotland. Elsewhere in Ireland it is most likely that the early Brittonic speakers came from south-west England, Wales and Brittany, while the first Goidels, between 100 and 50 BC, came from Gaul, probably via Britain. The direct influx from Gaul took place after St Patrick's mission in the middle of the fifth century AD. The heroic age of the Irish epics (or Táin stories) is placed by T. F. O'Rahilly between 50 BC and AD 50; but more recent authorities, such as Kenneth Jackson, prefer the fourth century AD, arguing that the rule of the royal dynasties could not have arisen before the third century.

The proto-historic period of Ireland, which depends on oral traditions, covers the seven hundred years 200 BC to AD 500. In this time history was mingled with bardic mythology. Most scholars believe that the heroes of the epics are composite figures, and that the bardic tales contain a good deal of lively propaganda. One source of evidence is the *Lebor Gabála*, the Book of Conquest, a collection of legends dating from the sixth to the twelfth centuries; they claim that the Irish people came originally from Spain, under their leader Partholón, on the feast of Beltine. The Irish epics depict an aristocratic warrior society not unlike that of *Beowulf*, in which the focus of life is the festive hall built of timber. Halls like Tara, belonging to the royal house of the

Cruachain, were surrounded by hill fortifications.

T. F. O'Rahilly in *Early Irish History and Mythology* (pp. 15-17) divides the early Celts in Ireland into four groups:

1. The Cruthin, or Pretani, differing little from the Brittonic-speaking peoples who settled in northern Britain.
2. The Builg, known in Ireland as the *Firbolg* or *Erainn (Iverni)*, who were of the same stock as the Belgae of southern England.
3. The Lagin, two of whose tribes, the *Domnainn* and *Galioin*, overcame the Erainn and settled in Leinster, south of the Liffey. Their original home was in Armorica (Brittany), but they later provided themselves with fictitious Goidel pedigrees.
4. The Goidels or Q-Celts, who came from southern Gaul, soon after Caesar's conquest (about 50 BC). There is no evidence that these Goidels sailed directly from Gaul until St Patrick's time.

On Ptolemy's antiquated map, showing the inhabitants of Ireland, all must have been Brittonic-speaking, because tribal names have the characteristic consonant *p*, where Goidelic would have *q*, e.g. in Mana*p*ii. In other words, the final two of the above groups had not yet arrived.

About the Cruthins little is known, except that they lived in Antrim and the western part of County Down; the name fell into disuse in the eighth century AD. One group of the Cruthin was known as *Dál nRaidi*, a name which links them with the Picts who lived north of the Clyde-Forth line of the Antonine Wall in Scotland. The name *Pict* has no ethnic authenticity and was probably a slang term of the Romans in the third century AD. Race mythology in Ireland gave out that the Pretani who visited their shores were diverted by the local inhabitants to settle in Scotland and northern England; the theory arose from Bede's untrustworthy account of the Picts in Book I, chapter 1 of *The Ecclesiastical History of the English Nation*. Another group, who inhabited the eastern part of County Down, the *Ulaid*, gave their name to the province of Ulster. In the Ulaidian Cycle of legends their legendary king, Conchobar, ruled in Emain, near Armagh.

The first element of *Firbolg* means 'man' (cf Latin *vir*); the second element (originally *builg*) signifies 'the god of light-ning'. Legend has it that the Erainn invaders or Firbolg came to Ireland under Nemed mac Agnomain, a Mediterranean ancestor of the Britons, who died on an island in Cork harbour. Nemed was a fictitious figure, whose death near Cork was designed to associate the Erainn with Munster. The historical Erainn, who were at the height of their power before 300 BC, must have spread throughout Ireland, but were defeated in Leinster and the west country by the Laginian invaders. O'Rahilly calls the southern dialect of the Brittonic-speaking Erainn 'Invernic'.

The Lagin people, who reached Ireland in the third cen-tury BC, gave their name to the province of Leinster. They established themselves in the west of Ireland by overcoming the Firbolg and compelling the defeated to find refuge in the western islands of Scotland. They were able soldiers, who served as mercenaries to the kings of Tara. The Laginian sub-group, the Domnainn, seem to have originated in Devon, but some part of them was turned away from Leinster to settle in Ayr, Renfrew and Lanark in Scotland. The names Domnainn and Galioin fell into disuse when their social status declined, upon their becoming vassals of the Goidels. The Laginians, as a whole, sought to rehabilitate themselves with the newcomers by finding a spurious Goidel ancestor.

The ethnic situation in mid-Ireland (Leinster and Connacht) was at this time very mixed. O'Rahilly believes it was virtually impossible for genealogists to distinguish the various P-Celt elements, Cruthin, Bolgic and Laginian (op. cit. p. 98). The Irish national movement can therefore be dated from the invasion of the Goidels about 50 BC, under the legendary leader, Tuathal Techtmar. *Tuathal* means 'ruler of the people' or simply the community itself and *Techtmar* means 'journey-ing from afar'. A poem of eighty-three quatrains, composed by Mael Mura of Othian about AD 885, describes Tuathal's conquest of the Brittonic peoples. Though the account has fictitious details, the historicity of the expedition is not in doubt. It landed successfully on the north-east coast of Leinster and made the Laginians and remnants of the western Erainn vassal peoples who were compelled to pay tribute. Tuathal established himself as King of Tara, and created for his followers a territory in the Midlands by appropriating land from four contiguous counties. This settlement was called *Mide* ('the middle district'), from which is derived the name 'Meath'. The tribute imposed continued to be reluctantly paid until the eighth century.

Important political changes attributed to Tuathal must have taken much more than a generation to implement. Indeed, the conquest of all Ireland was not complete until the fifth century. Genealogical mythologists, bent on national harmony, sought to show that every pre-Christian king had a common Irish ancestry, and that Tuathal was an exile returning to assert his rights from usurpers. He was claimed as the descendant of *Míl Espáne* (Latin *Miles Hispaniae*) 'soldier of Spain', and his followers became the Sons of Míl, whose wife's name *Scotta* is simply the Latin for 'Irishwoman'. *Scotti* being wrongly believed to be related to *Scythi*, the country of origin of the Goidels was actually held to be Scythia.

Legend records that there was another landing of the Goidel invaders in the south, at the mouth of the Kenmare river in County Kerry, led by Mug Nuadat; this expedition was apparently unopposed, and the forces advanced across the River Shannon into western Ireland. *Conn* and *Eógan* being ancestral gods of the Goidels, the followers of the leaders became known in Ireland as *Connachta* and *Eóganachta* respectively, the former being the source of the name of the province of Connacht.

The Goidel dynasty of Irish kings, founded by Tuathal, lasted for six centuries. Their symbol was the goddess Medb of Tara, though the seat of rule was in Cruachain. Some of the epic tales recount the pseudo-history of provincial kings, whose enmity and conflicts provide a lively picture of Celtic life in this barbarous age. As the tales are traditional, they are anonymous, and usually in prose; the best are preserved in three principal manuscript collections of the eighth to the twelfth centuries: The Book of the Dun Cow, the Yellow Book of Lecan and Rawlinson B502. The characters are fictional, and much of the legend is connected with the seasonal festivals. Supernatural figures take a hand in human events, and imagination often takes the reader to the invisible Otherworld, an Elysium beyond the western sea. In this realm the joys of eating and loving were those principally esteemed. Tragic love is a dominant theme, and the virtues of courage, honour, loyalty and hospitality are extolled.

The smallest group of tales is the mythological, which includes 'The Wooing of Étaín' (a ninth-century text in three episodes). The hero is the god Midir, whose home is in the land of Promise. Étaín is wife to the King of Tara, and is supernaturally reborn as her own daughter, such complications being an intriguing aspect of Celtic romance. 'The Battle of Moytura', another tale in this group, is informative about the Irish pantheon; it describes a war against the race of giants (*Fomoiri*), who lived in Ireland before the coming of the first invaders, by *Tuatha Dé Danann* ('the tribe of the goddess Dána'). From this legend it is learnt that the principal god in prehistoric Ireland was Lug of the Long Arm, universally respected among the pre-Roman Celts. But there were subsidiary native deities, such as Manannán, Dagdá, besides gods of the crafts who presided over honest workmanship. Many of the pre-Goidelic deities were supposed to have taken refuge in the megalithic burial-mounds, for instance Dagdá at New Grange on the River Boyne, when the last conquerors overcame the Erainn and Laginian people. The daughter of Dagdá, Brigit, was also a tribal goddess of the Brigantes of northern England.

The best-known tales of Ireland are, however, in the Ulster Cycle, which belongs to the earlier half of the eighth century. These are legends of the Ulaid, concerning their 'endemic warfare' with the Connachta. It is characteristic of the Irish heroic age that the popular imagination should be caught by 'The Cattle-Raid of Cooley' (*Táin Bó Cualnge*), which concerns the theft by Queen Maeve's men of a bull belonging to King Conchobar of Ulster. The hero of this story was Cú Chulainn, who preferred a brave man's death to an inglorious obscurity. His tragedy compels the slaying in single combat of his foster-brother, implying the heart-felt clash of his duty, as soldier, and the loyalty of a kinsman. Another popular tale, which appears again in the Book of Leinster, is 'The Exile of the Sons of Uisliu'; it concerns the treachery of King Conchobar mac Nesa of the Ulaid, and the prophesied tragedy of Derdriu (the Deirdre of Celtic-inspired poetry), who is the daughter of a *file* or bard. Here the double theme is honour in love, and the disloyalty of a king who breaks his bond.

In the Cycle of Kings there is a story of 'Cano son of Gartnán', which is one source of the Tristan legend. Another celebrated figure of legend is Finn mac Cumaill of the Fenian Cycle, who appears in a number of ballads of *Duanaire Finn*, collected in the twelfth century. These relate the adventures of the *fiana*, or warrior-friends of the hero, as told by his son, the poet Oisín, from whom MacPherson borrowed for his *Ossian*, and whom Yeats revived in his early poetry of the Irish Literary Renaissance. Some of the ballads are in dialogue form, with the poet supposedly narrating his legend to St Patrick — a fictional licence. Finn, meaning 'white', is in no sense a tribal hero, but speaks, through Oisín, for Ireland as a whole; he is an unhistorical warrior-hunter, whose superhuman achievements suggests a divine descent. Such another was Cormac mac Airt, grandson of Conn, and hero of a hundred battles, who was credited with introducing the water-mill to Ireland. Tara, with its five radiating roads to the rest of Ireland, reached the height of its fame under Cormac's rule.

During the Roman occupation of Britain there seems to have been no movement of settlers from the Continent to Ireland. The historical period in Ireland begins shortly after the Roman departure, and is now taken to coincide with the arrival of Palladius in AD 431, whose Christianising achievements in Ireland have been widely confused with those of St Patrick. In the early Latin Annals of Ulster, which were compiled in the late fifteenth century by Mheg Uidhir (died 1498), AD 431 is the first date to appear. The much earlier Ulster Chronicle, on which the Annals depend, belongs to the seventh or eighth century, and was probably compiled in the monastery of Bangor. It shows obvious acquaintance with *Ecclesiastical History of the English Nation* (AD 725-31), since it uses Bede's Anno Domini system of dating. The legend of St Patrick is based entirely on two seventh-century sources, Muirchú's Life and the Tírechán's Memoir. He landed in Ireland in AD 432, visited Rome in 442, and died in 461; but not until twelve years after his arrival was he granted land in Armagh on which to build his church.

The transition from mythology to Irish history seems to have begun with Niall of the Nine Hostages, a warrior who led raiding expeditions on declining Roman Britain and Gaul, and was supposed to have been killed by lightning while abroad, about AD 405. Two of his sons headed dynasties in Donegal and Ulster, and claimed overlordship of the whole of Ireland.

Behind the mission of Palladius must be seen the visit of Rome's envoy to Britain in AD 429. As Palladius was Dean of Auxerre, he was well known to Germanus, and probably crossed from Britain to Ireland via south-west Wales. He was the founder of three churches in Wicklow, and did most of his missionary work in Leinster, the south and the Midlands. This is a principal reason why St Patrick confined his ministration to the north-east of Ireland. Even before Palladius, parts of the south and south-east coasts had probably been Christianised by British priests. D. A. Binchy in 'Patrick and his Biographers' (*Studia Hibernica*, vol. 2, (1962)) has shown that Irish loan-words from Latin, such as *Cresen* ('Christian') and *domhnach* ('church', Lat. *dominicum*) were in use before the advent of Palladius. At the time of the introduction of the monastic system to southern Ireland, monks had not yet appeared in the Church of England and Wales, and one theory is that the system was instigated by Christian emigrants from St Martin of Tours.

The cult of monasticism apparently initiated by St Martin was to some extent superseded by the more flexible and educative system of St Patrick. The virtues of this saint, which singularly fitted him for his role of Apostle, were human understanding and diplomacy. Muirchú's biography records that St Patrick's first diplomatic move was to visit the court of *Loegaire* (son of Niall) at Tara. Though this king was never converted, and Tara remained pagan until AD 565, most rulers were tolerant of the Christian movement. St Patrick's *Confession* makes it clear, however, that he was sub-jected to criticism and mockery of every description. The social and political conditions of rural Ireland were far from easy to modify according to Christian principles. There were no towns, and in the boggy interior of the country means of communication were rare. The religious structure of his small, fortified monastic establishments was dependent on the goodwill of tribal chieftains and kings, both exercising despotic powers.

As a Roman citizen, St Patrick believed in the hierarchical principle of the Catholic Church in Gaul, where some think he was trained. Having lived and served as a slave in Ireland in his youth, he knew the language and barbarous way of life, and wished to return and convert the pagan masters. Establishing himself in Armagh, only two miles west of Emain, he created four bishoprics, and put a trusted disciple in charge of each diocese. But the bishop, who was in charge of ritual, sacraments and ordination, played a lesser role in church affairs than the abbot who headed a monastery. The cornerstones of the religious community in Ireland became the ubiquitous monk and the hermit in his cell. Individualistic developments in the Celtic church of Ireland, for instance in fixing the date of Easter, may be ascribed to the severance of its connection with the Roman See after the fall of the capital to the barbarians.

St Patrick is credited with introducing the art of writing in roman letters about the middle of the fifth century. Among his reforms was the suppression of pagan divination, which broke the hold of druid priests over a superstitious people, while increasing the influence of the *filid* or learned bards, when they had mastered writing in Latin. Wisely, the monks did not interfere with the traditional poetry of panegyric, devoted to the praise of ancestors. St Patrick's loyal helpers were largely imported from Gaul and Britain. His unprecedented contribution to Irish culture was contact with Latin civilisation, which helped to humanise a ruthless aristocracy, and gradually brought a measure of literacy to the people.

The first royal personage to become a Christian was King Oengus of Cashel in AD 490. A generation after Patrick's death, a distinctive national church had been established, with an hereditary succession of abbots at the head of monasteries. Wherever there was a monastery, art and trade flourished, and the seeds of a township were sown. As the church waxed in influence, so the power of Tara waned. The last royal festival held there was in 559, though the title 'King of Tara' survived until AD 1170.

The earliest monastic seats of learning were Clonard and Moville, founded by different St Finnians in 520 and 540 respectively; there was another at Bangor in County Down, founded by St Comgall in AD 555. These monasteries were the birthplaces of Irish history and poetry, and gradually became important library centres. From reasons of policy, monastic orders stimulated the zeal for missionary work, and the ideal of the wandering scholar, who was to dominate learning in the Middle Ages. But at the same time a native restlessness was created, characteristic of the intelligent Irishman. By the seventh century AD, religious centres of learning in Ireland were in close association with leading monasteries in France, Switzerland, Italy and Germany. Chronicles were being written by clerics, but not always accurately dated; the age of history was about to be born. The studies of St Patrick, written by Muirchú and Tírechán in this century, were among the first attempts at chronological writing in Ireland.

The wise, learned and gentle St Finnian of Clonard was a greater scholar than St Patrick, and his monastery in Meath became a training school for religious teachers. The idea was to fit them for the task of founding similar institutions elsewhere. Some three thousand disciples passed through his hands, and the renowned Twelve Apostles of Ireland were judiciously selected from among them. Of the rest, it is said that none went away unrewarded. Among those honoured was Columcille, a man of aristocratic birth who became the notable St Columba of Iona. Part of this missionary's design was to minister to the permanent settlement of the Ulaid Irish on the coast of Argyll in Scotland. The reason for this emigration was the diminished influence of the Ulaid in Ulster, where the High Kingship in the north was centred upon the sons of Niall.

The Scots colony in Argyllshire, known as Dalriada, was headed by Fergus Mor, a descendant of Niall of the Nine Hostages; his sister, Erca, became the grandmother of Columcille, whose name means 'dove of the cell'. The second element of this name was added when the child demonstrated a devotion to the life of the church. Columcille, or *Columba*, was born in Donegal in AD 521, and became the foster-son of a priest, who ensured that he received an education befitting his aristocratic birth. While still young, Columba entered the services of the church and established a monastery at Derry in 546. A Celt of typical impetuosity, a scribe and a poet, he diligently sought biblical manuscripts to copy. One of the latter was the immediate cause of his departure from Ireland; the legend in the *Life*, written by Adamnán, ninth Abbot of Iona (AD 679-704), is the following:

St Finnian of Moville possessed a rare copy of the Mosaic Law, *Psalms* and four Gospels in Jerome's new Vulgate translation, which he jealously guarded. After the evening service, Columba used to conceal himself in the church and secretly copy this manuscript without the abbot's permission. When discovered, he claimed a humanist's right to keep the copy for study; but Diarmit, the first Christian king of Tara, ruled otherwise, under the Brehon Law. This imagined injustice was followed by another incident, in which the son of the King of Connacht sought sanctuary with Columba, having accidentally killed a follower of Diarmit's in a heated argument arising from a hurling match. The religious right of sanctuary was violated, and the offender put to death. Columba, in a rage, procured a large force from his royal kinsmen, and defeated an army of Diarmit's, with the loss of three thousand men. The church synod therupon compelled Columba to expiate this inhumanity by exile beyond sight of Ireland, that he might procure as many converts among the heathen as the men he had slain.

Columba was forty-two when he set sail from Derry, with twelve disciples and friends, in the spring of AD 563, the primary object being to forward his mission among the Picts of Caledonia. His was by no means the first pilgrimage there, since he was preceded by Saints Ninian, Brendan and Kentigern. He could not have found a more suitable retreat than Iona, only eighty miles from Ireland; here he built a church and laboured for the next thirty-four years of his life. The site of his monastery was thought to have been used for a temple of the druidic Moon Cult; but archaeological investigation has shown no signs of human life on the island before the arrival of St Columba. His monastery, which was a little north of the present buildings, eventually housed about one hundred and fifty monks and scholars. The first-comers planted corn, and are said to have existed on a broth made of nettles until they could import cattle and sheep, as well as oak-beams to build their monastery. They bred their own seals for winter clothing, using the oil as fuel for lighting.

Icolmkill (the Irish name for Iona) became holy ground for the Scottish converts whom Columba fathered; the first king of the Royal House of Scotland was crowned there in AD 574. Kings of Scotland were buried in Iona from AD 685 to the eleventh century, including Kenneth MacAlpin (860), Duncan (1040) and Macbeth (1057). The Irish shrine contained the remains of Cormac mac Airt, and two kings of Connacht, who became monks of Iona in the eighth century. From 1187 to 1228 Norse kings of the Isle of Man were interred in another shrine. But in AD 795 Norsemen attacked the island and killed the abbot and many of the monks. The raids were repeated in 802, 806 and 825, and with the decimation of the island population, the centre of the Columban church was moved to Kells in Ireland and Dunkeld in Scotland.

The Columban church developed distinctive characteristics, but functioned as a missionary and educational monastery, rather than a community of hermits. Students came from afar to learn the arts of its scriptorium. The day's work was divided into three labours: prayer, the monk's appointed menial task, and reading. No one was allowed to possess property of his own, and all had to be prepared to travel at short notice. Columba possessed a commanding presence and voice, and the discipline of this monastery was exemplary. One of his earliest tasks was to communicate personally with King Brude of the Picts (564). Being a skilful navigator, he travelled most of the way by water, and took with him wellspoken persons of Cruthin descent, who knew the Pictish language. Columba's undoubted gift, as Adamnán shows, was to allay pagan superstitions and subvert the authority of the druids; he gained the confidence and the friendship of Brude, without converting him, and was able to extend his influence in the Western Isles and the region of Loch Ness. His method was that of compromise and dignified example, without immediate radical change.

The Norse pirates who attacked Ireland for the first time in AD 795 were Norwegians from Rogaland, the region round the Stavanger Fjord; the principal reason for their incursions seems to have been shortage of food for the growing population. The seas they traversed demanded large, keeled galleys to enable the invaders to overcome the lighter Pictish vessels controlling the northern islands off the coast of Scotland. The Norsemen first took possession of the Hebrides and the Isle of Man, and governed them as a single kingdom in the ninth century. Their onslaught upon Ireland's west and east coasts and neighbouring holy places abruptly ended the Age of Saints.

The first foreign king, Thorgest, established himself in AD 839 and, styling himself the Abbot of Armagh, practised pagan incantations at the sacred altar of St Patrick. Limerick and Dublin became two of the most important Norse centres of operation, until the Norwegian power was halted by a Danish fleet and land army in 850. Northern Ireland then became a battle-ground between the *white* heathens (Norwegians) and the *black* heathens (Danes), so called because the latter wore dark, metal body-armour. The success of the Danes was short-lived, for two years later Olaf the White set up a dual Viking kingdom in Dublin, which became a busy centre for Norwegian shipping. He fortified the town on the site where the castle still stands.

The Vikings of Ireland did not remain as colonists, though most adopted Christianity, and many took wives from among the Irish. They were responsible for, and named, many of the present seaport towns, but this development was not to the advantage of the internal rural economy. Ireland was divided by feuds between the major kingdoms, such as Leinster and Meath, and handicapped by a lack of central government; it was not indeed until 980 that the Norwegians were successfully opposed by the kings of Meath and Munster. In 1002 the country was united for the first time under a national king, Brian mac Cenneidigh (Kennedy), or Brian Boru, but he unfortunately died at the Battle of Clontarf (1014) in his seventy-third year.

The intermarriage of Irish women and Viking invaders began at the aristocratic level, for political reasons; but by the mid-ninth century every social stratum was affected. Although not many brides entered into such unions voluntarily, the marriages were more acceptable if the husbands were Christians. Most Norsemen returned to their homeland, but many were assimilated to the Gaelic-speaking population; while Irish boys and girls were sometimes adopted by Norse families as foster-children. The occupation lasted for nearly two hundred years, and during this time the young Irish who changed their nationality or religion were called *Gall-Gaels* or 'foreign Irish'. The term *Gall*, originally applied to emigrants from Gaul, had by the ninth century come to mean an 'alien'.

The pinnacle of Irish civilisation was undoubtedly reached between AD 450 and 800. The reputation of the monasteries for learning and for the style of writing evolved in the Irish scriptoria was respected throughout Britain and Europe. Among the evangelists who founded monasteries or taught beyond the shores of Ireland, were the *sapientes* St Brendan, St Aidan, St Columbanus, St Gall and John Scotus; they travelled to countries as remote as Holland, France, Germany, Switzerland, Austria and Italy, and Celtic monasteries were maintained in such distant places as Bobbio and Taranto.

The noblest examples of Celtic book illumination are the Book of Durrow (*c*. AD 630), the Book of Kells (*c*. 760-820) and the Lindisfarne Gospels (*c*. 698), the first two being preserved in the Library of Trinity College, Dublin, the last in the British Library. The Trinity College books were products of almost antithetical monastic styles; but they agree in their curvilinear trumpet and spiral designs, the interlacing decorations being derived from metalwork of La Tène culture. The ecclesiastical iconography and symbolism must have been inspired by Byzantine, Syrian or Coptic craftsmen. Calligraphy is in typical Irish rounded uncials, of impeccable taste, with elaborate initial capitals. This style of penmanship was a cultural development of the ancient cursive, for which St Columba was largely responsible; it is recorded that he himself copied over three hundred manuscripts, one of which, the Cathach, is the earliest extant manuscript in Irish majuscule.

Durrow was a monastery in Meath founded by Columba before his exile; he was also, through St Aidan, the founder of the monastery on Lindisfarne in AD 635, with the result that many of its monks were sent to Ireland for training; there are many resemblances between the Book of Durrow and the Lindisfarne Gospels. In the scriptorium illuminators painstakingly designed colour-schemes and decorative pages, and may have had some training as goldsmiths or enamel-workers; but they had no hand in the preparation of the text, for calligraphy was a separate scribal art. The decorative panels of the Book of Durrow, with animal motifs, are thought to be of Germanic inspiration. How the various influences were acquired, cross-fertilised and assimilated is an unsolved problem, but the product implies a cultural traffic between the La Tène Celts and eastern Europe, Asia and North Africa. The dignified designs are full of imagination, and without trace of geometrically abstract formality.

The Book of Kells contains the four gospels, with loss of five pages and the coloured portrait of St John. Its chequered history suggests that it was begun in Iona late in the eighth century and transported for safety to Kells in AD 804, when the Vikings threatened to attack the island. An entry in the Annals of Ulster (AD 1007) says that it was later stolen from the sacristy for its gold decorations, but recovered months afterwards buried beneath some distant turf. This book was then prized for its reputed preservation of the holograph of St Columba; now it is treasured as probably the most magnificent illuminated volume in any culture. The baroque splendour, unique matching of colours, and asymmetrical conception are supremely Celtic and harmonious; yet four artists are thought to have taken a hand in the designs. Ornamental capitals adorn the beginning of every paragraph, and curious animal tracery enhances the beauty of each page. The exuberant iconography displays the fantasy of a graphic artist, whose imagination was at once Asiatic, African and modern.

Such ecclesiastical industry preserved texts in Latin, mostly borrowed from the Vulgate, and its design was to stimulate monastic pride in the possession of fine books. Celtic books used in western Britain and Ireland sometimes contain interesting relics of folklore, preserved in the Anglo-Saxon glosses of Hibernian Latin texts. Such a work is the *Lorica* of Gildas, written in a literary Latin dialect of the sixth century, though the extant manuscripts are of later date; one of the latter was associated with Aethelwald, ninth-century Bishop of Lichfield. *Loricas* are Christian prayers for protection, and have resemblances to pagan charms and leechdoms, in which a cloak to protect the superstitious from demons is sometimes mentioned.

The utilitarian *lorica* was a corselet, originally made of leather, later of chain-mail. In the Vulgate of Epistle to the Ephesians (VI.14), St Paul uses the phrase *loricam justitiae* symbolically; and the Irish Liber Hymnorum contains a prayer of St Patrick, known as 'The cry of the deer' (*fáeth fiada*), which revives the Psalmist's tradition of such a cloak in the Old Testament. The tunic is named a *byrne* in *Beowulf* 405-6. One exceptional value of the *Lorica* of Gildas is its rich alien vocabulary of anatomical terms, some borrowed from Hebrew or Arabic; in a single instance, the text was embedded in a monastic herbal.

In the seventh century literature in the native tongue, Irish Gaelic, was still the function of the bard or *file*, and the *ollamh*, or man of learning, who enjoyed the social status of a professor. Such a man was MacLiag of King Brian's court at Cashel in southern Ireland; he was the author of *The War of the Gael and the Gall*, recording the Irish struggle against the Norsemen. This work became a rallying point for all future attempts of the Irish to execrate foreign invaders. Only in the eleventh century did the Irish monasteries begin to cultivate the language of their countrymen, though Old Irish had appeared in writing as early as AD 650.

The characteristic nationalism of the Irish people was the product of their clans, family ties, religion, legends and Goidelic speech. Clan affiliations were an endless source of political rivalry and disunity, but a semi-feudal society was constrained by the Book of Rights and the Brehon Law to give freemen and intellectuals a stake in the community. The Book of Rights, drawn up about AD 900, aimed to regulate the succession to the High Kingship, nominally centred on Tara. This office, known as that of *ard rí*, could only be held by one of the provincial kings ruling in Leinster, Meath, Munster or Aileach (formerly Ulster). Each could compete, on equal terms, to become 'King of Erin', and receive (once only) the tribute due to the principal monarch. The Book was revised a century later, under the direction of King Brian, whose surname Boru means 'of the tribute', in order to abolish the vested rights of the descendants of Niall. In practice, the Book of Rights empowered the High King to maintain a national army, and arranged conditions under which subsidiary kings paid rents and tributes, or rewarded services in cattle, money, jewels, slaves or weapons. Only founders of a royal line were permitted to use the patronymic prefixes *O* (grandson) and *Mac* (son).

The *brehons* of Ireland, originally the 'lawgivers', were later to comprise legal experts, pleaders and judges, who decided penalties, and were allowed a share of the fines they imposed. There was a graduated scale of fines, known as *eric*, not unlike that of the Anglo-Saxons. For the aristocracy there was an 'honour price', half of which was forfeited if the dependant was deemed guilty of falsity, slander or betrayal. The Brehon Laws also called *Cáin Padraic*, were supposed to have been codified by St Patrick; their value is that the statute enshrines the social and intellectual traditions of Ireland, going back many centuries.

Irish law is complicated and certainly older than St Patrick's time. Patrick substituted the principles of the New Testament for those of the Old. By the third century AD, the law was fast becoming a closed preserve of learned arbitrators. The common law, in reality, contained few legislative enactments; it was fundamentally the expression of public opinion. The *Senchus Mór*, in four parts, was a treatise on contracts, loans, pledges, fees and rights of property, including those of the church; but an important section was devoted to criminal offences. The force of public opinion was so important that little physical enforcement of the law became necessary; and this applied even to observance of the Sabbath day. The Brehon Laws remained operative until the sixteenth century, but were often contested in court after the introduction of the Anglo-Norman code. The only legal code that is older was that of Greece and Rome.

Contrary to general belief, Greek was not taught in Ireland until the ninth century; Irish scholars who knew the language were mostly educated abroad. Although the able scholar St Columbanus, who founded the monastery at Bobbio in northern Italy in AD 613, had collected a library of 666 manuscripts, its tenth-century catalogue revealed that they were of Latin authors. The Book of Armagh (about AD 807) contains a linguistic curiosity — the Lord's Prayer in Latin, but reproduced in Greek characters. The languages conventionally taught in the monastic and bardic (non-church) schools were Latin and Irish. The first Old Irish writing in roman characters appeared in the seventh century, so that the earliest Irish literature is contemporaneous with that of the Anglo-Saxons. At the end of the ninth century, Ireland produced a scholar-king of Cashel (Munster), Cormac mac Culennáin, who was skilled in languages, including Old English and Danish; he wrote a Glossary, called *Sarnas Cormaic*, containing much cyclopaedic information. A much-loved churchman, he also produced the lost Psalter of Cashel, and was killed in battle in AD 908.

Old Irish had been standardised by the time of the Viking invasions; apart from some place-names, the loan words from Old Norse were related to trade, clothing and seafaring. *Erse*, for the modern revived vernacular, is Scots dialect for 'Irish', and strictly applicable to Scots Gaelic only.

The known history of languages begins with writing, and the Ogham inscriptions had their origin in pre-Christian Ireland. Invariably they consist of proper names in the genitive case, inscribed on the edges of large stones. Letters are represented by one to five notches, which are at right-angles or $45°$ in relation to a basic line. The incisions are to the left, to the right, or across this line, the short rectangular notches representing the five vowels of the roman alphabet, and the longer ones fifteen consonants.

Wherever the Celts lived they left a legacy of place-names, which persist, though not in the original orthography. Such names tend to recur in different regions; for the Celts were rural people, little given to gregarious communities, except for defence. They valued kinship, on which was founded tribal life and ownership of property. Land-owners in Ireland were wealthy principally in cattle, and the economy had little use for a coinage. The social unit was a family of four generations, in possession of cultivated land. Kings or queens could be chosen only from the progeny of a common great-grandfather.

The Celtic craftsmen were the first transmitters of Mediterranean civilisation to the British Isles; their curvilinear art was an inspiration both to the Saxons and the Norsemen. The Celts' tribal structure was not obliterated from rural society by the Romans, the Norsemen or the Anglo-Saxon invaders. They gave names to rivers, mountains and other geographical features, wherever they settled. They assimilated learning eagerly, and were zealous in disseminating it, through missionary foundations. Their organisation of social services through the monasteries was extended all over western Europe; and one of their greatest achievements was the codifying of common law for men living in competitive communities. They evolved a magnificent Celtic script, and beautiful manuscripts with colourful illuminations. Their early Catholic faith was not too rigid or orthodox; and because of it they became the preservers of Latin learning throughout the Dark Ages. They cherished the arts of music and oral poetry. They instructed kings to exalt godliness and service above personal ambition, thereby curbing the lawlessness of many barbarous peoples.

Ireland is justly regarded as the microcosm of the Celtic way of life; its undisciplined history can be attributed largely to a want of experience of Roman organisation. The Celts did not learn the value of civil institutions, because they had little knowledge of urban civilisation. The romantic conception of honour, characteristic of heroic ages, arose from the conduct of wars indispensable to the Celtic aristocracy. Christianity curbed some aggressive proclivities, and sublimated amoral impulses by diverting the energies of clansmen into social and economic channels. It did not, however, subvert clannish patriotism, or the duties of the *cenedl*, which permitted the continuance of blood feuds, the exaction of blood money, and other responsibilities of kinship communities.

Yeats described the Irish as a traditional race 'haunted by

people and places'; and Ernest Renan wrote in *The Poetry of the Celtic Races*:

> The essential element of the Celt's poetic life is the adventure . . . the pursuit of the unknown. . . . This race desires the infinite, it thirsts for it, and pursues it at all costs, beyond the tomb.

II

Language, Myth and Legend in Early Irish Literature

Irish literature in Gaelic (the earliest) is found first in manuscripts of the eleventh or twelfth century. Writing in the vernacular was, however, preceded by nearly five centuries of Irish literature in Latin, closely related to the European tradition. The alphabet of Irish scribes consisted of Roman manuscript letters, and in its characteristic 'pointed' form of uncial took three centuries to evolve. This MS style was retained in the printed characters introduced in 1551 — so late, because in Ireland the printing trade was strictly controlled by the government.

There are only eighteen letters in the Irish alphabet, thirteen consonants and five vowels, the missing characters of English being j, k, q, v, w, x, y, z. Many Irish characters are inevitably unphonetic in application. The 'acute' accent over a vowel is simply a mark of length.

Books printed in Irish are still regrettably few for a country whose Old Irish (700-1100) is the principal source of knowledge about the Celtic group of languages. The original tongue, fostered by a limited scholarly class, was highly inflected, but inadequately supplied with symbols for its sounds. Examples of Old Irish are to be found only in glosses to Latin manuscripts, preserved, for the most part, in Continental libraries.

Middle Irish (1100-1550), with simplified declensions and conjugations, was the language of most early manuscripts. The earliest work in Middle Irish was *Lebor na h-uidre*, or The Book of the Dun Cow (1106), compiled in part at the monastery of Clonmacnois, on the River Shannon, in County Westmeath; it consists mainly of romantic stories belonging to the Ulster cycle, the core of which is *Táin Bó Cuailnge* (The Cattle-Raid of Cooley). The Book of Leinster (1160) in Trinity College, Dublin is in similar vein, but its main historical interest is confined to that kingdom. The other important codices of the Middle Irish period are: The Yellow Book of Lecan, *Leabhar Breac* ('The Speckled Book'), The Great Book of Lecan (1417), The Book of Ballymote (*c.* 1450), The Book of Lismore, The Book of Fermoy, and The Book of Hy Maine.

Sagas were originally written in a mixture of rhythmical prose and verse, later in ballad form. The bardic poets, not unlike those of Wales, were the principal preservers of the Irish tradition, and therefore resided with the aristocratic families, both Gaelic and Anglo-Norman (the 'Old Foreigners'), when the latter had become hibernicised. Manuscripts were copied by lay scribes, principally in the fourteenth century.

The pagan heroic period, dating from about the time of Christ, was succeeded by an age of Christian poets living in the country, hermits observant of nature, nostalgic and religious. Historically and socially, such authors were dedicated to an ideal political order, of which Ulster, Leinster and Munster were the leading centres. The second element in provincial names, *-ster*, came from Old Norse *staðir* meaning 'places'.

Irish literature in the vernacular is less well known than it ought to be, mainly because the bulk remained too long in manuscript form. When the national poets were driven underground, they invariably personified Ireland under secret feminine names, such as Kathleen Ni Houlahan or Dark Rosaleen.

Borrowings from other languages during the period of standard Gaelic were mainly from Latin, Scandinavian and French; but these have been outnumbered by English loanwords since the sixteenth century. Irish was never a language that easily admitted alien coinages. Like German, it translated metaphorical innovations by employing native elements.

The mythology of Ireland begins with the Book of Conquest, *Lebor Gabála* (*c.* 1050), which recounts the invasion of Partholón after the Flood. O'Rahilly (op. cit.,

p. 75) sees this as a learned invention, in which the name Partholón is derived from Latin *Bartholomaeus*, whom Jerome characterised as 'the son of him who stayed the waters'. Geoffrey Keating in the seventeenth century, among many historians, gave some credence to invasions that were a complete fabrication, because the poetic symbolism had impressed credulous minds among the Irish aristocracy. Partholón's invasion (the first of five) came at a time when Ireland was peopled with Fomorians, regarded as demons from the sea; it proved ineffectual, because the invading force was destroyed within a week by an outbreak of plague.

The Celtic deities were all vaguely connected with lands across the sea, but were not an organised community comparable to the Olympian hierarchy, though *Lug* had a similar supremacy to Zeus. The intervention of supernatural powers in human affairs was, too, not unlike that of the Homeric epics, except that the Irish had two Otherworlds, one reached by entry into an ancient burial mound, the other by journeying across the sea, as in the Irish romantic tale 'The Voyage of Bran'.

The state of society reflected in the best known Ulster Cycle corresponds to that of Caesar's Gaul, before the abolition of druidism in the reign of Tiberius. Kings did not make the laws, but carried out those adopted by their assembly of freemen, called the *oenach*; underprivileged classes, churls and slaves, had no voice in a community that was aristocratic and freedom-loving. The bulk of the plebeian population lived in awe of the magical powers inherent in Celtic nature-worship. If the warrior class, equally superstitious, displayed no fear in their pursuit of honour and the prowess of arms, it was because druidic discipline had insinuated a belief that the souls of men are immortal.

Roman observers were of the opinion that the southern Gauls shared the philosophy of metempsychosis (transmigration of souls) with Pythagoras; but this is doubtful (see Alfred Nutt, *The Voyage of Bran* 1897, Vol. II). Nutt had reservations about affinities of the Celtic Happy Otherworld to the Greek Elysium. Like many superhuman heroes of Irish legend, Pythagoras declared Hermes to have been his spiritual ancestor, and was assured of his presence in a previous existence at the Siege of Troy. Proximity of the Greek settlement of Massilia (Marseilles) would explain some cultural influence upon the southern Gauls; but the pantheism of Pythagoras was unlike the nature-worship of the Gallo-Celts (Nutt preferred to style it 'panwizardism') in that the Greek doctrine was ethical rather than religious. Immortality of the soul does seem to imply affinity with the divine; but it also implies the soul's independent existence before, as well as after, bodily life.

Greek mythic literature was wholly pagan; that of the Celts reflects an earlier dispensation filtered through Christian traditions preserved in the monasteries. Consequently, Celtic gods are not the heroes of sagas; they are merely the instruments for shaping human destinies, by enabling the protagonists to change their shapes at will. As Nutt suggests, 'When the gods enter the world of mortal heroes, they must bow to the conventions of heroic legend' (p. 195). This obviously made it easier for later Christian recorders to 'turn the mythology into history'.

Since the tribal life and folklore of the Goidelic population of Britain were little affected by the Roman occupation, it is not surprising to find that the enduring aspects of fairy-lore, fantasy, illusion and romance, stem from the Gaelic tradition. The remainder of Celtic Britain, which had been within the reach of Roman culture, was seemingly influenced through trade and conquest from across the Irish Sea. Says J. R. R. Tolkien in his essay 'On Fairy Stories':

> The realm of fairy-story is wide and deep and high and filled with many things: all manner of beasts and birds are found there; shoreless seas and stars uncounted; beauty that is an enchantment, and an ever-present peril; both joy and sorrow as sharp as swords. In that realm a man may, perhaps, count himself fortunate to have wandered, but its very richness and strangeness tie the tongue of a traveller who would report them.
>
> (*Tree and Leaf*, p. 11)

The archaic form of *faërie* (usually trisyllabic) was Old French in origin; Spenser's use of it in the title and content of his great epic-romance (written in Ireland) would have been inconceivable without the complex Arthurian cycle that preceded it. Canto X of the second book of *The Faerie Queene* incorporates a commentary on the early Brittonic kings, as received from the *Chronicles* of Hardyng and Holinshed.

Fairies were in the first place beings imaginatively associated with the phenomena of nature, and not therefore supernatural. They belonged, as Tolkien says, to 'the Perilous Realm' (magic, enchantment, art itself) whose paths seldom cross those of mundane human existence. *The Lord of the Rings* was an experiment in restoring the original concept of 'faerie'. Tolkien believes that the origin of fairy tales is to be associated with that of language itself. Of its characteristics, he regards 'invention' as more important than anthropological considerations; 'the incarnate mind, the tongue, and the tale are in our world coeval' (*Tree and Leaf*, p. 27).

The Celts' sagas, as a whole, belong to a period of great unrest for their settled agricultural way of life, beginning some five centuries before the birth of Christ. The literature reveals gifts of inventiveness quite unlike anything that emanated from the great classical cultures. What follows is broadly an appraisal of creative writing that appeared in the Celtic languages between the sixth and twelfth centuries AD.

Myles Dillon, in the introduction to his edition of *Irish Sagas* (1968), mentions four cycles on which scholarly translations or modern renderings are based:

The Mythological Cycle, which concerns Celtic magic and the Irish Otherworld, conceived as a haven of refuge in the Western Sea, and sometimes referred to as the Land of the Living (*Tir-nambea*).

The Ulster Cycle, (see p. 7) with a modicum of history behind it, but ignoring the probable truth, that the Ulaid were defeated by the Connachta.

The Fenian Cycle, which consists of tales about the warrior band *fian*, as well as myths of the deity Lug.

The Historical Cycle (related to the Ulster Cycle) comprising tales of the ancient kings of Ireland.

There is much linguistic evidence that most of the extant manuscripts were based on earlier ones now lost, the difference in provenance sometimes being several centuries. The scribal tradition of fidelity to archaic forms was, however, a strong one.

Two events in Irish history powerfully affected the transmission of texts in different ways; they were the advent of Christianity and the irruption of Norwegian and Danish invaders at the end of the eighth century. The Christian influence did not get under way until the seventh century; by then the monastic tradition of solitary asceticism had played a significant role in the development of Irish individualism. Even more important was the influence of abbots in the secular education of the *plebs*. The dioceses of bishops were largely associated with the royal forts of small kingdoms; nevertheless abbots proved to be better situated to acquire political power. Monastic scribes were in close touch with the *filid* and improved their knowledge of Irish legends in the pagan oral tradition. The scriptoria of monasteries showed enterprise in taking down (perhaps improving) tales that had previously been the sole property of the *filid*. Children of influential landowners were the first to benefit from the opportunities of monastic education for laymen.

This beneficent source for the propagation of literature in the venacular, as well as Latin, was unfortunately driven underground by the Viking invasions; but these were confined largely to coastal areas. The Norsemen needed bases for sea-borne raids upon Wales, Cornwall and Anglo-Saxon England. Consequently it was the northern and eastern monasteries whose intellectual activities were curtailed by Norse violence. The educative scope of monasteries soon moved to the midlands and the west of the country, the part that was frequented by hermits, whose poetic instincts were deeply stirred by the nature-loving songs, myths and tales of the pagan tradition.

The scribal revolution affected prose and poetry, and had reached Ulster by the ninth century. There seems to have been no aesthetic preference for either medium in the remarkable Ulster Cycle; its purpose was to handle themes, historical and literary, relating to the royal houses of the province. Truth, as the modern historian knows it, was of no greater importance to creative imaginations, using the Irish language, than myth and legend. But the break in the *filid* tradition led to lively experiments in the forms and structure of occasional verse. The progressive monasteries had religious scribes, using Latin, as well as secular ones to record the vernacular antiquities of the laity. Among the latter, before the Viking invasions, there was a strong preference for legends about sea-voyages, for instance those of Bran and St Brendan. The real problem that has vexed most scholars of Early Irish is the probable difference between scribal versions of the eleventh and twelfth centuries, and the oral tradition of the three preceding centuries.

What was the motive prompting these early voyages (*immrama*)? The *Immram Brain* (Voyage of Bran), according to Kuno Meyer, would have been in writing by the seventh century. But most were the product of insecure churches and monasteries during the Viking occupation. Anchorites convinced themselves that they could find peace in some haven, usually an island, by sailing west or north in the Atlantic. A Litany of Pilgrim Saints was in existence about the time when the *Céli Dé* (Culdees, or 'companions of God') initiated their reform movement, which resembled that of the Benedictines on the Continent. The best known of the voyages, because written in Latin, was undoubtedly the *Navigatio Sancti Brendani Abbatis*, of which there are no less than 129 manuscripts. Brendan, Abbot of Clonfert, was born in County Kerry, and died in the last quarter of the sixth century; so that his venture should have had nothing to do with Viking invasions. It is significant, however, that no version was probably in existence before the ninth century, the original being in Irish. Vernacular accounts maintain that Brendan was persuaded to leave his country by Matthew XIX, 29, which says: 'Anyone who has left brothers or sisters, father, mother, or children, land or houses for the sake of my name will be repaid many times over, and gain eternal life.'

Brendan departed from Ireland in three skin-covered curraghs, each containing thirty persons; but he took no provisions for a voyage that lasted five years. After many adventures, including supernatural intervention by devils, goblins and sea-monsters, the voyagers reached an island where they could not land, although it was inhabited. By means of a wax tablet dropped to them from above, they were advised to return to Ireland, and to seek out a more promising destination. This was done, and a new company of sixty men re-embarked on a wooden ship, only to discover that the *terra secreta* they sought was already occupied by a hermit, dressed in feathers. He died and was buried by the voyagers. Brendan finally journeyed to the islands of Aranmore and Inis Da Druma, before sailing back to Ireland. There is no account of his doings after his second return.

Most voyages, e.g. those of Cormac in Adamnán's *Vita Columbae*, were in quest of a true *terra deserta*. Columba warned Cormac that he would fail, because one of his comrades had left his monastery without the abbot's permission. His was not the only venture that was marred by the presence of interlopers. Ecclesiastical voyages embody a good deal of pre-Viking folklore; so does the secular voyage of *Immram Brain*, in which the god Manannán, who dwelt in the Isle of Man, drives a chariot over the sea. Here is a lyrical passage that illustrates the sea-fever of Bran and his comrades (Kuno Meyer's translation):

> Sea-horses glisten in summer
> As far as Bran has stretched his glance:
> Rivers pour forth a stream of honey
> In the land of Manannán son of Lér.
>
> Though but one chariot-rider is seen
> In Mag Mell [The Happy Plain] of many flowers
> There are many steeds on its surface,
> Though thou seest them not.
>   . . .
> Along the top of a wood has swum
> Thy coracle across ridges,
> There is a wood of beautiful fruit
> Under the prow of thy little skiff.
>
> A wood with blossom and fruit,
> On which is the vine's veritable fragrance;
> A wood without decay, without defect,
> On which are leaves of a golden hue.

Whatever the circumstance of the voyage, there was invariably an appeal to some literate society in touch with a Christian church that did not inhibit Irish lyrical enthusiasm.

The *Immram Curaig Máele Dúin* in the Yellow Book of Lecan, is perhaps the earliest of the voyage manuscripts, dated about 1106. Thirty-four islands were visited in this Irish Odyssey, each vying with the last in the eccentricity of its events. In H. P. A. Oskamp's translation one of the hero's adventurers, from which I quote, took place on island 11:

When those apples came to an end for them, and they were suffering from extreme hunger and thirst and almost dead, and when their mouths and their noses were full of the stench of the sea, they saw an island and a fort therein. There was a white, high wall around it as if the wall was made of lime and as if it was all one rock of chalk. Great was its height from the sea; it almost reached the clouds. The fort was open; snow-white houses were there, like the wall. They went into the house that was the largest of them and there was nobody in it but a small cat in the midst of the house playing on four stone pillars. It used to leap from one pillar to the other. It looked a little at the men and did not cease from its play. After that they saw three rows on the wall of the house round from one door-post to the other. First a row of golden and silver brooches and their pins were in the wall. Another row then of large necklets like hoops of tubs, of gold and silver, and a third row of great gold-hilted swords of gold and silver. The cubicles of the house were full of white quilts and white garments. They saw then an ox with a flitch of boiled bacon in the midst and large vessels with good intoxicating liquor.

'Is it for us that this has been left?' said Máel Dúin to the cat, and the cat did not cease from its play. Then Máel Dúin realized that the food they saw had been left for them. They drank and ate and slept and they put the leavings of the drink into the pots and they stored the leavings of the food and then they discussed departing. One of the three fosterbrothers of Máel Dúin said: 'Shall I take with me one of these necklets?' 'No', said Máel

Dúin, 'the house is not without guard.'

Nevertheless, he *takes* one till he reached the midst of the enclosure. The cat followed them and leapt through him like a fiery arrow and *burns* him so that he became ashes. It went back and settled on its pillar. Máel Dúin spoke to it with words and placed the necklet in its former spot and cleansed the ashes from the floor of the enclosure and cast them on the shore of the sea.

And then they went into their boat and praised and magnified the Lord and thanked Him.

(The Voyage of Máel Dúin, pp. 121 and 23)

The two verbs in italics illustrate the translator's grammatical comment that 'the present and preterite are used . . . without distinction, as in the Icelandic sagas'. The Norse sagas of the Middle Ages were in all probability derived, both in form and spirit, from Irish forebears.

Many incidents, such as the one described above, recall pagan taboos, with which the Christian epilogue is often in ironical contrast. Some critics, therefore, treat the adventures as allegories.

Besides anomalies of the animal kingdom the early sagas introduce many creatures of prehistoric myth, with which modern readers are better acquainted. The English word *leprechaun* (OED seventeenth century) first appeared in its Irish form in *Echtra Fergusa Maic Léti* (The Adventure of Fergus Mac Léti), an exercise in Brehon poetry of the law-schools, belonging to the Ulster Cycle. This tale originated in the eighth century, when the Feni (Goidels), the Ulaid and the Laigin divided the rule of Ireland. Fergus, King of the Midland Goidels at Tara, was the owner of a magic sword called Caladbolg, whose etymology reminds us of King Arthur's Excalibur (from Celtic Latin *Caliburnus*). After a strenuous civil war, Fergus was resting on an unknown shore when he was suddenly attacked by water-sprites, called *lúchorpáin* (meaning 'tiny bodies'). These he easily overcame, and spared, provided they would teach him how to swim underwater. The leprechauns consented, on condition that Fergus should avoid the forbidden Loch Rudraige. Tempting fate, however, Fergus eventually overcame the monster that lived in this lake, but died from exhaustion as he set foot on shore.

According to O'Reilly's *Irish Dictionary* and Supplement (1817), numerous spellings, other than 'lúchorpáin', are found in Old and Middle Irish. Texts of the latter period reveal that the leprechaun had become a pigmy cobbler 'for ever mending a single shoe' (OED). The creature is also described in Irish folklore as a sprite who invariably carried a purse containing a shilling.

The barrows on the north side of the River Boyne, near Drogheda, were among many ancient burial grounds pillaged by the Danes; they are associated in Irish folklore with the *aes sidhe* ('people of the hills'), who may have been ancient gods or fairies. Legend has it that these tumuli go back to the Tuatha Dé Danann, and were originally dwelling-places, not tombs. Newgrange, the best known, is over three hundred feet in diameter, and seventy feet high. Early Irish for a male fairy was *fer-sidhe* (pronounced 'far-shee'), and for a female one *bean-sidhe* ('woman of the hill'), from which the word 'banshee' is derived. The latter sprite was believed to wail outside the window of a person about to die.

'A shadowy sense of vagueness, vastness, uncertainty' hangs over the mythological period of Old Irish writing, according to Douglas Hyde in that indispensable book *A Literary History of Ireland* (1899, p. 293). Hyde's was the first comprehensive study to gather the complex strands of the Ulster legends, a cycle that has proved fertile in propagating indigenous literature. Hyde acknowledged his indebtedness to other works of primary historical value, which were written in Irish in the early seventeenth century; they are Geoffrey Keating's *History of Ireland*, completed by 1640, and circulated in manuscript, but not printed until 1811 (English translation, New York 1866); and the Annals of the Four Masters, compiled by a group of antiquaries at the convent of Donegal (1636), and later translated into English by John O'Donovan.

These and other sources enabled Hyde to furnish the social background essential to an understanding of the heroic period. One reason for the skeletal nature of most of these saga manuscripts he attributes to the scarcity and expense of parchment. The organisation of a royal palace is admirably pictured, and the aristocratic habit of foster parentage explained. The vogue of the female warrior and war-teacher in Alba (Scotland), which figures not only in the Deirdre episode, serves curiously to remind us of the significance of taboos (*gessa*) in the Celtic tradition.

The folio vellum manuscripts of early Irish literature have been justly described as 'miniature libraries'. The Red Branch tales of the Ulster Cycle are no exception. The Ulaid of north-eastern Ireland were probably the first to provide a saga-sequence resembling a national epic. An epyllion, or minor epic, such as the *Táin Bó Cuailnge* (often abbreviated to 'The Táin') should not be compared, on aesthetic grounds, with the *Iliad* or the *Aeneid*; but it bears resemblance to *Beowulf* and the *Nibelungenlied*. The function of all heroic compositions is very similar. 'The Táin' is important as the earliest vernacular saga of western Europe. As in the Hebrew Pentateuch, only a few of the emotive passages are in verse; all the narrative is cast in prose.

Scholars usually agree that the action of 'The Táin' represents a period some two thousand years before the present time. That these stories must be older than AD 130 is indicated by no mention of the province of Meath, although places within that area are actually involved. What the Ulster Cycle represents is an oral tradition of folklore of an area somewhat larger than modern Ulster. The Cú Chulain saga acquired national importance through the enterprise of the *seanchaidhe* or storyteller. As there are several different versions of the same tale, it is almost beyond the powers of an editor to establish a canon. The land to which the Ulaid belonged lies east of Loch Neagh, and is not far from the present city of Belfast. The royal palace at the capital, Emain Macha, destroyed in AD 332, lay somewhat to the south-west; the remains, near Armagh, are now called Fort Navan. Cú Chulain himself came from Cuailnge and Muirthemne in County Louth.

Since the sources of 'The Táin' and ancillary tales are composite (from the Book of the Dun Cow, the Yellow Book of Lecan and the Book of Leinster), translators of an holistic turn of mind sometimes unite them to produce a synoptic version, somewhat like the Odyssey of Homer or the Gospels of the New Testament. Two such modernisations spring to mind, *Cuchulain of Muirthemne* by Lady Augusta Gregory (1902), and *The Tain* by Thomas Kinsella (1970). An advantage of the resulting saga is that it brings into prominence the 'Exile of the Sons of Uisliu', notable for the moving tragedy of Deirdre, as well as the evil results of Conchobar's unprincipled rule. Lady Gregory chose as a suitable folktale medium the Anglo-Irish dialect of Kiltartan near Coole Park in the West of Ireland, and produced a paraphrase of editorially selected material, in order to make the story tasteful and readable for educational purposes.

The *remscéla* (preliminary tales) are essential for a proper comprehension of the saga; without those it lacks motivation for some of the central features. Partially to remedy this, Kinsella in the Oxford edition of 1970 resorted to the twelfth century Book of Leinster (*c.* 1160) which is fuller and clearer on certain points, but suffers from what the translator named a 'florid adjectival style' (p. x). His version is as nearly as may be a faithful translation, something difficult to achieve, since there are inconsistencies and barren patches of narrative, not to mention diversity of tone in the disparate contributions. The naming of places Kinsella found to be of exceptional significance in the saga's itineraries; and this was to become a feature of medieval Irish literature. On the other hand, as compared with Anglo-Saxon literature, the women have 'strong and diverse personalities', which adds considerably to the dramatic value of the stories.

The saga of Cú Chulain concerns a group of warriors, descended from gods, called the Champions of the Red Branch, a name derived from one of three great halls at Emain Macha in which they assembled. Divine origin renders it plausible that personal prowess should, under stress, be supernatural. But besides its mythology *The Tain* interestingly reflects the social conditions of a primitive barter society, whose tribal strength depended on the possession of cattle, sheep, horses, female slaves and household goods, rather than on money or the holding of land. Bulls with preternatural endowments, through re-incarnation, often figure largely in the legends of pastoral societies; and Medb or Maeve of of Connacht (not strictly a queen, but a female warrior) coveted her husband's white-horned bull, named Findbennach, a creature of immense strength and size. It was Medb who instigated the raid against eastern Ulster, a community notable for its obstinate Pictish independence, in order to secure Donn, the Brown Bull of Cuailnge.

The Tain begins with a petty squabble between Medb and her husband Ailill over their possessions, which Kinsella entitles 'Pillow Talk'.

'You amaze me,' Ailill said. 'No one has more property or jewels or precious things than I have, and I know it.'

Then the lowliest of their possessions were brought out, to see who had more property and jewels and precious things: their buckets and tubs and iron pots, jugs and wash-pails and vessels with handles. Then their finger-rings, bracelets, thumb-rings and gold treasures were brought out, and their cloth of purple, blue, black, green and yellow, plain grey and many-coloured, yellow-brown, checked and striped. Their herds of sheep were taken in off the fields and meadows and plains. They were measured and matched, and found to be the same in numbers and size. Even the great ram leading Medb's sheep, the worth of one bondmaid by himself, had a ram to match him leading Ailill's sheep.

From pasture and paddock their teams and herds of horses were brought in. For the finest stallion in Medb's stud, worth one bondmaid by himself, Ailill had a stallion to match. Their vast herds of pigs were taken in from the woods and gullies and waste places. They were measured and matched and noted, and Medb had one fine boar, but Ailill had another. Then their droves and free-wandering herds of cattle were brought in from the woods and wastes of the province. These were matched and measured and noted also, and found to be the same in number and size. But there was one great bull in Ailill's herd, that had been a calf of one of Medb's cows — Finnbennach was his name, the White Horned — and Finnbennach, refusing to be led by a woman, had gone over to the king's herd. Medb couldn't find in her herd the equal of this bull, and her spirits dropped as though she hadn't a single penny.

Medb had the messenger Mac Roth called, and she told him to see where the match of the bull might be found, in any province in Ireland.

'I know where to find such a bull and better,' Mac Roth said: 'in the province of Ulster, in the territory of Cuailgne, in Dáire mac Fiachna's house. Donn Cuailnge is the bull's name, the Brown Bull of Cuailnge.'

(The Táin, pp. 54-5)

The badinage of this domestic episode is characteristic of Irish humour; the more extravagant the situation, the greater the amusement extracted from it. The most formidable warriors whom Cú Chulain defeats were, ironically, trained by the same instructor — the Amazon Scathach of Alba. The genuine chivalry of a warrior's behaviour has much of the quixotry that colours the eccentrics of Cervantes.

The northern Irish social system depicted in *The Tain* has the same cultural level as that of Scotland and northern England; frequent interchanges between Ulster and Alba, bardic as well as military, are fundamental to the appreciation of the saga. Scathach had an individualistic method of training warriors for single combat, a system of 'feats' or manoeuvres, not fully understood. Bloodthirsty descriptions of pitched battles include details of weaponry, scythed chariots, protective clothing and the practice of beheading distinguished victims for trophies. Largely through such particulars, the historian places the events in the Iron Age, shortly before the Roman invasion of Britain (see especially Kinsella chapter IX, and Gregory chapter XI). Unfortunately for the hero's personal fate, he is dogged by the antipathy of Morrigu, goddess of war. Here is an illustrative passage from the latter chapter:

As Cuchulain lay in his sleep one night a great cry from the North came to him, so that he started up and fell from his bed to the ground like a sack. He went out of his tent, and there he saw Laeg yoking the horses to the chariot. 'Why are you doing that?' he said. 'Because of a great cry I heard from the plain to the north-west,' said Laeg. 'Let us go there then,' said Cuchulain. So they went on till they met with a chariot, and a red horse yoked to it, and a woman sitting in it, with red eyebrows, and a red dress on her, and a long red cloak that fell on to the ground between the two wheels of the chariot, and on her back she had a grey spear. 'What is your name, and what is it you are wanting?' said Cuchulain. 'I am the daughter of King Buan,' she said, 'and what I am come for is to find you and to offer you my love, for I have heard of all the great deeds you have done.' 'It is a bad time you have chosen for coming,' said Cuchulain, 'for I am wasted and worn out with the hardship of war, and I have no mind to be speaking with women.' 'You will have my help in everything you do,' she said, 'and *it is protecting you I was up to this, and I will protect you from this out.*' '*It is not trusting to a woman's protection I am in this work I have in my hands,*' said Cuchulain. 'Then if you will not take my help,' she said, 'I will turn it against you; and at the time when you will be fighting with some man as good as yourself, I will come against you in all shapes, by water and by land, till you are beaten.' There was anger in Cuchulain then, and he took his sword, and made a leap at the chariot. But on the moment, the chariot and the horse and the woman had disappeared, and all he saw was a black crow, *and it sitting on a branch*; and by that he knew it was the Morrigu had been talking with him.

(Cuchulain of Muirthemne, pp. 165-6)

In the reading of Lady Gregory's dialogue, the intonation (or tune) of the speaker characterises the dialect of the west, in which the tale is written. Furthermore, there are idiomatic turns of phrase and syntax, indicated in the words italicised.

It is not easy for a critic to pass judgement on the Ulster Cycle in modern translation, especially as worth depends frequently on the period of original composition. Hyperbole and repetitive similes tend to mar the descriptions. The style of Old Irish romance of the sixth and seventh centuries is crude and formulaic, reflecting a state of society in which emotions were undisciplined. Warriors appear armed at royal feasts, and fight to the death over the best cuts of roast meat. Excitement is sustained by declamation (the *rosg* style) and by the constant occurrence of happenings that are unexpected. There is a grim irony in the code of honour itself; for heroes often behave like headstrong adolescents. The fate of great men is pathetic, rather than tragic; the tone of inevitability in the widow's laments confirms this. Bonds of kinship arising from the custom of foster-parentage seem to be stronger than those of family — a circumstance that often complicates issues of loyalty.

During the seventh century the ties between Ireland and Scotland were strengthened by adventurous warriors, the *fiana*, who supported a ruler of Irish extraction, King Aedán, in his struggle against the Angles. The origin of this *fiana* band is to be found in the Fenian Cycle of the third century AD; but recorded adventures in Leinster, Connacht and Munster are mostly fictional. So are the concocted genealogies of the principal figures. The legendary head of the *fiana* was Finn mac Cummaill (the Irish King Arthur), whose son Oisín and grandson Oscar had as principal companions Cailte and Diarmaid, the latter the handsomest warrior in Ireland. This band, said to have descended from the Firbolg people, was independent of the kingdom of Tara. Neither 'fiana' nor 'Fenian' is etymologically related to the name Finn (earlier spelt Fionn).

The Fenian Cycle is mainly of Middle Irish provenance, and notable from two aspects, the use of magic and a strict ritual of initiation. Membership of the group necessitated the stoical endurance of exacting physical tests; it also called for surrender of family ties, and a dedication to nature in its starkest form, because Fenians abhorred gregarious town life. They were expected to be familiar with all the practised forms of Irish poetry. According to legend, Finn (the 'fair'), whose seat was at Almhain, Co. Kildare, lived to a great age. He was the son of Cumall, hero of thirty battles, and learnt the art of divination from a poet living by the River Boyne, who allowed him to eat the Salmon of Knowledge. The reverence of Fenians took the form of hero-worship, rather than belief in the traditional gods. The tales say that Finn was once at war with Aedh, the sun-god, who was also master of the Otherworld.

The fued between the *fiana* and Tara, as described in the

Annals of the Four Masters, places the death of Finn in AD 286; his company consisted of 150 officers, each at the head of twenty-seven warriors. Keating's view of them in the *History of Ireland* is pragmatic:

> They were nothing more than members of a body of *buanadha* or retained soldiers, maintained by the Irish kings for the purpose of guarding their territories and of upholding their authority therein. . . . They were quartered on the people from November Day till May Day, and their duty was to uphold justice and to put down injustice on the part of the kings and lords of Ireland, and also to guard the harbours of the country from the oppression of foreign invaders. After that, from May till November, they lived by hunting and the chase, and by performing the duties demanded of them by the kings of Ireland, such as preventing robberies, exacting fines and tributes, putting down public enemies. . . .
>
> The warriors had the flesh of the wild animals for their food, and the skins for wages. During the whole day, from morning till night they used to eat but one meal, and of this it was their wont to partake towards evening. . . . Then they began to supple their thews and muscles by gentle exercise, loosening them by friction, until they had relieved themselves of all sense of stiffness and fatigue. When they had finished doing this they sat down and ate their meal.

The Fenian (also called the Ossianic) Cycle is different from that of Ulster in conception and in its love of Gaelic folklore; this difference is perhaps the reason for its appeal to the western Highlands of Scotland. Hyde writes of the tales in the *Literary History of Ireland* (p. 375):

> They were most intimately bound up with the life and thought and feelings of the whole Gaelic race, high and low, both in Ireland and Scotland, and the development of Fenian saga, for a period of 1,200 or 1,500 years, is one of the most remarkable examples in the world of continuous literary evolution.

The stories and ballads were undoubtedly composed for a stratum of society that was not an aristocratic ruling class.

The warrior invariably fights on foot; is a defender of a cause, not the instrument of maintaining a king in power. There are fewer champions renowned for single combat; their enthusiasm is for hounds, hunting and wild life. The fairy element is accompanied by many supernatural transformations. In *Duanaire Finn*, a verse-tale in the Book of Leinster, Finn, while in a vale of yew trees, is taken prisoner by phantoms. As one finds in The Arabian Nights, the most grotesque figures have their likeable and humorous side. For the prevailing tone of the Fenian Cycle is romantic and retrospective, that of a Christian ballad-writer reluctantly separated from his pagan past.

The *fiana* tradition was strongest in Leinster, but rival companies were active in Munster and Connacht. The *Duanaire Finn*, the Leinster chieftain's 'poetry-book' (also admired in Scotland) extols the hero Goll mac Morna of Connacht, who was Finn's enemy; but with the typical magnanimity of a warrior he protected Finn when he was ambushed. Goll was rewarded by marrying Finn's daughter; her loyalty was such that she refused to desert her husband in dire extremity, when he was compelled to quench thirst by drinking sea-water.

The natural successors to Finn the poet-warrior were Oisín, the supposed composer of the Ossianic ballads, and Cailte, who was credited with the authorship of 'The Colloquy of Oisín and St Patrick' (*Acallam Oisín Agus Phaidraig*). Oisín lost his son Oscar, bravest of the brave, at the Battle of Gaura (*Cath Gabhra*), which marked the close of Fenian supremacy.

There are two long, but distinguished, documents in the Fenian Cycle: 'The Colloquy with Ancient Men' (*Acallam na Senorech*) and 'The Pursuit of Diarmaid and Gráinne' (*Toruigheacht Dhiarmudu agus Ghráinne*). The prose text of the first is to be found in the fifteenth-century Book of Lismore where the stories take the form of a topographical guide to the sad wanderings of Oisín and Cailte, after the Battle of Gaura. Oisín soon leaves his companion to live with his mother in her *sidh* dwelling; but Cailte goes from place to place with the remnants of his clan, reviewing the glories of the Fenian past. The reader is told how Finn prophesied the coming of St Patrick; Cailte's task is to conduct the saint to memorable scenes of legendary interest. We are expected to suppose that the guide lived some hundred and fifty years after the battle. Patrick baptises Cailte and his men, and shows a courteous regard for their deeds of daring, as well as the poet-leader's outbursts of song, full of the joys of nature and the chase. Fairy-folk mingle constantly with mortals, and St Patrick is given power over these super-natural creatures.

Though there are various sources for the legends, a single author seems to have been responsible for their compilation; there is a later ballad version in which hero and saint some-times appear as figures of fun. Myles Dillon in *Early Irish Literature* (p. 40) ascribes the spirit of these caricatures to an aftermath of 'anti-clerical humour'.

'The Pursuit of Diarmaid and Gráinne' is a tale of consider-ably later provenance (seventeenth century), though a gloss to the 'Eulogy to St Columba' (ninth century) makes a palpable reference to it. This story was a source of the 'Tristan and Iseult' romance of Arthurian legend; it is also a parallel version of the fate of Deirdre in the Ulster Cycle. Finn was already advanced in years after the death of his wife Maighneis, but became betrothed to Gráinne, the daughter of King Cormac mac Airt. Gráinne had not, as yet, seen Finn, who was older than her father; and being a beauti-ful but wilful girl eloped with the reluctant Diarmaid. Their life in the forest, in which they have the help of a faithful dog, is told in several tenth-century sagas. Finn repudiated Gráinne, and was therefore compelled by the king to leave Tara; but the ban was subsequently revoked, and Finn then married another of the king's daughters Ailbe.

The pursuit of the fugitive lovers takes them to the west of Ireland, Limerick and Sligo. There is the inevitable penalty for sacrificing loyalty to passion. The story makes it clear that Gráinne was selfish and irresponsible. However, for a time they were happy, and she bore Diarmaid four sons. Their many adventures came to an end with the mortal wounding of Diarmaid by the wild boar of Ben Gulbain (modern Ben Bulben); Finn, who instigated the hunt, possessed the power to save Diarmaid, but deliberately avoided doing so. King Cormac, the sage, left several dicta, one on women, which was the result of disillusionment with his daughter:

> They have tell-tale faces,
> they are quarrelsome in company,
> steadfast in hate,
> forgetful of love, . . .
> arrogant and disingenuous,
> abettors of strife,
> niggardly with food,
> rejecting wisdom, . . .
> exceeding all bounds in keeping others waiting,
> tedious talkers,
> close practitioners,
> dumb on useful matters,
> eloquent on trifles. . . .
> Better to crush them than to cherish them.
> They are waves that drown you,
> they are fire that burns you.
>
> (Meyer's trans. in *Selections from Ancient Irish Poetry*, pp. 106-8)

The Historical Cycle is a miscellaneous series covering the succession of Irish kings to the time of the Norse invasions in the eighth century. Legend sometimes succeeds in confirming the claims of genealogies, for the Irishman's pride in his family-tree was universal, as Hyde explains in *A Literary History of Ireland*:

> Under the tribal system, no one possessed lawfully any portion of the soil inhabited by his tribe if he were not of the same race with his chief. Consequently even those of lowest rank in the tribe traced and recorded their pedigree with as much care as did the highest. . . . All these genealogies were entered in the local books of each tribe and were preserved in the verses of the hereditary poets. There was no incentive to action among the early Irish so stimulative as a remembrance of their pedigree. It was the same among the Welsh, and probably among all tribes of Celtic blood.
>
> (pp. 71-2)

Myles Dillon in *The Cycles of the Kings* (1946) thinks that most of the seventy fragmentary tales that comprise the series have small literary value. Thirteen centuries are involved, beginning in the third century BC, with Labraid Loingsech, and ending with Brian Bóramu (Boru), who became High King at the commencement of the eleventh century.

The principal royal figures are Conn of the Hundred Battles, Cormac mac Airt and Niall of the Nine Hostages. Stripped of their supernatural imaginings, these were probably rulers of physical or intellectual ability; their existence is verified in the Annals of the Four Masters. According to these annals, Conn lived in the second century AD, and overcame the five provincial kings of Ireland. Cormac was the grandson of Conn and the reputed founder of Tara; he reigned for forty years (AD 227-66) and was blessed with great wisdom and astuteness; Finn mac Cummaill was associated with the history of his reign. Niall of the Nine Hostages (reigned AD 379-405) was one of five sons of Eochu Muigmedón; his mother was the daughter of Scal the Dumb, legendary king of the Saxons. It was Niall who helped the clans of Dalriada to overcome the Picts of Alba (Scotland). From his son Owen were descended the great Tyrone family of the O'Neills. Of Niall's nine hostages, five were taken from the provincial Irish rulers, and four from Scotland. Niall met the death already described in the land of Gabrán, king of Scotland.

To 'The Adventures of the Sons of Muigmedón', translated by Myles Dillon in *The Cycles of the Kings*, a moral tag is appended, the following being the gist of the story:

One day the five sons went hunting and they lost their way in the forest and were enclosed on every side. They lit a fire and cooked some of their game and ate till they were satisfied. They wanted water, and Fergus set out in search of it. He found a well, but there was an old woman guarding it. She was as black as coal. Her hair was like the wild horse's tail. Her foul teeth were visible from ear to ear and were such as would sever a branch of green oak. Her eyes were black, her nose crooked and spread. Her body was scrawny, spotted and diseased. . . .

'You are horrible,' said the lad. 'Ay,' said she. 'Are you guarding the well?' said the lad 'Ay,' said she. 'May I fetch some water?' said the lad. 'Ay,' said she, 'If you give me one kiss on the cheek.' 'No!' said he. 'You shall have no water from me,' said she. 'I give my word,' said he, 'that I would rather die of thirst than kiss you.'

Fergus returned without water, and each of the brothers went in turn. Only Fiachra spoke temperately to the hag, and she promised that he would visit Tara. And that came true, for two of his descendants, Dá Thí and Ailill Molt, became kings of Ireland, but none of the descendants of the other three.

At last it was Niall's turn to go. When the hag asked him for a kiss, he consented and lay down with her. Then, when he looked upon her, she was as fair a girl as any in the world. She was as white as the last snow in a hollow. Her arms were full and queenly, her fingers long and slender, her legs straight and gleaming. She had two golden shoes on her bright little feet, and a precious purple cloak about her, held by a silver brooch. Her teeth were like pearls, her eyes large and queenly, her lips of Parthian red.

'You are fair, woman,' said the boy. 'Ay,' said she. 'Who are you?' said the boy. . . .

'King of Tara, I am Sovranty. I shall tell you its virtue. Your seed shall be over every clan. There is good reason for what I say.'

She bade him return to his brothers with the water, and told him that he and his race would be kings of Ireland for ever, except for Dá Thí and Ailill Molt and one king from Munster, namely Brian Bórama. As he had seen her, horrible at first and beautiful in the end, so also is sovranty; for it is most often won by war and slaughter, but is glorious in the end. He was to give no water to his brothers until they granted him seniority over them, and that he might raise his weapon a hand's breadth above theirs. He returned with the water and exacted the promise. . . .

(*The Cycles of the Kings*, pp. 39-40, §§ 9-17)

Early historians apparently supplemented the Historical Cycle from surviving annals, such as those of Tigernach, who died in 1088. He was educated at the monastery of Clonmacnois (founded in AD 544), of which he eventually became abbot, was familiar with historians such as Josephus and Bede, and considered that reliable sources (some quoted) were available in Ireland from about 300 BC.

The importance of the four cycles for Irish literary history is the picture of social and political life that they reveal. By the fifth century buildings were constructed of stone, wood, turf and clay; the Celt's staple food was meat, broth made of beef, and milk; bread was not used, since grain was grown for cattle. The simply fed population was able to support itself without external trade, and business within the country was transacted without the need of coinage. Even handcrafts owed little to Continental example. There were towns of only moderate size, but no organised means of controlling civic life.

Rulers were chieftains and leaders rather than kings, their despotic power being limited by tribal custom. Their aristocratic status depended on lineage, privilege and style of living; but they were responsible for the welfare and actions of their dependants, having to respect the rights of each class. The individuality of the Irish tribesman was sacrosanct; a man's word was traditionally held to be his bond. Important as kinship was, justice for all freemen superseded it.

A distinctive mark of the free-born and noble child of both sexes was upbringing by foster-parents, in which there were obligations on both sides. In the Irish tradition, hospitality from others was a right, not a favour. Noblemen expected this privilege to be extended also to retainers. The code of laws governing such customs was, however, complicated; and this meant that every ruler had to employ a *brehon* on the establishment, as well as a minstrel. The recorder of royal deeds was also responsible for the family genealogy. When Christianity came to Ireland, the pagan deities moved underground, and the tribal past was preserved in story and song.

Though not much is known about the early history of poetry in Ireland, we are told that the training of a professional poet (*filí*) was exacting. Originally he was a magician, sage and judge, as well as the great man's euhemerist. The pioneering poetry of the legendary Milesian, Amergin (the Irish equivalent of Welsh Taliesin) often took the form of incantations and charms, of which the following is a typical example:

> I am the wind which breathes upon the sea,
> I am the wave of the ocean,
> I am the murmur of the billows
> I am the ox of the seven combats,
> I am the vulture upon the rocks,
> I am a beam of the sun,
> I am the fairest of plants,
> I am a wild boar in valour,
> I am a salmon in the water,
> I am a lake in the plain,
> I am a word of science,
> I am the point of the lance of battle,
> I am the god who creates in the head the fire
> Who is it who throws light into the meeting on the mountain?
> Who announces the ages of the moon?
> Who teaches the place where couches the sun?
>
> (Sharp, *Lyra Celtica*, p. 3)

By St Patrick's time the archival function of the *filí* had not changed, but his manifold tasks were lessened by the introduction of writing. Neither reading nor secular literacy was, however, widespread until the tenth century. By then the poet had become a family bard, whose political influence was considerable, and was wielded by inciting or restraining hostile acts against rival rulers. The itinerant bard was the medieval counterpart of a modern press agent or public relations officer. His feats of memory may still have been considerable, but monastic scribes were capable of providing copies of what had once been traditional oral poetry. By the fifteenth century it was found necessary to limit the bard's political influence by law.

Both the *filí* and the bard of the Middle Ages wrote encomiastic poetry, and used verse for prosaic topics, such as genealogy or law. Dallán Forgaill, a famous member of the *filid* class, composed his *Amra*, 'Eulogy of Colm Cille', after the death of St Columba, using an alliterative technique to imprint his lament in the memory of the listener. Family eulogy remained the principal task of the professional poet, but when feats of arms were described they were often fanciful. The chief poet of Ireland was known as the *rig-ollam*.

The earliest alliterative line was called *reicne decubaid*; it consisted of two or three words beginning with the same letter followed by one that did not alliterate, e.g. Lóvĕly thĕ̽ lańd ŏ̽f Múnstĕ̽r. There was little attempt at rhythmic beauty, and less at rhyme; and the number of syllables in the line was immaterial. Rhymed quatrains, resembling ballad verse, were a novelty of the late Middle Ages, which compelled the poet to attend to the rhythm of a group of lines in elementary stanza form. Rhyme was an embellishment derived from the singing of Latin hymns, beginning in the sixth century; it became effective only when the significance of stressed syllables was recognised. The most commonly employed line was one of seven syllables, later technically called 'trochaic tetrameter catalectic', e.g. in Húge ŏ̽ld trées eñcóm-pãss ĭ̽t. Stanza forms, with a regular count of syllables, emerged in the seventh century. Douglas Hyde claims that the following lines from 'The Lament of Queen Maev' represent 'the exact versification of the original', preserving the Irish use of alliteration and vowel rhyme:

> <u>M</u>ochorb's son of <u>f</u>iercest <u>f</u>ame,
>   <u>K</u>nown his <u>n</u>ame for bloody toil,
> To his <u>g</u>ory <u>g</u>rave is <u>g</u>one,
>   He who <u>sh</u>one o'er <u>sh</u>outing <u>M</u>oyle.
> <u>K</u>indly <u>k</u>ing, who <u>l</u>iked not <u>l</u>ies,
>   <u>R</u>ash to <u>r</u>ise to <u>f</u>ields of <u>f</u>ame,
> <u>R</u>aven-<u>b</u>lack his <u>b</u>rows of <u>f</u>ear,
>   <u>R</u>azor-<u>sh</u>arp his <u>sp</u>ear of <u>f</u>lame
>   (*Literary History of Ireland*, p. 274)

Eleanor Knott's *Irish Syllabic Poetry* (1928) shows that the principal embellishments allowed to a poet were (a) alliteration of successive stressed syllables (*uaim*); (b) assonance (*amus*) as in line 5 above; (c) rhyme (*comhardadh*), which might be internal (as in line 4) or final; and (d) consonance (*uaithne*), which called for a trained ear for phonetic similarities. After stressed vowels the consonants were divided into six classes: (1) *c* [k], *p*, *t* (voiceless plosives); (2) *b*, *d*, *g* (voiced plosives); (3) *ch* [χ], *ph* [f], *th* [θ] (the corresponding voiceless fricatives); (4) *bh* [v] *dh*, *gh*, *l*, *mh* [v] or [w], *n*, *r* (voiced fricatives, grouped with liquid, nasal and trilled consonants); (5) *ll*, *m*, *nn*, *ng* [ŋ], *rr*; and (6) the sibilant *s*. For rhyme, the major division of consonants was thus palatal and non-palatal groups. The consonant after a stressed vowel might rhyme only with one of its own group. Douglas Hyde holds that form, rather than substance, supplied the elegance of the true poet's technique.

The Book of Ballymote (*c.* 1400), compiled by scribes three of whose names are known, was a miscellany of diverse documents, which included copies of the *Dindsenchas*, or topographical poems, and the Book of Rights, as well as a list of the principal Irish poets, with their schools and techniques. The writing of topographical verse was considered an advanced accomplishment; but the chief value of the *Dindsenchas*, whether in verse or prose, is the light thrown on the sources of place-names, and the rules of metrical composition. In topographical poetry alliterative quatrains invariably contain verses of seven syllables, the final words of lines two and four being longer than those of lines one and three. Rhyme in the middle of a line is most common in the last couplet.

An important section of the Book of Ballymote is devoted to the classification of satire (*áer*) into three types: *aisnes* (declarative), *ail* (insulting) and *aircetal* (incantational). The last is found principally in verse, and is of great diversity (see Mercier, *The Irish Comic Tradition*, pp. 108-9). Satire in early Irish poetry was usually expressed in the brevity of the quatrain. Nearly always it was directed at individuals, not at moral issues or human vice and folly; several had as their victims monks or ministers of the Christian church. Saints, like Columcille, sometimes feared and placated poets whose criticism took the form of derogatory verses. He is said to have performed two miracles in order to prevent the banishment of errant poets from Ireland. Keating's *History* reminds us that the *filid* were exiled on three previous occasions for personal lampoons. There are obvious satirical touches in the *Instructions of Cormac* and in the *Triads of Ireland* (to be discussed later).

There is considerable variety in Irish poetry before the close of the fifteenth century; the most significant categories are the heroic, the elegiac, the religious and the gnomic. Heroic verse of the seventh and eighth centuries is essentially that of an aristocratic class, and is incidental to the prose sagas. Though the actual manuscripts belong to the Christian era, they reflect the semi-barbarous state of a primitive pagan society. Here is the description of Cú Chulain in his chariot:

He who sits in that chariot,
Is the warrior, able, powerful, well-worded,
Polished, brilliant, very graceful. —
There are seven sights on his eye;
. . .
There are seven kinds of fair hair on his head; —
Brown hair next his head's skin,
And smooth red hair over that;
And fair-yellow hair, of the colour of gold;
And clasps on the top, holding it fast; —
Whose name is Cuchullin,
Son of Aodh, son of Agh, son of other Aodh. —
His face is like red sparkles; —
Fast-moving on the plain like mountain fleet-mist;
Or like the speed of a hill hind;
Or like a hare on rented level ground. —
It was a frequent step — a fast step — a joyful step; —
The horses coming towards us: —
Like snow hewing the slopes; —
The panting and the snorting,
Of the horses coming towards thee.
(Sharp, *Lyra Celtica*, p. 7, from H. MacLean's *Ultonian Hero Ballads*)

The passage is remarkable for its mythopoeic exaggeration, graphic similes and explosive action, all characteristic of the Celtic heroic temperament.

It is in assessing the lyric-elegiac group that the difficulty of evaluation lies for a modern English reader. As John Montague pointed out, 'Irish literature in English is in the uneasy position that the larger part of its past lies in another language' ('In the Irish Grain', *The Faber Book of Irish Verse*, pp. 21-2). In closely observing nature, early lyrical poetry was unique for its time, partly because Ireland did not share the cultural traditions of the rest of Europe. 'Deirdre's Lament for the Sons of Uisnach', in the verse paraphrase of Samuel Ferguson (1810-86) is a poem in its own right; here the first seven stanzas are offered:

> The lions of the hill are gone,
> And I am left alone — alone —
> Dig the grave both wide and deep,
> For I am sick, and fain would sleep!
>
> The falcons of the wood are flown,
> And I am left alone — alone —
> Dig the grave both deep and wide,
> And let us slumber side by side.
>
> The dragons of the rock are sleeping,
> Sleep that wakes not for our weeping —
> Dig the grave, and make it ready,
> Lay me on my true-love's body.
>
> Lay their spears and bucklers bright
> By the warriors' sides aright;
> Many a day the three before me
> On their linkéd bucklers bore me.
>
> Lay upon the low grave floor,
> 'Neath each head, the blue claymore;
> Many a time the noble three
> Reddened their blue blades for me.
>
> Lay the collars, as is meet,
> Of the greyhounds at their feet;
> Many a time for me have they
> Brought the tall red deer to bay.
>
> In the falcon's jesses throw,
> Hook and arrow, line and bow;
> Never again, by stream or plain,
> Shall the gentle woodsmen go.
>
> (Sharp, *Lyra Celtica*, p. 8)

Occasional objections are raised to nineteenth century versions of this kind, notably by Kenneth Jackson in the preface of *A Celtic Miscellany* (pp. 8 and 12); he argues that they merely attempt to 'render the spirit', in a whimsical or sentimental fashion that is atypical of the poet's expressed emotions. Ferguson was, however, as well acquainted with the Irish language he translated, as he was with 'dark broodings over a mighty past'.

Until the advent of the Normans, the Irish Christian church was isolated from the forms of Catholicism that prevailed throughout the old Roman Empire. There was among worshippers a constant struggle between natural and organised religion. An Irishman's instincts in matters of faith did not take kindly to external restraint. Tales about saints tended to be as apocryphal as those about heroes. On the other hand, lyrical hermit poetry provided some of the most attractive literary compositions extant. 'The Deer's Cry', attributed to St Patrick, is a poem probably of eighth-century vintage; a translation (with text) appeared in the *Thesaurus Palaeohibernicus* of Stokes and Strachan (1901-10, CUP Vol II, p. 354). The present extract is from that source:

> I arise to-day
> Through the strength of heaven:
> Light of sun,
> Radiance of moon,
> Splendour of fire,
> Speed of lightning,
> Swiftness of wind,
> Depth of sea,
> Stability of earth,
> Firmness of rock.
>
> I arise to day
> Through God's strength to pilot me:
> God's might to uphold me,
> God's wisdom to guide me,
> God's eye to look before me,
> God's ear to hear me,
> God's word to speak for me,
> God's hand to guard me,
> . . .

Christ to shield me to-day
Against poison, against burning,
Against drowning, against wounding,
So that there may come to me abundance of reward.
        . . .
I arise to-day
Through a mighty strength, the invocation of the Trinity,
Through belief in the threeness,
Through confession of the oneness
Of the Creator of Creation.

> (*Selections from Ancient Irish Poetry*, ed. Kuno Meyer,
> pp. 25-7)

The legend runs that King Laoghaire set an ambush to prevent Patrick from going to Tara to convert pagan subjects.
The saint, however, sang this hymn, thereby deluding the
would-be assassins into believing that he and his monks were
a group of wild deer, passing by with a fawn.

The seemingly prosaic gnomic verses of Irish tradition are
as instructive as those of the Anglo-Saxons. A gnomic utterance contains condensed wisdom, expressed in a felicitous
form. Kuno Meyer edited and translated two volumes of the
first importance in *Triads of Ireland* (Dublin 1906) and
Instructions of King Cormac (Dublin 1909); he dated both
groups of sayings not earlier than the ninth century. To
writing of this origin Irish literature seems to owe something
of its incisive analogy, poetical simplicity and aptness of
phrase. Matthew Arnold, in *The Study of Celtic Literature*,
lecture 6, saw this gift as a 'certain condition of spiritual
excitement'; in it distinctions of verse and prose fall away.
He also speaks of 'the Titanism of the Celt, his passionate,
turbulent, indomitable reaction against the despotism of fact'
(p. 118). Arnold might have added the Gaelic thinker's gift
for satire, and perception of humanism, as revealed in the
following *Triads*:

> Three fair things that hide ugliness: good manners in
> the ill-favoured; skill in a serf; wisdom in the misshapen.
> Three sparks that kindle love: a face, demeanour, speech.
> Three glories of a gathering: a beautiful wife, a good
> horse, a swift hound.
>   . . .

Three laughing-stocks of the world: an angry man, a jealous man, a niggard.

Three signs of ill-breeding: a long visit, staring, constant questioning.

Three signs of a fop: the track of his comb in his hair; the track of his teeth in his food; the track of his stick behind him.

. . .

Three excellences of dress: elegance, comfort, lastingness.

Three candles that illume every darkness: truth, nature, knowledge.

Three keys that unlock thoughts: drunkenness, trustfulness, love.

. . .

Three things that ruin wisdom: ignorance, inaccurate knowledge, forgetfulness.

. . .

Three angry sisters: blasphemy, strife, foul-mouthedness.

Three disrespectful sisters: importunity, frivolity, flightiness.

Three signs of a bad man: bitterness, hatred, cowardice.

(Meyer, *Triads of Ireland*, pp. 102-4)

The literature above considered was written in 'Irish Celtic', an archaic language examined briefly in Part III of W. B. Lockwood's *Languages of the British Isles, Past and Present* (Deutsch 1975), in which his 'Sketch of Old Irish' occupies pages 81-89. It is necessary only to add that different orthographies of the scribes reflect the unphonetic character of the spellings they employed. The lack of system is apparent in the habits of writing proper names. For example, *Gráinne* [graːnja]; *Guairé* [guarja]; *Leabhar na H-uidre* [lowar na hiːra]; *Táin* [toin]; *Tighearnach* [tiarnaχ]; *Uisliu* [Iʃlu]. Modern writers on Old Irish prefer to simplify the full spellings; but a reader unskilled in the Celtic language still finds it difficult to determine the quality of many consonants and vowels, especially if the latter occur in unstressed syllables. Glide-vowels, moreover, tended to become dialectal diphthongs, but the date of change remains a matter of speculation. The fortunes of Irish, as a spoken language after the Norman invasion of 1169, must be left to another chapter.

III

Ireland, 1100-1800: The Historical Background

When Brian Boru was killed at the Battle of Clontarf in 1014 Ireland had achieved an enviable culture, which in the next hundred and fifty years was far from static. The advent of Norman-Welsh barons in the reign of Henry II radically changed the way of life, the rule of law and the system of government. Ireland was long in recovering from feudal neglect of its indigenous civilisation, as modified by the Vikings. The country's last autonomous High King was the able Turloch O'Connor of Connacht (1119-1156), whose ecclesiastical achievement was the Synod of Kells in 1152, when the country was divided into thirty-six dioceses. During O'Connor's rule, St Malachy of Armagh returned from a mission to Rome in 1142 with a group of Cistercian monks from St Bernard of Clairvaux; they settled on the River Boyne and built the first Gothic church in Ireland.

As part of the Cluniac reforms of the twelfth century, Pope Gregory VII required the church in Ireland, as well as Irish monasteries, to conform to western ecclesiastical ideas. But Irish conservatism looked upon all reformers as Ostmen (aliens); while the Archbishop of Canterbury, to whom the Irish bishops were asked to pay allegiance, was regarded as an interloper. At this time there were four Irish dioceses, at Armagh, Dublin, Cashel and Limerick. The first step to reform was the creation of a common liturgy for the church in Ireland. Just before the accession of O'Connor, Celsus of Armagh (whom the people called Cellach) was named first Archbishop of Ireland, his local title being Coarb ('saintly successor').

The principal Ostmen towns in the twelfth century were

the seaports of Dublin, Wexford and Waterford, but prejudice against the Gall-Gael inhabitants seems to have disappeared by 1155, when the English Pope Adrian IV (whose secular name was Breakspeare) authorised Henry II to take over Ireland, implement the diocesan system and reform the administration of the country. There is doubt about the authenticity of this commission, named *Laudabiliter*, but there is none regarding the manner in which it was carried out. The feudal dispossession, from baronial Wales, was not unexpected. The principal agent was the Earl of Pembroke, supported by his Anglo-Flemish community; he had received an invitation from the exiled King of Leinster, Dermot MacMurrough, whose countrymen charged him with oppression of the nobility. Henry II authorised Welsh intervention, in exchange for the vassalage of the dispossessed ruler. Dermot then lived at Bristol for some months before moving to St David's, where he prepared a joint expeditionary force.

The FitzGerald family of south-west Wales were descended on the maternal side from Nesta, daughter of Rhys ap Tewdwr, King of Dyfed. The Geraldines had many relatives, with the result that the first invasion of Ireland was largely a family venture, offering prospects to its members of individual advancement. In 1169 the force landed near Wexford, under Robert FitzStephen and Maurice Prendergast, an experienced soldier who came from the region of Ross, where Henry I had planted a colony of Flemings. The party consisted of thirty nights, sixty armed infantrymen and three hundred archers. They were joined by Maurice FitzGerald and Raymond le Gros; and a year later, at Waterford, by Richard FitzGilbert de Clare, Earl of Pembroke, known in Ireland as Strongbow. After the capture of Dublin in 1171 Dermot MacMurrough died, and Strongbow became the first Norman King of Leinster. Dublin remained the capital of the English rulers from that date, and was the first city in Ireland to receive a municipal charter (1192).

Strongbow was, however, out of favour with Henry II, and, fearing the repercussions of a separate Norman kingship in Ireland, submitted to his ruler when Henry moved into south Wales. The king crossed to Ireland in October 1171 with an army of four thousand and stayed for six months to secure the allegiance of Irish rulers, including Pembroke's. This move was ostensibly in the interests of church unity. Leinster was made a sub-earldom of Pembroke, and the FitzGerald barons were confirmed in possession of the lands with which they had been rewarded for military services by Dermot.

By the Council of Lismore (1171) King Henry introduced the laws of England to Ireland, although it was not made clear to what sections of the population they applied. At Waterford and Dublin Irish rulers, including the *árd rí* (High King), recognised Henry's suzerainty and protection, in return for annual tributes. The Irish church accepted the validity of the English king's commission from the pope, in the hope that centralised rule would lead to religious concord; and the long-awaited reforms were adopted at the Synod of Cashel in December 1171. No Irish primate was acknowledged, and the liturgy was to be that of the Church of England. All these decrees were approved by Pope Alexander in 1172.

Henry decided that the Ostmen seaports of Limerick, Cork, Waterford and Wexford, were to remain commercial and shipping centres, garrisoned and controlled by the Crown. He nominated Hugh de Lacy as Justiciar or royal representative in Ireland, the territory assigned to him incorporating the greater part of the county of Dublin, to the detriment of the rulers of Meath. This defensible area was deliberately anglicised and came to be known as the English Pale.

Accounts of Strongbow's conquest of Ireland are invariably one-sided, being dependent on the *Expugnatio* of Giraldus Cambrensis, who accompanied Prince John to Ireland in 1184. This partisan witness saw the Irish as 'a race constant only in inconsistency, to be reckoned upon for nothing but their instability' (*Conquest of Ireland*, Bk II, ch. 1); but Edmund Curtis, the modern historian, describes the Norman invaders as 'gentlemen buccaneers'.

Nevertheless, Norman feudalism, as developed in England in the twelfth century, was the only viable means of controlling the acquired territory of the Irish patriarchies. The

hereditary kingdoms of the Celts were too small and antagon-
istic to survive. In spite of ardent nationalism, their patriotism
was local and clan-centred. Military resistance was poorly
organised and the equipment amateurish, except in the case
of the Ostmen, who were seamen and traders. These Gall-
Gaels promoted the wealth of the rural community through
their dealings in cattle.

Though Henry II established feudalism in Ireland with
little bloodshed, his authority was limited to the southern
and eastern regions. But he set the pattern for further
aggrandisement; and Maurice FitzGerald, a soldier of ability,
thought it possible for the small task force of 1171 to have
conquered the whole of Ireland. The policy behind the king's
appointment of Hugh de Lacy was to counterbalance the
power of the 'race of Nesta', in the person of the Earl of
Pembroke.

One of de Lacy's first steps in Meath was to rid himself
treacherously of the petty King of Breffni, Tighernan
O'Ruairc (Tiernan O'Rourke), which he did at a political
parley. Giraldus Cambrensis accused the Irish party of
double-dealing (*Conquest of Ireland*, Book I, ch. 40); but
there was mistrust and broken faith on both sides, the
Justiciar's party prevailing because it was secretly and better
armed. Nothing could stop the ruthless Anglo-Normans from
confiscating the property of Irish landowners, and supplan-
ting the officers of the church. In the four provinces of
Ulster, Connacht, Leinster and Munster, feudal landlords
took over, as they did in Wales. In 1173 the king's son,
Richard, was made Guardian of Ireland, with estates in
Wicklow and Wexford. Four years later the king's other son,
John, became Lord of Ireland and seized the barony of
Louth.

The leading families came to Ireland in three stages, with
the Earl of Pembroke, with King Henry II, and with Prince
John. Their households were the forebears of the Anglo-Irish
magnates, four of whom married Irish princesses to ensure
permanence. The rapacity of most lords was the cause of
Ireland's subsequent misfortunes. The principal families were
the various FitzGeralds of Offaly, Kildare, Munster and
Desmond; the FitzGilberts deriving from Strongbow, whose

line included the Lords of Wexford, descendants of Will de Valence; the de Lacy's of Ludlow who settled mainly in Meath; the du Bourgs or de Burgo's (later Bourkes) who found a place in Connacht and married into the O'Brien family — a branch of this family, the Mac Williams, became prominent in Mayo; the Butlers of Ormond, descendants of Theobold Walter, 'La Botiller', butler to Prince John; and the Mortimers, who became Earls of Ulster or Lords of Trim. Scarcely less influential were the Berminghams, Carews, de Courcys, Gautiers and Verduns; Bertram de Verdun had accompanied Prince John to Ireland, as his steward. All were freebooters of feudalism, who turned the Irish peasantry into serfs, known as *betaghs*, or 'food-providers'.

By the Treaty of Windsor (1175), about half of Ireland (the western regions) remained under the *árd rí*, Rory O'Connor of Connacht. He was to regard himself as liege of the English king, responsible for maintaining peace in his realm, and collecting the tribute of hides exacted of the vassal state. This tribute was apparently never paid. Rory died in 1198, and was succeeded by his brother, Cathal; but the shadowy independence of Connacht ended in 1224.

The Irish resistance movement began as a result of the defeat of Strongbow by Donal O'Brien near Limerick. Its primary purpose was to re-assert the rights of Irish land-owners, denied by Anglo-Irish courts; but militarily it had not the means to achieve much success. By the beginning of the fourteenth century most of exploitable Ireland was in the hands of Welsh or English feudal landlords. Leinster and five of the smaller kingdoms had completely lost independence. Only the north-west of Ireland, under the O'Neills and O'Donnells had not submitted; Connacht was conquered by Richard de Burgo in 1235.

When Strongbow died in 1176, Leinster, with its five modern counties, was taken over by the Crown, as the legitimate successor, Isabelle de Clare, was too young to manage her affairs. Native chieftains retreated to the mountains and forests of Leinster, leaving the cultivated lands to the barons. To extend his power, with limited human resources, Henry II granted the 'kingdom of Cork' to Milo de Cogan and Robert FitzStephen (illegitimate son of Nesta and of Stephen, one-time Constable of Cardiganshire), thereby unjustly displacing Dermot MacCarthy, King of Desmond. Similarly, the Welsh Lord of Brecon, Philip de Braose, was made titular 'King of Limerick'; but Donal O'Brien denied occupation until his death in 1194. Antrim and Down were independently conquered in 1177 by John de Courcey of Somerset, who became known as Prince of Ulidia, ruling from Downpatrick. He built stone castles in strategic positions and founded four Benedictine abbeys, but was deprived of independence by King John in 1205.

King John, the first Plantagenet king to limit baronial power in Ireland, re-established the O'Brien family in Thomond (Limerick) and the O'Connors in Connacht. To administer his policy, he appointed Meiler FitzHenry as Justiciar (1200-8) and effectively applied the laws of England, with the jury system introduced by Henry II. Dublin Castle, seat of the government, began to be built. The political blunder, however, was the failure to integrate families of the 'five bloods' in the new realm, by offering earldoms to their heads. These were the families from which the Irish High Kings had been chosen: the MacCarthy's, the MacMurroughs, the O'Briens, the O'Connors and the O'Neills.

Laurence O'Toole, last of the Irish archbishops and mediator at the Treaty of Windsor, had died in 1180, his successor being the English bishop, John Comyn, who commenced the building of St Patrick's cathedral in Dublin. King John instructed that bishops should be appointed in nine sees, as the nucleus of the state church of Ireland; but Gaels (native Irishmen) were excluded from ecclesiastical office, except in Armagh, Cashel and Tuam. Feudal bishops, who adminstered their own courts and knew no Irish, were entirely foreign to Celtic custom.

Two events of importance marked the turn of the thirteenth century, the meeting of the first Irish Parliament in 1297, and Bruce's invasion of Ireland, 1315-18. The Anglo-Irish Parliament met through the enterprise of John de Wogan of Pembroke, who became Irish Justiciar in 1295. Edward I wanted and obtained Irish assistance in his wars against Scotland, and to this end his deputy called together representatives of nine counties and five 'liberties', in addition to the earls and leading ecclesiastics. This parliament did not meet again until 1310.

The Bruce invasion was the result of the Battle of Bannockburn in 1314, when the Scots recovered their freedom; Edward Bruce of Galloway, the brother of King Robert, sought to rouse the Gaels of Ireland against the English by landing in Ulster with a force of six thousand mail-clad, experienced warriors. Winning successive victories over Roger Mortimer and Edmund Butler, Bruce was soon crowned King of Erin in Dundalk, only to see his ally, Felim of Connacht, defeated at the Battle of Athenry in August 1316. Robert Bruce joined Edward later that year, and caused devastation in central Ireland; but the brothers were unable to capture the well-defended city of Dublin. Robert immediately returned to Scotland, and his brother was able to make so little headway that he was killed in battle near Dundalk in October 1318. The misery of the country during this war is reflected in the Remonstrance sent to Pope John XXII in 1317.

In Ulster and the west of the country the Irish chieftains were gradually able to recover petty kingdoms, as well as castles that went by default, when an Anglo-Irish family disappeared from the scene. The power of resistance in Ulster was increased by the 'gallowglasses' (mailed axe-men) from the Hebrides, and the fighting zeal of the local kerns. The regression of English power in Ireland began in the reign of Edward III (1327-77) and the situation deteriorated during the succeeding century, as the aspiration of the Anglo-Irish for Home Rule made its appearance.

It was fortunate that the Norman barons, like the Danes and Norwegians before them, were soon assimilated to the native population, either through marriage or property interests, during the fourteenth century. By 1360 the use of the French language was rare in Ireland; for the Anglo-Irish had adopted native dress and customs. To meet this development the Statutes of Kilkenny were passed in 1367 by the Anglo-Irish Parliament; they forbade loyalists, at the risk of high treason, to speak Irish, dress in the native fashion, encourage 'foster' parentage, or recognise Brehon laws. The effect was to make the English of the Pale intolerable jingoes.

Indeed, the Kilkenny laws of Lionel Duke of Clarence, in the reign of Edward III, were a diplomatic disaster, because the repressive legislation was anti-social in intention; communication between neighbours was made impossible by the enactment's threefold classification. These were named as English-speaking loyalists of the Pale; the 'degenerate' English, with Gaelic manners, considered to be of doubtful allegiance; and his Irish enemies, pariahs excluded from the protection of the law. Because they inhibited reconciliation between governing and governed, the statutes were rarely enforced, but the spirit of their conception stimulated rebellion. Yet the statutes remained in force for two hundred years.

The king's Justiciar in Ireland was now called the Lord Deputy, or Lord Lieutenant. His office was no sinecure, and, being indifferently remunerated, did not attract men of the highest rank. Those who came were often ignorant of Irish affairs, yet expected to make the incumbency self-supporting by coercing Irish parliaments to approve of taxation without Gaelic representation. The important Anglo-Irish families, FitzGeralds and Butlers, remained loyal to the Crown until the Wars of the Roses, it being in their interests to do so, as some owned property in England and Wales. A document of 1395 records that the Earl of Ormond (a Butler) spoke both English and Irish fluently.

One of the objects of the Kilkenny Statutes had been to make the Anglo-Irish lords responsible for their Irish retainers and armed forces, which were growing in numbers. No effort was, however, made to increase the English-speaking population by immigration, or to improve the standard of education. There was a progressive decline of the English language until the seventeenth century, and a corresponding growth of Irish literature in manuscript. The official languages of debate in the Irish Parliament were French and English.

In 1394 Richard II visited Ireland to retrieve the realm's dwindling fortunes; he was accompanied by Thomas Mowbray and other peers, and a considerable army. The plan was to enlarge the English Pale of Meath and Dublin, to pardon the 'rebel Irish' (*hibernicised* Normans) and to confirm the Irish chiefs in the land they had possessed since the reign of Henry II, expecting in return their honourable allegiance. The innovation was that Richard now offered native Irishmen legal status under the Crown. The terms resembled those of the Remonstrance of 1317, and Richard received the homage of all chiefs, except Turloch O'Donnell, and a vassal of his named Maguire. On the most important of the Irish leaders he conferred knighthoods; but the ceremony, as described in Froissart's *Chronicles*, indicated a characteristic reluctance on the part of the recipients.

Unfortunately, Richard's diplomatic settlement lacked the power of enforcement, especially in the remoter parts of Ireland. In Leix and Offaly, where *urrighs*, or under-chiefs, of the MacMurrough family brooked no interference, allegiance was sorely tested. These chieftains were not represented in Parliament, and if they had been, would not have acquiesced in its Anglo-Irish leanings. Art Kavanagh of Norragh defied the Lord Deputy, Roger Mortimer, Earl of March, and the latter was killed at the Battle of Kellistown (1398). Richard II returned to Ireland to avenge Mortimer's death, but his heavily armed troops were found to be useless in the wild hill-country. Kavanagh, avoiding all engagements except a parley, retorted that he was the rightful King of Ireland. The episode is colourfully described in Jean Creton's *Histoire du Roi d'Angleterre Richard* (1399). When the king received the news of Bolingbroke's landing at Ravenspur, he was compelled to return to England, and to his own eventual dethronement.

Thus Leinster, the first province to fall in the Norman-Welsh invasion, struck a blow for Irish liberation. Two-thirds of Ireland was now partitioned between the Anglo-Irish earls and the Gaelic chieftains; the Irish language became universally current. Art Oge MacMurrough Kavanagh, remained King of Leinster from 1376 to 1417; but he voluntarily became a liege-lord of Henry V before his death in 1418. With him, the title of 'king' in Ireland disappeared. There were, however, over fifty comparable rulers, and political unity (Ireland's greatest need) was as distant as ever.

The office of King's Lieutenant was continued, but little influence could be exerted outside the English Pale of Meath and Leinster; the honour of conducting what was virtually a Dublin-centred government was twice held by Sir John

Talbot (1414 and 1442), who figures in Shapespeare's *Henry VI*, part I. During the reigns of the Lancastrian kings many English-speaking persons returned to England; and, except in the demesnes of the entrenched March lords, the Anglo-Irish population dwindled.

Richard, Duke of York, held four lordships in Ireland; he became Lord Lieutenant after Talbot in 1447, and during the next thirteen years was responsible for Irish support of the Yorkist cause. A supporter of Home Rule, he became so popular in Ireland that twenty-four chieftains, led by the powerful O'Neills, swore allegiance to him. George, Duke of Clarence (of Shakespeare's *Richard III*) was born to York in Dublin. Richard's elder son, Edward, Earl of March, was crowned King Edward IV in 1461, and the four Irish lordships were then absorbed by the Crown.

Desmond, of the FitzGerald family, now superseded Butler, the Lancastrian, as the principal earl of Ireland, and Thomas of that sept deputised for George, Duke of Clarence, as Lieutenant, until 1467. But the following year Thomas Desmond was beheaded for treating with the king's enemies and supporting Home Rule, the Crown invoking the Statutes of Kilkenny. This came as a shock to the Irish people, for Desmond was a man of culture, and founder of the Collegiate Church School at Youghal, an enterprise in higher education. Thomas, Earl of Kildare (another FitzGerald) filled the vacant lieutenancy from 1470 to 1477. His son, Gerald (whom the Irish called Garret More), became virtual ruler of Ireland from 1477 to 1513; and in his time the Irish Parliament, summoned in various places, increased its status as a power in the community.

Kildare's proximity to Dublin made it feasible for the viceroy to use his personal influence over the Great Council, the Parliament and the cultural life of the capital, now the hub of English pragmatism in colonial rule. Gerald the Great (Garret More) was the first Lieutenant to introduce muskets for arming the guards in Dublin. He is said to have been a governor of good humour, as well as action, and gifted with an incisive readiness of speech. Although his sympathies were unashamedly with the House of York, his strong and beneficent rule induced the Tudor monarch, Henry VII, now controller of the Yorkist estates in Ireland, to retain Gerald's services as King's Lieutenant. But during Kildare's governorship, two stooge pretenders to the English throne, Lambert Simnel of Oxford and Perkin Warbeck of Tournai, were supported by some Irish chieftains. For these Yorkist plots Kildare was replaced, and Sir Edward Poynings was despatched with a thousand men to suppress the stirrings of Home Rule, with which Kildare was known to be associated.

Poynings assembled Parliament at Drogheda in 1494, and charged Gerald Kildare with high treason for inciting rebellion among the Irish, by rallying support for these imposters; he was also accused of the offence of billeting troops on English subjects in the Pale. The fearful representatives were persuaded, and Kildare was imprisoned in the Tower of London. The indictment ended the division of Ireland which was associated with the Home Rule movement, and steps were taken towards political union, under English rule. The Statutes of Kilkenny were re-enacted; English writs were to be regarded as valid, and Englishmen alone were permitted to fill responsible offices. By these Poynings Laws (1495) the Irish Parliament became subordinate to the Privy Council of the Lord Lieutenant, who in turn was responsible to the king's Council in Westminster. Henry VIII, in 1541, became the first English monarch to accept the crown on behalf of the kingdom of Ireland, as well as England.

When Poynings left Ireland at the beginning of 1496, the widowed Kildare was restored to his lieutenancy, having taken as his second wife the king's cousin, Elizabeth St John, by whom he had five sons, all of whom unfortunately died as rebels at Tyburn in 1537. The effect of the new laws was to weaken the powers of the Irish Parliament, but to strengthen those of the king's deputy. Kildare's second spell of rule was spent in quelling Irish feuds and restoring the balance of power among the leading families. At the age of fifty-four he was killed by a musket shot in September 1513, conducting a minor skirmish against the O'Mores of Leix.

The death of Garret More marked the end of an epoch, in which medieval Ireland changed its social and political character from a rural and Gaelic community to a partly urbanised and cosmopolitan one. The growth of towns had been fostered by Henry II's confidence in free trade. From the twelfth century Dublin was the principal commercial port, modelled on the English liberty of Bristol. All Irish seaport towns owed their origins to Viking enterprise, and Waterford, Cork, Limerick and Galway were granted similar liberties to Bristol. Galway became the western centre of the fishing industry, in which Loch Corrib was then of considerable importance. A walled town by 1270, Galway received royal charters in 1396 and 1484; only two other towns had been founded in the kingdom of Connacht by the earlier of these dates, Athenry and Sligo. Thirty-three Irish towns are known to have existed by the year 1300.

The political influence of the Irish towns became increasingly important with their growth; for their populations were mixed, with a strong infusion of non-Gaelic elements, such as Scandinavians, French and Flemish. The seaport towns resisted not only feudalism, but the pressures of the Irish chieftains, and were invariably loyal to the king; but the Lord Lieutenant took the unfortunate view that such towns should be responsible for their own defence, from the sea as well as the land.

Inland villages and towns of the Middle Ages were at first places of refuge for *betaghs* who wished to escape the servitude of the manorial system. These villeins of feudalism were nominally emancipated by an edict of Edward III in 1331, which took time to become legally effective. *Betaghs* continued to be disposed of, like chattels, along with the land; but if they decamped to a town 'for a year and a day', they were entitled to freedom. Those voluntarily freed by the landowners, as an act of piety, were compelled to pay rent for the land on which they gained a livelihood. When the *betaghs* were liberated, the majority of farmers became pastoralists, rather than tillers of the soil. This fourteenth-century change coincided with the disappearance of manorial feudalism.

The names of inland towns show that their inhabitants were predominantly Irish. Some of the towns disappeared in the fourteenth century, because the Statutes of Kilkenny forbade tradesmen to traffic with the 'Irish enemy'. Some economists hold that the ban on Irish fairs and markets was a cause of trade depressions, with which Ireland was constantly threatened. Towns of the south and the east were usually the more prosperous.

In Ulster the principal centres of growth were the church towns of Armagh and Downpatrick, though Carrickfergus appears frequently in the historical records; they were predominantly Irish settlements. In Munster, the characteristic medieval town to survive was Kinsale. Towns were governed by burough councils, which tended to become oligarchies of leading families, and English in their citizens' political leanings, dress and style of living. An important contribution of the towns to social culture was the bilingualism of the majority, the languages of communication being English and Irish.

The event that most affected the structure of Irish society in Tudor times was the Reformation. Indeed, the Protestant religion, more than internal rebellion, gave an impetus to the second conquest of Ireland, although the Irish firebrand, Silken Thomas, Lord of Offaly, provided the spark to the conflict. This militant figure was a grandson of Garret More, and the son of Garret Oge (Gerald the Younger), who succeeded his father as Lord Lieutenant of Ireland. Through the machinations of his political rivals and incitement from Cardinal Wolsey, Garret was confined to the Tower, and falsely rumoured to be dead. His son Thomas, who gained the sobriquet 'Silken' from the ostentatious uniforms of his bodyguard, was deputising for his father from 1534; he immediately rose in the Council to challenge the authority of Henry VIII. In the tumult that arose the leading conspirators, including Thomas, were arrested and hanged like common criminals at Tyburn. The rebellious elements were quelled by Sir William Skeffington's occupation of Dublin and capture of Maynooth Castle, the entire garrison of which was put to the sword. This ruthless intimidatory act ended the power of the Geraldine family.

Thomas Cromwell, new Chief Minister, and the Reformation Parliament of 1529-36 then set about reforming the Irish church, bringing it into line with the Church of England. The first steps were the dissolution of the abbeys and monasteries, the acquisition of their property by the Crown, and the withdrawal of church representation in the Irish Parliament. By the Act of Supremacy, Henry VIII was declared head of the Church of Ireland, an unprecedented move, which was opposed by most churchmen, including the influential English. A majority of the bishops seems to have agreed to the rejection of the pope's authority, but there was practically no change in church services. The sacraments continued to be administered in Latin, but sermons were delivered in English. The first Prayer Book of Edward VI was actually printed in Dublin in 1551.

With Henry VIII established as King of Ireland in 1541, the office of the King's Lieutenant, and Kildare's aristocratic Home Rule terminated. The new Irish civil service, headed by the Lord Deputy, Sir Anthony St Leger, comprised English or Anglo-Irish officials only, and Ireland was granted its own law courts. But though representation in the Parliament was enlarged, and included a few important chiefs, jurisdiction was limited to the anglicised part of the country. With the many Gaelic chieftains, the conciliatory Deputy entered into territorial treaties, upon their acknowledgement of the king's authority. The first English colonisation was attempted in County Down in Ulster during the reign of Edward VI, when the Crown offered Sir Nicholas Bagenal land in the Mourne area belonging to the Abbey of Newry. Except for five years in the time of the Catholic Queen Mary, when papal authority was nominally restored, Protestants gained ground in Irish affairs, since they could not be legally dispossessed of the church land they had acquired through the Surveyor General, Walter Cowley. Not only church lands were expropriated; many chiefs forfeited estates through so-called treasonable acts, decided by packed juries. The injustices which accompanied the 'plantation' of English owners were the cause of much Irish bitterness. Gradually, however, exiled Anglo-Norman lords were allowed to return, among them Thomas Butler, Earl of Ormond, who accepted the new faith, being related to the Tudor line through Henry VIII's second wife, Anne Boleyn.

The new English colonies were intended to act as buffer zones, and colonists were bound to improve their quit-rent estates by building in stone, and to provide forces to the

Lord Deputy's defence of the realm. Thus were introduced the English county divisions of Ireland. Unjust appropriations of land at the expense of hereditary chieftains were resisted for the next fifty years, during which many traditional Irish families disappeared. The rule of Queen Elizabeth, whose strength was in Meath, Leinster and Ormond, spelt the end of Gaelic as well as feudal government, saw the annulment of Brehon law on freehold property, and abolished the elective status of chiefs by Tanistry. The Irish question was exacerbated by so-called 'tame' Irishmen who chose, for security reasons, to co-operate with the new government.

The Irish Parliament meeting early in 1560 was bent on permanent social changes, though it represented only ten counties. Its chief instrument was the Act of Uniformity, imposing the Prayer Book of 'the Queen's religion' on worshippers who could barely understand English, and allowing Latin as the only alternative. Queen Elizabeth sought to avoid religious persecution, by instructing the Lord Deputy not to press the oath of supremacy; but a number of officials, including bishops, were nevertheless deprived of their office. The Act of Uniformity divided Ireland into two camps, of Butlers and Geraldines, the latter now represented by the O'Neill and O'Brien families. In 1562 Shane O'Neill of Ulster diplomatically accepted from the queen the title of Lord of Tyrone; but he championed the retention of the Brehon Law of Tanistry. His only service to the Crown was to rid the glens of Antrim of James MacDonnell and the Hebridean Scots, a thorn in the flesh of the English Deputy, Sir Henry Sidney (1565). But O'Neill was murdered by the militant Scots two years later.

Deputy Sidney had insufficient money or arms to reform Ireland in accordance with the Tudor Protestant ideal. The main sources of rebellion were the absence of secure land-ownership and religious intolerance, which played into the hands of the Jesuits sent to promote the Counter-Reformation. In the south came an influx of land-seekers from Devon, including exploiters such as Sir Walter Raleigh and Sir Humphrey Gilbert, who with Crown connivance established themselves near Cork, in Munster. In this area, and in Connacht, many risings took place, Fitzmaurice's revolt in

Kerry (1579) being the most significant; for it was supported by Philip II of Spain and Pope Gregory XIII. Within a month Fitzmaurice was killed in a skirmish; but the conflict continued for a year before the insurgents were victorious at Glenmalure in 1580. In the suppression of guerrilla warfare (1583), in which Sir Walter Raleigh had a hand, the Earl of Desmond lost his life. Of the atrocities committed there are many accounts, among them Edmund Spenser's *View of the Present State of Ireland*, in which he wrote of the population's decimation: 'in short space, there was almost none left, and a most populous and lentiful country suddenly left void of man and beast' (p. 104).

After every uprising the policy was to colonise offending areas with settlers of English origin. Five hundred thousand acres of Munster soil were expropriated in 1586, of which half was allocated to Englishmen, preferably Protestants, on quit-rent terms; forty thousand acres went to Sir Walter Raleigh.

Twenty-seven counties were now represented in the Irish Parliament; but in 1580 its powers had been shorn by the creation of a Star Chamber, called the Court of Castle Chamber, operating from Dublin. This court was a pillar of strength to English officialdom, taking orders directly from Westminster. To boost the cultural supremacy of Dublin and the Pale, Trinity College was founded in 1592.

The last of the northern Gaelic lords, Red Hugh O'Donnell of Tyrconnell, was elected in the same year; he was the spirited instigator of the Catholic Confederacy of 1594-1603. Its struggle for power lasted ten years, largely because Ireland remained a side-issue with the Tudor monarchy; neither money nor manpower was in sufficient strength to maintain the new English colony. O'Neill and O'Donnell were well armed with disciplined troops, and were emboldened by moral as well as physical support from the pope, the Scots and Philip II of Spain. When Sir Henry Bagenal was defeated at Clontibret in 1595, both confederates were declared traitors; but temporising negotiations compelled them to be pardoned, without conceding their demand for religious toleration.

Meantime the strength of the government's army was raised

to seven thousand men; but a three-pronged attack on Ulster in 1597 proved unsuccessful. In the summer of 1598 Sir Henry Bagenal was defeated and killed, with the loss of fifteen hundred men, at the Battle of Yellow Ford, on the Blackwater. O'Neill was in a position to oust the Munster colonists, and to attempt re-instatement of the Geraldines, when his success rallied thirty thousand rebels to his cause. Queen Elizabeth reacted by appointing the Earl of Essex as Lord Deputy of Ireland, with an army of seventeen thousand. His wavering policy and successive defeats in Wicklow in four months reduced his force to a quarter of its size. Essex had no alternative but to negotiate a truce with O'Neill, whereupon he was recalled by the queen, disgraced, and executed for treason in 1600. He was succeeded in Ireland by Charles Blount, Lord Mountjoy.

The new Lord Deputy was resolute and ruthless, with a well-equipped army of twenty thousand, deployed to carry out his scorched-earth tactics, rather than seek engagements. Mountjoy gained the upper hand by creating conditions of famine, including the destruction of crops; in crushing the southern rebellion he was helped by the President of Munster, Sir George Carew, who did nothing to stop the annihilation of garrisons. Stern action in the south was a preliminary to tackling the root of rebellion in Ulster. O'Neill had secured his position with fortified entrenchments on the approach from Dublin, and it became expedient to capture Derry, so that he could be attacked from the north.

Philip II of Spain died in 1598, but in September 1601 his successor, Philip III, despatched a force of four thousand, under Juan D'Aguila, to land at Kinsale on the southern coast; O'Neill and O'Donnell had to march the length of Ireland to meet them. When they arrived the seaport was already besieged by Mountjoy's forces. A decisive battle outside the town was fought on the day before Christmas, in which O'Neill was defeated, with the loss of nearly all his Scots mercenaries, one of the Spanish regiments, and some fifteen hundred of his Irish troops. Kinsale's Spanish defenders capitulated, and O'Donnell took ship to Spain, where he died at Salamanca, from suspected poisoning, the following year. Such penury and famine were then inflicted on Tyrone that resistance became impossible. O'Neill reluctantly surrendered a week after the death of Queen Elizabeth in March 1603. James I had claimed to be a friend to O'Neill and restored his earldom, with most estates, but abolished for ever the lordships of 'countries' and captains of 'nations', which were characteristic of the tradition of Tanistry; above all, he undermined the patriotic bardic stimulus. The English king introduced an Act of Oblivion in 1604, which promised protection to all loyal Irishmen, irrespective of former affiliations; but he did not grant freedom of worship. In 1607 O'Neill and ninety-nine northern chieftains therefore left Ireland, and the former died in Rome in 1616.

Shires, sheriffs and English law were introduced throughout the country in the first quarter of the seventeenth century, when Sir John Davies became the first Attorney-General. A royal commission confirmed all titles to land on the respective merits of the claimants. It found that religious divisions were not clear-cut, but townsmen tended to be Protestant in sympathy (though most towns had Catholic mayors until 1624), while countrymen were predominantly Catholic. Under the early Stuarts there was little religious persecution; but the commission discovered that recusancy and its effect upon the right to hold public office were emotive issues. Recusants could sit in Parliament and might have gained broader recognition had it not been for the Gunpowder Plot of 1606. In England, the king had diplomatically opted for the Established Church; in Ireland Catholics (especially Jesuits) and Puritans came to be regarded by the English Parliament as potentially seditious.

The Plantation of Ulster was the provocative event of James I's administration, being preceded by an Act of Parliament that attainted fugitive lords and expropriated their property. Under Brehon law this land did not, in fact, belong to the chieftains. Great hardship descended upon dispossessed tenants who tilled the soil. The State left Antrim, Down and Monaghan virtually untouched, but acquired by legal process most of the six counties of Armagh, Cavan, Derry, Donegal, Tyrone and Fermanagh, altogether half-a-million acres, part of which was designed for colonisation. 'Undertakers' enjoyed the privilege of disposing of Crown land to English and Lowland Scots settlers, on a quit-rent basis, the understanding being that allotments might be sublet to Irish tenants. The Lord Deputy, Sir Arthur Chichester, protested against this procedure, and thought that half the land should have remained in the possession of freeholders.

The Established Church inherited large endowments of what had been a predominantly Catholic area, and new boroughs were to be governed by Protestants, including Scots Presbyterians. London City acquired on lease part of northern Derry, in which it developed the modern town of Londonderry, for the benefit of Scots and English settlers. The Scottish land-barons, James Hamilton and Hugh Montgomery, acquired large tracts of land near the town of Belfast, which had grown up round John de Courcy's fortress of 1177. Such developments explain the rise of Presbyterianism in the province of Ulster, but this did not make much impact until after 1660. Nevertheless, the apparent success of the Ulster experiment led to lesser ones, aimed at strengthening the Protestant and loyalist influence in Ireland. Other schemes were introduced in Longford, Carlow, Wicklow, Wexford and Leitrim, where the Irish were dispossessed of a quarter of their land in return for security of tenure on what remained. Within a generation Gaelic landlordism was virtually extinguished and the bulk of the Catholic rural population converted to cottagers and tenants.

To confirm these measures and secure a Protestant majority in Parliament, thirty-nine new boroughs were created, on the recommendation of regional sheriffs. In 1614 a deputation of recusants approached King James I on religious disabilities; though it was unsympathetically received, eleven of the new buroughs were discarded and compulsory church-attendance was not enforced. But the principal Catholic grievances, land and religion, remained. The industrial enterprise of Richard Boyle, Earl of Cork, who had bought Sir Walter Raleigh's estates for a thousand pounds, changed that part of Munster to a largely Protestant area. A large capital investment developed the iron and linen industries; and Boyle took over the College of Youghal, which the Earl of Desmond had founded.

The exploitation of Ireland reached its peak under the Earl of Strafford, Sir Thomas Wentworth (1633-40), whose strategy was to limit the power of Protestant capitalists in Ulster and Munster, by offering alluring concessions to the Catholics, in return for exactions levied to aid the cause of Charles I; his principal targets were the City of Londonderry in the north, and the Earldom of Cork in the south. Expecting repercussions, he raised among the dispossessed a private army of nine thousand men; but although his economic policy led to some prosperity, the promises were not fulfilled, because of anti-Catholic feeling in England. Strafford was recalled, impeached and executed in May 1641. His splendid army was then disbanded, and two Puritan Parliamentarians, Borlase and Parsons, were appointed as joint Deputies.

An Irish Catholic rebellion broke out in August 1641, the leaders of which were Rory O'More and Felim O'Neill; their attempt to capture Dublin was foiled. In Ulster, however, ten thousand defenceless colonists were killed, and their massacre induced the Long Parliament to pass the Adventurers Act, which declared the property of rebels forfeit to speculators who offered an acceptable sum for the conduct of war. By this Act the king was forbidden to grant pardons to the Irish leaders; but he retaliated by persuading the Scots to join his party, and General Munro landed in Ulster with a strong force in April 1642. The revolt in Ireland preceded the Great Rebellion in England by nearly a year, and was not quelled until 1649.

The effect of the Civil War in England was to re-align the political groups in Ireland; changes began with the exclusion of Catholics from Parliament. The king appointed James, Earl of Ormond (a Protestant) as his Deputy in Dublin to oppose the power of Borlase and Parsons; but the principal rallying points for the Protestant cause became Derry and Cork. The expelled Catholic parliamentarians responded by setting up an independent body, known as the Catholic Confederation of Kilkenny (1642); Ormond served as a kind of go-between with the king. The situation was extremely complex; as few could foresee the outcome of the power-struggle in England, affiliations in Ireland tended to be fluid. The Catholic Confederation was essentially royalist, and therefore included some loyal Protestants.

Effective military action was placed in the hands of two professional Irish soldiers from the Continent: Owen Roe O'Neill, nephew of the Earl of Tyrone, who commanded in Ulster; and General Preston, who was in charge of the south; the latter was defeated by Ormond at New Ross in 1643. Six months later the Papal Nuncio, Rinuccini, arrived from Rome, with financial support from the French king, Louis XIV; he injected a religious enthusiasm into the cause, and O'Neill gained a notable victory over the Parliamentarian army at Benburb, Tyrone, in the summer of 1646.

After his defeat at Naseby (1645) Charles I was in need of reinforcements from Ireland, for which he promised the removal of all Catholic disabilities; but Rinuccini advised against external aid to a Protestant king, whose promises were unlikely to be fulfilled. Ormond had no alternative but to hand over Dublin to Cromwell's forces, under Colonel Michael Jones, who frustrated Preston's attempt to seize the city at Dangan Hill. Then Murrough O'Brien, Earl of Inchiquin and President of Munster (supporting the Parliamentarians) overcame a Catholic army at Knockanoss in November 1647. Munster, in consequence, did not suffer from the severities of retribution inflicted on Wexford and Ulster.

Oliver Cromwell became Lord Lieutenant of Ireland in August 1649, accompanied by an army of twenty thousand Roundheads. He showed no quarter to Irish Catholics and peers; terrorism was the approved method of intimidation, and almost the entire royalist populations of Drogheda and Wexford were sacrificed. By proclamation, he forbade all 'popish' ritual in the churches. Resistance virtually collapsed with the death of O'Neill at Cavan in November 1649, and of Rory O'More a few years later. The only occasion on which Cromwell was repulsed was at Clonmel in 1650, just before his return to England. He left Ireton, his son-in-law, as Lord Lieutenant in command of the Parliamentary forces. With the surrender of Limerick, Galway and Ulster in 1651-2, the Irish war was practically over, and some thirty thousand of the rebel forces were granted permission to leave the country for France and Spain. Irish labourers emigrated in numbers to the West Indies. As a result it is estimated that the humiliated population was reduced to about five hundred thousand.

The Rump Parliament, after Pride's Purge of 1648, passed an Act of Settlement for Ireland in August 1652; its inequity was excused on the ground that Cromwell had to defray the costs incurred in suppressing the rebellion. Nine counties were confiscated to the Commonwealth, and Clare and Connacht remained the only parts of the country available to Irish landowners. All the gentry were given smaller estates west of the River Shannon, but the labouring classes were left where they lived to cultivate the land occupied by Cromwell's soldiers, to the number of nineteen thousand, or by English adventurers. This unpopular scheme of trans- plantation, which placed more than half of Irish land in the hands of the Protector's men, took two years to com- plete. Towns were secured under English Protestant control, and the Catholic Church was disestablished. From 1653 to 1659 Ireland was under the more sympathetic rule, first of Cromwell's son-in-law, Charles Fleetwood, and then of his own son, Henry Cromwell. The harshest settlement to which Ireland was ever subjected materially boosted Protestant landlordism in the country, and the English grip on the com- mercial and civic life of the towns. Both sections prospered for a time, because free trade was established throughout the united kingdoms of England, Scotland and Ireland.

At the Restoration of Charles II in 1660, it was the Crom- wellian generals Monk and Coote, in Scotland and Ireland, who took the initiative, by declaring public support for a free Parliament under a constitutional monarchy. The new king, though well disposed, could do little to restore the rights of dispossessed Irishmen, because his power was limited by the English Parliament, which was not sympathetic to Catholics. A second Act of Settlement (1660) restored eighteen dispossessed peers, but not the estates of 'rebels' who formed the Catholic Confederation of Kilkenny. A few of the landlords were permitted to return from their exile beyond the Shannon. From 1661 the Lord Lieutenant was again Ormond, now elevated to a dukedom for his service to the royalist cause. His Court of Claims, which operated for six years, restored to the original owners a third of the land occupied by Cromwell's soldiers; but some three thousand transplanted owners failed to benefit, and Ulster was the province that suffered most.

The proportion of Catholics to Protestants a decade after the Restoration is thought to have been about eight to three, in a country now officially Anglican, though most of the lower and middle class was non-conformist. Though Catholics enjoyed the vote, and could sit in the Irish Parliament, the latter was subservient to the English one, and seldom met. Religious tolerance was rendered impossible by the unwillingness of Irish priests to disavow the pope's right to depose a dissenting monarch. The supremacy of the English Parliament was shown by the withdrawal of the right of free trade, thereby protecting the English cattle market from Irish competition. From 1666 to 1690 no Irish Parliament was assembled, though Charles II had died in 1685, and was succeeded by the Catholic king, James II. Under his rule, Stuart Ireland honoured its first Catholic Lord Deputy (1687), in the person of Richard Talbot, Earl of Tyrconnell. This was in keeping with the king's two Declarations of Indulgence (1687-8), which enabled the Catholics in both countries to hold office. These declarations were a prime cause of James's deposition in the bloodless revolution of 1688, and the call for William of Orange and his Stuart queen, Mary.

Ireland rebelled once more in July 1689, James personally conducting the campaign, supported by Louis XIV of France, with whom the exiled king had found refuge. The Patriot Parliament he called, which included most of the Anglo-Catholic peers, was so busy redressing Catholic wrongs, that it neglected to secure the seaports. The first to be besieged was Londonderry, where incredible hardships were suffered for three and a half months, before the blockade was relieved. The Protestant forces held out in Ulster until William of Orange landed; with his mercenaries their strength was increased to thirty-six thousand. The Jacobite army was augmented by seven thousand auxiliaries from France. At the Battle of the Boyne (1690) King James's resistance was irresolute; he fled to Dublin, and from there to France. The consequences of this defeat were disastrous for Irish Catholics, who fought under Tyrconnell merely to survive.

Tyrconnell, before his death in 1691, handed over the Irish command to Brigadier Patrick Sarsfield, a popular figure trained at a French military college; he was soon joined by Marshall St Ruth of France, who enrolled in Ireland an army of fifteen thousand. When William III returned to England after his entry into Dublin, his command was taken over by General Godert de Ginkel of Utrecht. The campaign moved to central and western Ireland; for in the south John Churchill, then Earl of Marlborough, was in possession of Cork and Kinsale. Ginkel triumphed brilliantly in this second stage at Aughrim (where St Ruth was killed), and at the siege of Limerick (July to October 1691); by the terms of the treaty that he negotiated, eleven thousand of the Irish army under Sarsfield emigrated to France, to distinguish themselves in Europe, rather than swear allegiance to William III. Ten years later the able Hollander, de Ginkel, was made second in command to the Duke of Marlborough in his Continental campaigns.

The articles of the Treaty of Limerick, which Sarsfield adroitly secured, undertook not to deprive freedom-fighters of their privileges and Irish estates. The avowed object was to restore the *status quo* under Charles II, but the terms were not ratified *in toto* by the Whig Parliament of England, which delayed approval for eight years. Some four thousand Jabobite supporters lost their property. The mainstay of their cause had been new Gaelic peers and the old Norman aristocrats, but both disappeared, with Sarsfield, as a power in Irish affairs. After three conquests of Ireland since Elizabeth, the burden of English colonisation had increased, and the centuries-old possessors of the land were self-exiled or extirpated. Catholics were not only excluded from Parliament by the Test Act of 1691, but deprived of the vote; they could not bear arms, serve on juries, teach or practise the law. The woollen trade was crippled by an Act of 1699, which stopped Irish producers from selling anywhere else than in England, where the goods bore a heavy import duty, to protect the English industry.

A number of Penal Laws were passed by the Irish Parliament between 1695 and 1715, the most effective against Catholics concerning estate succession. Unless he conformed in religion, the eldest son was largely relieved of his inheritance, and the land divided equally among the deceased's next of kin; many well-to-do families were impoverished by this subdivision. No priest was allowed to say Mass unless he was registered. Catholics were debarred from public education, unless it was Protestant and in English. No papist could even reside in the towns of Galway and Limerick. An elaborate scale of rewards for informers was drawn up by the Anglo-Irish minority Parliament responsible for the laws to stamp out underground movements, such as the agrarian Whiteboys of Tipperary, who came to the fore in 1761.

Reaction to these oppressive enactments left indelible marks on the character of the people: furtive and sullen silence; retaliatory attacks by night, upon individuals or their cattle; perjured testimony; a disposition to oppose anything English on the slightest ground whatever. Catholics were joined by out-of-work Presbyterian weavers in the north, whose threatened livelihood incited many to emigrate to America and to resist England there in the War of Independence.

Such was the condition of affairs when Jonathan Swift, born and educated in Ireland, produced his Irish Tracts, such as *Drapier's Letters* and *A Modest Proposal* (1720-9). In *A Proposal for the Universal Use of Irish Manufacture*, he wrote:

> Whoever travels this country, and observes the face of Nature, or the faces and habits and dwellings of the natives, will hardly think himself in a land where either law, religion or common humanity is professed.

> (*Selected Prose*, Irish Tracts, p. 396)

Swift was a member of the Anglo-Irish aristocratic caste, an Anglican divine with no love for papists or Presbyterians; but he despised the unjust laws and absolutist policy of the Whig Protestant ascendancy. Absentee landlordism was among the great evils; for many of those who lived in England from rents in Ireland were indifferent to, or unaware of, the misery under which tenants existed. Poverty was a by-word, and Swift devoted a third of his income to charity when he discovered that thirty thousand beggars were on the roads, a considerable proportion of them in Dublin. Worse was to come; for in 1740 a famine carried away nearly half a million people. The population's decline had been accentuated by the departure of one hundred and twenty thousand men to join European armies in France, Spain and Austria.

When Queen Anne, the last of the Stuarts, died in 1714, the succession went to the Georges of Hanover, who were German-speaking, and therefore content to leave the conduct of political affairs to the Whig Parliament. By the second decade of the century it was realised that Catholicism in Ireland was ineradicable. Yet the Toleration Act of 1719, granting freedom of conscience, was negated by the retention of the Test Act of 1691, though it made concessions to well-to-do Catholic merchants. It is estimated that during the eighteenth century some five thousand Catholic families became Protestant. For forty years (1724-64) Ireland was governed by the Anglican Archbishops of Armagh, Hugh Boulter, John Hoadley and George Stone, whose task was to further economic policies that continued to protect English commercial interests. Under the Declaratory Act (1719), Ireland was subjected to the various statutes approved at Westminster. So subservient had the Irish Parliament become that there was 'no change in its representation by election throughout the reign of George II. The House seldom met, and the Lord Lieutenant did not find it necessary even to reside in Ireland, except for short periods; Lord Townshend in 1767 was the first Deputy to live in the country since the Hanoverian succession. But in the reigns of George I and II stately buildings began to dignify the city of Dublin; Phoenix Park was the creation of the Deputy, Lord Chesterfield, in 1745.

It was owing to the Anglo-Irish influence of Jonathan Swift, Bishop George Berkeley, Dr Charles Lucas ('the Wilkes of Ireland') and Edmund Burke that the situations in Ireland began to improve after 1760. Deism and scepticism in the mid-eighteenth century helped to relax the tensions of the religious struggle among the Protestant population of Irish towns; the social atmosphere became more favourable to tolerance, and to the creation of the opposition Patriot Party (1760-82), headed by Henry Flood, Henry Grattan and

James Caulfield, Earl of Charlemont. The first aim of these Irish Whigs was the abolition of the Penal Laws; the second, to secure for Irish citizens of the sister kingdom the legal rights enjoyed by Englishmen under Magna Carta and subsequent enactments, such as the Habeas Corpus Act.

Grattan, a splendid orator, would not accept office under the government, fearing it might hamper his freedom to criticise and to initiate reforms. When the American War of Independence broke out in 1775 the time was opportune for England to conciliate Ireland; troops had to be withdrawn, and the country was not readily defensible against England's other opponents, France, Holland and Spain. The outcome was the formation of the Protestant Irish Volunteers (1778), approved and armed by the mother country, to a strength of eighty thousand, commands being set up in both Leinster and Ulster. In 1779 John Hely-Hutchinson, a barrister of Trinity College, published the *Commercial Restraints of Ireland*, his plea for Free Trade, which was piloted through the English Parliament by the Tory Prime Minister, Lord North, in the same year. The repeal of the Test Act followed in 1780, and then the relaxation of penal laws against Catholics. By Gardiner's Second Relief Act (1782) Catholics were enabled to acquire and bequeath freehold land, and to open their own schools, but not to vote in elections. The Irish Parliament forthwith gained legislative independence.

Led by the younger William Pitt, the Tories returned to power in 1783, and the new Prime Minister realised that the Irish problem was far from settled, because its Parliament lacked an administration through which to govern. Ireland remained a Protestant junta controlled by its viceroy, and backed by 'Orangemen', the secret society formed after the Battle of the Boyne. From this organisation arose the separatism of Ulster, which has plagued Irish politics to the present time. Pitt's solution of the anomaly of two Parliaments under one king was some form of assimilating 'Union'. This was forced upon him by constant disagreement over commercial treaties. The power of the Regent, when the king's health rendered him unfit to rule, raised other issues, complicated by the aloofness of Grattan, by the political atmosphere of the French Revolution, and by England's declaration of war against France in 1793. This brought many Irishmen into the English armies.

In the latter emergency the Irish Volunteers were disbanded and replaced by a Protestant militia and a yeomanry in the English oligarchy's pay. The defence of Ireland was entrusted to this new force of sixty-five thousand men. None the less, in 1798 Wolfe Tone and his league of United Irishmen, supported by France, fomented insurrections in Ulster and Wexford. French and Dutch expeditions by sea failed to materialise, because one was scattered by a storm, the other defeated at the Battle of Camperdown. In Ireland the brief struggle was resolved at Vinegar Hill, where numbers of insurgents lost their lives. The projected Union of England and Ireland in 1799 was designed to prevent further disaffection, while England was involved in a mortal struggle against Napoleon. The Irish Parliament resisted the measure for a year, but was eventually won over by bribes and new peerages costing more than a million pounds, which was added to Ireland's national debt. Under the Act of Union in 1800 the country was to be represented in the English Parliament by one hundred members in the House of Commons and twenty-eight peers in the House of Lords. Catholics were to receive the vote, but not the right to stand for election; their disabilities were not finally removed until 1829. Free trade between the two countries was, however, guaranteed.

These seven hundred years, during which there were four conquests — those of Strongbow, Mountjoy, Cromwell and William of Orange — proved to be a vital period in Irish history, responsible for most of the country's problems. The gaelicisation of the Norman barons by the end of the thirteenth century, e.g. of the White Knights of Glin and Kerry, was due in large measure to marriages or concubinage with Irish women. Since the church required no validating ceremony, secular marriages were the order of the day until the seventeenth century. This practice facilitated divorce, by permitting a sequence of opportunist, but lawful, marriages, resulting in not infrequent lawsuits. Some of these were due to canon law on the subject of propinquity, which forbade wedlock between cousins, even of the third degree. Moreover, under Brehon law, a dowry paid to a husband by a wife's family (sometimes by subscription) had to be refunded if he divorced her. With persons of high rank dowries were usually high, and sureties for repayment had to be provided.

In the Middle Ages patronymics, and sometimes nick-names, were used instead of surnames. The prefix *fitz* (son of) was the Anglo-Norman equivalent of *mac*; occasionally the suffix *-son* came into use in Norman areas, but seldom after the fifteenth century. In the case of a daughter, the prefix was *ní* or *nín*. If a son bore the same name as his father, the adjective *óg* (*oge*, 'junior') appeared after it. The honorific suffix *mór* (more) after a chieftain's name signified 'the great'.

Neo-Gaelic lordships that followed mixed marriages with Norman barons brooked no interference in the pursuit of feudal power by the latter, especially in relations with Irish sub-chiefs, from whom fees or produce in kind was exacted. Members of Irish clans were liable to be called upon for military service, unless they were churchmen, or of the pro-fessional class (e.g. lawyers, bards or physicians). The *kern* was commonly a freeman soldier unable to afford armour; a *gallowglass* was a fully armed mercenary, entitled to quarters, and of sufficient standing to employ a paid atten-dant resembling a knight's squire. Until the sixteenth century horsemen followed the Celtic practice of riding without proper saddle or stirrups, which made them more vulnerable in battle than they should have been.

The Irish church's attitude to marriage was characteristic of its peculiar isolation and privilege, which included heredit-ary election within the family until the thirteenth century, and enforced payment of tithes from the twelfth century. Monasteries during the Middle Ages became increasingly secularised; for monks and abbots, ignoring papal injunctions on celibacy, openly took wives, and so tended to reside at home. The Normans seem to have been responsible for the introduction of many Cistercian foundations to Ireland. The Irish tradition of ascetic life was kept mainly by anchor-ites in the orders of friars, who often lived in cells attached to a church.

It is difficult to understand the worsening political situation in Ireland until it is realised that the early kings were leaders of people, as well as patrons of religious institutions, but *owned* no territory. Possession of land was a feudal concept, introduced in the Middle Ages with papal sanction by Norman overlords of the twelfth century. The servile condition of the rural population was a Gaelic concept, for serfdom had by then ceased to exist in the Holy Roman Empire. The pattern of land ownership was not, in fact, changed until the passing of Statute 33 Henry VIII, during the deputyship of Sir Anthony St Leger, when Irish and Anglo-Irish lords became nominally tenants-in-chief under the Crown; but in effect they owned their estates. Henry's implementation of the religious Reformation was a more difficult task, because of its international repercussions.

This was a principal reason for the English plantation policy between 1565 and 1576, and the reaction to it which resembled a Catholic crusade against the regime of Queen Elizabeth, especially after she was excommunicated by the pope in 1570.

The plantation scheme made little headway at first until steps were taken by Sir Henry Sidney to occupy monastic land in Ulster, Munster and Connacht. Up to 1568 the administration of Ireland had been singularly inept, because the queen was niggardly in support of the Deputy, and indifferent to the fate of the warring Gaelic factions. Eventually Secretary of State, William Cecil, envisaged a series of 'private-soldier colonies', consisting of volunteers who had served, or had personal interests, in Ireland. The upshot of this nascent colonialism was increasing resentment, and ultimately hatred. It is imperative to grasp the causes of administrative errors of judgement, if the historical picture has not already made this clear.

Henry VIII extinguished a Norman-Hibernian culture which, however imperfect from the humanist viewpoint, meant much to the inhabitants of Ireland. Unfortunately accounts presented by English intellectuals, such as Sir Thomas Smith and Edmund Spenser, as well as politicians and annalists, were uniformly antipathetic to the Irish way of life. Here are two opinions recorded by N. Canny in *The*

Elizabethan Conquest of Ireland, pp. 124 and 135:

> Matrimonie emongs them is no more regarded in effect
> than conjunction betwene unreasonable beastes, perjurie,
> robberie and murder counted alloweable.... I doubte
> whether they christen there children or no, for neither
> finde I place where it should be don, nor any person able
> to enstruct them in the rules of a Christan....
> (Henry Sidney, 'Report on the State of Religion in Munster',
> 1567)

> A barbarous country must be first broken by a war before
> it will be capable of good government; and when it is fully
> subdued and conquered if it be not well planted and
> governed after the conquest it will eftsoons return to the
> former barbarism.
> (John Davies, *Discovery*, p. 208)

The humanist philosophy behind colonialism in the
Elizabethan age saw English plantation plans as a dutiful
mission to civilise degraded peoples, whom the English
regarded as savages and pagans. Several of the queen's
Lieutenants, such as Sidney, had served diplomatically in
Spain, and so modelled their attitudes on Spanish Con-
quistadors, who cynically pretended to uplift Amerindians.
This mistaken colonial policy was repeated in the English
plantation of the Virginia Company in 1607.

The new English idealism had serious consequences for the
three strata of Irish population, viz. the indigenous Gaelic
majority, the Anglo-Irish feudal order, and the 'civilised' élite
who occupied the Pale along with Irish labourers and tenants,
whose indifferent mastery of Irish was accompanied by a
broken English patois. Society within the Pale was, indeed,
of mixed intellectual capacity; consequently there was a
variety of shades of political opinion, not entirely in accord
with the thinking of the English social order. Many of the
Dublin gentry still favoured traditional Gaelic customs and
dress. Only the moneyed gentry and the merchant class of
eastern coastal towns, aspiring to gentility, were likely to be
anglicised. This was the group that sent sons to English
universities for legal or classical education, and at one time

filled the administrative posts in Dublin. But with the advent of Deputy Henry Sidney in 1565, officials from England were appointed who were more sympathetic to the new land policy of 'surrender and re-grant'; and this led to divided loyalties within the Pale. A thorough command of the Irish language even came to be regarded as a disqualification. Disaffected young gentlemen from the Pale and from Munster towns were now sent to Catholic universities on the Continent, instead of Oxford and Cambridge.

In the eighteenth century the predominantly Catholic population of Ireland rose from two and a half million to five and a half million, but Catholics possessed only about fourteen per cent of the land. The increasing demand for food could not have been met but for improved cultivation of the potato. The impoverishment of the people, who were discriminated against by the Penal Laws, constituted a social problem that only a few thinkers, such as Edmund Burke, were able to appreciate. By the reign of Queen Anne the Church of Ireland, affiliated to the Anglican Establishment in England, was alone recognised, although its members numbered only ten per cent of the people; the word 'Protestant' virtually meant a communicant of the Anglican Church. The Scots Presbyterians of Ulster, a leading non-conformist group, suffered similar disabilities to the Catholics. They could not hold public office, being suspected of Jacobite sympathies; marriages celebrated in their church were not recognised, and this meant that their children could be disinherited, a situation that prevailed until 1782. Many Ulster people emigrated to America, and were prominent in opposing Britain in the War of Independence.

Vis-à-vis religious affiliations, the political situation in Ireland until the reign of George III was grotesque; for citizens were taxed without representation, and the executive that actually governed the country was out of touch with the legislature to which it was responsible. Yet the new Parliament House in Dublin, completed in 1739, was as lavish as the official residence at the Castle. The golden age of Anglo-Irish ascendancy came in the latter half of the eighteenth century, when the principal streets of Dublin were widened, and magnificent buildings in grey stone began to appear;

these included the façade to Trinity College, the Inns of Court, the Royal Exchange and the Custom House. Georgian houses, memorable for their neo-classical plaster-work, were erected, for instance in St Stephen's Green; palladian country houses appeared on the private estates of the gentry. Dublin Castle, with elegant interior decorations, stood in extravagant contrast to the dire poverty of the bulk of the people. When Britain embarked upon war against revolutionary France in 1793 it was clear that the anomalies of the Irish discontents had to find a more realistic solution.

IV

Irish and Anglo-Irish Literature, 1100-1800

The term 'Anglo-Irish', as applied to literature, is not strictly valid until the latter half of the seventeenth century. The adventurers from Wales who conquered Ireland in the twelfth century were not English, for they spoke no tongue descended from West-Saxon, but used a French dialect or Flemish. Throughout the Middle Ages Irish continued to be the language of literature, alongside Latin. English had little impact upon Irish literature until after the second conquest, when James I (a Scot) succeeded Queen Elizabeth.

The bardic tradition was not immediately broken by the advent of the Normans. While the courts of chieftains and kings remained they were cultural centres for the poetry of praise and propaganda. Gaelic Ireland was unique in its partiality for rural life; as there were few large towns, centuries elapsed before urban dwellers were looked upon as leaders of thought. The mystical element so prevalent in medieval lyrical poetry arose mainly from anchorites who wrote in seclusion.

The Old Irish language preserved by the scribes was conservative, because the oral practice of bards was to standardise the literary medium. Conventions were, however, somewhat relaxed following the introduction of Scandinavian settlers in the ninth century; and were modified again with the coming of the Norman ruling class, which was dominant until 1250. After that the foreigners were culturally absorbed and became speakers of Gaelic. A compromise was reached between the standard language of scholars and the down-to-earth speech of the people. The poets themselves helped by expanding the compass of their talents.

Middle Irish was undoubtedly the dominant language in the fourteenth century, as is shown by the directive Edward III gave (in French) to the Sheriff of Kilkenny in 1360. This document is preserved in the Archives of the Diocese of Ossory:

> As many of the English nation in the Marches and else-where have again become like Irishmen, and refuse to obey our laws and customs, and hold parliaments after the Irish fashion, and learn to speak the Irish tongue . . . we order . . . that any one of English race shall forfeit English liberty, if after the next feast of St. John the Baptist he shall speak Irish with other Englishmen and meantime *every Englishman must learn English* and must not have his children at nurse amongst the Irish.
>
> (Quoted by D. Hyde in *A Literary History of Ireland*, pp. 608-9)

Other documents reveal that Norman and Welsh landowners gradually adopted Irish names, such as MacWilliam, MacGibbon and MacKeon; and with rare exceptions those who sat in Dublin's Irish Parliament were monoglots. On this account Irish-medium colleges were instituted in France for the benefit of young men seeking university education abroad.

Modern Irish dates from the reign of Queen Elizabeth; the inception is usually assigned to the Battle of Kinsale (1601). This was a flexible form of speech, used by the majority of speakers outside the boundaries of the Pale, which consisted then of four counties. A good example of early modern Irish as a cultured literary language is the writing of Geoffrey Keating only a few decades later; but its circle of appreciation was limited to a small educated class. Neither the printing of an Irish New Testament in 1603, nor the appearance of a Catholic Catechism in 1611, succeeded in keeping this literary language alive.

The classical period of Irish writing (*c.* 1300-1650) seems to have ended with the Cromwellian invasions, which provided the starting point for dialectal variations among the semi-literate peasant population. When a standard language was found necessary for education, English was the obvious choice to supplant the dialects.

Queen Elizabeth had before ordered a fount of Irish type to be made in roman characters, to print the Anglican Catechism of 1571. But the reaction to anything emanating from the Protestant English queen produced another type devised by exiled monks in Belgium, for the purpose of Catholic counter-propaganda. This type better preserved Irish manuscript characteristics, and was used to print books in Louvain and Rome for circulation in Ireland. A century later the Louvain type proved itself to be the more acceptable for Irish Gaelic literature. In 1680 an improved design by Joseph Moxon, author of *Mechanick Exercises* (1678 and 1683), began to be employed, even by the Church of England. Moxon had been invited to restore this type by the scientist Robert Boyle, son of Richard Boyle, first Earl of Cork; Boyle ordered it, at his own expense, for the printing of Bishop Bedell's Irish translation of the Old Testament. Moxon must have obtained samples of the Louvain type from the Irish scholar, Andrew Sall, of Douai; his upright version remained in use for over a hundred years.

In the mid-seventeenth century when Gaelic Ireland was stripped of its political power, and the right of the people to be educated in their own language had been withdrawn, there was a progressive decline in the use of Irish as a literary language; and in this unhappy situation Anglo-Irish literature was born.

The eighteenth century was nevertheless crucial for the reproduction of Gaelic literature. Often printers in Ireland had to use roman type for lack of supplies of Irish characters, and this practice has continued sporadically from 1735 to the present time. But 1788 saw the production of new Irish founts, which were encouraged by the Gaelic Union of the nineteenth century. Now, however, the Irish character is preserved principally for aesthetic or antiquarian purposes; appreciable differences from roman type are observable in the seven letters *a, d, f, g, r, s* and *t*.

In spite of the educational ban for two centuries, Irish was kept alive in the domestic circle until about 1750 and perpetuated in books coming from foreign presses, including an eighteenth-century one in Paris. The lifting of the ban made it possible for Charlotte Brooke to publish in Dublin her

Reliques of Irish Poetry, in vernacular type, in 1789. It is worth mentioning at this point that the Irish Archaeological Society, from its foundation in 1841, encouraged the study of the vernacular, and its work was continued by the Gaelic League from 1897.

Thomas MacDonagh's *Literature in Ireland* (1916) makes an eloquent appeal for the cultivation of Anglo-Irish, not as a parasitic dialect of English, but as a literary language in its own right, capable of communicating the manners, customs, traditions and outlook of a Gaelic people, and comparable in richness to the art of any other European nation. He maintains that Irish speech has a distinct rhythm; that English as spoken in Ireland has a 'more deliberate way of pronunciation' (p. 65); and that there is in it a prose intonation, which is saved from monotony 'by the natural rise and fall of the voice' (p. 72). As a result, there is in Anglo-Irish a more reasoning, 'conversational tone, which disallows inversions' and quaint words (p. 73). The principal contribution of poets is seen as 'a music that at once expresses and evokes emotion' (p. 81). Novelists of the nineteenth century have added a droll whimsicality, which is 'different from humour proper' (p. 13). How Anglo-Irish developed such linguistic capabilities is explained in his chapter IV:

> The syntax of the Gaelic language — and it is the syntax that matters rather than the introduction of foreign words — is fixed and in all important features not likely to undergo modification. The verb will precede its subject, the adjective will follow its noun to the end. Similarly English in Ireland will not conform to Gaelic rules. . . . More important are the use in Irish of the concrete as against the English use of the abstract; the use of the adjective in preference to the verb; the use of periphrasis to avoid trusting to voice emphasis the meaning of the sentence. . . .
>
> Modern Irish is much more in line with Old Irish than is Modern English with Old English. This has saved Irish from the introduction of words that are rather labels than names. . . .
>
> On the other hand Irish has on the whole remained un-

affected by things that have very greatly affected almost all other modern languages — by the printing press, by modern commerce, by modern science and the rest. The result is that it has not been unified. It is still rich in dialects and in variant forms. No single literary, commercial or journalistic language exists. . . . The vocabulary of the language is very large. It would seem that the people, thrown back on themselves and on nature, not forced to invest technical terms for the new things of civilization, have gone on with the minute study of the old things. They have named all the facets and distinguished all the moods. With this they have retained an ease for full expression that English does not know. . . .

One fears to draw conclusions too general from particular points of difference between Irish and English, in vocabulary and in grammar. . . . There are wide differences, which prove different mental habits, different social conditions, different literary traditions. English writing is full of metaphor that cannot be understood without knowledge of historic events which have not affected Ireland: Shakespeare's plays are indeed, as has been said, nothing but strings of popular sayings. Irish has a different set of historic memories and of popular sayings. These have come into Anglo-Irish, but not in full force, and Anglo-Irish is the simpler for it. New images have to be supplied from current life in Ireland; the dialect at its best is more vigorous, fresh and simple than either of the two languages between which it stands. It is indeed by its colloquial directness that you will know the true Anglo-Irish work. . . .

To the new generation of Irish readers who know the two languages, many otherwise fine books are spoiled or at least made a little foolish and ridiculous by the grotesque disguises under which Irish words appear in them. . . . The pity of it is that it is in Ireland that Irish meets this fate. . . .

(pp. 42-52)

The Battle of Clontarf (1014), with its appalling loss of life among Irish chieftains, is fully recorded in the 'Wars of the Gael and the Gall', part of the Book of Leinster (1150). The account in this manuscript is incomplete, but an intact version remains in the transcript made by Michael O'Clery in 1635. The importance of the battle was the termination of the political domination of Ireland by Norwegians and Danes; but disaffection in isolated pockets continued for at least seven years. Brian Boru faced the task of rebuilding devastated churches, monasteries and schools; but it is known that Glendalough, Clonard and Armagh were sacked as late as 1016-21, and that bardic schools also suffered from the Danish depradations.

Bardic training centres continued to provide poets for the leading families for four centuries, but during that period saga-writing showed no sign of progress. A tendency to resort to repetitive skills in laudatory verse was inevitable, when the office of bard became hereditary. The technical advance in writing religious and secular lyrics was, however, notable, though much of this writing disappeared from family archives during the Anglo-Norman occupation of the country.

By a strange coincidence memorable work of the O'Daly families has, however, survived, some of remarkable sensitivity. Muireadach Albanach (Murdoch the Scotsman) was a member of the O'Daly family of Meath and grandson of a professor of poetry at Clonard. His poems were addressed to members of the O'Brien family of Thomond, who helped him to escape from the wrath of O'Donnell at the beginning of the thirteenth century. According to the Annals of the Four Masters, he had killed his patron's steward in a quarrel at Lisadell near Sligo; but his friends helped him to escape to Argyllshire, where he became the leading poet of Scotland. From there he travelled to Greece, Palestine and the Far East, but was allowed in return for some laudatory verse to go back to Ireland, with a pardon from his chief. The Scottish Book of Lismore contains several poems, one of which 'On the Death of his Wife' is illustrated by the four stanzas below, in Frank O'Connor's version:

> I parted from my life last night,
>   A woman's body sunk in clay:
> The tender bosom that I loved
>   Wrapped in a sheet they took away.

The heavy blossom that had lit
  The ancient boughs is tossed and blown;
Hers was the burden of delight
  That long had weighed the old tree down.

And I am left alone tonight
  And desolate is the world I see
For lovely was that woman's weight
  That even last night had lain on me.
. . .
My body's self deserts me now,
  The half of me that was her own,
Since all I knew of brightness died
  Half of me lingers, half is gone.

                    (*Faber Book of Irish Verse*, pp. 91-2)

Notwithstanding its conservatism of form, Irish poetry of the Middle Ages subtly reflects disturbance and change, but with spiritual qualities that are free from external influence. The audience was obviously susceptible to emotions only partly expressed, the rhythm supplying the other imponderables. The paradox is, in fact, achieved of conditioned training, divesting itself of artifice and the fetters of arbitrary rules.

Ireland's greatest religious poet, Donnchadh mór O'Dála (O'Daly), also wrote in the first half of the thirteenth century, and died in 1244. He is represented by some four thousand lines of verse, and was apparently a cleric who lived in County Clare, though he was buried in the abbey of Boyle, in County Roscommon. The tone of his poetry is certainly in the monastic tradition, as the pilgrimage confession 'At Saint Patrick's Purgatory' shows. Here are five stanzas of Sean O'Faolain's translation:

> Pity me on my pilgrimage to Loch Derg!
> O King of the churches and the bells —
> Bewailing your sores and your wounds,
> But not a tear can I squeeze from my eyes!
>
> Not moisten an eye
> After so much sin!
> Pity me, O King! What shall I do
> With a heart that seeks only its own ease?

> Without sorrow or softening in my heart,
> Bewailing my faults without repenting them!
> Patrick the high priest never thought
> That he would reach God in this way.
>   . . .
> On the day of Doom we shall weep heavily,
> Both clergy and laity;
> The tear that is not dropped in time,
> None heeds in the world beyond.
>   . . .
> O only begotten Son by whom all men were made,
> Who shunned not the death by three wounds,
> Pity me on my pilgrimage to Loch Derg
> And I with a heart not softer than a stone!
> (Greene, *An Anthology of Irish Literature*, vol. I, p. 174)

In this rendering the translator rarely departs from the Irish medieval tendency to make the line of verse an independent metrical unit. O'Faolain indulges only twice in inversions of word order (lines 4 of stanza one, and 2 of stanza five). MacDonagh (op. cit. p. 110) says of earlier lyric verse that the language is usually clear, direct, hard, delicate and bright, and this is true of the few poems of O'Daly's that survive. Douglas Hyde translated another poem, which admirably preserves the skilful internal rhyming, assonance and alliteration of the Gaelic poet's schooling.

> Not on the world thy love bestow,
>   Passing as flowers that blow and die;
> Follow not thou the specious track
>   That turns the back on God most high.
>
> But oh! let faith, let hope, let love,
>   Soar far above this cold world's way,
> Patience, humility, and awe —
>   Make them thy law from day to day.
> (*Literary History of Ireland*, p. 468)

This poet is not to be confused with Angus O'Daly, the Red Bard and renegade, who was said to have been in the pay of Lord Mountjoy to satirise Gaelic and Anglo-Norman Munster families; but the bard, in defiance of all custom, met his death in Tipperary.

The abundant anonymous poetry of the thirteenth century has several examples of a sophisticated, brittle wit, anticipating the spirit of English Cavalier poets, but without its cynicism. The talent of translator Frank O'Connor does ample justice to the poem 'I Shall not Die':

> I shall not die because of you
>   O woman though you shame the swan,
> They were foolish men you killed,
>   Do not think me a foolish man.
>
> Why should I leave the world behind
>   For the soft hand, the dreaming eye,
> The crimson lips, the breasts of snow —
>   Is it for these you'd have me die?
>
> Why should I heed the fancy free,
>   The joyous air, the eye of blue,
> The side like foam, the virgin neck?
>   I shall not die because of you.
>
> The devil take the golden hair!
>   That maiden look, that voice so gay,
> That delicate heel and pillared thigh
>   Only some foolish man would slay.
>
> O woman though you shame the swan
>   A wise man taught me all he knew,
> I know the crooked ways of love,
>   I shall not die because of you.
>
> *(Penguin Book of Irish Verse*, p. 66)

The medieval family poet was not a musician, according to Douglas Hyde (op. cit. p. 496); he was a verse-maker, who constructed poems after the complex models of the seminary. When a bard presented a panegyric to a patron, the poem was taught to a harper and/or singer, who accompanied him to court. The classical metres of the Irish bardic tradition continued in use until the middle of the seventeenth century. But by the sixteenth century some bards had become so insolent and hospitality-demanding that Statute 28 Henry VIII was passed to limit their activities. Hyde maintains that many accusations against them, including Spenser's, were libellous, and that bards 'fairly reflected public opinion'.

But the minstrelsy survived, and two poets of the seventeenth century demonstrate the resurgence. Teigue Dall O'Higgin (*Dall* signifies 'blind') gained an immense reputation in a lifetime spent mainly in County Sligo. He became a favourite with the neighbouring Gaelic aristocracy, and possessed a remarkable instinct for conveying the social environment in which he moved. Without satire, he rebukes Irish pride and advocates unity, rather than rivalry, among the leading septs. The language of his verse is invariably dignified and lucid, as Robin Flower shows in his translation of 'The Good Tradition':

> Ah! liberal-handed lady, though
> Round Eire's shore the generous wave
> Ebbs now, in thee 'tis still at flow;
> No marvel that the bard's thy slave.
>
> A lady passionate for song,
> True friend of all the bardic kind,
> Who cleaves to her can scarce go wrong;
> Song to her loaned doth interest find.
>
> The good tradition holds no more
> Of open-handedness to art;
> On later manners men set store
> And close their purse-strings and their heart.
>
> Now that the giving spirit's gone
> And wealth and art are by the ears,
> That poet's mad who labours on
> And gives to song his wasted years.
>
> In ancient Ulster as of old
> Dwelt Liberality of right;
> Now Ulster hearts are changed and cold,
> From all that province she takes flight.
>
> She's chased from Munster; Connacht too
> Gives her no welcome as of yore;
> The hapless hunger-stricken crew
> Know Liberality no more.

She's known no more where the wide plain
Of Leinster spreads beneath the skies;
Unless another shape she's ta'en,
That hides her from the poet's eyes.

A mist has caught her from our sight,
A druid mist that hides her o'er;
Ask but a lodging for the night
And all men turn you from the door.
                    (*An Anthology of Irish Literature*, pp. 196-7)

O'Higgin died tragically, about 1617, at the hands of a ruthless marauding band.

The suppression of bardic schools at the end of the sixteenth century at least produced some major improvements in the practice of vernacular poetry. Rules and technicalities were discarded that had been in vogue for at least a thousand years. One effect was to place poetry within the reach of many educated writers of the middle class who wished to please their own public. The loss of hundreds of archaic words resulted in a diction less formidable and pedantic. In musical quality alone, the new-found language discovered Celtic subtleties, to this day associated with the Gaelic of Western Scotland and Ireland. Instead of prolonging effete metrical patterns, poets ventured to modulate by the manipulation to vowel sounds, to secure certain emotive effects. The method had its dangers, but also many advantages, especially when new lyrics were accommodated to traditional song-settings.

Egan O'Rahilly (1670-1726) was a Jacobite poet of Kerry, writing at the time of the Fall of Limerick. 'A Grey Eye Weeping' laments the woes of his country and mocks the Anglo-Irish gentry in the person of 'Valentine Brown', on behalf of an embittered emigrant. The lamentations, either in elegy or invective, resemble denunciations of a biblical prophet. O'Rahilly's majestic style favours lengthened lines, without rhyme, in which he secures a Whitman-like effect through the sonorous variation of vowel sounds. It is difficult to simulate this in translation; but 'Brightness of Brightness' is perhaps the best example.

A change in the attitude of creative writers to their medium was inevitable in the eighteenth century. The humanistic arts were at home in Dublin, and most of the leading poets, among them Thomas Parnell and Oliver Goldsmith, elected to write in English. Both were born and educated in Ireland, but apparently knew no Gaelic. Parnell acknowledged discipleship of Pope; Goldsmith was more familiar with French writers, such as Voltaire, Marivaux and Buffon, than with Geoffrey Keating. Though Lissoy in Westmeath was once proposed as the idealised location of Goldsmith's 'Deserted Village', Auburn has no real Irish background. Macaulay, hardly one to be moved by the *perfervidum ingenium Scotorum*, was not mistaken when he wrote:

> The village in its happy days is a true English village. The village in its decay is an Irish village. The felicity and the misery which Goldsmith has brought close together belong to two different countries, and to two different stages in the progress of society.
>
> (*Poems of Oliver Goldsmith*, p. 173)

Goldsmith's essay on 'Carolan, the Irish Bard' (1670-1738) is hardly more than a facetious portrait of a comic Irish prototype, ironically mistaken for an heroic Pindar (see *The Bee and Other Essays*, pp. 257-60).

Carolan's songs figure more sympathetically in the translations of Charlotte Brooke, who is known to have died in 1793, four years after the publication of her *Reliques of Irish Poetry*. She was neither a blue-stocking nor a patroness of letters, but her father took infinite care with her education; she taught herself Irish, in order to understand the hearts and minds of the peasantry near her home in Kildare. Charlotte's poems characterise the romantic propensity of a revived interest in Celtic studies. The publication of *Reliques* was an historic occasion, for it was the first book printed *in Ireland* to contain characters of Gaelic type. The aim was to discountenance the clamour over Macpherson's *Ossian*, by presenting the original text on which the translations were based.

Charlotte's literary father, Henry Brooke, was a Protestant, at one time the possessor of a house at Twickenham, and a friend of Pope. He wrote plays (one censored in England on political grounds), and acquired fame as the author of *The*

Fool of Quality, a poem in five books, that ran into several editions, and was much praised by John Wesley. His unmarried daughter devoted her life to his care, and survived him by only a decade, during which she wrote his biography and edited the collected works. These in retrospect are of meagre literary merit. Her *Reliques* emulated the similar researches of Thomas Percy, who actually encouraged her to publish the compilation; Blake's influential patron, William Hayley, who had the ear of William Pitt, did the same.

A. C. H. Seymour's *Memoir* of Charlotte Brooke (1816), is a pietistic biography in 125 pages, which contains letters and juvenilia; but it is principally valuable for explaining the genesis of her collection; moreover, it gives extracts from the critiques of contemporary reviewers. By them the resemblance to Macpherson's *Ossian* was immediately noticed, and the poems were generally admired for their simplicity and pathos; one caviller, however, smiled condescendingly 'at the excess to which she carried her enthusiasm' (*Memoir*, p. 45). The enthusiasm is accounted for in the following encomium of the Preface (pp v and vi):

> There are many complex words that could not be translated literally, without great injury to the original. . . . The number of synonima in which it abounds, enables it, perhaps beyond any other, to repeat the same thought, without tiring the fancy or the ear. There are upwards of forty names to express a *Ship* in the Irish language, and nearly an equal number for a *House*.
>
> It is really astonishing of what various and comprehensive powers this neglected language is possessed. In the pathetic, it breathes the most beautiful and affecting simplicity; and in the bolder species of composition, it is distinguished by a force of expression, a sublime dignity, and rapid energy, which it is scarcely possible for any translation fully to convey; as it sometimes fills the mind with ideas altogether new, and which, perhaps, no modern language is entirely prepared to express. One compound epithet must often be translated by two lines of English verse, and, on such occasions, much of the beauty is necessarily lost; the force and effect of the thought being weakened by too slow an introduction on the mind.

Translations are invariably tinged by the taste in poetry of the period to which they belong. Eighteenth-century readers were fond of universal principles, and sought them in grammar, science and Newtonian mathematics; some believed that the proper language of poetry was discoverable in a dynamic law, of which the all-pervading neo-classical diction was a suitable expression. Such a rational style was probably least well-adapted to the spirit of Celtic heroic or lyrical poetry. Gray's experimental pindaric ode, 'The Bard', sounds hollow after the opening stanza.

A large proportion of the poems in the *Reliques* is written in ballad measure; but full command of this deceptively facile stanza form came to fruition only in Charlotte's final romantic tale, 'Mäon', addressed to Mr and Mrs Trant; for here she was able to give full rein to her fancy. In the translations proper footnotes are often more illuminating than her labours to capture the poignancy of a dramatic situations; for instance, in 'The Lamentation of Cucullin over the Body of his son Conloch':

> O thou lost hope of my declining years!
> O cruel winds that drove thee to this coast!
>   Alas! could Destiny afford
>   No other arm, no other sword,
>   In Leinster of the pointed spears,
> On Munster's plains, or in fierce Cruachan's host,
>   To quency in blood my filial light,
> And spare my arm the deed, my eyes the sight!
>   . . .
> O that to Lochlin's land of snows
>   My son had steer'd his course!
> Or Grecian shores, or Persian foes,
>   Or Spain, or Britain's force!
>
> There had he fallen, amidst his fame,
>   I yet the loss could bear;
> Nor horror thus would shake my frame,
>   Nor sorrow be — Despair! —

(Reliques, pp. 26-8)

Each poem is preceded by an 'advertisement', which is in reality an explanation of its content and stylistic difficulties, or a reference to the source of the text and the antiquarian detail. She borrowed freely from researchers in the Royal Irish Academy, such as O'Connor, O'Halloran, Vallancey and J. C. Walker, whose *Historical Memoirs of the Irish Bards* (1786) is constantly called upon. The annotations are profuse, and furnish fascinating observations on such topics as the activities of the Fenian militia (pp. 39-42), the impact of Christian missionaries on the tradition of military glory (pp. 82-3), the relation of chess to the ownership of land (p. 85) and the origin of church bells (pp. 91-2).

The style of the late Augustans is at its most characteristic in the odes and elegies. Fitzgerald, writing in the reign of Queen Elizabeth, thus described the ship on which he is about to set sail to Spain:

> Stout is my well-built ship, the storm to brave,
>   Majestic in its might,
> Her bulk, tremendous on the wave,
>   Erects its stately height!
> From her strong bottom, tall in air
> Her branching masts aspiring rise;
> Aloft their cords, and curling heads they bear,
> And give their sheeted ensigns to the skies;
> While her proud bulk frowns awful on the main,
> And seems the fortress of the liquid plain!
>
> (*Reliques*, pp. 182-3)

Charlotte thought the elegy form was peculiarly suited to the Irish language, because of its usually plaintive and sentimental note. One (undated) 'To the Daughter of Owen', by the poet O'Geran, was a particular favourite that she was at pains to translate in its native grace, without resorting to periphrasis:

> Sweet! do not thou a like misfortune prove!
> O be not such thy fate, nor such they love!
> Let peril rather warn, and wisdom guide,
> And from thyself thy own attractions hide!
> No more on that bewitching beauty gaze,
> Nor trust thy sight to meet its dazzling blaze!
>
> (*Reliques*, pp. 195-6)

The moralising tone, emphasised by the four marks of exclamation, recalls much minor poetry of the eighteenth century; *bewitching* and *dazzling* are trite epithets that fail to make the desired impact.

Speaking of Miss Brooke's letters, as genuine expressions of personal circumstance, Seymour rightly commends the 'uncommon facility' of the writing. Perhaps Miss Brooke's deepest qualities are displayed, not in the poetry, but in the prose. This confession seems to come from the heart:

> *Now* I see matters in quite another point of view. — I see, to demonstration, that one must be in a manner 'absent to the body' in order to be 'present to the Lord.' — I see the vital necessity of renouncing self altogether — of losing *all* that Adam *found*, in order to *find* what he *lost*. Long experience has convinced me of this necessity — and argument could now as soon make doubt of my existence, as of a truth to which that existence is itself the witness. . . .
>
> Is not here a circumstance that one who did not know me, would take to be a certain mark of an advanced state of grace! — yet it is *not* so. — My views and pursuits — hopes, fears, desires, and prayers are all *converted*, it is true — but my spirit and temper are still the same. — Indignity would I am sure, if offered, offend me, as much as ever; and disappointment in those things for which I Have not lost my relish, vexes me for the moment, just in the same degree as it would have done ten years ago. Though *to God* I am humbled almost to annihilation of self — yet, to my fellow-creatures I am proud still. My pride does not prevent me from condescending to my inferiors, provided they don't *forget their distance* — nor to my superiors, *when they don't take airs upon it*, — but when either of these things befal, then I *feel* that I am proud, though I don't always let it be *seen*. . . . I have neither rank, nor wealth, nor power, nor beauty, — nor any thing else whatever, that is material, to offer upon the Altar of faith, obedience, and love.
>
> (*Memoir*, pp. 87-9)

(Miss Brooke actually misquotes II Corinthians V. 8, which reads 'willing rather to be absent *from* the body, and to be present *with* the Lord'.) Pride in the integrity of the human personality, as this passage discloses, is most relevant to the

Celtic spirit, and altogether compatible with natural piety, whatever the creed observed. The clannishness of the eighteenth-century Irish resulted from an innate sense of class, in which different levels of civilised behaviour were distinguished. Without the distancing here required, agreement on personality judgements would have been impossible. Comparative freedom from social pretension was due, in a measure, to the Celtic instinct for friendliness and conviviality. Refinement of manners did not exclude the acceptance of class, provided offence was not given. Irish democracy has always embodied the notion that every class is socially responsible for the welfare of all the others.

Much is to be gleaned of Anglo-Norman times from a Munster historian John McCraith, whose *Triumphs of Turlough O'Brien* was written about 1459. Annalists and chroniclers played a major role in the writing of prose from the thirteenth to the seventeenth century. The function of an annalist was simply to record events from year to year; the words *annals* is first noted in the OED from Edmund Campion's *History of Ireland* (the Dedication to Thomas Wentworth in the 1633 edition). The term *chronicle* (of Old French origin) appeared in English three centuries earlier, and referred especially to the kind of records in which facts are baldly narrated without any attempt at literary style.

Edmund Campion's *History of Ireland* (1571) does not belong to either of the above classes. Nor is it a history in the modern sense of 'a systematic account of events treated as natural phenomena' (OED § 5). Campion's is a Catholic's impression of what he observed on a journey of less than ten weeks through the country of his birth. He did, however, consult 'rolls, records and scattered papers', as well as the writings of Giraldus Cambrensis and later chroniclers. Annals in the vernacular he had to forego, lacking knowledge of the Irish language. Campion's education at St John's College, Oxford, led to a fellowship, which shows that he was then an Anglican; but from 1571 he spent several years at Douai, where he joined the Society of Jesus. His preaching to recusants in London during 1580 was thought to be seditious, and led to his torture and execution the following year.

There is no Catholic partisanship in the views on Ireland
expressed by Campion, though the account fulsomely praises
the part played by religious houses in Ireland's history. Full
recognition is given to the English Crown's right to continue
to exercise authority. Holinshed's *Chronicles of England,
Scotland and Ireland* (1587) borrowed extensively from
Campion (see R. B. Gottfried's facsimile edition, 1940,
p. v), while Spenser in his *View of the Present State of
Ireland* (1596) helped himself indirectly through Holinshed.
Gifts of scholarship and style are immediately visible in
Campion's *History*, in spite of its lack of proportion, owing
to the haste in which the study was compiled. The following
passage has the merit of closely observed domestic custom,
as well as clarity and humour:

Cleare men they are of Skinne and hue, but of themselves carelesse and bestiall. Their Women are well
favoured, cleare coloured, faire handed, bigge and large,
suffered from their infancy to grow at will, nothing
curious of their feature and proportion of body.

Their infants of the meaner sort, are neither swadled,
nor lapped in Linnen, but foulded up starke naked into a
Blanket till they can goe, and then if they get a piece of
rugge to cover them, they are well sped. Linnen shirts the
rich doe weare for wantonnes and bravery, with wide
hanging sleeves playted, thirtie yards are little enough for
one of them. They have now left their Saffron, and learne
to wash their shirts, foure or five times in a yeare. Proud
they are of long crisped glibbes, and doe nourish the same
with all their cunning: to crop the front thereof they take
it for a notable peece of villany. Shamrotes, Water-cresses,
Rootes, and other hearbes they feede upon: Oatemale and
Butter they cramme together. They drinke Whey, Milke,
and Beefe broth, Flesh they devoure without bread, corne
such as they have they keepe for their horses. In haste and
hunger they squele [*sic*] out the blood of raw flesh, and
aske no more dressing thereto, the rest boyleth in their
stomackes with Aquavitæ, which they swill in after such
a surfeite, by quarts & pottles. Their kyne they let blood
which growen to a jelly they bake and over-spread with

Butter, and so eate it in lumpes.

One office in the house of great men is a tale-teller, who bringeth his Lord on sleepe, with tales vaine and frivolous, whereunto the number give sooth and credence. So light they are in beleeving whatsoever is with any countenance of gravitie affirmed by their Superiours, whom they esteeme and honour, that a lewd Prelate within these few yeares needy of money, was able to perswade his parish: That S. *Patricke* in striving with S. *Peter* to let an Irish Galloglass into Heaven, had his head broken with the keyes, for whose releife he obtained a Collation.

Without either precepts or observation of congruity they speake Latine like a vulgar language, learned in their common Schooles of Leach-craft and Law, whereat they begin Children, and hold on sixteene or twentie yeares conning by roate the Aphorismes of *Hypocrates*, and the Civill Institutions, and a few other parings of those two faculties. I have seene them where they kept Schoole, ten in some one Chamber, groveling upon couches of straw, their Bookes at their noses, themselves lying flatte prostate [*sic*], and so to chaunte out their lessons by peece-meale, being the most part lustie fellowes of twenty five yeares and upwards.

(*A Historie of Ireland*, pp. 17-19)

Glibbes (parag. 2) were the thick masses of hair worn on the forehead, and overshadowing the eyes. *Shamrotes* (same paragraph) happens to be the first citation in the OED (sixteenth century) appearing alongside the modern spelling. The etymological source is Irish *seamróg*, the common trefoil, which St Patrick of legend adopted to illustrate the mystery of the Trinity.

Ireland before the seventeenth century was not a land of national cohesion, politically or socially; a common language was no solvent of tribal separatism and pride, which was fostered by the genealogist of each sept. By the time of the English Renaissance the clan in Ireland had failed to fulfil its purpose; but the annalist remained to eulogise its past. One such, Dugald mac Firbis (1580-1660) was a descendant of the scribe who helped to compile the fifteenth-century

Yellow Book of Lecan, for the O'Dowds in County Sligo. Dugald settled in Galway in the reign of Charles I, and compiled his famous nine Books of Genealogies in the College of St Nicholas, during the Cromwellian occupation. Much early Irish history, including a large part of the Annals of the Four Masters, is based on his researches into the records of Irish kings and chieftains, not excluding the families of Danish descent. Dugald's conclusion in Book Nine favours the Milesian race, but with some degree of scepticism:

> Here is the distinction which the profound historians draw between the three different races which are in Erin. Every one who is white of skin, brown of hair, bold, honourable, daring, prosperous, bountiful in the bestowal of property wealth and rings, and who is not afraid of battle or combats, they are the descendants of the sons of Milesius in Erin.
>
> Every one who is fair-haired, vengeful, large, and every plunderer, every musical person, the professors of musical and entertaining performances, who are adepts in all druidical and magical arts, they are the descendants of the Tuatha De Danann in Erin.
>
> Every one who is black-haired, who is a tattler, guileful, tale-telling, noisy, contemptible, every wretched, mean, strolling, unsteady, harsh, and inhospitable person, every slave, every mean thief, every churl, every one who loves not to listen to music and entertainment, the disturbers of every council and every assembly, and the promoters of discord among people, these are of the descendants of the Firbolg, of the Gailiuns, of Liogairné, and of the Fir Domhnann in Erin. But, however, the descendants of the Firbolg are the most numerous of all these.
>
> This is taken from an old book. And, indeed, that it is possible to identify a race by their personal appearance and dispositions I do not take upon myself positively to say, for it may have been true in the ancient times, until the race became repeatedly intermixed. For we daily see even in our own time, and we often hear it from our old men, that there is a similitude of people, a similitude of form, character, and names in some families of Erin compared with others.
>
> (Hyde, *A Literary History of Ireland*, p. 563)

Other important annalists of the seventeenth century include Roderick O'Flaherty and the O'Clery family, some of whose work is preserved by the Royal Irish Academy. Michael O'Clery of the Franciscan order (1575-1643) was the most voluminous of Irish antiquarians, and was therefore employed as chief compiler of the Annals of the Four Masters (1636). He travelled throughout Ireland, assembling material on the lives of the early Irish saints, which he published in Louvain in 1645; he was also responsible for the *Lebar Gabala* or Book of Invasions (1630-31) to which reference has already been made. The expense incurred in the compilation of the Annals of the Four Masters was defrayed by Ferral O'Gara, Prince of Coolavin, Co. Sligo, an Anglican graduate of Trinity College, Dublin.

As usual with early chronographers, these Annals begin with Noah's flood in the year 2242, a date arrived at through the traditional Septuagint calendar. The long intervening period before the advent of Christianity is filled with undependable legends of invaders, settlers, and family lists of kings. Little more credence can be given to the events of the first eight centuries of the Christian era; fact is inevitably entangled with fiction until the late medieval period. The fourth-century campaigning in Britain and Gaul of Niall of the Nine Hostages, to bolster Irish settlements against attacks from the Picts of Alba, was one of several events that may be called historical. Another was Fergus Mór's establishment of the Scottish kingdom of Dalriada at the beginning of the sixth century AD. A third was the obvious affiliation between the church in Wales and the church in Ireland. The British chroniclers Gildas and Nennius seem to have drawn much of their material from this Irish source. In Ireland documents were plentiful; but annalists were merely industrious scribes, who copied manuscripts, but had little or no critical faculty for evaluating the credibility of witnesses. History begins when some part of this faculty has been trained and developed.

One difference between annals and seventeenth-century history may be illustrated by comparing the Annals of the Four Masters with Geoffrey Keating's contemporary *History of Ireland*, although in the present century the latter has become a masterpiece of mixed acceptability. Keating was born some time during the 1570s in Burgess, Tipperary, being of Norman extraction; the Irish surname was *Céitinn*. In Ireland he must have attended a bardic school, for at least eighteen poems are known to be of his composition. Theological training was probably gained at an Irish College in Bordeaux, which was founded about 1603; there he qualified as a Doctor of Divinity. He returned to Ireland, as curate at Tubrin, when times were difficult for Catholic priests, especially for a preacher as eloquent as Keating. A sermon maliciously reported to Carew, President of Munster, resulted in the Penal Laws being invoked against him. He found a retreat in a cave in the Glen of Atherlow, where he planned the writing of an Irish history on new lines. Disguised, he visited monasteries in many parts of Ireland, especially in the south, the object being to copy or consult manuscripts, a majority of which have now passed out of existence. This historian is thought to have died about the year 1650.

The *History of Ireland*, written between 1629 and 1634, is in elegant Irish, claimed as the classic model of prose in the seventeenth-century vernacular. This was probably the last word to reach the public in manuscript form. Numerous scribal exemplars are extant, the earliest Kildare copy, dated 1640, being in the Library of the Franciscan Monastery in Dublin. Keating's *History* did not, however, appear in print, until Book I was published by Halliday of Dublin in 1811. An English translation was made by John O'Mahoney, and published in New York in 1866. The range of literary and other references was astonishing. Here is an extract from the Preface:

> I have seen that the natives of Ireland are maligned by every modern Englishman who speaks of the country. For this reason, being much grieved at the unfairness those writers have shown to Irishmen, I have felt urged to write a history of Ireland myself.
>
> (Hyde, *Literary History of Ireland*, p. 556)

There follows, in the opening chapter, the main burden of the author's complaint:

There is no historian who has written upon Ireland since the English invasion, who does not strive to vilify and calumniate both Anglo-Irish colonists and the Gaelic natives. We have proofs of this in the accounts of the country given by Cambrensis, Spenser, Stanihurst, Hanmer, Camden, Barclay, Morrison, Davis, Campion, and all the writers of the New Galls. . . . They write not of their piety or their valour, or of what monasteries they founded, what lands and endowments they gave to the Church, what immunities they granted to the ollamhs, their bounty to the ecclesiastics and prelates of the Church, the relief they afforded to orphans and to the poor, their munificence to men of learning, and their hospitality to strangers, which was so great that it may be said, in truth, that they were not at any time surpassed by any nation of Europe in generosity and hospitality, in proportion to the abilities they possessed.

(ibid., pp. 557-8)

Keating's work remained the only reputable history of Ireland until the middle of the nineteenth century; by this time Irish had ceased to have any literary currency. The word *history* is used by Keating in its most liberal medieval sense, to include documented as well as legendary material in the form of anecdote. There is no trace of bardic archaism in his scholarly style; he denies himself the rodomontade of ancient dramatic or epical manners, and restricts the didactic tendency to poetry. Purity and clarity are the merits of his narrative style, revealed even in translation:

Mochua and Columcille were contemporaries, and when Mochua or Mac Duach was a hermit in the desert the only cattle he had in the world were a cock and a mouse and a fly. The cock's service to him was to keep the matin time of midnight; and the mouse would let him sleep only five hours in the day-and-night, and when he desired to sleep longer, through being tired from making many crosses and genuflexions, the mouse would come and rub his ear, and thus waken him; and the service the fly did him was to keep walking on every line of the Psalter that he read, and when he rested from reciting his psalms the fly rested on the line he left off at till he resumed the reciting of his psalms. Soon after that these three precious ones died, and Mochua, after that event, wrote a letter to Columcille, who was in Iona, in Alba, and he complained of the death of his flock. Columcille wrote to him, and said thus: 'O brother,' said he, 'thou must not be surprised at the death of the flock that thou hast lost, for misfortune exists only where there is wealth.' From this banter of these real saints I gather that they set no store on worldly possessions, unlike many persons of the present time.

('Mochua's Riches', P. S. Dineen's translation, 1908,
History of Ireland, III.71)

Standish O'Grady, writing just before the nineteenth-century literary revival, thought that Keating's conception of history should neither be rejected nor retained. He writes:

What the present age demands upon the subject of antique Irish history — an exact and scientific treatment of the facts supplied by our native authorities — will be demanded for ever. It will never be supplied.

(*History of Ireland*, II.16)

The rise of Anglo-Irish literature in the eighteenth century, though not as yet quite distinctive, was attributable to the emergence of an educated Protestant class in Dublin and the Pale, of which Trinity College was the nerve-centre. Swift, Berkeley, Burke, Farquhar, Murphy, Goldsmith and Sheridan all enjoyed the benefit of such a background. These writers, and the actor Charles Macklin, formed the core of the new movement, residing much of their time in London or its neighbourhood, in order to be at the heart of governmental power and social influence. They were writers with a spirited command of the English tongue, Jonathan Swift (1667-1745) being by far the most distinguished. This observant parson of Laracor in Meath revealed a personality entirely relevant to the social, economic and political developments of his age. But it was not until after 1713, when the disillusioned politician had moved into the Deanery of St Patrick's, that his Irish blood was roused, and he became the mouthpiece of

Ireland's inarticulate discontents. Many English-speaking Protestants have since been among the stout defenders of the Irish cause, among them Robert Emmet, Edward Fitzgerald, Theobald Wolfe Tone and Henry Grattan.

Swift has been rebuked for his tongue-in-cheek denunciation of the Irish language; for in sharing the prejudices of clerics such as Ussher and Woodward, he thought it demonstable that the irrational pronunciation of Gaelic put a brake on the country's intellectual advancement, as well as its progress in commerce and industry. In 1729 he expressed the hope that the Irish language would be abolished, because

> this would, in a great measure, civilize the most barbarous among them, reconcile them to our customs and manner of living, and reduce great numbers to the national religion, whatever kind may then happen to be established. The method is plain and simple; and although I am too desponding to produce it, yet I could heartily wish some public thoughts were employed to reduce this uncultivated people from that idle, savage, beastly, thievish manner of life, in which they continue sunk to a degree, that it is almost impossible for a country gentleman to find a servant of human capacity, or the least tincture of natural honesty; or who does not live among his own tenants in continual fear of having his plantation destroyed, his cattle stolen, and his goods pilfered.
>
> (*Prose Works*, vol. VII, p. 133)

This attitude was typical of the man who opposed the abolition of the Test Act in Ireland, and who was repeatedly passed over in his quest for a bishopric, because he was out of favour with Queen Anne.

Although he had supported Harley's Tory ministry while in England, Swift was an uncompromising Whig in his political sentiments. He had studiously avoided becoming a professional writer by preserving anonymity in all his published work, except *A Proposal for Correcting, Improving and Ascertaining the English Tongue* (1712). While writing *Gulliver's Travels*, a characteristically Irish voyage story, he became disturbed by the increasing subordination of Ireland to the interests of the English government of Walpole, and consequently advocated a boycott of English manufactures. *The Letters of M. B. Drapier* (see p. 78) began to appear in 1724; the spelling chosen represents that of the French original; *draper* (first recorded in *Piers Plowman*, 1362) is, however, the only orthography noted in the OED. That Swift did not intend the *i* to be pronounced is shown in the rhyme of the following couplet: 'But to this parchment let the *Drapier*/Oppose his counter-charm of *paper*'. ('*A Simile*, on our want of silver, and the only way to remedy it', 1725).

The *Drapier Letters* consisted of five documents which, by persistence and over-emphasis, achieved their end in compelling Walpole's administration to withdraw a monetary patent that constituted a monopoly. This patent, granted in 1722, was corrupt at base, since it granted the interest to the King's mistress, the Duchess of Kendall, who received a bribe of £10,000 from William Wood, so that he might avail himself of a profit of £40,000. The patent allowed Wood, an ironmonger, to mint copper coins for fourteen years, in excess of what the Irish community required; the protests from the commissioners of revenue in Dublin were completely ignored. Statistics showed that the debased coinage would carry a loss of 150 per cent to the Irish people. Two years elapsed before an enquiry was ordered by the Privy Council; Swift intervened in the knowledge that Ireland strongly wished to be responsible for its own currency.

The last of the *Drapier Letters*, addressed to the whole people of Ireland, was responsible for a warrant issued to arrest Harding, the printer; but he was never prosecuted, and a reward of £300, offered to anyone disclosing the name of the author, was not taken up. The cancellation of the patent meant that Wood and the Duchess of Kendall had to be compensated.

The disastrous situation in Ireland went beyond the unsatisfactory state of monetary matters. Between 1720 and 1729 Swift published a number of papers that cover the spectrum of evils under which Irishmen laboured, through no fault of their own. These pamphlets are reprinted in volume VII (*Historical and Political Tracts – Irish*) of the *Prose Works*, edited by Temple Scott, 1897-1908. Principal reasons for the problems were the separation of the executive in

Ireland from the legislative body in England; the continuance of rotten boroughs in the electoral system; and the practice of bestowing patronage, peerages and pensions which the Crown upheld.

Swift's *Proposal for the Universal Use of Irish Manufacture* in 1720 (see p. 78) broke a silence of six years after the Dean's return to Ireland. The political circumstances that gave rise to it are well known. An Act had been passed in March of that year for 'better securing the Dependency of the Kingdom of Ireland upon the Crown of Great Britain'. Most Irish legislation since the Navigation Acts of 1663 had been prompted by the mercantilist theory that succeeded feudalism. This doctrine suggested that the main energies of the nation should be directed to the pursuit of wealth, in terms of money, which was to be measured by the influx of precious metals. The power of a mother country could only be ensured by an excess of exports over imports, and by directing the flow of capital into the most effective channels. This policy tended to ruthless exploitation of colonies like Ireland, which was Britain's largest after America. It was not until 1776 that the alternative policy of *laissez-faire* was encouraged by Adam Smith's *The Wealth of Nations*.

William Molyneux, M.P. for Dublin University (Trinity College), had been one of the first, in 1698, to argue that Ireland should not be treated as a colony; his pamphlet was entitled *The Case of Ireland's Being Bound by Acts of Parliament in England, Stated*. Under the Protestant ascendancy Catholics were deprived of the rights of citizenship, and found all their institutions in the hands of a religious minority; the few legislative powers of the Irish Parliament were constantly hamstrung by the intervention of the Privy Council. Swift, though a pillar of the established church in Ireland, perceived clearly the adverse effects upon a population that was deliberately browbeaten into a state of rebellion.

Swift's pamphlet published in 1724, *The Truth of Some Maxims in State and Government examined with reference to Ireland*, examines the mercantilist theory closely, and employs the phrase *British Empire* at the beginning of the seventh paragraph. No earlier usage has come to notice; the OED observes, under *Britain* (p. 1113), that the term was only brought into vogue in 1868. Swift here assumes that human (or natural) rights exist by universal consent, as a tenet of common political wisdom. Swift numbers among the fallacies of progress, three assumptions: (1) that the dearness of things necessary for life, in a fruitful country, is a sign of wealth; (2) that low interest rates are an indication that plenty of money is available; when people no longer know how to dispose of their money, the price of land invariably rises; 'consequently absentee landowners leasing farms are forced to increase rents; (3) that people themselves constitute the riches of a nation; this, he says, would be true in Ireland, were it not for large families and resulting unemployment, leading to the poverty of many. Nearly half the population of Ireland, he pointed out, consisted of professional paupers. Swift actually approved the emigration of Ireland's surplus population to America.

The Present Miserable State of Ireland (an undated paper, probably written in the latter part of 1726) was an important document, written shortly after Swift had had an interview with Walpole. It criticises William of Orange's Act prohibiting the exportation of wool manufactured in Ireland, a bill that was conceived to silence the clamours of competitive English weavers. This led to large-scale retrenchment of Irish workers in this trade, and to the current excess of imports over exports. Swift wrote:

> There are thousands of poor wretches who think themselves blessed, if they can obtain a hut worse than the squire's dog-kennel, and an acre of ground for a potato-plantation, on condition of being as very slaves as any in America. What can be more deplorable, than to behold wretches starving in the midst of plenty!
>
> We are apt to charge the Irish with laziness, because we seldom find them employed; but then we don't consider they have nothing to do. . . . The want of trade with us is rather owing to the cruel restraints we lie under, than to any disqualification whatsoever in our inhabitants.
>
> (*Prose Works*, ed. T. Scott, VII, p. 164)

A Short View of the State of Ireland (1728) is one of the tracts most frequently quoted by historians; its English printer, Mist, was actually prosecuted. Here are the fourteen points that made Swift's skilfully argued pamphlet famous:

I shall only enumerate by rules generally known, and never contradicted, what are the true causes of any country's flourishing and growing rich, and then examine what effects arise from those causes in the Kingdom of Ireland.

The first cause of a Kingdom's thriving is the fruitfulness of the soil, to produce the necessaries and conveniences of life, not only sufficient for the inhabitants, but for exportation into other countries.

The second, is the industry of the people in working up all their native commodities to the last degree of manufacture.

The third, is the conveniency of safe ports and havens, to carry out their own goods, as much manufactured, and bring in those of others, as little manufactured as the nature of mutual commerce will allow.

The fourth, is, That the natives should as much as possible, export and import their goods in vessels of their own timber, made in their own country.

The fifth, is the liberty of a free trade in all foreign countries, which will permit them, except those who are in war with their own Prince or State.

The sixth, is, by being governed only by laws made with their own consent, for otherwise they are not a free People. And therefore all appeals for justice, or applications, for favour or preferment to another country, are so many grievous impoverishments.

The seventh, is, by improvement of land, encouragement of agriculture, and thereby increasing the number of their people, without which any country, however blessed by Nature, must continue poor.

The eighth, is the residence of the Princes, or chief administrators of the civil power.

The ninth, is the concourse of foreigners for education, curiosity or pleasure, or as to a general mart of trade.

The tenth, is by disposing all offices of honour, profit or trust, only to the natives, or at least with very few exceptions, where strangers have long inhabited the country, and are supposed to understand, and regard the interest of it as their own.

The eleventh is, when the rents of lands, and profits of employments, are spent in the country which produced them and not in another, the former of which will certainly happen where the love of our native country prevails.

The twelfth, is by the public revenues being all spent and employed at home, except on the occasions of a foreign war.

The thirteenth, is where the people are not obliged, unless they find it for their own interest, or conveniency, to receive any monies, except of their own coinage by a public mint after the manner of all civilized nations.

The fourteenth, is a disposition of the people of a country to wear their own manufactures, and import as few incitements to luxury, either in clothes, furniture, food or drink as they possibly can live conveniently without. . . .

A man who lives in a solitary house far from help, is not wise in endeavouring to acquire in the neighbourhood, the reputation of being rich, because those who come for gold, will go off with pewter and brass, rather than return empty. . . . Our misfortune is not altogether owing to our own fault, but to a million of discouragements.

The conveniency of ports and havens which Nature bestowed us so liberally is of no more use to us, than a beautiful prospect to a man shut up in a dungeon.

As to shipping of its own, this Kingdom is so utterly unprovided, that of all the excellent timber cut down within these fifty or sixty years, it can hardly be said that the Nation hath received the benefit of one valuable house to dwell in, or one ship to trade with. . . .

No strangers from other countries make this a part of their travels, where they can expect to see nothing but scenes of misery and desolation. . . . If we do flourish, it must be against every law of Nature and Reason, like the thorn at Glastonbury, that blossoms in the midst of Winter.

(ibid pp. 83-8)

Though Swift was no economist, he had fundamental principles, such as the right of a people to be governed by its own laws, which made his concept of rational freedom helpful at a critical time. What he managed to do was to unite Irishmen of different factions in a sense of nationhood. But in so doing, he overlooked the fact that native Irishmen had no real rights as free men, as long as the Anglo-Irish alone enjoyed the privileges he assumed all to possess.

The skill of indictment displayed in the above passages has none of the macabre irony of *A Modest Proposal*, but there are glimpses of a nascent Anglo-Irish satirical vein for which eighteenth-century expatriates were largely responsible. The temper of invective is seen to better advantage in Swift's verse lampoons, especially those on Wood's Halfpence. *Prometheus* (1724) contains an excellent example:

> Ye Pow'rs of *Grub-Street*, make me able
> Discreetly to apply this *Fable*;
> Say, who is to be understood
> By that old Thief *Prometheus*? WOOD.
> For *Jove*, it is not hard to guess him;
> I mean *His Majesty, God bless him*.
> This Thief and Black-Smith was so bold,
> He strove to steal that *Chain* of *Gold*,
> Which links the *Subject* to the *King*,
> And change it for a *Brazen String*.
> But sure, if nothing else must pass
> Between the *King* and US but Brass,
> Altho' the *Chain* will never crack,
> Yet *Our Devotion* may *Grow Slack*.
>
> But *Jove* will soon convert, I hope,
> This *Brazen Chain* into a *Rope*;
> With which *Prometheus* shall be ty'd,
> And high in Air for ever ride;
> Where, if we find his *Liver* grows,
> For want of *Vultures*, we have *Crows*.
>
> (*Poetical Works of Jonathan Swift*, p. 279)

No national group sailed nearer the wind in the risk of libel than the Irish, and this courageous lampooner was no exception; in spite of the Penal Laws, he sheltered successfully behind anonymity, so that the burden of responsibility fell chiefly on English printers.

One paradox of Swift's mastery of the English language is his flyting technique, shown in the amusing way he adapted satire to the Gaelic tradition. In preserving its comic and fanciful aspects, he developed an innate gift for parodying the style of eccentrics and pseudo-classicists, whom he read with much critical enjoyment. Irish was being taught at Trinity College in his time by Paul Higgins, possibly as a means to Protestant conversion; but interest in the subject declined after the Battle of the Boyne. That Swift ever took such teaching seriously is as unlikely as that he was conscious of his own prejudice. Only an egocentric reasoner, assured of the rightness of his judgements, could have committed himself to the following:

In one of the advertisements I encountered near a hundred words together, which I defy any creature in human shape, except an Irishman of the savage kind, to pronounce; neither would I undertake such a task, to be owner of the lands, unless I had liberty to humanize the syllables twenty miles round. The legislature may think what they please, and that they are above copying the Romans in all their conquests of barbarous nations; but I am deceived, if anything has more contributed to prevent the Irish from being tamed, than this encouragement of their language, which might be easily abolished, and become a dead one in half an age, with little expense, and less trouble.

How is it possible that a gentleman who lives in those parts where the *town-lands* (as they call them) of his estate produce such odious sounds from the mouth, the throat, and the nose, can be able to repeat the words without dislocating every muscle that is used in speaking, and without applying the same tone to all other words, in every language he understands. . . . The Scotch cadence, as well as expression, are offensive enough. But none of these defects derive contempt to the speaker; whereas, what we call the *Irish brogue* is no sooner discovered, than it makes the deliverer in the last degree ridiculous and despised; and, from such a mouth, an Englishman expects nothing but bulls, blunders, and follies. Neither does it avail whether the censure be reasonable or not, since the fact is always so. And, what is yet worse, it is too well known, that the bad consequence of this opinion affects those among us who are not the least liable to such reproaches, farther than the misfortune of being born in Ireland, although of English parents, and whose education has been chiefly in that kingdom.

'On Barbarous Denominations in Ireland', *Prose Works*, VII, pp. 345-6)

V

Anglo-Irish Relations since 1800

Universal depression came with the conclusion of the Napoleonic wars; there were a number of factors headed by the unexpected population growth. The Industrial Revolution was accompanied by great inequalities of wealth. Improved transport and communication systems meant the greater mobility of educated persons. In areas where Anglo-Saxon institutions had scarcely penetrated, national self-interest became unusually lively.

The Irish question after 1800 was difficult on two grounds, ownership of land and religious division; Ulster was a particularly troublesome area. After the Union, clashes between church and state commenced with the disabilities of Catholics. Daniel O'Connell (1775-1847), a barrister educated at Douai and Lincoln's Inn, signed a petition for the emancipation of the Catholics in 1805, and formed the Catholic Association in 1823 as a way of raising funds ('Catholic rent') to alleviate the post-war poverty of the predominantly Catholic peasantry. He was repeatedly returned to Parliament, and used constitutional procedures and public demonstrations as a means of securing reforms.

Many changes were necessary, as Ireland doubled its population during the first half of the nineteenth century. After 1817 the country was plagued by a succession of famines, the direst of which was the Great Potato Famine of 1845, lasting for five years. During the Duke of Wellington's premiership, O'Connell steered the Catholic Emancipation Act through Parliament (1829). Thirteen years later his motion to repeal the Act of Union was defeated, largely because he was opposed by Ulster dissenters, voting with

English Conservatives. For nearly a century the House of Lords proved the major obstacle to Irish reform, repeatedly rejecting desirable acts that were passed by the Commons.

O'Connell was the initiator and orator of the first liberation movement and anticipated Gandhi in advocating the non-violent repeal of the Act of Union. For a generation he was the moving spirit behind the resistance of the Irish peasantry, who were a fertile seed-bed of discontent, comparable to that of the Russian muzhiks. His chief journalistic spokesman was an able Protestant lawyer, Thomas Davis, founder of *The Nation* newspaper, an enterprise in which he had Catholic allies in Gavan Duffy and John Dillon. In 1842 this group founded the popular movement known as Young Ireland.

The land problem can be briefly described as follows. The Irish landlord rented land to graziers (the owners of cattle herds) and to cottiers, who were the highest bidders among small peasant farmers. The staple diet of the latter was the potato and buttermilk. Grain crops, butter and pigs were invariably reserved for market sales in order to pay the cottiers' landlord. The peasantry were, in effect, labourers living from hand to mouth on the tillage of sometimes a quarter of an acre. Their scourge was the middle-man, who acted as an agent and collector of rents, and who figures so evilly in Irish fiction, e.g. in Maria Edgeworth's *Castle Rackrent*, as the callous evictor of those who were unable to pay. The feuds of dispossessed peasants against their masters were matched only by the revenge they took against constables and plain-clothes spies, who were their principal accusers. The Penal Laws existed undisguisedly to favour the minority Protestants at the expense of all Catholics, unless they were engaged in trade. But in spite of provocation, the Catholic Church opposed physical force against Anglican persecution, and discouraged Irish separatism as the sin of rebellion.

After 1800 the Scottish Presbyterian peasants of Ulster enjoyed rights and security of land tenure denied to their Irish counterparts. The linen and shipbuilding industries enabled the north to surmount the famines that were to decimate the population of the rest of Ireland. But Ulster

Protestants practised discrimination against Catholics, in the farming as well as industrial communities. The Orange Order of 1795 had been the first of the societies with militant aims to become the activists of modern Irish history by frustrating governmental attempts at religious toleration. Formed after the fateful defeat of the United Irishmen at the Battle of the Diamond, its avowed aim was to defend the Protestant Constitution, without weighing the cost of resultant religious warfare.

Not all fervent Irish nationalists were Catholics; exceptions were Henry Grattan, Theobald Wolf Tone, Edward Fitzgerald and Robert Emmet. Thomas Davis championed Young Ireland against Anglo-Saxon domination, characterised by economic materialism. He was a middle-class lawyer and Benthamite, a representative example of the non-violent, cultural nationalist. His policy of agrarian reform was designed to halt the depopulation of Ireland, a country which he argued could support twenty-five million people. Since there was no peaceful ecumenical means of dispossessing covetous landlords, he failed to impress the Ulster Orangemen, and was ignored by most Protestants, who profited from the preservation of the feudal tradition of land ownership. Davis could not speak the Irish tongue, as O'Connell could; yet in *The Nation* he made the preservation of the indigenous language a corner-stone of editorial policy.

Throughout his turbulent career for the liberation of Ireland, O'Connell was harrassed by official and political opponents, while most of the associations he formed were eventually suppressed. After his election to Parliament in 1828, he refused to take the oath of supremacy, and was not allowed to take his seat until the next election. As a tribute for services to the nation, he was awarded an annual allowance to cover his expenses. In 1844 he successfully appealed against a conviction and fine for causing disaffection in Ireland.

In the period of agrarian unrest (1840-70) over two million Irishmen emigrated to different parts of the world, principally to England, the colonies and the United States. The famine of 1845, when Ireland's population was about eight million, was aggravated by England's adherence to the principle of Free Trade and her refusal to ban profitable exports from Ireland, while that country was suffering under this crisis. The Irish naturally blamed the Union for their distress. In considerable numbers poverty-stricken country-men sought employment in Belfast's cotton and other industries; there was a fivefold *increase* in that city's population between 1800 and 1850. The shipbuilding yards of Harland and Wolff augmented Belfast's labour force from 1858.

Robert Peel's constabulary was most unpopular in Ireland during the potato famine; but in 1846 he succeeded in repealing the Navigation Acts and the Corn Laws, which made the importation of low-priced grain from America possible. The disaster was alleviated only by charity from England and the United States, which supported a third of the population. The Encumbered Estates Act of 1849 was designed to enable ruined land-owners to sell their properties, mainly to English and Scots speculators. The country was depopulated of its peasants, to the embarrassment of industrial towns, especially in England. As the new owners of estates were English-speaking, the Irish language lost thousands of speakers. There was no material decrease, however, in adherence to the nationalist cause.

Daniel O'Connell, the incomparable demagogue of Irish history, died in Genoa in May 1847, when the potato famine was at its height. He had made peace with the new Whig government under Lord John Russell in England, and then turned upon the firebrands of Young Ireland, who never forgot his unfulfilled promises. His political function had obviously been that of catalyst to arouse the Irish from their servility. He has not, however, won the affection of literary historians, in whom Thomas Davis, James Mangan, the poet, and Gavan Duffy inspired greater veneration.

The hard fact was that England retained thirty thousand troops in Ireland to prevent insurrection, and three quarters of these guardians of the peace were recruited from the Irish peasantry. Among the radicals, ascendancy now passed to new organisations, such as The Tenant League and the Irish Confederation; the latter was under the chairmanship of Smith O'Brien, with the eloquent John Mitchel as his principal activist. The tithe war (or rent strike) became a provocative plan of campaign; but after a scuffle with the constabulary at Ballingarry in 1848, both ring leaders were arrested, condemned and sent to Van Diemens Land (Tasmania), from which they finally escaped to California.

After the outbreak of typhus, the social and political condition of Ireland in the mid-nineteenth century was pitiable. Thomas Carlyle, the critic of Chartism, was sent to report, and after a circular tour of the island under the guidance of Gavan Duffy, he described the situation as 'the abomination of desolation'. A papal legate, Archbishop Cullen, was despatched from Rome to Armagh in 1850, in order to reform the Irish Catholic Church, which seemed the only hope of social regeneration. This ecclesiastic was a puritan, who declared all forms of Irish radicalism to be heresy. He roundly condemned journalistic and literary incitement like that practised by Duffy, Mangan and Mitchel in *The Nation*, and set in motion an era of literary protest, which culminated in the writings of James Stephens (not the poet), Yeats and James Joyce. Duffy was so dispirited when he believed that Archbishop Cullen was in league with the English Whig government that he emigrated to Australia in 1855.

The Fenian movement of 1858, whose aim was Home Rule, was initiated by the Irish Republican Brotherhood, whose guiding hand was Stephens, popularly called 'Mr Shock'. He had gained experience in France during the revolution that produced the Second Republic, and he studied the Irish discontents by walking the length and breadth of his native land, a distance of over three thousand miles. The policy of the Fenians, as outlined by John O'Leary, editor of the *Irish People*, ignored Archbishop Cullen, in holding that the only solution lay in preparedness. Neither he nor Stephens relied on the support of one class; least of all did they court the peasant farmer, the prosperous middle class, or the Catholic clerics. As Joyce reminded us in *Ulysses*, one of the Fenians' slogans was 'No priests in politics'.

The Fenian demand for independence was equally strong among exiles in the urban areas of America, who raised funds for transmission to the mother country. Irish-Americans formed their own brigade and fought with distinction in the Civil War on the side of the Union. But these emigrés took little part in raising the secret Irish Army at home; the latter never became effective because it was lacking in arms. The day of liberation, in Stephens's judgement, was to come in December 1865. But the plot was discovered by the English authorities three months earlier, and the ringleaders, including O'Leary, were tried and sentenced to penal servitude. The only man to escape the retribution of the law was Stephens, who reached the United States via Paris in the middle of 1866. After a futile insurrection in February 1867, the Fenian movement fizzled out for a generation.

In 1869 Gladstone disestablished the Church of Ireland, which was supported by an eighth of the population, the viable religions being predominantly Catholic and Presbyterian. But his attempt at conciliatory action in the Land Act of 1870 was ineffectual. The Home Rule League, which owed much to the humanist Isaac Butt, was founded in 1873, and the Land League in 1879; both enjoyed the support of the patriot Protestant, Charles Stewart Parnell, whose mother was American. He was of Anglo-Irish descent, and entered Parliament in 1875, stepping naturally into the leadership vacated by the death of Daniel O'Connell. Ten years later Parnell, supported by Michael Davitt, had four-fifths of the Irish members of Parliament behind him.

It was Parnell who, in 1880, initiated the practice of 'boycotting' land agents who evicted tenants. The first victim was Captain Boycott of Lough Mask, who was compelled to hire Ulster Orangemen as labourers, and invoke the protection of the English military for the gathering of his potato crop. The amended Land Act of 1881 was the result of Parnell's cautious co-operation with the Liberal leader Gladstone, who was now regarded as 'the friend of Ireland'; the new law offered peasant farmers just rents, fixed tenure and the right to sell. Yet it was not until the enactments of 1885, 1887, 1891 and 1903 that the land war ended, these laws making the farmers landed proprietors, instead of tenants.

George Moore, the novelist, who was living in Paris at the time, was himself an absentee landlord, and wrote in *Parnell and His Island* (1887)

In Ireland there is nothing but the land; with the exception of a few distillers or brewers in Dublin, who live upon the drunkenness of the people, there is no way in Ireland of getting money except through the peasant . . . rent is a tribute and nothing else.

(pp. 6 and 8)

Under the new laws, feudalism in Ireland came to an end, and arbitrary eviction disappeared. The Wyndham Land Act of 1903 provided a hundred million pounds to buy up the peasants' land debt; but unfortunately, the best land was already in the hands of graziers.

In 1884 Parnell founded the weekly newspaper *United Ireland*, with the voluble William O'Brien as his editor; it soon had a circulation of over a hundred thousand. Parnell's greatest strength was, however, the hold he maintained on the popular Irish nationalist party, which captured all the Commons seats of Leinster, Munster and Connacht. Members received no salaries, and Irish nominees for election were usually men without private income, so that living expenses had invariably to be met from funds raised in America.

The first Home Rule Bill was introduced by Gladstone in 1886, when in his seventy-seventh year, the plan being to grant Ireland its own Parliament, and an independent administration. After two months' debate, the Bill was defeated by the efforts of Randolph Churchill and the Conservative party, supported by the House of Lords and those Unionists who had defected from the Liberal Party. Home Rule was unfortunately associated with Popery, a religious prejudice that not even majority opinion could eradicate. A second Home Rule Bill was proffered in 1892, and passed by the Commons, but rejected by the Lords. Meantime Parnell had been discredited by an unfortunate divorce action; as a result, he lost his leadership, and died in 1891 at the young age of forty-five.

Not until 1906 did the Liberals under Campbell-Bannerman return to power, and the prospect of Home Rule was reopened. The strongest opposition to Home Rule now came from the Orange Order of Ulster, whose festival, held on 12 July, celebrated the anniversary of the Battle of the Boyne and the overthrow of England's Catholic king. Ulster Unionists wanted to keep the British and Imperial connection at all costs, and formed themselves into an activist society indistinguishable from the Orange Order, except that their policy was public and political; whereas Orangemen, who associated in masonic lodges, were a secret brotherhood, no less influential in the province. The Ulsterites (mainly northern farmers and the working-class) were determined to keep their province Protestant. The province consists of six north-eastern counties: Antrim, Armagh, Derry, Down, Fermanagh and Tyrone, and still has a population nearly half that of the rest of Ireland; but only in the last two of these counties do the Catholics slightly exceed the Protestants.

The most vociferous religious group was the Presbyterians, who reacted with the Calvinist fanaticism they inherited from their forebears in Charles I's reign. This faction, being of Scottish descent, had maintained close associations with Dalriada since the fourth century. Since the Restoration, Ulster had helped to relieve population pressures in south-western Scotland, and thus the Presbyterians became the dominant influence in northern Ireland. They had imbibed republican ideas from America and France, but remained loyal to the Union with England by progressively dissociating themselves from Irish nationalist movements.

In 1910 Sir Edward Carson, an astute and experienced lawyer from Dublin, took charge of the Irish Unionists' cause, and confronted John Redmond, leader of the Irish Nationalist Party, who was Parnell's successor. This was at a time when the Irish literary and cultural Renaissance of the eighteen-nineties had achieved much success in arousing national pride and racial identity. The most distinguished authors wrote in English; but the Gaelic League, founded in 1893 by Douglas Hyde, proved a rallying point for half a million people, still using the vernacular. A movement, styled *Sinn Féin* (implying 'self-help'), was initiated by Arthur Griffith in 1899, with the object of fostering Irish industries by boycotting English imports. In this combination of circumstances, the final battle for Home Rule became a prickly issue for the English Parliament. Nevertheless, Asquith and Redmond carried the enabling motion through, by means of the Parliament Act of 1911. This inhibited the peers from effectually vetoing Bills passed by the House of Commons; at the expiry of two years, any enactment approved by the Lower House would automatically become law.

Ulster Orangemen immediately organised themselves to resist incorporation in an Irish self-governing state. The Solemn Covenant of September 1912, signed by two hundred thousand Unionists, declared Ulster's intention to fight for the maintenance of its rights under the Crown. Political camps in Ireland began to arm, when the Home Rule Bill was passed by the House of Commons in January 1913; but the outbreak of World War I fortunately delayed implementation of the Act until the signing of the Peace Treaty.

There was much diversity of opinion about Home Rule during the war, and the threat of conscription, though apparently not enforceable in Ireland, helped to provoke the Easter Rising of 1916; it was instigated by the Irish Republican Brotherhood. Public buildings in Dublin were occupied by Patrick Pearse, James Connolly (a Marxist) and their Volunteers, and an Irish Republic was proclaimed. British occupation forces ended the insurrection by bombarding the city for four days, after which fourteen ringleaders were shot under martial law, by orders of General Maxwell. Éamon de Valera was fortunate to escape, though jailed in England for several years. The severity of this action and the execution of Roger Casement as a spy (August 1916) occasioned lasting bitterness in nationalist Ireland; this is reflected in Sean O'Casey's *The Plough and the Stars*. The rebellion served to promote public sympathy for Sinn Féin, which had displaced the moderate policy of Redmond by 1919. In that year the Free State of Ireland was proclaimed by *Dáil Éireann* (the national assembly), under the leadership of de Valera and Griffith; the militant Volunteers at once became the Irish Republican Army, still known to the public as the IRA.

Independence was given to Ireland, excluding Ulster, in December 1920, by an Act amending the earlier Home Rule law, introduced by Lloyd-George's coalition government.

De Valera returned from America, but the transfer of power did not take place immediately. This was due to a clash of authority between the Republican de Valera group (Sinn Féin) and the Free Staters under Michael Collins and Richard Mulcahy. The situation was not improved by the presence of the Black and Tans, or military police, sent to stiffen the Royal Irish Constabulary. Their operations, especially in Cork, were a political blunder, causing violence and suspicion between the parties. What was virtually an Anglo-Irish war lasted until July 1921.

The Sinn Féin party, which obtained a majority at the first two elections, wanted a republic, and refused to form an Irish government with dominion status only. In December 1921 a compromise was reached in London and a treaty signed, whereby the Home Rule representatives accepted the Irish Free State as a member of the Commonwealth, under the British Crown. This momentous occasion, which cost Lloyd George his premiership, is described by Winston Churchill in *The World Crisis: The Aftermath* (1929). On the issue of the British connection, de Valera decided to resign, Arthur Griffith becoming President of the Executive Council in 1922, with Collins as Chairman of the Provisional Government. After the election in June of the same year, civil war broke out between the Free State (i.e. the treaty) party and the Republicans, which caused the irreparable destruction of the Public Record Office in Dublin. Ten days after Griffith's death from a heart attack, Collins was ambushed and shot in Cork; their successors were W. T. Cosgrave and Kevin O'Higgins. Though de Valera had taken no active part in the latest troubles, he was imprisoned in Ireland. In 1927 he abandoned the Sinn Féin cause, and founded the Fianna Fáil party, which agreed to the oath of allegiance, so that its members could occupy seats in the Dáil.

When de Valera undertook to form a government in 1932, he declared the IRA an illegal organisation and restored Ireland's economy by ending the boycott of Britain he had earlier advocated. The Free State Party later changed its name to Fine Gael, and sent its extremists, the Blue Shirts, to fight for General Franco in Spain, under Eoin O'Duffy. The Catholic Free State of Éire was officially created by plebiscite in 1937, with the Dáil's 144 members as its House of Representatives, and the President as Head of State. He was empowered to appoint the Prime Minister and to exercise all legal powers of a ruler, including command of the army. The upper house, the Senate, was to have sixty members, eleven nominated by the Prime Minister, and the rest elected by the Dáil. Fianna Fáil remained the dominant political party for most of the next forty years, until the coming of the National Coalition in February 1973; this coalition became feasible when the partition of Ireland ceased to be the major issue, and economic problems needed to take precedence.

The Northern Ireland House of Commons (Stormont) functioned from June 1921, representing a large part of Ireland's population, who occupy only seventeen per cent of the land; Protestant Unionists (about sixty-two per cent of Ulster's people) usually muster four-fifths of the seats. The integrity of this legislature, as well as the religious group it represents, was safeguarded by the Ireland Act of 1949, the year in which the government of John Costello declared the rest of Ireland a republic.

The industrial output of Northern Ireland exceeds that of the rest of the country, but until recently only ratepayers were entitled to vote. Since the introduction of adult suffrage in 1970 the causes of unrest in Ulster have been (a) Catholic disabilities in public office, and (b) provocative acts of violence, including sectarian murder, by groups that are broadly classified as republican, because they disavow the British connection. On the other side, the Unionist party, which excludes Catholics, steadfastly rejects government from Dublin. The Ulster Parliament, with forty-eight members, sends twelve representatives to the English House of Commons, and accepts the latter's overruling decisions on foreign policy, defence and income tax.

The verdict of history honours Daniel O'Connell and Arthur Griffith as outstanding figures of Ireland's tragic story since 1800. Though both spoke and sought to preserve Gaelic, trusting in cultural values as the foundation of nationalism, they differed in personality and political aspirations. Sinn Féin was the brain-child of Griffith, but it denounced labour discord and dictatorial socialism. Griffith, however, became disillusioned with the form of government he was called upon to administer; he seems to have realised that what he could obtain from a reluctant England did not square with his ideal.

That Ireland's troubles were aggravated by unwarranted oppressions is no longer doubted. Scots and Welsh were not, like the Irish, deprived of their land by external force, or of their culture and language by alien systems of education. Ireland was anglicised by law, so that a social compact was scarcely possible. As England's first experiment in colonisation, the mistakes made were costly to a succession of governments. Colonialism was synonymous with exploitation, even if the English brand was less paternalistic than that of the Roman Empire. The irony of Ireland's situation in the days of Yeats and Maud Gonne was summarised by Douglas Hyde in an address to the National Literary Society of Dublin in 1892. He was quoting the views of Mazzini:

> We ought to be content as an integral part of the United Kingdom because we have lost the notes of nationality, our language and customs. It has always been very curious to me how Irish sentiment sticks in this halfway house — how it continues apparently to hate the English, and at the same time continues to imitate them; how it continues to clamour for recognition as a distinct nationality and at the same time throws away with both hands what would make it so. . . . We find ourselves despoiled of the bricks of nationality. The old bricks that lasted eighteen hundred years are destroyed.

As long as Ireland was part of the United Kingdom, the language problem remained a bone of contention. The vernacular was still spoken in country villages, smaller towns, and isolated areas, such as the islands of the west coast. But as the medium of education was English, vernacular speakers had declined from about 1750; much less Irish was heard in the eastern provinces, and it was virtually non-existent in the cities of Dublin, Belfast and Cork. Many patriot writers,

James Clarence Mangan among them, were unable to speak Irish. Douglas Hyde, the Protestant author who became first President of Éire (1938-45), devoted the last fifteen pages of *A Literary History of Ireland* to the people's educational grievances.

The Commissioners of Education in Ireland found in 1825 that about half a million speakers still used the vernacular (see Hyde, op. cit. p. 625). But German observers, not long after this report, thought that figure was considerably under-estimated. Hyde blamed the Board of National Education and its policy of uniformity for the decline of Irish in the nineteenth century. The Irish-speaking child, he said, was being taught to read and write a language he did not speak at home. English ought to have been taught as a second language, through the medium of Irish, and the curriculum should have included *Irish* history, in order to halt the undoubted anglicisation of the people.

But the issue was not as readily soluble as Hyde imagined. At the time of the Union, educational facilities in Ireland were preponderantly in the hands of 'hedge' schools. Classes were, in fact, held in the open air, until indoor schooling was organised by the Christian brothers and Ursuline sisters, who catered only for Catholics. When the Church of Ireland established non-sectarian schools under the aegis of the Kildare Place society, Catholic children were forbidden to attend. The Catholic Church obviously considered illiteracy preferable to non-Catholic instruction. It was thus difficult for the authorities to provide national education for such a mixed population, while financial assistance had perforce to be given to private as well as public schools. There were over 3,500 national schools by 1850, yet the illiteracy rate was then 47 per cent of the total population (see R. Dudley Edwards, *An Atlas of Irish History*, Methuen, 1973, p. 228).

To promote the teaching of Irish in the schools, a number of books in print would have been a *sine qua non*; but the Gaelic literary tradition was largely an oral one. When the Church had abandoned Latin (or Norman French) in services, English was the natural choice to replace it, because that was the language of the professional classes, who desired a reasonable standard of education for their children. The foundation of the Gaelic League in 1893 arose from the demand for Home Rule; but the cold fact was that a knowledge of English was a necessity to secure desirable employment.

One can observe the educational problem clearly by reading the opening chapters of Maurice O'Sullivan's autobiography, *Twenty Years A-Growing*, published in 1933. The first passage illustrates the child's dilemma concerning the home language, while being schooled in English:

> With that the man spoke out in Irish for he had no knowledge of English, or, if he had, he did not let on.
>
> 'What sort of talk has that man?' said I to the woman who had me in her arms.
>
> 'That's Irish.'
>
> 'What's Irish?'
>
> 'Oh, wait now,' says she, 'till you go home, that is the time you will have the Irish.'
>
> 'Where is my home? We have no Irish at all in this home here.'
>
> 'This is not your home, Maurice, but the Blasket.'
>
> (op. cit., p. 7)

The passage below reflects the reaction of an English-medium teacher to a parent who has decided to take the child from such a school:

> She said no more but went out, I following her, till we reached the place where my father was. She gave him a thousand welcomes and spoke gently at first; but looking at her I could see that she had no good intentions. It was not long before she spoke her mind:
>
> 'Arra, musha, you ought to know what you are doing,' said she, 'taking the child home when he is just learning his scholarship, and if you left him here he would have a livelihood for ever.'
>
> 'Och, my pity for your head,' replied my father, 'I don't know what livelihood he would get but only to let him follow his nose in the end of all.'
>
> 'Well, Shaun,' said she, 'I always thought you had some sense until to-day, and you do such a thing to the poor boy. In the first place he will lose his English, and so he

will be a fool when he grows up a stripling, if he lives so
long. Where will he go, and how will he get work without
the English?'
'Isn't it better still for him to have the two languages?'
said my father. 'And another thing, you don't know what
way will Ireland turn out yet. Maybe the foreign tongue
will go under foot,' said he, with a laugh.
'Och,' said she, 'the way with you is, live horse and you
will get grass.'

(ibid. pp. 18-19)

Altercation on the educational front shifted in the
eighteen-nineties to the new university campuses of Dublin,
Belfast, Cork and Galway. But much progress was nevertheless made through academic research into the past of the
Gaelic languages. After Edward Lhuyd had broken new
philological ground, more than a century elapsed before
Bopp discovered that the Celtic languages belonged to the
Indo-European family. Irish language studies during the
nineteenth century began to make great strides, as texts in
manuscript form became available for investigation. John
O'Donovan published his *Grammar of the Irish Language*
in 1847 and his edition of the *Annals of the Four Masters*
in 1848-51; as a consequence, he was invited to become the
first Professor of the Irish Language at Queen's College,
Belfast. Another scholar of note was Eugene O'Curry, who,
though self-educated, lectured at the Catholic University in
Dublin on the *Manuscript Materials of Ancient Irish History*,
published in 1861. In the Public Records Office, William
Maunsell Henderson's great erudition produced the *Chronicon
Scotorum* (1858) and a translation of the *Tripartite Life of
St Patrick* (1871).

The study of Celtic languages was finally put on a modern
scientific basis by J. Caspard Zeus in *Grammatica Celtica*
(1853); and he was ably succeeded by several other Germanic
scholars, such as Ebel, Windish, Zimmer and Thorneysen.
The influential journal *Revue Celtique*, was founded in Paris
in 1870. In Ireland the greatest contributions to the study
of the Celtic past were made by Whitley Stokes and Standish
James O'Grady. The latter's *History of Ireland*, published in

1878, was a landmark in bringing to life the heroic period of Irish folklore. The purpose of his admirable rescension was explained in the compiler's Introduction:

> The bardic literature of ancient Erin would fill, perhaps, a hundred volumes such as the present. When completed, the piled up mass would be without harmony, meaning, or order. The valuable and the valueless would be mingled together. . . . Moreover, the genesis of these tales must be ascribed to peoples separated from one another by wide tracts of country and distances of time, so that contradiction and confusion are inevitable. The result would be a huge literary chaos, not a work of art, and this would be true even if the tales were reduced each to its pure epic elements. . . .
>
> The bardic mind affected a certain fastidiousness in its mode of treating the heroic period. A conventional set of ideas were deemed poetic, and all outside that was unpoetic. We can see how some such traditions clung around the mind of Homer. . . . This has been my object to represent, as in a picture, the state of society which obtained in this country in ancient times, which, though distant in one sense, are near in many others. . . .
>
> One of the most interesting features of early Irish civilisation, the religious feature, is also unfortunately the most obscure. In the absence of clear philosophical statements by the monks, we are obliged to fall back upon the tales and poems. . . . Now, if we had a sufficient quantity of pre-Christian Irish literature, there would be no loss sustained by the unfortunate reticence of the ecclesiastics; but this is not so. The bards were but the abstracts and brief chronicles of their own time, and in their hands the ancient tales and traditions varied from century to century, acquiring more and more a new complexion as the ages ran on. . . .
>
> The advent of Christianity ruined the bards. The missionaries felt instinctively that the bards were their enemies. . . . The degradation of the bardic class was therefore essential to the success of the missionaries. Both could not live in the same country. . . . St. Patrick, and his compeers and fellow-missionaries, seem to have been rude, uneducated

men. Their Latin is rude, clumsy, and ungrammatical. His own compositions are so bad, that they have been considered forgeries. . . .

On the other hand, in the time of Adamnan, three centuries later, the monks had perfected a splendid Latin style, enriched with contributions from the Greek and Hebrew, and giving the reader the impression that they were the intellectual lords of the land. In the bardic literature of this period, we look in vain for anything which might be considered in profane literature the equivalent of 'The Life of St Columba.'

In fact, the positions of the contending parties had been reversed. The bards now amused only farmers and tradesmen, while the monks crowned kings, and trained the minds of princes. The consequence was, that secular literature did not flourish, or flourished only in the monasteries, where it was not the chief thing, but an ornament of the monastic mind.

(op. cit., vol. 1, pp. ix-xvii)

One outcome of the spade-work of philologists, historians and folklorists was a timely revival of interest in Ireland's medieval and Tudor manuscripts; for those in private hands were fast disappearing. Some Irish poets of the nineteenth century composed in the vernacular; others who had the knowledge preferred to translate. Some account of their writings will complete the present chapter. Preference is given to poets who were personal translators, such as Callanan, Ferguson and O'Connor; secondary composers like Mangan, who relied on the English renderings of O'Daly, O'Curry, and other translators, are discussed in the next chapter.

The first translator of note was a minor poet, J. J. Callanan, born in 1795, who was much influenced by the English romantics, especially Byron. His principal work consisted of free translations of traditional ballads, or the re-vamping of Jacobite songs in the facile measures of Thomas Moore. Callanan's restless spirit found expression in nostalgic sentiment, lacking the depth of feeling one associates with the imagination. Although Charles Gavan Duffy included six of Callanan's poems in *Ballad Poetry of Ireland*, a book that was reprinted forty times between 1845 and 1869, all, except the original composition 'Gougaune Barra', are the poetry of escape, in which romantic topography has an exaggerated importance. The title celebrates a beauty-spot on the once-wooded lake of county Cork:

There is a green island in lone Gougaune Barra,
Where Allua of songs rushes forth as an arrow;
In deep-valley'd Desmond — a thousand wild fountains
Come down to that lake, from their home in the mountains.
There grows the wild ash, and a time-stricken willow
Looks chidingly down on the mirth of the billow;
As, like some gay child, that sad monitor scorning.
It lightly laughs back to the laugh of the morning.

(Ballad Poetry of Ireland, p. 183)

When Duffy founded *The Nation* in 1842, he and his collaborator, Thomas Davis, enlisted the help of young poets in order to remind the dispirited nation of the greatness of its past. From the literary aspect, this was a misguided aim of the Young Irelanders, since the primary motive was political, therefore journalistic. Sean O'Faolain put the case concisely in his study of *The Irish*:

Their weakness and bad example was to subserve literat
ure to opinions, to political dogmatising, to nationalist
'right' and 'wrong' which, by directing the eye away from
the literary object to the political goal, introduced a new
falsity and undid a certain amount of their appeal to
realism.

(p. 135)

Few Irish poets of the nineteenth century, in a natural desire to interpret the Celtic spirit, escaped this criticism. There was, however, a translator of the ancient poets, whose talent and individual strength made a signal contribution; this was Samuel Ferguson (1810-86), whose long life spanned many vicissitudes in the Irish scene; experience taught him wisdom and forbearance. Ferguson was born in Belfast of a middle-class Scots family; he read law at Trinity College Dublin, and was called to the bar in 1838. His real interests were, however, antiquarian; he therefore chose to accept a

Deputy-Keepership in the Dublin Record Office and was knighted for his services in 1878. Four years later Ferguson was elected President of the Royal Irish Academy. His patriotism was such that he declined to publish his many books anywhere but in Ireland, which limited their distribution. He also showed a deliberate preference for Irish themes.

Ferguson was a gifted Irish scholar, with a fondness for using Gaelic refrains in lyrical verse. His translations from the vernacular are among the most elegant of his achievements, because they are sincere renderings, though not literal. An example of this quality has already been cited in the paraphrase 'Deirdre's Lament', on p. 50. Ferguson's poems first saw the light in *Blackwood's* and the *Dublin University* magazines; but a number were collected in *Lays of the Western Gael* (1867), based largely on the Red Branch cycle of Ulster legends. The gusto of his ballad writing is admirably revealed in 'The Burial of King Cormac':

> They loosed their curse against the king;
>   They cursed him in his flesh and bones;
> And daily in their mystic ring
>   They turn'd the maledictive stones.
>
> Till, where at meat the monarch sate,
>   Amid the revel and the wine,
> He choked upon the food he ate,
>   At Sletty, southward of the Boyne.
>
> High vaunted then the priestly throng,
>   And far and wide they noised abroad
> With trump and loud liturgic song
>   The praise of their avenging God.
>
> But ere the voice was wholly spent
>   That priest and prince should still obey,
> To awed attendants o'er him bent
>   Great Cormac gather'd breath to say, —
>
> 'Spread not the beds of Brugh for me
>   When restless death-bed's use is done:
> But bury me at Rossnaree
>   And face me to the rising sun. . . .

Then northward forth they bore the bier,
    And down from Sletty side they drew,
With horsemen and with charioteer,
    To cross the fords of Boyne to Brugh.

There came a breath of finer air
    That touch'd the Boyne with ruffling wings,
It stirr'd him in his sedgy lair
    And in his mossy moorland springs.

And as the burial train came down
    With dirge and savage dolorous shows,
Across their pathway, broad and brown
    The deep, full-hearted river rose;

From bank to bank through all his fords,
    'Neath blackening squalls he swell'd and boil'd;
And thrice the wondering gentile lords
    Essay'd to cross, and thrice recoil'd.
(Taylor, *Irish Poets of the Nineteenth Century*, pp. 113-15)

The greatest merit of Ferguson's translations of ancient Irish legends is their narrative skill and momentum. Yeats, admiring the simplicity and sincerity, called Ferguson 'the one Homeric poet of our time' (*Davis, Mangan, Ferguson*, p. 31). Narrative vigour is to be observed, even when the poet resorts to the difficult medium of blank verse, as in 'Conary':

    One I saw
Seated apart; before his couch there hung
A silver broidered curtain: grey he was,
Of aspect mild, benevolent. compact,
A cloak he wore of colour like the haze
Of a May morning when the sun shines warm
On dewy meads and fresh ploughed tillage land
Variously beautiful, with border broad
Of golden woof that glittered to his knee
A stream of light.
                (Taylor, op. cit. pp. 38-9)

Though there are some lapses of craftsmanship in Ferguson's epic *Congal* (1872), most critics consider that there is more to praise than to blame; only a technically competent poet could have attempted so exhausting a theme after Wordsworth and Tennyson in the nineteenth century. Ferguson was indeed the only poet of his time to capture the bardic spirit, and it was no surprise when a second series of *Lays of the Western Gael* appeared in 1880. All his poems were eventually collected and edited by A. P. Graves in 1918. It was discovered that Ferguson had actually suppressed some of the Young Ireland poems, believing that his sincere patriotism might be mistaken for a dubious nationalism. Ties with the Young Ireland movement were probably loosened by the death of Thomas Davis in 1845, an event which the poet commemorated in his famous 'Lament':

> Young salmon of the flood-time of freedom
>   That swells round Erin's shore,
> Thou wilt leap against their loud, oppressive torrents
>   Of bigotry and hate no more!
> Drawn downward by their prone material instinct,
>   Let them thunder on their rocks, and foam;
> Thou hast leaped, aspiring soul, to founts beyond
>   their ranging,
>   Where troubled waters never come.
>   • • •
> O brave young men, my love, my pride, my promise,
>   'Tis on you my hopes are set,
> In manliness, in kindliness, in justice,
>   To make Erin a nation yet;
> Self-respecting, self-relying, self-advancing,
>   In union or in severance, free and strong,
> And if God grant this, then, under God, to Thomas Davis
>   Let the greater praise belong!
> ('Lament for the Death of Thomas Davis', Taylor, op. cit.,
>   pp. 141-3)

Yeats's courageous praise of Ferguson has not earned consensus of approval, partly because it was an ultra-gracious expression of his personal indebtedness to that writer. Among other critics, Thomas Kinsella thought that the estimate of *Congal* and related epic pieces was overrated, because it condoned Ferguson's randomness of approach and antiquated enthusiasm, which are always the enemies of finished work.

That mercurial figure of the present century, Michael O'Donovan (1903-66), who frequently wrote under the pseudonym of Frank O'Connor, was a translator of a different mould. Though a self-made writer, who had acquired book-learning by his own efforts, he was deferential towards academic scholarship, and was in constant demand at United States universities. As an impecunious youth, O'Connor was spurred on by his friend, Daniel Corkery, to learn Irish; and he zealously copied early poetic texts, a habit which taught him to memorise passages that he loved.

O'Connor's first employment was as County Librarian, successively at Cork, Sligo and Wicklow, where he was enabled to satisfy his avidity for reading. In 1927 he visited Paris and met James Joyce, the encounter finally deciding him to write in English. Before 1930 most of his literary contributions appeared in the *Irish Statesman*. His first collection appeared under the title *Guests of the Nation* in 1931. Between that date and 1963 the writer also published seven volumes of verse translation, covering every period of Irish poetry.

O'Connor was a master of sonorous Irish speech, and an impressive conversationalist, who despised oratory, especially in religion and politics; for like Yeats, he disapproved of all forms of fanaticism. The conscientious craftsmanship in whatever he undertook was revealed in constant revision to improve what he had already published. The poetry was in sharp reaction to the romantic element in Victorian English verse; outspokenly, he recommended the Irish poets of the eighteenth century. One of O'Connor's services to the literature of his country was his appraisal and translation of poems by Egan O'Rahilly (see p. 97), Eileen O'Leary and Brian Merriman. A splendid example of the translator's vigour and clarity is the rendering of O'Rahilly's poem 'The Reverie':

One morning before Titan thought of stirring his feet
   I climbed alone to a hill where the air was kind,
And saw a throng of magical girls go by
   That had lived to the north in Croghan time out of mind.

All over the land from Galway to Cork of the ships,
   It seemed that a bright enchanted mist came down.

Acorns on oaks and clear cold honey on stones,
    Fruit upon every tree from root to crown.

They lit three candles that shone in the mist like stars
    On a high hilltop in Connello and then were gone,
But I followed through Thomond the track of the hooded
                                                    queens
    And asked them the cause of the zeal of their office
                                                    at dawn.

The tall queen, Eevul, so bright of countenance, said
    'The reason we light three candles on every strand
Is to guide the king that will come to us over the sea
    And make us happy and reign in a fortunate land.'

And then, so suddenly did I start from my sleep,
    They seemed to be true, the words that had been
                                                    so sweet —
It was just that my soul was sick and spent with grief
    One morning before Titan thought of stirring his feet.
        (Greene, *Anthology of Irish Literature*, vol. I, pp. 235-6)

One of O'Connor's memorable translations was of 'The
Lament for Art O'Leary', a 'keening' poem, which preserved
the wailing ritual that accompanied Irish burials, a practice
which J. M. Synge was still able to observe on the Aran
Islands. Keening took the form of recitative, the principal
mourners in Eileen O'Leary's 'Lament' being the wife and
sister of the deceased, Arthur O'Leary. This man was an
outlawed officer of the Austrian army, a Catholic who was
murdered in 1773 for refusing to sell his horse to a Protestant
named Morris, at the regulation valuation of five pounds.
His wife, Eileen, who incidentally was the aunt of Daniel
O'Connell, pursued the responsible detachment of soldiery,
and had the guilty persons withdrawn from the neighbourhood. Rumour had it that Morris was afterwards killed in
Cork by O'Leary's sister:

            My comfort and my friend,
            Master of the bright sword,
            'Tis time you left your sleep;
            Yonder hangs your whip,
            Your horse is at the door,

Follow the lane to the east
Where every bush will bend
And every stream dry up,
And man and woman bow
If things have manners yet
That have them not I fear.
· · ·
Could my calls but wake my kindred
In Derrynane beyond the mountains,
Or Capling of the yellow apples,
Many a proud and stately rider,
Many a girl with spotless kerchief,
Would be here before tomorrow,
Shedding tears about your body,
Art O'Leary, once so merry.
· · ·
But cease your weeping now,
Women of the soft, wet eyes
Till Art O'Leary drink
Ere he go to the dark school —
Not to learn music or song
But to prop the earth and the stone.

(*Penguin Book of Irish Verse*, pp. 83-6)

Perhaps the most important eighteenth-century poet whom O'Connor helped to rescue from oblivion, through English translation, was Brian Merriman (1747-1805). This man was a mathematics teacher in Limerick just before his death; but little is known of his antecedents, except that he was of Protestant parentage, and came from County Clare. As a result of O'Connor's interest, *The Midnight Court* was published in London in 1945; the original text had been made available by the Irish Text Society in 1911. O'Connor's care in preserving the poet's tone in translation is amply demonstrated in a number of revisions.

Merriman was the first Gaelic poet to compose in heroic couplets; but the Augustan flavour of *The Midnight Court* belongs as much to the original version as to the translation. The style is reminiscent of the writing of Swift and Goldsmith. Skilful handling of the metrical form is evident in the following passage, which John Montague headed 'The Maiden's Plight':

I fasted three canonical hours
To try and come round the heavenly powers;
I washed my shift where the stream was deep
To hear a lover's voice in sleep;
Often I swept the woodstack bare,
Burned bits of my frock, my nails, my hair,
Up the chimney stuck the flail,
Slept with a spade without avail;
Hid my wool in the limekiln late
And my distaff behind the churchyard gate;
I had flax on the road to halt coach or carriage
And haycocks stuffed with heads of cabbage,
And night and day on the proper occasions
Invoked Old Nick and all his legions;
But 'twas all no good and I'm broken-hearted
For here I'm back at the place I started;
And this is the cause of all my tears
I am fast in the rope of the rushing years,
With age and need in lessening span,
And death beyond, and no hope of a man.

(*Faber Book of Irish Verse*, p. 166)

If one may rely on the suggested date of composition (1780), this poem of over twelve hundred lines belongs to no contemporary school of Gaelic craftsmanship. The Court was set up in the spirit of Connacht folklore, and the characteristically Irish approach to absurdity in no way conflicts with this; it appears, for instance, in Merriman's naturalistic attitude to the celibacy of priests. But the verse is as devoid of the florid or lyrical note, as it is remarkable for clarity and vigour in its expression.

The Midnight Court seems to have been designed as a comic satire with the intent of exposing the evil of 'arranged' marriages. Often the sexes were ill-matched for reasons of age or physical incapacity. Merriman confirms that in the eighteenth and even later centuries there was undoubted unwillingness among young men to marry, low wages being offered as a ground for enforced celibacy. The frankness of O'Connor's English translation met with immediate disfavour from the Board of Censors.

Educated prose writers since the age of Swift, such as Goldsmith and Sheridan, elected to write in English, even when of Irish descent; for the principal use of prose in Ireland was to advance thought by argument. Since the age of reason Irishmen had learnt to disentangle history from myth, religion from legend; but it was mainly through English that distressed writers were able to reach the minds of political oppressors. The truth about anti-feudalistic Ireland before the seventeenth century began to emerge in the prose demonstrations written in the nineteenth and twentieth centuries. For although Irish individualism had stoutly in the past protested against Norman feudalism, Gaelic literature was never anything but aristocratic. The common people did not begin to figure in Irish writing until the eighteenth century, though even then the tenant-farmer remained a peasant.

It is refreshing, therefore, to come across a book in modern Irish, about life at another social level, which might indeed belong to the Middle Ages. Maurice O'Sullivan's *Twenty Years A-Growing* is the autobiography of a Blasket islander, translated by M. L. Davies and G. Thomson. E. M. Forster's Introductory Note calls this 'an account of neo-lithic civilisation from the inside' (p. v), in contradistinction to the objective account of the Aran islanders presented by J. M. Synge. The translators say that the Irish dialect of English differs from standard English in its unconscious memories; that it is a new, direct and witty language, moulded in idiom to the old way of thinking, but wanting the stamp of the ancient poetic tradition, and therefore more restricted in range (pp. ix to x). Here is a passage in which a few vernacular terms were retained whenever they were appropriately untranslatable. Idiomatic turns of phrase or syntax have been italicised:

> In a little while we met my two aunts. They *tore me asunder* with kisses, for women are the very devil for *plámás*, [coaxing talk] so that I did not like to meet them at all. Why wouldn't they *take it fine and soft* like a man? Not at all, they must be fawning on you every time they come across you. . . .

It was a custom in the district, when a boy was wearing his first suit, for him to go from house to house through the village, and *it is he would be puffed up* with pride coming home in the evening with all the money he was *after getting* during the day. . . .

We sat *in to* the table and they began conversing in Irish. I sat listening to them shyly, like a dog listening to music, but I could not make any sense out of it. I slipped across to my aunt and gave her a nudge in the back: 'What sort of talk is that going on between my father and the other man?' said I.

'That's Irish, *astor*, [treasure] said she, putting her arms round me and kissing me.

I would *rather the frost than that to be done to me.* When I got myself free of her I slunk away to the door, where I watched the people passing up and down, thinking still of the silly ways of women *that you can't speak to them* without their *leaping at* you.

My father, uncle and Martin were now pretty merry with *the* drink. 'Wait here till I get a *car*,' [carriage] said my father. 'I won't be long.'

(pp. 20-22)

Maurice O'Sullivan was fortunate in his translators. George Thomson was a Greek scholar, who learnt his Irish on the Blasket, largely from the author himself, to whom he became friend and career adviser; Moya Davies was a lover of the Celtic languages and Irish folklore. This ideal partnership was instrumental in preserving the nuances and idiom of the Gaelic original. Though O'Sullivan modestly minimised the extent of his education, his verse quotations show that he was familiar with traditional bardic poetry, as well as poets like Brian Merriman, and that he was thoroughly bilingual. Above all, he appears in the autobiography as a sensitive, open-hearted lover of nature and of folk music; his response to environment is one of the principal charms of the book. The Anglo-Irish dialogue of the Blasket islanders is a sheer delight; few novels and plays, not even Synge's, reveal so amusingly the west-countryman's perennial struggle to match his mother tongue in English. Not only is the dialect witty and graceful, but there is a notable fondness for proverbial sayings, racy oaths and expletives.

Here are some random examples of native idiom:

p. 27: The house *put great wonder on* me

     28: It would *raise the dead from the grave* to watch them dancing

     30: The people began to scatter homeward *to the white gable* (i.e. to bed)

     32: they are all *on the way of truth* now (dead)
We would not come home until *the blackness and blindness* of the night
what used you to be doing *in the run of* the day

     33: The *devil a bit* there was to buy

     35: There was *a head of* sweat on the players

     52: Oh, isn't it a big house! How was it built *at all*

  113: if they were not praising her *it is not day yet* (I should be surprised)

  126: I wanted no more than *the wind of the word*, for I was *blind* with sleep

  131: Och, that's talk *in the air* (wild)

  143: may the big fellow *take the head from your scroggle* if it isn't fine the way you are *after putting the yellow terror* on me

  148: now and then the leap of a pollock would send up a leap of foam which sparkled in the sun *the way it would put stars on my eyes*

  162: Oh, musha, *my pity on you entirely*, isn't it you who *has the skull of a chicken* to tell me there are people like that

  246: As sure as I live and *there's a cross on the ass*, said I, it is over the cliff you will go. I shouted *in the height of my head*

  253: the two of us *turned our faces up* into the island

  257: I shall be expecting you every day from this *out*

  263: She did not answer, but looked wonderingly at me *between the eyes*. 'Have you Irish', said I (do you speak)

  269: Well, *said I in my own mind*, it is not the windy day is the day for scallops

p. 274: I will be perished ... if I go on fasting like this, for *the soul will fall out of me* on the road

276: I don't know in the world what brings strangers *into* the Blasket to learn Irish, for ... when they come back to this place after leaving the Island they *have it thrown under foot* ... Will the day ever come when Irish will *be poured out* here, as English is *poured out* to-day?

280: He *put a whisper* in my ear

288: it is to the devil I *give* you if I *haven't the slant on you*, you dregs of the city
I think, Sullivan, *it is* in a temper *you are*

307: I have *made my white coat* at last (achieved what I wanted)

312: a small, short, haggard, rough-voiced fellow with a pale face and two eyes *like candles*

318: Did you never hear that a peeler is not to be trusted until he's seven years *under the clay*?

323: Musha, how are you *since*, daddo? (since last I say you)

Oaths, curses and expletives

38: Musha, *the killing of the cattle on* you if you haven't a noisy wind-pipe

151: *Your soul to the devil*, who will buy the fish?

162: *Great God of Virtues*

Proverbial wisdom

94: Did you never hear how the life of man is divided? Twenty years a-growing, twenty years in blossom, twenty years a-stooping and twenty years declining.

242: words do not fatten the friars

255: Bitter the tears that fall but more bitter the tears that fall not

256 however long the road there comes a turning

270: Bare is the companionless shoulder

281: the fat does not notice the lean

Syntax

p. 38: There was a fine burst of sunshine, my feet up on the ditch, *and I considering* where I should turn my face (absolute participial phrase)

48: *it is often* I was out and *it is only midnight* would bring me home (impersonal periphrasis with the verb 'be')

283: I . . . told him what was *after* happening to me since I left Mallow (adverb used as substitute for the pluperfect tense)

The conditional phrase *if so*, after adversative *but*, is used with several different connotations:

252: up he went with the stick, but, *if so*, the cow-seal leapt straight at him with open mouth (= when he did so)

272: I had four hours to spend in the city, but *if so* . . . I had no intention of leaving the station (= nevertheless)

272: When I had finished my task I handed in the paper, but, *if so*, even yet she did not speak a word (= when I did)

274: I walked ahead, but, *if so*, the farther I went the more the cross-roads were confusing me (= because I did so)

277: I thanked him and ran off, but, *if so*, my boy and girl were nowhere to be seen (= it so happened that)

279: I looked round at the people but, *if so*, I was not at all pleased with the way some of them were smiling (= when I did)

J. M. Synge, who studied Gaelic at Trinity College, when he visited the Aran Islands in 1898, found it necessary to procure a tutor to help him with the regional dialect; for this isolated community of speakers had for long been separated from linguistic developments on the mainland of Ireland. Some critics seem to have been under the impression that the dialogue of his plays was an artefact bearing slight resemblance to the speech of the peasants he created. Though *Twenty*

150 *Language and Society in Anglo-Irish Literature*

Years A-Growing was written a generation later than Synge's works, it echoes many of the dramatist's phrases and constructions. There appears, however, to be a greater variety of idiom at the command of the autobiographer from the Blasket islands, who actually maintained that the purest Irish was to be found in that hard-working but self-sufficient group of individualists.

O'Sullivan's patriotism, grounded in a love of the mother tongue, is of a kind that wins universal respect. The reception of *Twenty Years A-Growing* among the remnant of Blasket islanders was more important to its author than the impact of the translation upon Anglo-Irish readers. Yet the English version of his autobiography succeeded in giving it a permanence it would not otherwise have enjoyed. Among other idiosyncracies, it confirmed that the devil was still the pejorative ghost of Irish folklore; that the 'peeler' persisted as a derogatory symbol for the police force, vainly euphemised by calling it the 'Civic Guard'; that the priest remained as ubiquitous as ever in Irish society, and as powerless to subdue the ancient superstitions; that the Big House was yet held in awe as an emblem of the snobbish Ascendancy; that humour could still emerge naturally from the gaffs of peasants, whose astuteness fell short of coping with such bewildering experiences as a journey by train. For Maurice's migration from Dingle to Dublin is one of the most amusing chapters of the book.

A book of similar interest for the study of colloquial Anglo-Irish is the *Autobiography of Peig Sayers*, an Irish-speaking woman of peasant stock, who went to live on the Great Blasket after her marriage into the O'Sullivan family. Her story, as dictated to her poet-son in 1935, covers roughly the same period as *Twenty Years A-Growing* (1933). Bryan MacMahon later translated it into English, in a style befitting the narrator's origins. Born at Vicarstown, not far from Dunquin on the Dingle Peninsula, Peig received a brief but inadequate education for one who habitually spoke the West Kerry dialect.

As literature, the autobiography is insignificant; but there is wry humour in an account that shows how a person like Peig adapted herself to the usage of English. The extensive range of coloquialisms among the domesticated Irish is certainly enlightening. The syntax differs but slightly from that of the cultured Ascendancy, for English landlords were not immune to local influence. It is clear that Anglo-Irish, after the Famine, had become a brand of speech notable for the number of restorations from native Irish idiom.

Owing to its comparative isolation, the Gaeltacht area of West Kerry produced many lively but unconventional speakers. Theirs was still an oral tradition from the turn of the nineteenth century to the First World War, a period when economic conditions were so bad that people of both sexes dreamt daily of emigration to America. In fact, the Irish language declined there through lack of opportunity for the younger generation, who felt that continued use of the native tongue hampered prospects of employment. There were no longer agricultural or other inducements to live on the rock-bound Blasket Islands or the adjacent Dingle Peninsula.

Here are characteristic examples of native idiom to be found in *Peig*:

p. 14: her health and courage ebbed away until in the *heel of the hunt* the poor woman hadn't even the desire to live

He wouldn't travel as much as a *cock's step* from our house.

17: [she] wasn't able to do a *hand's turn*

you'll be the right *little ball* of a girl when you're wearing these

The dear woman thinks that it's *out of your poll* the sun rises

20: And what name have they *on you*? (given you)

25: If he *lobbed* that hill over there down on top of this hill here in order to please her she wouldn't be thankful

27: Master Daly was a good man, a clever teacher and a *great warrant* to solve every problem

28: I got a *clatter* of the palm of the hand from him that made me see visions

29: he could have been a big *bucko* of an Englishman over from the city of London! He hadn't one tittle of Irish *in his beak*

p. 33: Bad *cess* (luck) to ye . . . if ye haven't *the* foolish
chatter
Old Kitty was in her cabin before me, squatting
on her *hunkers* (haunches)

34: [I] rammed one of the halves right under my
oxter (armpit)

35: I stretched out my hand *class* (sort) of lazily
'twas against my will I *faced* (made) for the door

38: because of his rotten teeth he was making *no
hand* of the yellow-meal bread (no headway
with)

40: near the bridge *back* the road (at the back of)

42: Each of them was *wildout* about the drop of
drink (excited)

46: the foreign bucks were thoroughly disgusted at
their failure to land the priests *in a hobble*

47: They took out their pipes then, and my word *to
you* but they *knocked steam* out of them

49: 'twill be time *and plenty* to face southwards
about twelve o'clock
the biggest *ninnyhammer* in the country when he
has a drop taken

50: Isn't it many a day we'll spend in the graveyard, a
place where our *gums won't ask for food*

51: The bad times had a firm *hoult* (hold) of the poor
people

52: God have mercy on me *whatever*

55: when the *hot drop got under their teeth* it played
Molly Bawn to them entirely

57: a proper *moody-nahdy* he is

58: as light in his head as a *puck goat* (he goat)
Bad *scran* (food-refuse) to you, *how well* you
never lost the old habit

67: I had hung the *delph* on the dresser (crockery in
general, not necessarily from Delft)

69: we were all fairly attached to one another and
then I was *on the pig's back*

70: he *put the heart cross-ways* in me with his two
wild eyes (terrified)

74: The *Brass Buttons* are outside (peelers, police)

p. 75: your throat would land you in trouble, *my hayro* (cultic spelling of 'hero')

79: I would dress myself in an *óinseach*'s rags (female fool)

86: he was *speechifying* away with big *rocks* of words

91: I'll be *shortening my road* (returning home)

97: a powerful closely-set *mallet* of a dame

98: before long she was *fogging smoke* out of a big white clay pipe

she was on her *grug* there (cf p. 33, *hunkers*)

you could nearly have *shaved yourself* in the gloss he had *in* his boots

103: I was a *bouncer* of a young woman

104: a pair of policemen in battle-dress coming down the street and moving at a *right gait-of-go* (rapid pace)

108: a green tuft of grass growing on the other side of the *grype* (trench)

But, *man dear,* she looked like a small shaved drowned rat

if she had *gandy* (spirit) in her while ago she has very little of it left now

in God's name let none of ye tell him *but* a little (even)

122: he didn't know *from Adam* how to come *around* the money

124: light a *sop* of straw (piece)

125: he'd meet a live person who'd *cross-hackle* him (interrogate)

135: I almost *dropped life* and I was trembling from head to foot

138: they had a big *belter* of a servant boy with them ... a well-set, strong *scourger* of a lad ... the devil and all of a *whinger*

141: the fairies had *clodded* her

142: my little pup had a full *bandle* of his tongue hanging out (a two-foot measure, used in making flannel)

151: when we left the chapel there was right *tip-of-the-reel* and hullabaloo

p. 153 That you may life long in *the whole of* your health

159: Never mind, Peig! Marriage was *laid out* for you (made)

176: at that time poor people weren't *too hot in their skins* (well-off for food)

185: this was, as they say, '*laughter from the teeth out*' (grim laughter)

198: She got a *sugan* rope and tied it around the daughter's waist (made of straw)

202: without a trace of *dudeen* (short-stemmed pipe)

203: it fell on the threshold stone and was broken into *flitters* (splinters)

207: Take off the bandage *till* I see it (so that)
       He told me to *stoop* my leg with lukewarm water (bathe)

Oaths, curses and expletives

70: you thunderin' *straip* (forward girl)

108: God leave ye *yeer* strength!

165: *Sha*, be easy in your mind now!

202: I'd swear by all the *brindled bibles of the Pope*

Proverbial wisdom

26: Advising a rough-spoken woman is as senseless as striking cold iron with a rib of hair

33: Cat and skin go together, child!

37: when the cat is out the mice dance!

41: the help of God was nearer than the door!

58: Nobody is ever in a right hobble except the one who hasn't the use of her legs

91: Pounds vanish but pouts remain (said of an unfortunate marriage)

94: There's hope from a prison, but none from the grave

126: Even a noble horse can't run well for ever

140: The weakling as he can and the strong man as he covets

143: Far-off hills are green but not always are they grassy

p. 149:   There's no cure for misfortune but to kill it with patience!

   186:   The city has a broad entrance but a narrow exit

Syntax

   45:   what happened ∧ him?
          When he and the other three priests . . . had the dinner *eaten* (the normal word order in the perfect and pluperfect tenses)

   146:   trouble used ∧ knock her out completely

   204:   I don't think that there's another old woman alive who has more a mind for tobacco *that* I have

VI

Nationalism and the Language of Poetry

The Irish literary revival of the nineteenth century culminated in the early twentieth in the work of Synge, Yeats, Joyce and O'Casey, writers who became international figures, without losing their identity as Irishmen. A dilemma undoubtedly faced Irish authors who elected to write in English. There were several reasons for their language preference, one being that more people of Irish descent live abroad than in Ireland. Untold thousands emigrated to America and to the British colonies that became independent, or joined the English-speaking Commonwealth. The literary revival reached its peak in the period 1890-1920, but had spent much of its force by the nineteen-thirties, when Ireland had achieved independence.

Better to understand this movement, clear ideas are needed about the senses in which 'Anglo-Irish' is used for persons and for literature. The spiritual vigour behind the revival owed as much to popular thinking about the importance of nationalism, as to the origin and individuality of authors. Eminent literary personalities, such as Wilde and Shaw, for reasons of their own, isolated themselves from the movement, and did so initially by residing in London. Some considerations that motivated their self-exile will appear in the course of the present chapter; but the fundamental circumstance was their place of schooling and their home background.

Daniel Corkery, a school master of Cork, had two patriotic pupils, Sean O'Faolain and Frank O'Connor, who chose the medium of English to distinguish themselves as writers. In *Synge and Anglo-Irish Literatrure* (1931) Corkery investigated this problem from the national point of view; for he held this to be the only ground on which any literature can become distinctive. Since the eighteenth century, expatriation has, he says, become the badge of the Anglo-Irish author. Any writer who spends the whole of any year abroad is an expatriate, and he invariably writes for an alien market. Although he may draw his material from Irish life and associate himself with Irish culture, he effectively cuts himself off from political Ireland. In such a case, the acceptable moulds of Anglo-Irish literature cannot be distinguished from those of contemporary English, unless certain 'colonial' characteristics have been evolved, for instance, the portrayal of social peculiarities which merely entertain the Ascendancy's kinsfolk in England. Nearly all Anglo-Irish writers are therefore regarded by Corkery as 'spiritual exiles', and in this class he includes all who wrote for the Abbey Theatre before 1922.

Corkery ascribed the flux and uncertainty of the Irish mentality to the alien system of English education; the school-going child's sympathies for things Irish were continually affronted rather than refined: 'his education sets up a dispute between his intellect and his emotions' (p. 15). Since Ireland gained independence, this system of nurture has changed; but Anglo-Irish writers persist in writing for English and American audiences. The trouble seems to be that the break in Irish cultural traditions, expressed in literature, lasted too long to be overcome in a generation. Homeliness is not, Corkery maintains, a feature of the Irish novel, but satirical portraiture is. No great Irish novel will be written which does not take into account the religious consciousness of the people, their idea of nationalism, and their hunger for land.

In the event, Corkery demands more 'Irishness', cultural and political, in Anglo-Irish literature. He wrote in English himself, and was not opposed to a medium that ensures wider circulation of germinal ideas. An important distinction has, however, to be made between literature and sociology, for cultural clashes involve emotive nationalism as well as religious dissociation. The principal clash has been between indigenous Irishmen and settlers who once ruled the country. When Michael Davitt founded the Land League in 1879 (see p. 125) he took a decisive step towards involving the numerically strong peasant class in the politics of the country. This peasantry was then invested with dignity and a vague Gaelic virtue in the works of Synge and Yeats, which amounted to primitivism. This idealisation had nothing to do with the peasant's economic status; Irish patriots like de Valera even deprecated social advancements that smacked of English materialism.

From the eighteen-eighties the new land-owning Irish peasant class was determined to improve its public image, and resisted any idea of a noble savage inheriting traditional values from archaic literature. Hence the public demonstrations against Anglo-Irish plays such as *The Playboy of the Western World*; for this was mistaken as a typical instance of Anglo-Saxon bourgeois contempt for the Irish way of life. Those who wrote for the Abbey Theatre were of the Anglo-Irish class, with the wrong political background. That a writer was of Irish birth added nothing to his caste acceptability; he had to be a Catholic and a republican, who nourished his rancour by recalling the Penal Laws. This is the reason that articulate Anglo-Irish authors, who wrote between 1890 and 1920, became an isolated group, even if they identified themselves with the Corkery desideratum of 'Irishness'. It also explains why authors such as George Moore, James Joyce, Sean O'Casey and Liam O'Flaherty did much of their writing abroad.

O'Flaherty was born on Inishmore, the largest of the Aran Islands, and not only spoke Irish fluently, but understood the volatile character of the Irish people, for whom his stories were principally written. According to his latest critical biographer, A. A. Kelly, he has two speaking voices, and 'an Irish and English writing style':

> His Irish style appears only in some Aran and animal stories. This style uses short simple sentences and very few subordinate clauses. It avoids the relative pronoun which in Irish does not exist, using repetition instead. . . . No detailed study has been made of the effects of O'Flaherty's bi-lingualism and some useful research remains to be done in this field. (*Liam O'Flaherty the Storyteller*, pp. 128-9)

Language is more than a means of communication; it enshrines a cultural ethos; but O'Flaherty believed in the brotherhood of man. Though he wrote in both languages, he tried to avoid national sentiment when using English. Writing on 'Double Vision¹ in Anglo-Irish Literature', Andrew Carpenter makes a significant contribution to this difficult problem:

> I find a constant and pervasive sense of authorial doubt and questioning in Anglo-Irish literature — a questioning which may broadly be called *ironic*. . . . No one writing in Ireland . . . is both wholly Gaelic Irish and wholly inside the English language. The compromise each writer makes as he writes of Ireland in English, is almost a racial one. . . .
>
> To some extent, this awareness of two living cultures — the writer not feeling he belongs properly to either — accounts at the most obvious level for the Anglo-Irish writer's insecurity and his need to take up a position of ironic detachment from his creation: but this is only part of the reason. . . .
>
> Only after a process of linguistic and social self-definition can anyone born or bred in Ireland develop the confidence to react to the dualities of Irish life. . . . The Irish language may be seen as a pointless anachronism or as the key to national identity. . . .
>
> The world in which one sees two things at once becomes merely confusing, in life as in literature, without rigorous technical control. . . . What is important is that all these sets of visions are co-existent; after all, the tension between appearance and reality is at the heart of many works of literature in many cultures; but the simultaneous awareness of two appearances and two realities is, I am inclined to think, an important element in the tone of Anglo-Irish writing and the personality of the Anglo-Irish writer.
>
> (*Place, Personality and the Irish Writer*, pp. 174-84)

Thomas MacDonagh believed, with justification, that Anglo-Irish writers of the nineteenth century created a literary dialect in English, with a characteristic emphasis not

designed to provide local colour. The significant contribution
writers made to English was 'colloquial directness' (*Literature
in Ireland*, p. 34); but others of a general nature were shrewdness and whimsicality. In *John Bull's Other Island* (1904),
the Preface as well as the play, Bernard Shaw sought to
demolish the traditional view of the Irishman as a dreamer
and romantic idealist; gullibility in business dealings and
vulnerability to exploitation are, however, compatible with
otherworldliness. An English dramatist has not the Irishman's
verbal sharpness or the Frenchman's *riposte*, unless he
happens to be a Cockney.

The poetic renascence in Ireland was part of the Celtic
revival in Britain, which in turn was an off-shoot of western
European romanticism. Nationalism in Germany, and later in
Italy, preceded the romantic rebirth of literature, the
principal aim in newly-founded states being to arouse
patriotic sentiment. In the last decade of the eighteenth
century, Irish patriots who wrote English verse were a small
band, whose pathos was intended to echo the melancholy of
the Celtic past. The bloodthirsty sagas of early Irish, in fact,
rather suggest a measure of Celtic irresponsibility. It cannot
be urged that intellectual freedom in Ireland was inspired by
the internecine struggles of bardic literature, even after the
advent of Christianity.

Thomas Moore's friendship with Byron had some bearing
on his undoubted appeal to the national consciousness of
Ireland. To a people whose collective will was largely in a
state of disintegration, the only fanning of independence
feasible was in the realm of spirit; and most evidence of
rebellion in Moore's writing was temperamental fantasy. He
was born the son of a Dublin tradesman in 1779, and wrote
principally for an English-speaking public, to whose tastes
and manners he was compelled to conform. Except by the
standards of Georgian and Victorian taste, Moore was a
minor poet; yet his lyrical gift was greatly esteemed in his
own time. A man of considerable personal charm, his pleasing
voice and gentle manners made him a popular favourite in
upper-class London drawing-rooms, to which he was introduced by his patron, Lord Moira.

Though not so able a poet as Burns, Moore was his Irish

counterpart, and in *Irish Melodies* composed his own lyrics to music of the eighteenth century, harmoniously scored by Sir John Stevenson. These airs were first recorded in the seventeen-nineties by Edward Bunting; Moore received a hundred guineas for every poem printed by Power Brothers, the publishers. In the Introduction to the *Faber Book of Irish Verse* (p. 31), John Montague belittled Moore by saying, *inter alia*, that he made no acknowledgement to Bunting for his labours; but this is not true. For Moore did so in the Preface to the first collected edition of his poems in 1841, which Longmans reprinted in the 1865 edition of *Irish Melodies*. Here are the relevant passages:

To the zeal and industry of Mr Bunting his country is indebted for the preservation of her old national airs. During the prevalence of the Penal Code, the music of Ireland was made to share in the fate of its people. Both were alike shut out from the pale of civilized life; and seldom any where but in the huts of the proscribed race could the sweet voice of the songs of other days be heard. Even of that class, the itinerant harpers, among whom for a long period our ancient music had been kept alive, there remained but few to continue the precious tradition; and a great music-meeting held at Belfast in the year 1792, at which the two or three still remaining of the old race of wandering harpers assisted, exhibed the last public effort made by the lovers of Irish music to preserve to their country the only grace or ornament left to her, out of the wreck of all her liberties and hopes. . . .

But for the zeal and intelligent research of Mr Bunting, at that crisis, the greater part of our musical treasures would probably have been lost to the world. It was in the year 1796 that this gentleman published his first volume; and the national spirit and hope then wakened in Ireland, by the rapid spread of the democratic principle through-out Europe, could not but insure a most cordial reception for such a work. . . .

It was in the year 1797 that, through the medium of Mr Bunting's book, I was first made acquainted with the beauties of our native music. A young friend of our family,

Edward Hudson, the nephew of an eminent dentist of that name, who played with much taste and feeling on the flute, and unluckily for himself, was but too deeply warmed with the patriotic ardour then kindling around him, was the first who made known to me this rich mine of our country's melodies: — a mine, from the working of which my humble labours as a poet have since derived their sole lustre and value. About the same period I formed an acquaintance, which soon grew into intimacy, with young Robert Emmet. He was my senior, I think, by one class, in the university. . . . I found him in full reputation, not only for his learning and eloquence, but also for the blamelessness of his life, and the grave suavity of his manners. . . .

I have already adverted to the period when Mr Bunting's valuable volume first became known to me. There elapsed no very long time before I was myself the happy proprietor of a copy of the work, and, though never regularly instructed in music, could play over the airs with tolerable facility on the pianoforte. Robert Emmet used sometimes to sit by me, when I was thus engaged; and I remember one day his starting up as from a reverie, when I had just finished playing that spirited tune called the Red Fox, ['Let Erin remember the days of old'] and exclaiming, 'Oh that I were at the head of twenty thousand men, marching to that air!' . . .

Though fully alive, of course, to the feelings which such music could not but inspire, I had not yet undertaken the task of adapting words to any of the airs; and it was, I am ashamed to say, in dull and turgid prose, that I made my first appearance in print as a champion of the popular cause. Towards the latter end of the year 1797, the celebrated newspaper called 'The Press' was set up by Arthur O'Connor, Thomas Addis Emmet, and other chiefs of the United Irish conspiracy, with the view of preparing and ripening the public mind for the great crisis then fast approaching. . . .

To those unread in the painful history of this period, it is right to mention that almost all the leaders of the United Irish conspiracy were Protestants. Among those

companions of my own alluded to in these pages, I scarcely
remember a single Catholic. . . .

We are told of painters calling those last touches of the
pencil which they give to some favourite picture the
'ultima basia'; and with the same sort of affectionate
feeling do I now take leave of the Irish Melodies, — the
only work of my pen, as I very sincerely believe, whose
fame (thanks to the sweet music in which it is embalmed)
may boast a chance of prolonging its existence to a day
much beyond our own.

(op. cit., pp. vii-xxviii)

It is a pity that this Preface was not reproduced in A. D.
Godley's critically splendid Oxford edition of Moore's
Poetical Works in 1929, for it is full of biographical interest.
At Trinity College, where Catholics were not then *personae
gratae*, Moore became the friend and admirer of Emmet, and
he supplies an intimate account of the Provost's enquiry into
subversive activities, which led to his friend's untimely death.
Though the poet's political sympathies were with Whigs,
he was saved from Emmet's fate by the admonition of his
mother, who advised him to end his connection with the
Young Irishmen. The song 'Oh! Breathe Not his Name' is a
final tribute to Emmet. Moore's pamphlet novelette *The
Memoirs of Captain Rock* (1823) was, none the less, an
indictment of English misrule, which shows that the writer
possessed considerable moral courage.

Successive series of *Irish Melodies* were published, beginning in 1807 and ending in 1835. The poems number over
one hundred and thirty, and became popular in many
European countries; Moore himself mentions translations
into Latin, French, Italian, Russian and Polish. The *Irish
Melodies* were ranked by partial critics, such as Byron, with
Lalla Rookh as Moore's most enduring compositions. The
latter, an exotic oriental operetta, was written in 1817 at
the behest of Longmans, and Moore received £3,000 for the
copyright.

There is no need to quote from 'The Last Rose of Summer',
'The Minstrel Boy', 'She is Far from the Land', 'Oft in the
Stilly Night', 'The Harp that Once in Tara's Halls', 'The

Meeting of the Waters', 'Believe Me if all those Endearing Young Charms', 'The Time I've Lost in Wooing'. All are poems of sentiment, memorable for a neat turn of phrase and admirable singing quality, largely because of the tuneful music that accompanied them. Moore himself said that the popular, conventional verses were not intended as serious poetry. It is preferable therefore to recall stanzas that demonstrate Moore's philosophy in characteristic moods, the one convivial, the other cynical:

> Shall I ask the brave soldier who fights by my side
> In the cause of mankind, if our creeds agree?
> Shall I give up the friend I have valued and tried,
> If he kneel not before the same altar with me?
> From the heretic girl of my soul should I fly,
> To seek somewhere else a more orthodox kiss?
> No, perish the hearts, and the laws that try
> Truth, valour, or love, by a standard like this!
> ('Come Send Round the Wine', *Irish Melodies*, p. 23)

> But alas for his country! — her pride is gone by,
> And that spirit is broken, which never would bend;
> O'er the ruin her children in secret must sigh,
> For 'tis treason to love her, and death to defend.
> Unpriz'd are her sons, till they've learn'd to betray;
> Undistinguish'd they live, if they shame not their sires;
> And the torch, that would light them thro' dignity's way,
> Must be caught from the pile where their country expires.
> ('Oh! Blame not the Bard', op. cit., p. 29)

The Byronic influence in Moore's poetry is well illustrated in *Lalla Rookh*, modelled on the heroic couplets of 'The Corsair'. The first scene in Moore's romance introduces the minstrel Feramorz entertaining the heroine with the legend of 'The Veiled Prophet of Khorassan'. The setting is voluptuous, as becomes an eastern tale; but more impressive is the elaborate stage-rhetoric that colours the bard's Islamic prophecy:

> celestial warriors, then, when all
> Earth's shrines and thrones before our banner fall;

When the glad Slave shall at these feet lay down
His broken chain, the tyrant Lord his crown,
The Priest his book, the Conquerer his wreath,
And from the lips of Truth one mighty breath
Shall, like a whirlwind, scatter in its breeze
That whole dark pile of human mockeries; —
Then shall the reign of mind commence on earth,
And starting fresh as from a second birth,
Man, in the sunshine of the world's new spring,
Shall walk transparent, like some holy thing!
Then, too, your Prophet from his angel brow
Shall cast the Veil that hides its splendours now,
And gladden'd Earth shall, through her wide expanse,
Bask in the glories of this countenance!

                    (*Poetical Works of Thomas Moore*, p. 347)

Moore's versatility is to be seen at its best in the readable *Journal* and the verse satires; they tell us more about the Celtic spirit than his *History of Ireland*, compiled towards the end of his career for *Lardner's Cyclopaedia*. When he turned from verse to prose, Moore devoted many years to the *Lives* of Sheridan (1827), Byron (1830) and Lord Edward Fitzgerald (1831). Before Moore's death in 1852, Francis Sylvester Mahony of Cork (1804-66), created the Father Prout series of articles for *Fraser's Magazine* (between 1834 and 1836) and accused the song-writer of massive borrowing, in metaphor and phrase, from Greek, Latin and French sources. Mahony, besides being a poet and humourist, was a competent classical and French scholar, who had travelled extensively in Europe and Asia Minor. He translated *Irish Melodies* into Latin and Greek under the title of *Moore's Plagiarisms*, and produced evidence that 'Go where Glory waits thee' was a free version of an early sixteenth-century song by the Comtesse de Chateaubriand, favourite of Francis I. But like most allegations of this nature, the charge was overstated, if ever seriously maintained. In every aspect of authorship, Moore was the best critic of his own shortcomings.

The importance of *The Nation* in fostering Irish literary talent, while serving as an instrument of propaganda for the Young Ireland party, can hardly be overestimated; yet the supporters of the movement were chiefly Protestants. Ten poets writing in English established their reputations while they contributed to this long-lived weekly, which continued until 1891, and was then revived as *The Irish Weekly Independent* in 1897. One of these minor poets was Thomas D'Arcy McGee, who migrated to Canada, where he became one of the founders of that country's federal government. The *raison-d'être* of the journal was liberal nationalism, leading to independence for Ireland; two of Gavan Duffy's ablest associates were educated at Trinity College, namely Thomas Davis of Cork (1814-45) and John Dillon, a Dublin barrister (1816-66). In 1843 Davis anthologised one hundred and four poems contributed to the journal, under the title *The Spirit of the Nation*; this collection was reprinted fifty-five times in the next half-century.

Davis died of scarlatina three years before the abortive insurrection of 1848, which sent Gavan Duffy to a brilliant political career in Australia. Although Davis is represented in several Irish verse anthologies, he was not a great poet, not even an orator or a wit; but the selections in Duffy's *Ballad Poetry of Ireland* show that he was possessed of a vein of poetical feeling, and a gift for restraint, which at this time Ireland sorely needed. Davis's *Literary and Historical Essays*, written for *The Nation*, was also published by Duffy shortly after the patriot's death in 1845; and a glance at such articles as 'Our National Language' and 'Means and Aids to Self-education' indicates the wisdom of counsel, and the balance of his judgement. When Davis passed from the scene, the impact of *The Nation* upon the growth of Anglo-Irish literature was less fortunate; Sean O'Faolain explains the reason in the last chapter of *The Irish*:

A literature, one feels, must justify itself on its literary merits, not a factitious appeal. . . . The inspiration of the men who first set the modern literary revival on its way was nostalgic and sentimental. These men were the rebelly group known as the Young Irelanders. . . . They thus came after Catholic Emancipation, were contemporaneous with O'Connell, took part in the Tithe War, the fight for the Repeal of the Union of Britain and Ireland, the arguments over Education, the start of the land troubles. . . . To them O'Connell, who, as a pragmatic politician, had no time for Gaelic and said that he saw it die without regret, was too materialist, too vulgar, too cheap, not idealist enough to build up the soul of the people.

All that I have already said about the way in which the Rebel spends and wastes himself is true a hundredfold of these men. They did not devote their great talents to literature: they devoted them to literature in the interests of politics. Their interest was in functional literature, or as we now call it *littérature engagée*. Their literary work suffered accordingly; their political influence prospered.

Before a literary movement could develop in a strictly literary way Irish writers had to purify literature of this political impurity.

(pp. 130-32)

One poet who came to *The Nation* late in his career was James Clarence Mangan (1803-49); the second of his names is the pseudonym under which he first wrote for the *Comet* and the *Dublin Penny Journal*. The life of this Dickensian, pathetic eccentric was written in 1897 by D. J. O'Donoghue, who also published the *Poems* and *Prose Writings* (1903-4). Mangan wrote a brief autobiographical sketch of his bankrupt father and unhappy family life, which, however exaggerated, left ineradicable marks on his son's career, in drudgery, insobriety and addiction to opium. The only education he apparently had was from a benevolent priest, who taught him to read in the French, Spanish and Italian languages.

At the age of fifteen Mangan began to write poetry, to lighten his employment for long hours as a scrivener. The poems were only nominally translations, from German, Spanish, Turkish, Persian and Irish, for Mangan's approach was nothing if not original. It was not until 1830 that the poet earned a meagre living as a free-lance journalist. His talent was soon noticed by the antiquary, George Petrie, who in 1838 found him a post in the Irish Ordnance Survey. Later he was found part-time work as a librarian at Trinity College; but he seems to have had no secure position when he died of cholera in 1849. Mangan spent most of his life in the slum area of Dublin, and it is probable that his early death was due as much to poverty and physical exhaustion.

Edgar Allan Poe and Mangan died in the same year, and though there is no evidence that they were known to each other, there are similarities in their exotic romanticism and bravura style of verse. The energetic, emotional incandescence of Mangan owes something to Shelley; the meretricious, sometimes strident, language is largely his own, and may be observed in the patriotic (but exceptional) poem 'To My Native Land':

> And till all earthly power shall wane,
>   And Time's grey pillar, groaning, fall;
> Thus shall it be, and still in vain
>   Thou shalt essay to burst the thrall
> Which binds, in fetters forged by fate,
> The wreck and ruin of what once was great.
> (Greene, *Anthology of Irish Literature*, vol. II, p. 332)

It was only when he undertook to transmute Irish bardic poetry of the seventeenth century that Mangan found really congenial themes. The Wildean notion that 'nothing succeeds like excess' was a principle well grounded in Mangan, and it is, perhaps, the lack of restraint that denies him the title of major poet. Technical expertise, including deft repetition, came to him naturally, as in 'Dark Rosaleen'. This poem is said to have been inspired by *Róisín Dubh,* a lyric by an unknown Irish bard contemporary with Edmund Spenser. Mangan's version was several times revised to enhance its intensity and fluidity:

> Over dews, over sands,
>   Will I fly, for your weal:
> Your holy, delicate white hands
>   Shall girdle me with steel.
> At home in your emerald bowers,
>   From morning's dawn till e'en,
> You'll pray for me, my flower of flowers,
>   My Dark Rosaleen!
>   My fond Rosaleen!
> You'll think of me through daylight's hours,
> My virgin flower, my flower of flowers,
>   My Dark Rosaleen!

I could scale the blue air,
　I could plough the high hills,
Oh, I could kneel all night in prayer,
　To heal your many ills!
And one beamy smile from you
　Would float like light between
My toils and me, my own, my true,
　My Dark Rosaleen!
　　　. . .

O! the Erne shall run red
　With redundance of blood,
The earth shall rock beneath our tread,
　And flames wrap hill and wood,
And gun-peal, and slogan cry
　Wake many a glen serene,
Ere you shall fade, ere you shall die,
　My Dark Rosaleen!

　　　　('Dark Rosaleen', stanzas 5, 6, 7)

One important aspect of Mangan's originality was his choice of epithets; another, the ease of his transitions from one emotive effect to another; both contribute to the musical quality of the verse, which is Mangan's principal asset. These talents were very little acquired from the Irish poetic tradition. Mangan was well read in Goethe's *Faust* (Anster, the translator, was a personal friend), and the *German Anthology* (1845) was actually Mangan's first published book. It is likely that he learnt his art from Continental, as much as from English sources. In stanzaic verses containing short lines, it often happens that enjambement rhythmically separates a noun from its qualifier, e.g.

That, like his, it may defy all *other*
　Flames, while time shall roll! . . .

Truly have I been long years unheedful
　Of the thorns and tares, that choked the *weedful*
　　Garden of my mind! . . .

Well will I obey thy mystic *double*
Counsel, through all scenes of woe and trouble,
　As a magic spell! . . .

> This is truth's, is reason's deep revealing,
> Unto me from thee, as God's to a *kneeling*
>   *And entranced saint!*
>
> ('To Joseph Brenan', stanzas, 1, 3, 8 and 9)

Mangan's most memorable poems are those which reflect his hypochondriac melancholy, for instance, 'The One Mystery', whose last stanza was quoted by Yeats to show that the poet could embody 'the whole man', as well as his intellectual or aesthetic nature (see *Davis, Mangan, Ferguson*, ed. McHugh, pp. 22-4). One perceives a finely controlled strain of desolation in the unusual poem 'Siberia', especially in the last four stanzas. But the most moving and faultless of the autobiographical poems is 'The Nameless one', from which are taken here a few of the middle stanzas:

> Roll on, my song, and to after ages
>   Tell how, disdaining all earth can give,
> He [God] would have taught men, from wisdom's pages,
>   The way to live.
>
> And tell how trampled, derided, hated,
>   And worn by weakness, disease, and wrong,
> He fled for shelter to God, who mated
>   His soul with song —
>
> With song which alway, sublime or vapid,
>   Flowed like a rill in the morning beam,
> Perchance not deep, but intense and rapid —
>   A mountain stream.
>
> Tell how this Nameless, condemned for years long
>   To herd with demons from hell beneath,
> Saw things that made him, with groans and tears, long
>   For even death.
>
> Go on to tell how, with genius wasted,
>   Betrayed in friendship, befooled in love,
> With spirit shipwrecked, and young hopes blasted,
>   He still, still strove.
>
> (*Penguin Book of Irish Verse*, pp. 161-2)

Among the lesser poets who succeeded Mangan in public esteem were Aubrey de Vere (1814-1902) and William

Allingham (1824-89). Theirs was an imaginative, rather than a technical, poverty, though their work is represented in nearly every anthology. De Vere was a nature poet, who emulated Wordsworth, whom he met in 1841. He was a Protestant from County Limerick, and a major change entered his poetry when he embraced Catholicism in 1851. He began to write hymns, but few comparable to *'Dei Genitrix'*, in which he strikes a note of prophetic doom. His long poem *Inisfail, A Lyrical Chronicle of Ireland*, was published in 1862, and purported to be an imaginative reconstruction of legendary history in ballad form, as well as an expression of faith in the country's supernatural destiny; and this, notwithstanding the Great Famine, and general exodus of a depleted peasantry. In the Spring of 1849, de Vere had already written one of the most inspired poems on the Famine, the dirge-like 'Year of Sorrow', from which the following stanzas are taken:

> Once more the cuckoo's call I hear;
>   I know in many a glen profound
> The earliest violets of the year
>   Rise up like water from the ground.
>
> The thorn I know once more is white;
>   And far down many a forest dale
> The anemones in dubious light
>   Are trembling like a bridal veil.
>   • • •
> From ruined huts and holes come forth
>   Old men, and look on yonder sky!
> The Power Divine is on the earth:
>   Give thanks to God before ye die!
>
> And ye, O children worn and weak,
>   Who care no more with flowers to play,
> Lean on the grass your cold, thin cheek,
>   And those slight hands, and whispering, say,
>
> 'Stern mother of a race unblest,
>   In promise kindly, cold in deed! —
> Take back, O Earth, into thy breast,
>   The children whom thou wilt not feed.'

(Taylor, *Irish Poets of the Nineteenth Century*, pp. 89-90)

On Irish themes, de Vere's other verse publications were *The Legends of St Patrick* (1872) and *The Foray of Queen Maeve* (1882). Earlier in his career, he had taken a less optimistic view of the country's situation in the prose treatise, entitled *English Misrule and Irish Misdeeds* (1848). The history of Ireland in the nineteenth century owed much to works such as this, which include Gavan Duffy's *Young Ireland 1840-50*, and *The League of the North and South 1850-56*, written in Nice between 1880 and 1886, after the author had retired from public life in Victoria.

Allingham had married an Englishwoman, and came to live near Tennyson in Hampshire in 1863, from which date his readable *Diary* (1907) gains in significance. In the following year he published a romantic poem of 4,700 lines, entitled *Laurence Bloomfield*, written in heroic couplets, and composed with a view to needful social reforms. It describes the mass eviction of western Ireland's tenant farmers by unscrupulous land agents, such as William Carleton and his contemporaries had done in fiction.

The limited readership of Allingham's verse, after the initial impact of the literary revival, was partly due to the English cast of the poet's mind. It is also true that Irish poets immediately before Yeats were tardy in discovering the national characteristics that might bridge the country's sectarian quarrels. Victorian sentiment, like Allingham's, was inadequate to unify a contentious nation's cultural aspirations. William Butler Yeats (1865-1939) had some success in achieving this, and not merely because he was a writer of greature stature. As a young man, he had read Standish O'Grady's *Story of Ireland* with some enthusiasm; but like Hyde he realised that Anglo-Saxon, Celtic and Latin cultures had been mingled for so many centuries that an ethnic entity was an abstraction rather than a reality.

Was the National Literary Society's translation of old Irish sagas sufficient stimulus to create an artistically viable modern language? Hyde compromised between a dominantly English vocabulary and the idiom of dialects he knew. In his *Love Songs of Connacht* (1893) modes of thought, tricks of expression, syntactical arrangements, were all assimilated to an Anglo-Irish background. Other revivalists modified a similar hybrid to suit their own ends. Both Yeats and Hyde were rightly anxious to avoid all forms of political extremism.

Writers after 1890 fall naturally into two groups: those who continued to exploit the old Anglo-Irish conventions, and those who aimed to preserve essentially Celtic, if abstract qualities. The latter group included Yeats, Synge, Lady Gregory, Katherine Tynan, George Russell (AE) and James Stephens.

Yeats tended to be cosmopolitan, and owed something to Indian mysticism and French symbolism; his poetry is intellectual, but also evocative. He had the grace of a lyrical poet and a surprising nuance of felt rhythms that had no predecessors in English. It was not his 'Irishness' that set Yeats apart from most poets of his time. He was born in Dublin of Anglo-Irish Victorian parents, and was exposed to the scepticism of his father, John Butler Yeats, whose strong convictions influenced his son's literary life. William was not, indeed, a bright student, and declined to enter Trinity College, as his elders had done, preferring to attend an art school, in the footsteps of his father, while using his leisure time to write verse.

Most of Dublin's aspiring writers managed to temper their Irish romanticism with some realism; but Yeats had an introspective, aristocratic turn of mind, which seemed to distance him from contemporaries. Moreover, fifteen impressionable years were spent in London, reading William Morris, Francis Thompson, Ernest Dowson and Lionel Johnson, besides Spenser, Shakespeare and Blake. Pre-Raphaelite influences were discernible in his lofty manner, dandified clothes, flowing black tie and long hair. The neo-romantic bearing on Yeats's immature style took years to eliminate. Throughout his life Yeats was a laborious and painstaking writer of verse, four to seven lines representing an average day's work.

The second formative influence on the young poet's life was his meeting in 1885 with the Fenian leader, John O'Leary (1830-1907), who had just returned from exile in Paris. Yeats wanted to be in closer touch with the people, and O'Leary and Maud Gonne, an ardent feminist, enabled him to meet in debate young writers with similar aims. O'Leary had been sentenced to twenty years penal servitude (see p. 125), but fifteen had been remitted by the govern-ment, provided he lived abroad. A humanist of Trinity College, O'Leary was entirely without rancour towards those who disagreed with his views on the necessity for Irish independence. He lent Yeats the poems of Davis and other Young Irelanders with whom he had collaborated on *The Nation*, and the young man responded by joining his debating society.

Yeats disagreed with his father about the sort of poetry needed to break the spell of the *fin-de-siècle* writers he called the tragic generation, with whom he had associated in London. According to *Autogiographies* xxx, he sought a personal utterance, free from rhetoric and abstraction (p. 102). O'Leary helped him to obtain subscribers for his first volume of verse *The Wanderings of Oisín and other Poems* (1889); the 'Crossways' section began, prophetically, with the lines 'The woods of Arcady are dead,/And over is their antique joy'. The volume also included a fine lyrical narrative, 'The Stolen Child'.

It is true to assert that a new idealism in poetry grew out of Yeats's friendship with O'Leary. In the section of his next volume called *The Rose*, the poet introduced the occult at the end of a patriotic poem, entitled 'To Ireland in the Coming Times':

> Know, that I would accounted be
> True brother of a company
> That sang, to sweeten Ireland's wrong,
> Ballad and story, rann and song; . . .
>
> Nor may I less be counted one
> With Davis, Mangan, Ferguson,
> Because, to him who ponders well,
> My rhymes more than their rhyming tell
> Of things discovered in the deep,
> Where only body's laid asleep.
> For the elemental creatures go
> About my table to and fro,
> That hurry from unmeasured mind
> To rant and rage in flood and wind; . . .

While still I may, I write for you
The love I lived, the dream I knew.
From our birthday, until we die,
Is but the winking of an eye; . . .
I cast my heart into my rhymes,
That you, in the dim coming times,
May know how my heart went with them
After the red-rose-bordered hem.

(*Poems*, pp. 19-20)

This poem had a dual purpose: to express Yeats's admiration for Maud Gonne, and to placate O'Leary, who complained that the lyrics often lacked a genuine Irish spirit. The red rose in the last line was the symbol of eternal beauty used by the Rosicrucian Society, and figured in the ritual of the Society of the Golden Dawn, of which Yeats was a member. The Rosicrucian Order, claiming secret knowledge of magic, was founded in 1484, but not referred to in literature until 1614.

Though O'Leary regarded nationalism as essential to great literature, he denounced the Young Irelanders' injection of politics into poetry. There were other young disciples under his wing in Katharine Tynan, Stephen Gwynn, T. W. Rolleston, editor of the influential *Dublin University Magazine*, Douglas Hyde, founder of the Gaelic League, and George William Russell, the mystic who called himself AE, after the first two letters in the word *aeon*. Hyde was the only one capable of writing in Gaelic. While living in London, Yeats found refuge in the Irish Literary Club of Southwark, founded in 1880, at a time when about five thousand Irishmen were leaving their native land each month, in search of employment with better prospects. Ireland was anything but a nation of shop-keepers, like England, since only Belfast produced consumer goods in quantity. Seventy per cent of the population was on the land, and this peasant class Yeats came into contact with only while resident in Sligo. The Irish revival had little to do with the language and interests of the depressed class; Sligo, for instance, was a seaport, and the majority of the inhabitants were English-speaking.

The ideal of a national literature for Ireland, on which Gavan Duffy had set his heart when he founded The New Irish Library, no longer appealed to the new generation, John Todhunter, Hyde, AE and Yeats. Yeats was interested more in artistic autonomy for Ireland, than in political autonomy; he could not tolerate militant, patriotic rhetoric; he disliked even more the rough-and-tumble of literary animosity in Dublin, which he described as an 'unmannerly town' ('The People', line 3). Yeats's success was in creating a neo-Celtic romanticism, which was the fruit of his multifarious reading in Old Irish supernatural literature. This was in English translation, but Yeats transmuted it through a new symbolism imbibed from France. In narrative verse this was difficult to accept, but in lyrics and elegies, Yeats met with immediate approval:

> Yet they were of a different kind,
> The names that stilled your childish play,
> They have gone about the world like wind,
> But little time had they to pray
> For whom the hangman's rope was spun,
> And what, God help us, could they save?
> Romantic Ireland's dead and gone,
> It's with O'Leary in the grave.
>
> Was it for this the wild geese spread
> The grey wing upon every tide;
> For this that all that blood was shed,
> For this Edward Fitzgerald died,
> And Robert Emmet and Wolfe Tone,
> All that delirium of the brave?
> Romantic Ireland's dead and gone,
> It's with O'Leary in the grave.
>
> ('September 1913', *Poems*, pp. 46-7)

Such poetry appealed because it possessed what Yeats himself called 'rhythmical animation' ('What is Popular Poetry?', *Essays and Introductions*, p. 11). A ballad monologue, 'The Madness of King Goll' is impressive, because of its dramatic technique; this was the style that J. B. Yeats, the poet's father, had advocated, and involved the use of a *persona*, based on traditional Gaelic mythology.

When poets provide documentary evidence, the growth of an artistic mind is a profitable study. For Wordsworth there is *The Prelude*, for Keats the *Letters*, for Yeats the prose *Trembling of the Veil, Ideas of Good and Evil, Plays and Controversies* and *A Vision*. After the fertilisation of ideas through J. B. Yeats and O'Leary, there were other significant events in the development of W. B. Yeats: first, his luckless relationship with Maud Gonne, whom O'Leary had introduced, and whose social orbit and fount of revolutionary ideas was France. Then came the fruitful meetings with Lady Augusta Gregory and John Millington Synge, both in 1896. These authors filled the gap in Yeats's yearning for independent Ireland, caused by the death of Parnell in 1891. There was nothing specifically Irish in *The Wanderings of Oisín*, except the theme. The narrative was mannered, because it owed much to Spenser, to Shelley's *Prometheus Unbound* and to William Morris. Yeats did not, in fact, find a mature style until the period 1910-21, which was a time of considerable political and social unrest. Here is part of 'Easter 1916':

> Too long a sacrifice
> Can make a stone of the heart.
> O when may it suffice?
> That is Heaven's part, our part
> To murmur name upon name,
> As a mother names her child
> When sleep at last has come
> On limbs that had run wild. . . .
> We know their dream; enough
> To know they dreamed and are dead;
> And what if excess of love
> Bewildered them till they died?
> I write it out in a verse —
> McDonagh and MacBride
> And Connolly and Pearse
> Now and in time to be,
> Wherever green is worn,
> Are changed, changed utterly:
> A terrible beauty is born.

(Poems, p. 93)

Two of the Irish activists who participated in this rising, Patrick Pearse and Thomas MacDonagh (see pp. 128 and 159) were academics as well as poets. Britain being at war, they were summarily court-martialled and shot.

Autobiographies is a book essential to the understanding of Yeats. To the Hermetic Society, which used to meet in York Street, Dublin, he propounded that 'whatever the great poets had affirmed in their finest moments was the nearest we could come to an authoritative religion, and that their mythology, their spirits of water and wind, were but literal truth' (p. 90). A dozen pages later, he spoke of his plans as a poet:

> We should write out our own thoughts in as nearly as possible the language we thought them in, as though in a letter to an intimate friend. We should not disguise them in any way; for our lives give them force.... If I can be sincere and make my language natural, and without becoming discursive, like a novelist, and so indiscreet and prosaic, I shall, if good luck or bad luck make my life interesting, be a great poet; for it will be no longer a matter of literature at all.
>
> (pp. 102-3)

Utterances like this and the previous one induced T. S. Eliot to write in *After Strange Gods* that Yeats's supernatural world was a 'sophisticated lower mythology, summoned like a physician, to supply the fading pulse of poetry with some transient stimulus' (p. 46).

It is still difficult to trace in Yeats's work an ordered relationship with the nationalist movement; he is better to be seen as a mirror of the incoherence of his times; in his vision of Byzantium he made poetry out of the struggle of an enlightened individual to survive in the midst of chaos. No pretence was made to disguise his anti-rationalism; for Yeats's esoteric and hieratic symbols of faith had conviction, and there were many who shared his belief in the spiritual values of art. A reader can sense the lofty moral vision of his perceptions in the *obiter dicta* of his *Diary*, begun in 1909:

> One cannot sum up a nation intellectually, and when the summing up is made by half-educated men the idea fills one with alarm.

Emotion is always justified by time, thought hardly ever.

Hatred as a basis of imagination, in ways which one could explain even without magic, helps to dry up the nature and make the sexual abstinence, so common among young men and women in Ireland, possible.

The soul of Ireland has become a vapour and her body a stone.

. . . without culture or holiness, which are always the gift of a very few, a man may renounce wealth or any other external thing, but he cannot renounce hatred, envy, jealousy, revenge. Culture is the sanctity of the intellect.

You cannot keep the idea of a nation alive where there are no national institutions to reverence, no national success to admire, without a model of it in the mind of the people.

(*Autobiographies*, pp. 472, 487-9, 493)

The consistency and tenacity of Yeats's outlook bore fruit in the splendid verses of *The Tower, The Winding Stair* and the *Last Poems*, on which his reputation now mainly rests. These are not writings for readers who expect poetry to provide spiritual comfort; the themes are invariably internal conflict, associated with ageing, though not with despair; but the Christian consolations are bravely rejected. Language is reduced to its barest essentials, yet it loses none of its passionate, heroic dignity. This is how Yeats ends 'Coole Park and Ballylee, 1931':

We were the last romantics — chose for theme
Traditional sanctity and loveliness;
Whatever's written in what poets name
The book of the people; whatever most can bless
The mind of man or elevate a rhyme;
But all is changed, that high horse riderless,
Though mounted in that saddle Homer rode
Where the swan drifts upon a darkening flood.

(*Poems*, p. 140)

What do these three collections prove, if they do not show a shift of emphasis in the *Kathleen Ni Houlihan* pattern, to which O'Leary and Maud Gonne had previously persuaded him? Was it possible to find dignity in the romantic image of a race in defeat, as Christ demonstrated it in conquered Israel? The tragedies were not really comparable; for the Christian one was the reverse of a *national* movement, though there was poetry in it. Yeats's aesthetic devotion stopped short of religious dedication. But no modern poet planned a career more purposively than he did, as this passage from *The Trembling of the Veil* shows:

> I delighted in every age where poet and artist confined themselves gladly to some inherited subject-matter known to the whole people, for I thought that in man and race alike there is something called 'Unity of Being'. . . . Nations, races, and individual men are unified by an image, or bundle of related images. . . .
>
> I had seen Ireland in my own time turn from the bragging rhetoric and gregarious humour of O'Connell's generation and school, and offer herself to the solitary and proud Parnell as to her anti-self, I had begun to hope, or to half hope, that we might be the first in Europe to seek unity as deliberately as it had been sought by theologian, poet, sculptor, architect, from the eleventh to the thirteenth century.
>
> (Autobiographies, pp. 190-95)

It should be observed that Yeats bracketed 'theologian' with poet, sculptor and architect.

As time passes, it becomes clearer that Yeats was not a typical Irishman; he was too independent to cumber himself with Irish grievances, except as they touched his class. His abiding love was for poetry, mysticism and the so-called Union of Hearts. When he propounded the aims of the literary revival in *The Celtic Twilight* (1893), he was mindful of the thinking of Matthew Arnold in *The Study of Celtic Literature*, written twenty-six years earlier. Arnold had praised the fruits of the Celts' imagination in the works of Shakespeare and other poets. Yeats sought to achieve something more by transferring the concept of Irish nationality from the political arena to literature, and through the superiority of his class, as well as intellect, to enhance the status of the Irish people in the eyes of Europe. The force of his exhortation in 'Under Ben Bulben' is palpable:

> Irish poets, learn your trade,
> Sing whatever is well made,
> Scorn the sort now growing up
> All out of shape from toe to top,
> Their unremembering hearts and heads
> Base-born products of base beds.
> Sing the peasantry, and then
> Hard-riding country gentlemen,
> The holiness of monks, and after
> Porter-drinkers' randy laughter;
> Sing the lords and ladies gay
> They were beaten into the clay
> Through seven heroic centuries;
> Cast your mind on other days
> That we in coming days may be
> Still the indomitable Irishry.

(Poems, p. 185)

The 'indomitable Irishry' apparently meant more to Yeats than the peasantry, with whom his acquaintance was slight.

The literary revival, of which Yeats was indisputable leader, produced from among his circle of friends and contemporaries a few who resolutely declined to acknowledge discipleship. Among them was AE (George Russell) 1867-1935, a personality so admired that some called him the 'Socrates of Dublin', while others regarded him as a modern Irish saint. In his writings Russell proved to be an honest mystic and a sincere, though often exacerbated, nationalist, who wrote poetry only when he felt the urge to express himself 'artistically'; he was also an enthusiastic amateur painter. *Homeward* (1894) and *The Earth Breath* (1897) contain his most pleasing verses, and a small volume, called *Collected Poems*, appeared in 1913.

Talk with a writer so engaging and friendly was a memorable experience, and AE's conversation tolerated only occasional cynicisms, as when he said: 'A literary movement consists of five or six people who live in the same town and hate each other cordially'; or 'the only listeners in Dublin are tired talkers' (see Rodgers, *Irish Literary Portraits*, pp. 193 and 197).

The *raison d'être* of the revival in which Yeats and AE participated was the conviction that supporters should write and publish in Ireland. The theosophical movement in Dublin played a significant part in this plan, and began with the foundation of the Hermetic Society in 1885, and the Dublin Lodge in the following year. This was replaced by the Universal Brotherhood in 1897, all these societies being modelled on ones in England. Russell, Yeats, Charles Johnson and John Eglington were in the forefront of these theosophical groups, and studied the occult, as well as such movements as esoteric Buddhism, while conducting their own theosophical journals. One of the earliest fruits of these applied studies was Yeats's *The Celtic Twilight* (1893), actually written much earlier; it showed a clear link between mystical thinking and Irish nationalism, the medium of which was invariably English, and so alien to the Catholic community; AE's poem 'On Behalf of Some Irishmen Not Followers of Tradition', in spite of the unwieldy title, expresses the kind of enthusiasm that was then current.

> The worship of the dead is not
> A worship that our hearts allow,
> Though every famous shade were wrought
> With woven thorns above the brow.
> We fling our answer back in scorn:
> 'We are less children of this clime
> Than of some nation yet unborn
> Or empire in the womb of time.
> We hold the Ireland in the heart
> More than the land our eyes have seen,
> And love the goal for which we start
> More than the tale of what has been.'
> The generations as they rise
> May live the life men lived before,
> Still hold the thought once held as wise,
> Go in and out by the same door.
> We leave the easy peace it brings:
> The few we are shall still unite

In fealty to unseen kings
Or unimaginable light.
We would no Irish sign efface,
But yet our lips would gladlier hail
The firstborn of the Coming Race
Than the last splendour of the Gael.
No blazoned banner we unfold —
One charge alone we give to youth,
Against the sceptred myth to hold
The golden heresy of truth.

(*Penguin Book of Irish Verse*, pp. 313-14)

Poems by Russell bore other curious titles, such as 'Over-soul' and 'By the Margin of the Great Deep', some containing colourful descriptions of Irish landscape, in which epithets like 'sapphire' and 'amethyst' tended to dominate. These writings were the inspired, but gracefully controlled, out-pourings of a visionary with a practical turn of mind, quite unlike those of the better painter, William Blake. A mere utilitarian, but eloquent, statement of Russell's political ideals in prose appeared in *The National Being* (1916).

The most brilliant portrait of the man ΛE himself is to be found in George Moore's *Hail and Farewell* (1911-14). It reveals that part of Russell's charm was his ability to match impetuous speech with disarming personal relation-ships, of the kind that make literary movements enduring. Russell said that his greatest pleasure was the discovery of new poets, and he continued to unearth many during his seven-year editorship of *The Irish Statesman*, a weekly financed from the United States (1923-30). AE's literary friendships and undogmatic ideas were not diminished when he became the organiser of co-operative land-banks for the Irish Agricultural Society, in a patriotic attempt to improve initiative and uplift the country's economy.

Oliver St John Gogarty (1878-1957), who figures in episodes one and nine of Joyce's *Ulysses* as Buck Mulligan, was less important as a poet than as a literary personality. In later life he declined to write the life of Joyce, on the paradoxical ground that he was the saddest person he had ever met. Gogarty was a sceptic and an ebullient talker of a distinguished Irish cast of mind. He was also a specialist surgeon, remarkably well read in the classics, Dante, Shakespeare and Burns. His Celtic pride, fiery energy and coarse-grained humour, made him a formidable figure in Dublin's literary society. The fame of Gogarty as a raconteur and master of repartee was legendary. Some idea of this quality can be gleaned from his best known prose work *As I was Going down Sackville Street* (1937) and its auto-biographical companion *Start from Somewhere Else* (1955); both were written in America, when he had retired from professional life in order to become an author.

What emerges from these retrospective writings is a bawdy Chaucerian character, of the kind Dublin often produced (Brendan Behan was of a similar stamp). In his youth at Trinity College, Gogarty had been a champion cyclist, and at the height of his medical career gained fame for the exploit of escaping from kidnappers by swimming the Liffey in midwinter. He had apparently been captured by irregulars, to be murdered as a hostage. This event he celebrated by the gift of two swans to the river, Yeats being present at the ceremony.

> Keep you these calm and lovely things,
>   And float them on your clearest water;
> For one would not disgrace a King's
>   Transformed beloved and buoyant daughter.
>
> And with her goes this sprightly swan,
>   A bird of more than royal feather,
> With alban beauty clothed upon:
>   O keep them fair and well together!
>
> As fair as was that doubled Bird,
>   By love of Leda so besotten,
> That she was all with wonder stirred,
>   And the Twin Sportsmen were begotten!
>   (*Oxford Book of Irish Verse*, pp. 172-3)

This occasion signalled the subsequent appearance of *An Offering of Two Swans* (1923), a book of lyrical verse, reprinted in *Collected Poems*, published in New York in 1954.

As a friend and supporter of Arthur Griffith, Gogarty was quickly disillusioned, after the Civil War, with the government of de Valera; not until the presidency of Cosgrave did he accept the honour of a senatorship. When over fifty he regrettably decided upon the career of a free-lance journalist in the United States, a life of strenuous endeavour that was not very remunerative. When he died, he was buried, at his own desire, on the banks of a quiet fjord on the coast of Connemara.

James Stephens, reviewing *An Offering of Two Swans* in *The Dial* (June 1924) had this to say of Gogarty's verse:

> His poetry is not breathed in the Irish manner. It is more carved than flowing, but his master is Catullus rather than Herrick. . . . The Celt in Dr Gogarty is already promising that if he can forget his scholarship he will remember his ancestors, and sing like a lark instead of like a musician.
>
> (*Letters of James Stephens*, pp. 306-7)

In 1904 AE published the anthology *New Songs*, an epoch-making event for the young poets who had developed their talents with his encouragement and help. The first of these was Seumas O'Sullivan (1879-1958) whose *Twilight People* (1905) and *Verses Sacred and Profane* (1908) were meant to re-capture the pastoralism and idyllic beauty which he associated with the Irish peasantry; but this was a state few actually enjoyed. A third volume *The Earth Lover* introduced occasional town poetry; but the mood was the same — a mystical naturalism that derived from Russell, which led AE to think that a modicum of technical competence and rhythmical innovation was an adequate testimony of discipleship.

Another poet sponsored in *New Songs*, Padraic Colum (1881-1972), was advised by AE to concentrate on drama, where he fell under the spell of Yeats. He was co-opted onto the committee of the Theatre of Ireland in 1906. Yeats subsequently wrote in his *Diary* 'Colum is one victim of AE's misunderstanding of life that I rage over' (see Rodgers, op. cit., p. 199). But animosity apart, Colum's *Wild Earth*, published with supplementary poems in 1909, displayed a more rugged sense of the soil than O'Sullivan's;

these stanzas are from 'A Drover':

> O farmer, strong farmer!
> You can spend at the fair,
> But your face you must turn
> To your crops and your care;
>   . . .
> O the smell of the beasts,
> The wet wind in the morn,
> And the proud and hard earth
> Never broken for corn!
>
> And the crowds at the fair,
> The herds loosened and blind,
> Loud words and dark faces,
> And the wild blood behind!
>   . . .
> I will bring you, my kine,
> Where there's grass to the knee,
> But you'll think of scant croppings
> Harsh with salt of the sea.

(Greene, *Anthology of Irish Literature*, vol II, pp. 503-4)

Despite his conservative Catholicism, Colum had all the attributes of an original, because his naturalism was sparing in literary allusions.

James Stephens (1882-1950) did not figure in *New Songs* because, as an overworked solicitor's clerk, he was not discovered by AE until 1907. The *Collected Poems*, published in 1926, are, however, dedicated to Russell in the warmest terms. The collection, better called 'selection', embodied the best of six slender volumes of verse published between 1909 and 1925. Lightness of touch, and Georgian competence in the handling of a lyric, were qualities that AE's Edwardian taste encouraged in young poets, much to the disgruntlement of Yeats. Stephens soon became a spirited writer of prose, and his *Letters*, edited by Finneran in 1974, are a sheer delight of caprice and gentleness. He acknowledged obvious shortcomings as a poet, and confessed that, but for the discovery of Browning and Blake, and his desire to intensify life, he would not have written verse at all. AE adversely criticised the manuscript of *Songs of the Clay* (1915), in which Stephens attempted to break with the Georgian conventions, with the result that its publication was delayed for a year. 'The Centaurs' appeared in this volume:

Playing upon the hill three centaurs were!
They lifted each a hoof! They stared at me!
And stamped the dust!

They stamped the dust! They snuffed upon the air!
And all their movements had the fierce glee
Of power, and pride, and lust!

Of power and pride and lust! Then, with a shout,
They tossed their heads, and wheeled, and galloped round,
In furious brotherhood:

In furious brotherhood! Around, about,
They charged, they swerved, they leaped!
    Then, bound on bound,
They raced into the wood!

(Collected Poems, p. 18)

Repeating the last phrase or sentence of a stanza at the beginning of the next was a popular Irish means of securing continuity of rhythm and meaning, and was probably derived from a French source.

In editing his *Collected Poems*, Stephens rearranged those he wished to preserve in six books, giving each a novel title, the significance of which he did not explain. Superfluous exclamation marks in 'The Centaurs' are presumably his own; most were eliminated in Lloyd Frankenberg's reprint (*James Stephens: A Selction*, 1962).

F. R. Higgins (1896-1941) became the protégé of Yeats and was one of his ablest collaborators in the Abbey Theatre. A Protestant, in spite of his Irish appearances and county of origin (Mayo), he was educated in the east of Ireland and aspired to be an ardent nationalist. This is shown in his care to preserve an Irish colouring in what he wrote for the papers he edited, which were mostly trade journals. Higgins was a founder of the trade-union movement in Ireland; but his private life was dedicated first to poetry and later to drama. Like Thomas Moore, he wrote ballads to the tune of existing

Irish airs; but the language was often undisciplined and deliberately illiterate, like that of Rudyard Kipling. Three of his five volumes are generally held to contain his best verse, *The Dark Breed* (1927), *Arable Holdings* (1933) and *The Gap of Brightness* (1940). The most praised poem, 'Father and Son', was a tribute to the elder Higgins, who was a Meath engineer. It appeared in the first of these publications:

> Only last week, walking the hushed fields
> Of our most lovely Meath, now thinned by November,
> I came to where the road from Laracor leads
> To the Boyne river — that seemed more lake than river,
> Stretched in uneasy light and stript of reeds.
>
> And walking longside an old weir
> Of my people's, where nothing stirs — only the shadowed
> Leaden flight of a heron up the lean air —
> I went unmanly with grief, knowing how my father,
> Happy though captive in years, walked last with me there....
>
> For that proud, wayward man now my heart breaks —
> Breaks for that man whose mind was a secret eyrie,
> Whose kind hand was sole signet of his race,
> Who curbed me, scorned my green ways, yet increasinly
>   loved me
> Till Death drew its grey blind down his face.
>
> And yet I am pleased that even my reckless ways
> Are living shades of his rich calms and passions —
> Witnesses for him and for those faint namesakes
> With whom now he is one, under yew branches,
> Yes, one in a graven silence no bird breaks.
>
> (*Faber Book of Irish Verse*, pp. 264-5)

Contemporary with his friend Higgins was Austin Clarke (1896-1974), who admired Yeats with critical reservations. The development of Clarke's mind and art is self-revealed in *Twice Round the Black Church* (1962) and *A Penny in the Clouds* (1968). Like Joyce, Clarke was educated first in the Jesuit College of Belvedere, and then at University College Dublin, where he succeeded Thomas MacDonagh as English lecturer after the Easter rising of 1916. A capacity for independent judgement was, by Clarke's own account, repressed during schooling, with serious psychological consequences when he reached adulthood; but he learnt Gaelic and was able to master the intricacies of its grammar. Two instructors at the University were professors George Sigerson and Douglas Hyde, who were the leading exponents of early Irish literature, and convinced him of the excellence of vernacular poets of the eighteenth century.

It was Higgins who introduced Clarke to the poetry of Dowson and the *fin-de-siècle* decadent poets of England; but by the outbreak of World War I Yeats had become Clarke's major influence. In verse he described an interview with Yeats at the Savile Club in London, where Clarke soon found employment as a book-reviewer and freelance journalist. He did not find Yeats as co-operative with young talent as AE, Harold Monro, Desmond MacCarthy and Leonard Woolf.

Returning to Dublin a few years before the death of Yeats, Clarke was responsible for establishing the Dublin Verse-Speaking Society and the Lyric Theatre Company. During the next seventeen years he neglected pure poetry for verse drama. At the conclusion of this period Clarke's reputation was greatly enhanced by the independence of his criticism in *Poetry in Modern Ireland* (1951) and *The Celtic Twilight in the Nineties* (1969). In both these books he promoted the dignity and significance of the literary movement that Yeats and AE had initiated, while arguing for the greater importance of Sigerson and Hyde's translations of the Irish classics. The trouble had been that the poetry-reading public for Gaelic verse was too small to make it viable for the commercial publisher.

Clarke therefore contended that poetry written in the vernacular should return to the oral tradition of circulation. Though his own poetry was written in English, most of it had a distinctively Irish flavour. Unfortunately, a good deal to which he attached importance was obscure. This difficulty hampers most of the long experimental poems of the later period. They were all published in pamphlet form by his private press, the Bridge, which limited editions to about three hundred copies. The *Collected Poems* of Clarke, edited by Liam Miller in the year of the poet's death, was the product of drastic revisions, after he had prepared a holocaust of the manuscripts at the bottom of his garden. Perhaps the most significant of the separate publications were *Pilgrimage and Other Poems* (1929); *Ancient Lights* (1955), *Flight to Africa* (1963) and *Mnemosyne Lay in Dust* (1966). The earlier volumes had been much influenced by Clarke's fifteen years in London, and suffer from an adjectivally descriptive style, which often descends to wearisome particularity. The metrical experiments were, however, diverse, and include blank verse, at its best in the long narrative poem, *The Vengeance of Fionn* (1917).

The *Pilgrimage* poems of Clarke back to Ireland of the ninth century, which he styled the Celtic-Romanesque period, eminent in various art forms. Here began his resuscitation of the assonantal measures of the past — a hint given to him by George Russell. The first stanza of 'Ancient Lights' contains, for instance, the following cryptic lines:

> *I* had been *taught*, *beat* door, leaped *lan*ding,
> *Lie*d down the *ban*nisters of *naught*

'Respectable People', in the same volume, offers a rousing example of Clarke's middle style:

> *Thought rattles along the empty railings*
> Of street and square they lived in, years
> Ago. I dream of them at night,
> Strangers to this artificial light,
> Respectable people who gave me sweets,
> Talked above my head or *unfobbed*
> *The time*. I know them by each faded
> Smile and their old-fashioned clothes.
> But how can I make room for them
> In a mind too horrible with life?
> This is the last straw in the grave,
> *Propping the tear in which grief burns*
> *Away*. Shame of eternity
> Has stripped them of their quiet habits,
> *Unshovelled them out of the past.*
> Memory finds beyond that last
> Improvidence, their mad remains.
>
> (*Selected Poems*, p. 29)

The sentences or phrases italicised display the poet's novel habits of image-making.

Clarke's later work, for instance, *A Sermon on Swift and Other Poems* (1968) contains some pungent satire. There is a note of unconcealed modernity about 'A Jocular Retort':

> Criticus smiled as he wrote, and remarked
> In the Literary Supplement
> Of the London Times that Mr Clarke was
> A garrulous rambling old Irishman.
> No doubt I have become too supple
> For the links of those boastful manacles
> That hold back meaning, but I prefer it
> To being a silent Englishman
> Who cannot untie his tongue. So I pen
> On, pen on, talkative as AE was,
> When old. Because there is no return fare,
> Few friends come out of the Isle of AEaea
> Where lately my desires have been penned
>
> *(Selected Poems*, p. 135)

Clarke's animadversions on the corruption of post-independence Irish society have many subtleties of this kind; but he will never be the sort of poet to whom reading publics respond wholeheartedly.

Like Yeats, Clarke disdained the Americanised modernism of Ezra Pound and T. S. Eliot, though he did make a literary pilgrimage to the United States, and openly disavowed faith in poets such as Frost and Whitman. Yeats, he surmised, owed more to the symbolist movement in England of the eighteen-nineties than to any American force, except that of Emerson. Clarke took great pains not to emulate the technical experiments of Yeats; but the great works of that self-contained individualist were ever before him; he refers to them constantly in his critical circumspections on Anglo-Irish poetry after 1890. In Clarke's view the eloquence of Yeats owed much to the distinctly Irish rhythmical lilt of Burke and Grattan (see the article on Yeats in the *Dublin Magazine* XIV, April 1939, pp. 8 and 9).

It seems clear that the literary revival was, in its inception, an Anglo-Irish one, aimed at creating a national self-consciousness in English. Of the three great protagonists, Standish O'Grady, Douglas Hyde and W. B. Yeats, two were Protestants; but the real strength of the movement was its non-sectarian character. The leaders found that they had plenty of upper-middle-class supporters, who owed most of their taste in art to the past of the English Ascendancy. They felt that a narrow adherence to nationalism would stultify the mind. Yet a distinctive Irishness was thought to be a duty that every creative writer ought to preserve. Yeats and his confreres were divided only in allegiance to the literature of England, through which they received their poetical education. Thus Yeats wrote in 'A General Introduction for my Work':

> There are moments when hatred poisons my life and I accuse myself of effeminacy because I have not given it adequate expression. It is not enough to have put it into the mouth of a rambling peasant poet. Then I remind myself that though mine is the first English marriage I know of in the direct line, all my family names are English, and that I owe my soul to Shakespeare, to Spenser and to Blake, perhaps to William Morris, and to the English language in which I think, speak, and write, that everything I love has come to me through English; my hatred tortures me with love, my love with hate. . . . This is Irish hatred and solitude, the hatred of human life that made Swift write *Gulliver* and the epitaph upon his tomb, that can still make us wag between extremes and doubt our sanity. . . .
>
> No man can think or write with music and vigour except in his mother tongue. . . . Gaelic is my national language, but it is not my mother tongue.
>
> (*Essays and Introductions*, pp. 519-20)

Unfortunately the Catholic writer was not much stimulated by the Jansenism of the Irish Church, which favoured book censorship and was suspicious of the fruitfulness of the arts. When customary censorship was introduced during the First World War, and was tightened after the Easter Rising of 1916, Irish publishers found it difficult to pay their way, and Maunsell, the most progressive, had to abandon business.

The Irish Academy of Letters, established by Yeats in 1932, was designed principally to combat the restrictive effect of the Literary Censorship Act of 1929. One disastrous effect of this Act was to curb independence of thought, and curtail the creative work of the leisured class. Government support was now forthcoming for the materialistic new Irish bourgeoisie, whose literary outlook tended to be narrow, and whose taste was mostly philistine. Such was the situation which induced up-and-coming Irish writers to have their work published in England; they were unwilling to subserve Irish parochial interests or de Valera's political chauvinism.

In *The Fortunes of the Irish Language* (1954) Corkery blamed O'Connell for the Irish Party's failure to give the mother-tongue a permanent place in school education, and Davis for encouraging the idea that 'nationality could exist in two languages' (p. 116). Only after the Great Famine did John O'Mahony, a learned member of the diaspora in America, give birth to the concept of *Fenianism*, a movement to nurture the Gaelic language throughout Ireland, and not merely among the proletariat in the Gaeltacht. Had it not been for O'Mahony, the Gaelic League of 1893 might never have come into being, or its publication scheme put into operation. For literary productions in Gaelic had, from the outset, to be subsidised, in order to become competitive. Under Victorian imperialism the submergence of the Irish vernacular was by no means unique; Corkery might have mentioned many other countries besides India, Pakistan and Palestine, in which the national languages of indigenous peoples had to be reborn.

Dramatic Language in the Irish Theatre

The European Renaissance, in its westward path from the thirteenth to the sixteenth century, by-passed Ireland, and no interest in drama appeared there until the latter half of the seventeenth century. Partly because of the church's opposition, Ireland was the last country in Europe to promote the concept of national drama, and this had unfortunate social and linguistic consequences. The rise of literary drama at the close of the nineteenth century was due solely to the initiative of the Protestant Ascendancy. Traditional theatres in the larger cities were in the hands of entrepreneurs or actor-managers, such as Dion Boucicault at the Queen's Theatre, Dublin. Here, and at the other two theatres, The Gaiety and the Theatre Royal, bookings for plays of London origin were extremely heavy.

Dublin theatres had a two-century anglophile background, made possible by the liberal policy of Charles II, for they were founded after the Restoration of the Stuart kings. There was a regular theatrical traffic between Dublin and London, and this accounted for the success of dramatists of Irish origin such as Congreve, Farquhar, Steele, Goldsmith, Sheridan, Wilde and Shaw on the English stage. They were, in a sense, forerunners of the realistic drama on democratic principles that followed the revolution of Hendrik Ibsen on the Continent, and T. W. Robertson in England. Irish-born dramatists are credited with pert dialogue and satiric irony, especially at the expense of the English and their Penal Laws. As a generalisation, it is thought that they added finesse and polish to English comic writing.

In successive centuries the Sheridan and Boucicault families played significant roles in the development of Anglo-Irish theatre. The playwright Richard Brinsley Sheridan's father was an actor and teacher of elocution, who became an Irish expatriate, turned English lexicographer. Dion Boucicault the elder (1822-90), born in Dublin, and educated at London University, was the youthful author of *London Assurance* (1841), a comedy so successful that it was recently revived. His *Colleen Bawn* (1860), *Arrah-na-Pogue* (1865) and *The Shaughraun* (1875) set the fashion for Irish romantic melodrama, which it was easy for Bernard Shaw to debunk in the *Saturday Review* in 1896.

Boucicault retired to America in 1876 and died in New York. His son, Dion Boucicault the younger, was born there in 1859, and began a stage career twenty years later. He then transferred to Australia for a decade and to London in 1901, where he became manager of the New Theatre in 1915. The Irish plays of the elder Boucicault were designed for nostalgic approval abroad, rather than for home consumption. London actor-managers then used the Dublin theatres as they did provincial ones in England, with the result that many plays appeared there before they were taken to London. In this way, leading English actors were able to disseminate Whig policy on the Dublin stage until the outbreak of the First World War.

When Douglas Hyde established the Gaelic League in 1893, 855 in every thousand Irish people could not speak Gaelic (see Ó Cuív's *A View of the Irish Language*, p. 81). Only the principal towns of the west coast were Gaelic speaking. Hyde was of opinion that drama should prove an effective means of re-vitalising interest in the vernacular. But the Irish language was not, indeed had never been, a product of urban culture. Plays flourish where reasonably large audiences can patronise them. Most Irish towns were founded by Vikings, developed by Normans, and received their education at the hands of the English.

The first Irish play in the vernacular was probably Father Dineen's *Tobar Draoidheachta* (The Magic Well), produced by W. G. Fay for Arthur Griffith's Sinn Féin movement. This was followed by *Casadh an tSúgáin* (The Twisting of the Rope) in 1901, which Douglas Hyde devised to incorporate folk elements, such as singing and dancing. Folk-drama, intended for small-group entertainment, became a regular feature of the Irish Festival *Oireachtas*, initiated by the Gaelic League in 1897. *An Pósadh* (The Marriage), Hyde's second vernacular play, was not produced by the National Theatre until 1911. By 1913 there came into being a company of Gaelic actors, known as 'The Players', but the First World War soon put an end to its activities. After the Irish Civil War, a Dramatic Union was created, and subsidised by the Irish Government to produce plays in Gaelic during the summer months. But this body did not possess its own theatre, and the *Gaeltacht* consisted largely of isolated pockets in Donegal, Mayo, Galway, Kerry, Cork and Waterford, ninety per cent of Gaelic speakers living in the first named. Gaelic drama survived principally in two theatres, one in Dublin, the other in Galway, the latter producing such actors as Mícheál Mac Liammóir and Siobhán McKenna. In the Galway Gaelic Theatre, the *Taibhdhearc*, the best work in Irish vernacular drama has undoubtedly been done.

The dramatic revival of the eighteen-nineties was a Dublin growth, and the outcome of Anglo-Irish enterprise. The movement began tentatively with Yeats's founding of the Irish Literary Society in London in 1891, followed by a National Literary Society in Dublin the following year. Yeats felt, as did Shaw, that the English theatre was moribund in the hands of managers who were dedicated to the star-principle, to spectacle, elaborate scene-painting and the profit motive. Above all, Yeats was conscious of a lamentable lack of stage-worthy poetic plays. Contacts were made in London with Florence Farr, the actress, and George Moore, the novelist and playwright.

Before the birth of the dramatic revival, described in the *Samhain* articles of *Plays and Controversies* (1923), Yeats had written the verse plays *The Countess Cathleen* (1892) and *The Land of Heart's Desire* (1894), the latter being produced in London by J. T. Grein's Independent Theatre. Edward Martyn and Lady Augusta Gregory came into the theatre project only in 1898, when the former sought an Irish sponsor for his two plays *The Heather Field* and *Maeve*, published in 1890. From the discussions of these three enthusiasts the Irish Literary Theatre ensued in 1899, George Moore being drawn into the management by reason of his theatrical experience in London.

From the outset Yeats's leadership took the line that the Irish Literary Theatre (1899-1904) should not compete with the commercial theatres; his plan was to get the 'heroic age into verse, and to solve some problems of the speaking of verse to musical notes' (*Plays and Controversies*, p. 9). Plays were to be produced in prose and verse, but poetic drama was to be Yeats's special contribution. For this, acting had to be simplified and speech given precedence over gesture (op. cit. p. 47). 'Let us learn construction from the masters' he declared, 'and dialogue from ourselves' (ibid., p. 13). Irish dialogue in English would (he maintained) be lively and spontaneous, as long as it reflected folk speech. He therefore looked for suitable precedents in Ibsen's *Brand* and *Peer Gynt*, and the works of Strindberg, Björnson, Tolstoy, Hauptmann and Zola, hoping to supplant action with exchange of motives and conflicts of character.

The first season of the Irish Literary Theatre in May 1899 was an important event, for which George Moore had engaged actors in London and rehearsed them there. The chosen plays were Martyn's *The Heather Field* and Yeats's *The Countess Cathleen*, the venue being the Ancient Concert Rooms. A subscription list guaranteed expenses, but no one was called upon, because the deficit was met by Martyn himself, who came from a distinguished Catholic family, with an estate near Moore's in the west of Ireland. Without Moore's advice in construction, Martyn would have been an unlikely participant, because he had little sympathetic understanding of character. *The Heather Field* was regarded as true to the Celtic spirit, with its ancient reverence for natural beauty. Yeats admitted that he had no knowledge of theatre when he produced the first version of *The Countess Cathleen*. The play was opposed by a section of the press and the local student body, on the ground of alleged blasphemy, with the result that police protection had to be sought. The work was afterwards extensively revised; throughout his career Yeats learnt from audience reaction and actor experience, and so mastered his craft.

The intention was to open the 1900 season with a play in Gaelic, but nothing suitable could be found. Instead, an English company was invited to act in Martyn's *Maeve*, Moore's *The Bending of the Bough* and Alice Milligan's *The Last Feast of the Fianna*. The second of these was Moore's re-writing of Martyn's first play, *The Tale of a Town*, a problem drama deemed unacceptable in the form he had submitted it. There was much collaboration of this kind, especially between Yeats and Lady Gregory, which she described in *Our Irish Theatre* (1913).

In 1901, Frank Benson was engaged to produce three plays at the Gaiety Theatre for the October season, and achieved great success with *Diarmuid and Grania*, which brought scenes from Tara and Ben Bulben to the stage for the first time. This was a collaborative effort by Moore and Yeats, 'Moore accepting my judgement upon words, I his upon construction' (see Yeats, *Dramatis Personae*, pp. 62-4). One of Benson's functions was to train Irish actors, so that they would be able to take over the following year, when the Irish Literary Theatre performed AE's *Deirdre* and Yeats's *Cathleen Ni Houlihan*, with Maud Gonne in the latter title role. Both plays were later published, to fulfil Yeats's policy that the plays should be read, as well as seen and heard. Russell's admired play was fortunate in his hiring the services of the brothers William and Frank Fay, Irish actors who complemented each other and believed in the ideal of a national theatre.

In the six years of its existence, the Irish Literary Theatre produced twenty-one plays, including six by Yeats, two each by Martyn, James Cousins and J. M. Synge (*In the Shadow of the Glen*, 1903, and *Riders to the Sea*, 1904), and one each by Moore alone, Hyde and Lady Gregory. The other contributions were by Alice Milligan, Fred Ryan, Padraic Colum and S. MacManus, together with the collaborated work of Yeats and Moore.

The ablest expression of the Irish Literary Theatre's policy is to be found in Yeats's annual *Samhain* reports; for instance, this from the notes for 1902:

In Ireland, where we have so much to prove and to disprove, we are ready to forget that the creation of an emotion of beauty is the only kind of literature that justifies itself. . . . Irish writers of considerable powers of thought seem to have no better standard of English than a schoolmaster's ideal of correctness.

(Plays and Controversies, pp. 28-30)

This sounds like a counsel of perfection, but it brought new writers into the fold, such as Padraic Colum and Lady Gregory, whose first plays, respectively *Broken Soil* and *Twenty-five*, were produced in 1903.

So acclaimed were the artistic merits of the plays by London critics, that the players were invited by the Irish Literary Society in London in the same year to perform at the Queen's Gate Hall. Here they were seen by Miss A. E. F. Horniman, who had once been Yeats's private secretary. She was so impressed that she wrote offering to equip and maintain a small theatre in Dublin at her own expense, in order to supply the wants of the national movement. A suitable building was found in the Mechanics' Institute, and reconstructed at a cost to the donor of some £13,000. In December 1904, the Abbey Theatre, claiming to be a national body, licensed in the name of Lady Gregory, replaced the Irish Literary Theatre. The Abbey was the first Repertory Theatre created in the British Isles, its seating capacity being a mere 500, and its stage twenty by fifteen feet. The opening plays were *On Baile's Strand* by Yeats, and *Spreading the News* by Lady Gregory.

As there was both press and vocal opposition to the title of National Theatre, Yeats was provided with an opportunity to establish the principles upon which he hoped a national theatre would operate, when its programme was expanded on a seasonal scale. In the *Samhain* reports, which were continued until 1906, Yeats made the following arguments:

'Literature is the ultimate creator of all values', while at the same time representing 'one man's vision of the world' *(Plays and Controversies*, p. 56)
Opinion-ridden communities, created by the popular press, put 'creative minds into some sort of a prison' (p. 57)
No nation draws all its life out of itself. Therefore writers

are no less national who show the influence of other countries, or of the great authors of the world (p. 108)
'All language but that of the poets and of the poor ... is
bedridden'. Persiflage may express a deliberate enjoyment
of words, but it is not a true language. 'It is impersonal ...
on the edge of life; it covers more character than it dis-
covers'; yet all comedies tend to be made out of it
(pp. 120-21)
'Every change towards realism [has] coincided with a
decline in dramatic energy' (p. 127).

Two attractive plays of the new theatre proved to be
Cathleen Ni Houlihan and *The Pot of Broth*, in the latter
Lady Gregory had collaborated with Yeats. Her forte was for
comedy, and her amusingly observant prose became an
admirable foil to his verse. Lady Gregory was thoroughly
conversant with Gaelic, but Yeats was slow in acclimatising
to the language-habits of Irish speakers when they used
English. It was she who gave him the advice 'think like a wise
man', but express yourself like 'the common people'
(*Dramatis Personae*, p. 67). She declined to take any credit
for the 'bits of dialogue' she contributed to *The Pot of Broth*.

The Abbey Theatre encouraged many writers of fiction to
submit manuscripts to the Selection Committee, and these
became so numerous that Yeats felt compelled to draft a
memorandum of 'Advice to Playwrights', which was sent to
any author whose play showed some promise. Here are a
few of the memorable items:

A play to be suitable for performance at the Abbey should
contain some criticism of life, founded on the experience
or personal observation of the writer, or some vision of
life, of Irish life by preference, important from its beauty
or from some excellence of style; and this intellectual
quality is not more necessary to tragedy than to the
gayest comedy. . . .
Any knot of events, where there is passionate emotion
and clash of will, can be made the subject matter of a play,
and the less like a play it is at the first sight the better play
may come of it.

(Lady Gregory, *Our Irish Theatre*, pp. 101-2)

Yeats was immediately accused of moulding the new aspirants to his own ideals; but these were too personal to have much effect upon writers with different aims, such as Padraic Colum, Lennox Robinson and William Boyle. Among patriotic Irishmen Yeats was regarded as a decadent; he was known to support the doctrine of 'Art for Art's sake' and he openly disapproved of poetry with a political bias. Theatre audiences were often baffled by his poetic language, though they experienced its emotive impact. When public resentment was evident at the nature of the fare produced at the Abbey Theatre, Yeats bravely shouldered the responsibility. Not everyone, including the actors, thought that the 'literary' faction should take credit for the theatre's success. In *The Fays of the Abbey Theatre*, by W. G. Fay and Catherine Carswell, the authors had this to say:

> *The Abbey Theatre was first and foremost a theatrical, not a literary movement.* It was the creation not of men of letters but of actors. . . . The Irish experiment was the exact opposite of the Norwegian. Ibsen made a theatre to suit his plays. We of the Abbey made our theatre first and then got plays to suit it, which, I venture to submit, is the natural order. . . . If we had been limited by literary or political considerations we might have done some interesting work but we should have remained parochial.
>
> (pp. 106-7)

In a later book on the *Abbey Theatre*, Gerard Fay confides the information that

> Frank Fay worked away at Yeats as though he were preparing him for an examination. He never moved far from the question of the relationship between the actor and the poet and of what the poet should demand of the actor in declamation, elocution or just plain speech. . . .
>
> Their discussions on verse-speaking led to Yeats's abandoning some extravagant ideas he had picked up on the subject. They led to Yeats's having Frank Fay's voice in mind when he wrote some of his plays.
>
> (pp. 29-30)

Of twenty-six dramatic writings in *The Collected Plays of W. B. Yeats*, published in 1952, twelve are in verse, seven in prose (but for a song or two), and four contain a mixture of verse and prose. The two modernised versions of the Oedipus tragedies of Sophocles have the choruses wholly or partly in verse, but are otherwise in prose. Yeats's last verse play, *The Death of Cuchulain* (1939), is unusual in choosing prose for the prologue only. The dominant measure for poetic drama is blank verse, except in *The Green Helmet* (1910), which he designates 'an Heroic Farce'. Here he elected to employ free 'fourteeners' (lines varying from 13 to 15 syllables) — a colloquial ballad measure, skilfully devised to link the dialogue, though the results are sometimes prosaic.

Yeats was intent on securing the most suitable rhythm for an actor's delivery, and was sufficiently flexible to be independent of the dominant medium. Poetic language performed for him a similar function to religious ritual, and he strove to re-create vividly the nature of the ceremonial he presented. some characters were regarded as more prosaic than others; but he was willing to be guided by the spirit of a producer's interpretation, especially when a situation was seen in a new light through action on the stage. His reading of Jacobean drama made it possible to write verse that, metrically alone, was distinguishable from prose. He was influenced, equally, by his collaboration with Lady Gregory in prose plays.

Of all modern poets Yeats was the most skilful in the employment of rhyme, assonance, alliteration and the other accoutrements of Elizabethan rhetoric. *On Baile's Strand* has a chorus of singing women to enact the lyrical function, which is seldom long absent from Yeats's plays:

> May this fire have driven out
> The Shape-Changers that can put
> Ruin on a great king's house
> Until all be ruinous.
> Names whereby a man has known   5
> The threshold and the hearthstone,
> Gather on the wind and drive
> The women none can kiss and thrive,
> For they are but whirling wind,
> Out of memory and mind.   10

They would make a prince decay
With light images of clay
Planted in the running wave;
Or, for many shapes they have,
They would change them into hounds   15
Until he had died of his wounds

(*Collected Plays*, p. 262)

The second and sixth lines, by deliberately jolting the rhythm, contrive to relieve the metrical monotony of the octosyllabic chant. A more unconventional device was to modulate the verse by the use of approximate, sometimes dissonant, rhymes: *out*/*put, house*/ruin*ous* (pseudo-rhyme on unstressed syllable), *known*/hearth*stone* (rhyme on secondary stress), *wind*/*mind, wave*/*have, hounds*/*wounds*. Though the classification of these types has no great significance, several pairs do revive the Elizabethan habit of eye-rhyme.

For fifteen years after the Easter rising, Yeats wrote nothing for the Abbey Theatre, but his interest in drama was sustained by a study of Japanese *Noh* drama, which resulted in *Four Plays for Dancers*, composed between 1917 and 1920, for performance in private drawing-rooms. These short, semi-mythological plays were intended for a select, but imaginative, audience; all included musicians in the cast, players of drum, zither and flute. A decorative coloured back-cloth was used, but no scenery, and the actors wore masks, designed by Edmund Dulac, to conceal facial expressions, and make the language as impersonal as possible. The function of music was to intensify the speeches at appropriate points, while rhythmic dancing filled the intervals of silence, after the oriental fashion. In this esoteric plan passion was disembodied, and all imagery symbolic; but the masque appeared bloodless in the context of human relations. The bird symbolism in the musicians' songs is of considerable importance, for birds were used 'as symbols of subjective life' (see Note on 'Calvary' in *Plays and Controversies*, p. 458). In *At the Hawk's Well* there is the bird of prey; in *The Dreaming of the Bones* the crowing of the red bird of March, and in *Calvary* the white heron. *The Only Jealousy of Emer* begins with this song:

A woman's beauty is like a white
Frail bird, like a white sea-bird alone
At daybreak after stormy night
Between two furrows upon the ploughed land: . . .
How many centuries spent
The sedentary soul
In toils of measurement
Beyond eagle or mole,
Beyond hearing or seeing,
Or Archimedes' guess

(*Collected Plays*, pp. 281-2)

In the different stages of Yeats's dramatic development, the first was Victorian; for it produced a poetic style, partly in the spirit of Morris, and partly like the exquisiteness of Bridges. Even a bardolater would not have suggested that the blank verse was entirely successful. In *Four Plays for Dancers* the stylised language supports the observation of Sean O'Faolain that Yeats 'put a barrier between himself and his fellow men by the technique that he employed' (Rodgers, *Irish Literary Portraits*, p. 4). Plays are not stageworthy, where there is no clear location, nor much attempt at subtlety of character. Writing of the feminine element in poetry, Yeats himself said that it 'comes from the lack of natural momentum in the syntax' (*Letters*, p. 710).

Such momentum was, however, achieved in the problem phase of *Wheels and Butterflies* (1934), where Yeats chose to eschew rhetoric and his Sibylline approach to language. To recuperate from an illness, the poet spent a holiday in Rapallo, where he renewed earlier contacts with Ezra Pound. He had also just read his favourite French author, Balzac, and was prepared for a more naturalistic turn of mind. *The Words upon the Window-Pane*, a play about spiritualism, is consequently the most actable of Yeats's final groups of plays. It was successfully produced, both at the Abbey Theatre, and in America, and a little resembles the plays of T. S. Eliot after *Murder in the Cathedral*.

Lady Isabella Augusta Gregory (born Persse) (1852-1932) lost her husband Sir William Gregory (thirty-five years her senior) in 1892, and produced most of her literary work after that date. A pioneer in the field of Irish dialect literature, she had reached middle age before she learnt Irish. She was the author of thirty-five plays, in addition to two in which Yeats collaborated; translated plays of Molière, Cervantes, Sudermann and Goldoni; wrote selective versions of the Old Irish classics; produced a memoir on the Abbey Theatre; kept a journal (1916 to 1930), left an unpublished autobiography, now in print, entitled *Seventy Years*, and produced other works, such as *Poets and Dreamers* (1903), which was the first of her folklore studies. Here was an active and public-spirited life, the importance of which to Irish literary history is now being appreciated. A major contribution was her adaptation of the Kiltartan dialect of Galway, as a medium for dialogue in Anglo-Irish creative writing.

The Persse family of Roxburgh came to Ireland in the time of Cromwell from Northumberland, and were members of the Anglican Church. But William Gregory's influence, as a supporter of Catholic Emancipation, probably induced Lady Gregory to become a liberal, though her manner of life remained traditionally feudal. Augusta's interest in Irish folklore and mythology had, in truth, been aroused by her Catholic nurse, Mary Sheridan, who was employed by the Persse family for forty years. Her first literary affections were for Malory and the Scottish ballads in Percy's *Reliques of Ancient Poetry*. Though an enthusiast for Home Rule, she never became an Irish scholar, in the sense that she was unable to read Old Irish or compose in the modern vernacular. In 1892 her neighbour, Edward Martyn, presented her son Robert with a grammar and an Irish Bible, from which the would-be linguists could make a beginning. After her husband's death, Lady Gregory lived at Coole during the summer months, and in a London flat for the winter. She visited the Aran Islands for the first time in the summer of 1898, when Synge was in residence on Inishmore but the writers did not then meet.

Practical-minded Lady Gregory was an admirable director of the Abbey Theatre for a quarter of a century; for she was prepared to make sacrifices of time and money, and possessed a patient and equable temperament. Her authority and directness of purpose are apparent in *Our Irish Theatre*, a delightful account of the birth of the Abbey playhouse. An amusing exchange of letters with Yeats reveals the quality of her writing:

> Mr. Yeats wrote: 'I don't think you need be anxious about next year's theatre. . . . I have found a greatly increased friendliness on the part of some of the younger men here. In a battle like Ireland's, which is one of poverty against wealth, one must prove one's sincerity by making oneself unpopular to wealth. One must accept the baptism of the gutter. Have not all teachers done the like?' I answered that I preferred the baptism of clean water. I was troubled by the misunderstanding of friends.
>
> (Op. cit., p. 71)

The second chapter of the memoir contains lively pen-portraits of Lady Gregory's guarantors, Sir Frederick Burton, John O'Leary, W. H. Lecky and Douglas Hyde.

The most valuable part of the book is the record of Lady Gregory's own play-writing, which began with 'bits of dialogue' for Yeats, when he needed words that had 'the ring of daily life'. The earliest plays of Yeats to which she contributed were *Cathleen Ni Houlihan* (in which for three nights she played the lead), *The Pot of Broth* and *Where There is Nothing*, subsequently rewritten by Yeats as *The Unicorn from the Stars*. In later years Yeats was less appreciative of her work than he ought to have been, for she also contributed to five other plays, *The Hour-Glass*, *The King's Threshold*, *On Baile's Strand*, *The Shadowy Waters* and *Deirdre*; wrote scenarios for some of the plays of Hyde, and lent a helping hand in the Hanrahan stories of Yeats, on one of which Hyde's *The Twisting of the Rope* was founded.

Verse plays, which demanded closer audience attention to the language, were mainly the task of Yeats to provide. Lady Gregory felt it her function to comply with the popular desire for comedy; her plays were applauded as a relaxation, and were more influential than those of Yeats and Synge. Her short comedies were esteemed for liveliness by nearly all the critics. Yet she wished to disown her first venture, *Twenty-Five*, on the ground of sentimentality; for she tried to base all her writing on personal experience, and observed that romantic love was not a characteristic trait of the Irish. It should be borne in mind, however, that Lady Gregory was in her fiftieth year when she made her debut as a dramatist. The influence of Molière on her dramatic style was important; but she disapproved of the epithet 'farce', when applied to *Spreading the News* or *The Rising of the Moon*. Farce (she told Yeats) 'is comedy with character left out'; and to this he responded that melodrama is 'tragedy with passion left out' (see *Our Irish Theatre*, p. 106).

Spreading the News was performed at the opening of the Abbey Theatre in December 1904, and printed in *Seven Short Plays*, which she dedicated to Yeats in 1909. Like most of the plays in this volume, this is a comedy of humours, in the spirit of Ben Jonson and French taste; its Fair scene is laid in Cloon, which represented the town of Gort, only a few miles from Coole Park. Even more farcical is *Hyacinth Halvey* (1906), with a modicum of Shavian wit and improbability. Nowadays it seems juvenile to assume that country townsmen are so gullible. The technical skill and verisimilitude of the dialogue were what attracted Yeats. The dialect of the Kiltartan parish was soon accepted on the Dublin and London stages as thoroughly representative of the speech of western Ireland, where the typical peasantry undoubtedly lived. Kiltartanese appears, perhaps, to best advantage in *The Workhouse Ward* (1908) based upon the author's experience as a social worker; in it there is a considerable advance in the development of character.

MRS DONOHOE. Fair enough, fair enough. A wide lovely house I have; a few acres of grass land . . . the grass does be very sweet that grows among the stones. And as to the sea, there is something from it every day of the year, a handful of periwinkles to make kitchen, or cockles maybe. There is many a thing in the sea is not decent, but cockles is fit to put before the Lord!

MIKE McINERNEY. You have all that! And you without ere a man in the house?

MRS DONOHOE. It is what I am thinking, yourself might come and keep me company. It is no credit to me a brother of my own to be in this place at all. . . .

MIKE McINERNEY. . . . I'd like well to draw anear you. My heavy blessing on you, Honor Donohoe, for the hand you have held out to me this day.

MRS DONOHOE. Sure you could be keeping the fire in, and stirring the pot with the bit of Indian meal for the hens, and milking the goat and taking the tacklings off the donkey at the door; and maybe putting out the cabbage plants in their time. For when the old man died the garden died.

MIKE McINERNEY. I could to be sure, and be cutting the potatoes for seed. What luck could there be in a place and a man not to be in it? Is that now a suit a clothes you have brought with you?

MRS DONOHOE. It is so, the way you will be tasty coming in among the neighbours of Curranroe.

(*Collected Plays,* vol. I, *The Comedies*, pp. 101-2)

The excellence of Lady Gregory's comedies lies in their construction, her instinctive knowledge of the balance of parts that makes a sometimes frivolous play stageworthy. Many comic characters resemble fictional types found in the novels of Charles Lever and Samuel Lover; but most are based on the author's observation, tinged with the snobbery of her attitude towards them. Lady Gregory's humanity does ensure sympathy for all she creates; but imaginative depth was reserved for the more ambitious forms of drama.

In the Coole Edition of Lady Gregory's plays, edited by Ann Saddlemyer, the writings occupy four volumes: I Comedies, II Tragedies and Tragi-comedies, III Wonder and Supernatural plays, and IV Translations, Adaptations and Collaborations. The plays of three acts have not, in general, been as successful in production as the shorter curtain-raisers, a possible reason being that expansive talk tends to halt, rather than advance, the action. In whatever form she adopted, Lady Gregory was pre-eminently a myth-maker, who had learnt the importance of reaching a dramatic climax through ingenious or amusing situations. Her 'wonder and supernatural' plays, such as *The Golden Apple* (1920) and *Aristotle's Bellows* (1921), have paradoxically an air of reality, in spite of her imaginings. Though the prose language of these faery plays is not visible for verse drama, there are scenes which evoke as much poetry as Maeterlinck's *Blue Bird*.

Lady Gregory being an outspoken adherent of Home Rule, nationalism could not be kept out of her plays, especially the historical ones; she hoped the latter might prove serviceable for educational purposes. *The White Cockade* (1905), which is classified by Saddlemyer as a tragicomedy, reveals a mastery of dialogue and character unexcelled in her repertoire. The theme is James II's unheroic escape after the Battle of the Boyne. Legends of the Stuart kings she had gleaned from 'wise old neighbours who sit in wide chimney-nooks by turf fires' (*Collected Plays*, II, p. 301), as well as from songs circulating in Connemara. To *The White Cockade* she appended the following note:

> In these days, when so much of the printed history we were taught as children is being cast out by scholars, we must refill the vessel by calling in tradition, or if need be our imaginings. When my *White Cockade* was first produced I was pleased to hear that J. M. Synge had said my method had made the writing of historical drama again possible.
>
> (*Collected Plays*, II, p. 303)

The hero of this play is Patrick Sarsfield, Earl of Lucan, an idealist whose resourceful conduct after the battle was in contrast to the stark cowardice of the Stuart king. The white feather of the royal cockade was probably intended as a symbolic feature. But the character who steals the limelight on the stage is Mrs Kelleher, whose proverbial sallies provide the liveliest and most inventive speeches of the comedy. *The White Cockade* has a distinct kinship with the plays of Shaw. Only the regional characters employ the Kiltartan dialect consistently.

Lady Gregory's preference for folk plays was natural, if she was to give this language its fullest scope; she consequently considered *The Image* (1909) the best of her dramatic writings. Yeats, on the other hand, found the play tedious, because lacking in her usually crisp dialogue. There was a theory behind the title which held that everyone has a 'heart-secret' acting as a spur to the quality of his life, so long as the dream is not made known to his acquaintances. Once divulged to the world, it loses potency; for every image crumbles 'at the touch of reality' (*The Image*, p. 296). Without making her own dream explicit, Lady Gregory hoped that a new Ireland would rise up 'out of the foundations of the old, with love and not hate as its inspiration' (p. 297). What happens when a private dream is noised abroad is illustrated in the following dialogue:

> HOSTY. Well, it's the people of Munster are taken up in themselves with pride and with conceit! My joy that I was not reared among them, but in the bright beautiful province of Connacht!
>
> MRS COPPINGER. Let you keep your great praises of Connacht and your talk for them are the other side of the earth and cannot see into it, as I myself can see it over the mering wall, and the fields that are all a flag, and the thistles as hardy as our own and as bold. It is not here I myself would wish to stop, in a narrow barren place, where you never would get your fill of the world's joy. It's out to America I would go, and a fair wind blowing!
>
> HOSTY. I know well what it is you are dreaming to find before you in the States — beer from Denmark, honey out of Greece; rings and brooches and such things as are dear to women; high blood and grandeur and ringing of bells; a silver cushion having four edges, and you sitting on it through the day time the same as the Queen of Pride, and talking of the ways of the world and the war! But remember now I was in America one time myself!
>
> (p. 138)

Truth to life was unfortunately sought through volubility of the characters, rather than through the technique of suggestion. The pathos of the play consequently turns on a dreamer's waywardness, that of Malachi Naughton, the 'mountainy' man from the Connacht border, whose personality hints at the sadness of human separateness. In Irish comedy such a character is never at a loss.

The Kiltartan dialect was not altogether a satisfactory

medium for Lady Gregory's heroic plays, which Ann Saddlemyer calls tragedies. The most ambitious of the five were *Kincora* (1905) and *Grania* (1912); both are well constructed plays, and *Kincora* was the first historical drama performed at the Abbey Theatre. Its moral is the disastrous effect of divided loyalty. The prose speeches are sometimes flamboyant, and critical opinion tends to regard the play as melodrama, rather than tragedy. Yet in the persons of Gormleith and Grania, Lady Gregory created two of the most complex heroic figures of the Irish stage. Gormleith is conceived on the lines of Lady Macbeth, while the character of Brian Boru, the High King, carries suggestions of Alfred the Great; the dramatic climax of the play is the trial of the rebels in Act II.

The first draft of *Kincora* was tightened in 1909 to give the plot greater tragic cohesion; but the Coole edition preserves the original scenes in an appendix, and this enables the reader to understand the Queen's frustrations, which were partly due to her earlier marriage to a Dane. The tortured character of Gormleith is revealed in her conviction, not only that Brian's desire for peace in Ireland through asceticism, was illusory, but that his reliance upon the word of unknown prophets had become an outmoded superstition. The most effective use of Kiltartan speech is to be found in the dialogue of lesser figures, such as Brennain, Phelan and Rury.

Grania proved to be the most controversial of Lady Gregory's full-length plays, in reducing the cast to the three characters concerned in the love triangle; it never appeared on the stage for the possibly evasive reason that the author was unable to engage actors to her liking. Character limitation meant that the lovers had constantly to explain their own motives. The result was a problem play. The theme was Diarmuid's divided allegiance, for he had compacted with Finn, his chief, to observe a bond of compulsive chastity, which embittered all three parties. The runaway pair was required to send Finn an unbroken loaf every month, as a token of their trustworthiness. When this bond was broken, almost accidentally, Finn tracked Diarmuid down, and caused his death. The surprising *volte face* in Grania's affections is the real crisis of the drama; she demands the restoration of her original betrothal, and execrates Diarmuid for his unnatural coldness.

Grania is therefore a powerful psychological study, which departs from the original tale only in dispensing with the supernatural element. The problem starts in the first Act, with the betrothal itself:

> GRANIA. I asked the old people what love was, and they gave me no good news of it at all. Three sharp blasts of the wind they said it was, a white blast of delight and a grey blast of discontent and a third blast of jealousy that is red.
>
> FINN. That red blast is the wickedest of the three.
>
> GRANIA. I would never think jealousy to be so bad a smart.
>
> FINN. It is a bad thing for whoever knows it. If love is to lie down on a bed of stinging nettles, jealousy is to waken upon a wasp's nest.
>
> GRANIA. But the old people say more again about love. They say there is no good thing to be gained without hardship and pain, such as a child to be born, or a long day's battle won. And I think it might be a pleasing thing to have a lover that would go through fire for your sake.
>
> (*Collected Plays*, II, pp. 15-16)

Grania is a feminist, living in a world governed by men, and acts as she does in order to shape her own destiny. Irish tradition did not take kindly to her infidelity, even to denying her both stature and beauty.

Lady Gregory, however, solved one of the problems of historical drama and fiction. She understood that no one can reconstruct the minds and motives of historical persons without distortion. It has proved wiser and more practical for a writer to project the thinking of his or her own time back into the past, and so create characters that live, whimsical though they sometimes appear to be. George Bernard Shaw's *St Joan* is a fine example.

Shaw was not given to compliments, but described Lady Gregory as 'the greatest living Irishwoman'. Her most impressive achievement, after the organisation and virtual management of the Abbey Theatre, was the influence she exerted on the future of Irish drama. The folk-spirit was largely her creation, as was the stage-dialect that went with it, with all the beauties of rhythm and characteristic repetitions of phrase. Though the three seasons of the Irish Literary Theatre lasted only a week apiece, their impact on the writing of genuinely Irish plays, and a more natural style of acting, was immense. The conversational tone of Lady Gregory's plays was germane to the peasant way of life, as well as to the new literate class, for Irishmen were renowned as great talkers. Above all, she held doggedly to her faith in the small theatre for its merits in sustaining dramatic illusion.

The language tradition handed on by Lady Gregory to J. M. Synge (1871-1909) in 1898 grew out of her adaptation, rather than translation, of the legends of *Cuchulain of Muirthemne*. Synge, who was the son of a Dublin lawyer, read for a degree in Gaelic and History at Trinity College, while taking violin lessons in order to become a musician. To this end he lived first in Germany, then in Paris; but an inborn restlessness took him as far afield as Italy, because of an interest in Petrarch, Boccaccio and Dante. He spent five years on the Continent and became a competent linguist, thus being able to earn a living as a teacher of English and German. He was so nervous a performer on the violin that he abandoned music for French and Breton literature. When Yeats met Synge in Paris, he did not know that his Irish acquaintance had only another decade to live. He advised Synge to give up the precarious existence he was leading and study the life of the Aran islanders, for which his knowledge of Gaelic had prepared him. As it turned out, this knowledge was largely academic; but Synge had already mixed with vernacular speakers, when he met peasants of County Wicklow, as a young member of the Dublin Naturalists Field Club.

There is no body of Anglo-Irish dramatic work as unified as the group of plays which Synge left; they should not, however, be separated from the other prose writings, now available in the four-volume Oxford edition of the *Collected*

Works (1961-8), edited by R. Skelton. Autobiographical notes tell how a young man from a Protestant family, which had produced five bishops, became an agnostic at the age of seventeen; Synge deliberately sought isolation from relatives and friends, because he had no wish to debate his private convictions. His introspective nature found comfort in Wordsworth's poetry; but his own early verse is full of disillusionment. Synge visited the Aran Islands in the summer months of five successive years (1898-1902); his total stay was, however, only four and a half months, during which he made copious notes, and collected anecdotes and observations. When *The Aran Islands* was published in 1907, Synge acknowledged some indebtedness to Pierre Loti's *Pecheur d'Islande*, an analogous study on the peasant life of the Bretons.

The Aran Islands, as Synge pointed out, is indispensable to an understanding of the attitudes, beliefs and spiritual values of the plays' characters, though *Riders to the Sea* is the only one located on Aran. The people he made the basis of his art were primitive in their pursuits. The emotional involvement of a poet in the making shows itself in the impressive phrasing of Synge's dialogue. He sought to make the language used symbolic of a cosmic pattern, which he took to be the foundation of myth. Infinite pains were taken to express accurately the traditional elements of this community of fishermen. As a man trained in the thought processes of western civilisation, with its conventional values, Synge was concerned in *Riders to the Sea* to understand what made the islanders stoically resigned, even while they felt insecure. His mission, he told Yeats, was to 'unite asceticism, stoicism and ecstasy', because he felt that these three qualities had never yet come together in literature. ('The Cutting of an Agate', *Essays and Introductions*, p. 308).

Synge's reaction to the legendary past, as re-created in AE's poems and paintings, and Yeats's *The Shadowy Waters*, was characteristic. In 1904 he wrote to his friend Stephen MacKenna:

> I do not believe in the possibility of 'a purely fantastic, unmodern, ideal, breezy, springdayish, Cuchulanoid

National Theatre' ... No drama can grow out of anything other than the fundamental realities of life. ... I think the law-maker is tending to reduce Ireland ... to dismal, morbid hypocrisy. On the other hand I feel of course the infinitely sweet and healthy piety of a great deal of Irish life.

(Greene and Stephens, *J. M. Synge*, pp. 157-8)

Before the Aran period, Synge's life had been that of a would-be artist drifting without much purpose. In his first three plays the gods he seemed to invoke were the over-mastering forces of nature; they were quite as important to him as leading characters; they meant more than the spirit of nationalism, which Synge regarded as *hubris*. Their aspect might be fierce or brutal, joyous or benign; the mood is indicated by descriptive images whose power is felt, rather than understood. It is difficult to assign names to Synge's effects upon audiences of mixed sensibilities. Sardonic humour in the comic scenes is full of tragic irony, mingled with a grimness of intent that few city-dwellers would be able to appreciate; for they do not live in closest contact with nature. In the plays of Synge there is therefore no room for sentiment, and little for dramatic conflict; the dominant note is awe and acceptance of the unforeseen. A mind so ascetic and watchful as this is not moved by the consolation of philosophy. Synge's concept of pagan stoicism in characterisation would have been approved by Aristotle.

Synge was, indeed, the living exemplar of Lady Gregory's notion of the 'heart-secret'. Though a compassionate person-ality, he was so withdrawn that he had difficulty in getting to know the kind of Irishmen in whom he was interested. His acquired taste for French realism led him to choose characters that suited his mode of expression. The paradox of his prose style is that the tone of the dialect is poetic; the rhythm has a cadence more Latin than English, and the intonation needed should have a musical note. Synge is never as prosaic as Lady Gregory; nor has his language a special location, like Kiltartanese. The actors took time to accommodate to the archaic flavour, and the idiomatic inversions of syntax; for Synge's originality lay mainly in his close attention to idiom.

Novels and plays had already been written about Irish peasant life, which Daniel O'Connell thought to be the finest in Europe; but no one before Synge had so clear a vision of its dignity and composure. Success was due to his ability to transform the local into the universal; there is no sense of historical time to distract in his portrayal of peasant characters; they are valid for the heroic age as for modern times. What Synge communicates is their toughness to survive, or their resignation to accept the inevitable. They complain often, but an almost aristocratic spirit forbids them to quit. Yeats and Synge seem agreed that 'the sentimental mind is found among the middle class' (*Plays and Controversies*, p. 146).

There was a particular class of self-sufficient peasantry that Synge favoured, foot-loose tinkers, pedlars, herdsmen, beggars and the like. They accord with his romantic realism, and with the streak of violence incorporated in the plays. Years of vagabondage in Germany, France and Ireland had brought him into contact with life in the raw. The most attractive feature of Synge's individualism is dedication to the purity of art; in this he was especially moved by the works of Hauptmann, Racine and Anatole France.

A perverse criticism has argued that Synge invented a language that no Irishman ever spoke. Did the speech of Jacobean Englishmen resemble that which Shakespeare attributed to Hamlet, Othello or Lear? Synge's dialect did what it was intended to do — it depicts truthfully the culture of a small community living in isolation. The islanders were Anglo-Irish in the true sense that they were more bilingual than Synge himself, as the following passage shows:

Some of them express themselves more correctly than the ordinary peasant, others use the Gaelic idioms continually and substitute 'he' or 'she' for 'it,' as the neuter pronoun is not found in modern Irish.

A few of the men have a curiously full vocabulary, others know only the commonest words in English, and are driven to ingenious devices to express their meaning. . . .

Foreign languages are another favourite topic, and as these men are bilingual they have a fair notion of what it means to speak and think in many different idioms. Most of the strangers they see on the islands are philological students, and the people have been led to conclude that linguistic studies, particularly Gaelic studies, are the chief occupation of the outside world.

(*Four Plays and The Aran Islands*, p. 170)

Between 1903 and his death Synge wrote six plays, all, except *The Tinker's Wedding*, being produced at the Abbey Theatre. *In the Shadow of the Glen* was the first of these, a short tragicomedy based on a tale Synge had heard from Pat Dirane on Inishmaan; the setting is, however, an isolated small-holding in the Wicklow hills, where rain, mist and bog exert a depressing effect upon the inhabitants. Synge brilliantly captures the spirit of this place through the talk of four characters, but especially that of the leading figures Nora Burke and the Tramp. The latter has the role of an admonishing stranger in the home. His unconventional discourse with the husband, who has feigned to be dead in order to spy on his sex-starved wife, is a splendid example of the author's grim humour:

TRAMP *doubtfully*: Is it not dead you are?

DAN: How would I be dead, and I as dry as a baked bone, stranger?

TRAMP *pouring out the whisky*: What will herself say if she smells the stuff on you, for I'm thinking it's not for nothing you're letting on to be dead?

DAN: It is not, stranger; but she won't be coming near me at all, and it's not long now I'll be letting on, for I've a cramp in my back, and my hip's asleep on me, and there's been the devil's own fly itching my nose. It's near dead I was wanting to sneeze, and you blathering about the rain, and Darcy (*bitterly*) — the devil choke him — and the towering church. *Crying out impatiently*. Give me that whisky. Would you have herself come back before I taste a drop at all?

(*Plays and Poems*, pp. 86-7)

Only the sensitive but hardy Tramp is not overcome by the sinisister gloom of the glen's surroundings; his earthy wisdom resembles that of a wandering pilgrim. The final lines of the play are characteristic of Synge's ironic method with the folk-tale. The wronged husband is seen sharing a drink with Michael, perhaps realising that his young neighbour is the seduced party. The play is a fine demonstration of comic effects in Synge's puritanical frustrations, his melancholy attitude to ageing, and his unerring response to nature.

Short as *Riders to the Sea* is, there is justifiable comparison with Greek tragedy in the play's archetypal inevitability and lyrical power. There is also an undoubted likeness to the *Hippolytus* of Euripides; the Sea resembles the god Poseidon (Irish Manannán), to whom Bartley's death is ascribed. The mythological background is of great significance, and so is the wailing of women, who perform the function of the Chorus in Greek drama. The priest has a comparatively minor effect upon the play's morality, and helps to suggest the blend of pagan and Christian elements characteristic of the superstitions of Irish peasantry. Though the high incidence of death by drowning was due to the inability of most islanders to swim, fatalism decreed that the Sea should not be cheated of its 'riders'. Keening became an awe-inspiring accompaniment of burial, and was a cry of rage, as well as of despair.

Synge claimed that he introduced few words that he had not actually heard spoken. But there is obvious selectivity in his careful choice of language, subconsciously derived from his reading of Loti. Here are citations taken at random from *Riders to the Sea*:

> CATHLEEN: Is the sea bad by the white rocks, Nora?
> NORA: Middling bad, God help us. There's a great roaring in the west, and it's worse it'll be getting when the tide's turned to the wind. *She goes over to the table with the bundle*. Shall I open it now? . . .
> CATHLEEN: Give me the ladder, and I'll put them up in the turf loft, the way she won't know of them at all, and maybe when the tide turns she'll be going down to see would he be floating from the east. . . .
> MAURYA: It's a great rest I'll have now, and great sleeping in the long nights after Samhain, if it's only a bit

of wet flour we do have to eat, and maybe a fish that would be stinking. . . . Michael has a clean burial in the far north, by the grace of the Almighty God. Bartley will have a fine coffin out of the white boards, and a deep grave surely. What more can we want than that? No man at all can be living for ever, and we must be satisfied.

(Plans and Poems, pp. 96-7 and 105-6)

Though written in prose, this is scanable free verse, with a predominantly falling rhythm, notwithstanding the likeness to blank verse of the first line. Stressed syllables are so disposed and balanced with unstressed ones that comparison with musical composition is hinted.

Synge's most distinguished, but contentious, drama was *The Playboy of the Western World* (1907), a work complex in motivation, but simple in design. He said it was written to please himself, and intended as an extravaganza, preserving it from farce by serious episodes. His delight in rollicking and outlandish behaviour points to the influence of Rabelais, Molière, Cervantes and the Elizabethan comic dramatists. *The Playboy*'s language was too outrageous for the taste of members of the Gaelic League, and stormy scenes accompanied first productions in Dublin and America. Its later success before more mature audiences was due to the play's remarkable vitality. Synge wrote in his Preface:

In a good play every speech should be as fully flavoured as a nut or apple, and such speeches cannot be written by any one who works among people who have shut their lips on poetry.

(Plays and Poems, p. 175)

Church-going Irishmen were greatly offended by Synge's constant use of sacred and profane utterances in the dialogue. Although he made more than fifty changes to the original text, Synge retained references to events in the New Testament, and ignored warnings to mitigate his anti-clericalism. Press critics accused him of exaggerating eccentricities of the peasant class, and of traducing the character of Irish women; they were not placated when he reported amazement at the comic diversity of life beyond the River

Shannon. Since the Spanish Armada, the Irish had often defied the Ascendancy government by sheltering fugitive criminals; there was thus nothing extraordinary about a group of flighty women who regarded parricide as heroism. The first Act of *The Playboy* was accepted as farcical, but Dublin audiences were not objective enough to tolerate the roguishness that followed. The violence of the last Act proved the Achilles heel of the play; yet no voice was raised against the *volte face* of Pegeen, after the romantic love-scene with Christy, nor against the felony of Widow Quin, whose Elizabethan gusto at one stage nearly stole the play. Christy alone seemed capable of character development, starting with shallow vanity, and ending in self-assurance.

The ambivalence of *The Playboy*'s ironies was probably designed to keep the responses of a critical audience constantly on the alert. Was this, perhaps, why the play was later included in the Surrealist Manifesto (see Owen Quinn, *Envoy* III, 11, 1950) Synge ended all attempts to classify the play by insisting that a work of art needs no author-elucidation. Yeats and Lady Gregory made it clear that their theatre would not yield to attempts at play-censorship by mob disapproval.

Synge's colourful language was a composite dialect consisting of Wicklow, Kerry and Galway elements, though the scene of the play was laid in north Mayo. The following examples are arranged under five heads.

1. *Indigenous words: Creel* cart (one with detachable sides); *loy* (long-handled light spade); *poteen* (whisky illegally distilled from potatoes); *drouthy* thirsty); *streeleen* (light conversation); *banbhs* (piglets); *priesteen* (dimin: minor priest); *shebeen* (low-class wayside inn); *cnuceen* (hillock); I just *riz* the loy (raised); *thraneen* (shred); *cleeve* (basket); *turbary* (right to cut turf); *gob* (face); *felts* (fieldfares); *boreen* (small path or track); *cockshot-man* (aunt Sally at the Fair); *skelping* (whipping); *parlatic* (paralytic); *paters* (paternosters); *drift* (group, collection).

2. *Vernacular phrases*: the *scruff* of the hill (rough slope just below the crown); in the *gripe* of the ditch (belly); *penny potboy* (menial attendant at an inn); I'm *destroyed*

walking (exhausted); *famished* with the cold (nearly dead); a *bona fide* (genuine traveller, who might be served after licensed hours); the *butt* of his tail-pocket (bottom); *scribes* of bog (strips for peat-cutting); a *gaudy* officer (member of the uniformed militia); you've *a power* of rings (plenty); she'd be *stringing gabble* till the dawn of day (chattering); *grass* tobacco (dried, but not cured); *mitch off* (to desert or steal away); *whisht* your talking (be silent); a *lier on walls* (probably a 'lounge-lizard'); you'll meet the wisest old men, I tell you, *at the corner of my wheel* (while I am spinning); a man can't hang *by his own informing* (on his own evidence); *winkered* mule (blinkered); *old hen* (influenza); a *gallous* story (gallows).

3. *Idiomatic constructions:* You're *wanting*, maybe (wanted); It's a safe house, *so* (then); there's a sprinkling ∧ have done that among the holy Luthers of the preaching north (omission of subject relative); hanged his dog *from* the licence (to avoid paying); the naked parish where I *grew* a man (grew up to be); the rusted poison did corrode his blood the way he never *overed it* (got over).

4. *Other folk peculiarities*: I never left my own parish till Tuesday *was a week* (a week ago); sit down now while you're quiet *till* you talk with me (and talk); *Amn't I after* holding out with the patience of a martyred saint (haven't I been); you'll have great times *from this out* (in future).

5. *Oaths, imprecations and salutations*: May I meet him *with one tooth*; I will, *by the elements and stars of night*; God *increase* you!

Synge's other dramatic works, *The Tinker's Wedding, The Well of Saints* and *Deirdre of the Sorrows*, illuminate, if they do not expand, his methods. The good-humoured agnosticism of the first prevented the play's performance in Dublin during the author's lifetime. Michael Byrne and Sarah Casey were an admirable couple for exhibiting Synge's gift of flyting dialogue, one butt being the Chaucerian priest, who was reluctant to marry them for the modest fee of half a sovereign. The squalid humour of this comedy is both daring and restrained.

A rumbustious style serves to differentiate the tinkers' play from *The Well of Saints*, a static drama, in which the protagonists are a cripple and a blind man. Wildness of language had here to be curbed in the interests of verbal accuracy, which is helped by carefully detailed stage directions. The sacred settlement of Glendalough was the scene of this play, and its time the early nineteenth century. This Ibsenesque fable was designed to explore the existential effects of illusion and reality upon the personality of deprived individuals, who have lived in intimacy, either through marriage or other circumstances. Synge delicately captures the fantasies and ironies, especially of physical relationships; he shows skilfully that the heart is superior to the mind in gaining the mutual respect of such persons.

The last play, *Deirdre of the Sorrows*, is unique, not in being tragic wholly, but in the style which made it suitable for a well-known interpreter. This was Molly Allgood, whose stage name was Maire O'Neill, and whom the author intended to marry. The play was not completed to Synge's satisfaction before his death; but a version was agreed upon by Yeats, Lady Gregory and Miss Allgood, who directed it at the Abbey Theatre in 1910. It was then published by the Cuala Press, though differing considerably from Synge's manu-script drafts. The authentic text, edited by Ann Saddlemyer, is published in Skelton's Oxford edition of the *Works*. Act III was revised by Synge no less than eight times. One major difficulty was the language of the dialogue, which consider-ably modified vernacular Irish. T. S. Eliot said that his plays were written to find a language in which verse would be hardly distinguishable from prose; Synge had attempted the reverse. But because the legendary material was aristocratic in origin, he found it necessary to compromise by intro-ducing two characters of an intermediate social class, namely Lavarcham and Owen. Poetic prose is spoken throughout by Deirdre and her equals; in its sentences the stress is equally distributed to secure a rhythmical balance, giving the effect of free verse. Synge achieved remarkable results in modulat-ing the tempo of rhythms to avoid monotony; but there is none the less a loss of dramatic vigour in his transformation of narrative into epical or lyrical terms. That the rhythmical structure may be compatible with metrical lines is shown in the following random selections, where the units are separately indicated:

DEIRDRE: Wóods of Cúan, wóods of Cúan,
deár coúntry of the eást!
It's séven yéars we've had a life was jóy
                                        ónly,
and thís dáy we're góing wést,
thís dáy we're fácing deáth, máybe,
and deáth should be a póor, untídy thíng,
thoúgh it's a qúeen that diés.

LAVARCHAM: And yét you'd do wéll to be góing to your
                                        dún,
and nót putting sháme on her meéting
                                the Hígh Kíng,
and shé seámed and swéaty and in greát
                                        disórder
from the dúst of mány róads.
Áh, Cónchubor, my lád, beáuty goes
                        quíckly in the wóods,
and yoú'd lét a gréat gásp, I téll you,
if you sét your éyes this níght on Deírdre.
                        (*Plays and Poems*, pp. 258 and 260)

Each of the above units contains three to six stressed syllables, though the rhythm is somewhat different in the two speeches. The familiar tone of the second is underlined by the phrase *my lad* in addressing the high king. Many subtleties, such as this, are to be found in the talk of Lavarcham and Owen, designed to prevent the dialogue from becoming mannered.

In the *Antigone* of Sophocles, as in Synge's play, the dominant note of the heroine's character is resignation. The classical influence upon the spirit of Synge's plays is always near the surface, and was probably due to his admiration for Racine, and to the range of his translations. But the classical element of piety is replaced by egotism in *Deirdre of the Sorrows*, one result being an absence of dramatic tension in the conduct of the leading character. Moral dignity worthy of tragedy is also wanting in the male figures.

The peasant life which Synge made the substance of most

plays was not, indeed, ennobling; disadvantages were bigotry, superstition and sometimes defiance of the moral law; these the liberal agnosticism of the playwright was compelled to notice. According to Synge, the writer who never left Ireland inherited a narrowness of outlook from which it was difficult to escape. Ireland he visualised as 'the soul's dark cottage', battered by the ignorance of the masses, and this he was unable to contemplate philosophically. He was not, in fact, a philosopher, but an aesthete, in the healthy sense. Uneasiness of mind concerning patriotic self-sufficiency haunted all his plays; he spoke boldly about the crippling effects upon the mind of dishonesty, dependence and self-deception.

The first dramatist to advance from the lower classes through self-education was Sean O'Casey (1880-1964), who was born in Dublin, the youngest of thirteen children, eight of whom died in childhood. He was brought up in the Protestant faith by his widowed mother; his *Autobiographies* in two volumes vividly reflect the slum environment out of which his writing arose. The impoverished family lived in one of the many Georgian tenement houses in the north of Dublin, during a period when the population of the city numbered about a quarter of a million. Until his forty-fifth year O'Casey was a manual labourer, whose longest employment was with the Irish Railways, in whose service he helped Jim Larkin, an eloquent labour leader, to found the Transport Workers Union. The harsh circumstances of his youth made O'Casey an avowed socialist, which he remained for the rest of his life; but his ultimate position resembled that of Ruskin, rather than of Marx.

O'Casey learnt and taught Irish with the Gaelic League, and became Secretary of the new Irish Citizens' Army, about which he wrote his first book. This movement resulted from one of the writer's bitterest experiences, the eight-months' lock-out of striking employees in 1913. The flag of this army, designed by AE, consisted of a plough and seven stars on a blue background; during the subsequent unrest there was considerable rivalry between it and the tricolour of the Irish nationalists, consisting of green, white and orange perpendicular panels. O'Casey the trade unionist became disillusioned when the labour cause was ousted by the nationalist movement; for political power in Ireland then passed to the new bourgeois middle-class, which replaced that of the English Ascendancy, and allièd itself with the Catholic Church.

Among O'Casey's most formative influences were the plays of Shakespeare, contained in his late father's small collection of books, and the Authorised Version of the English Bible, from which his mother taught him; both figure prominently in the plays. For some years he himself taught at a local Sunday school. Occasional recreations were visits to the theatre, where the fare provided included Shakespeare, but consisted largely of the plays of Dion Boucicault (1820-90), such as *The Colleen Bawn* and *The Shaugraun*. The latter impressed O'Casey tremendously, when at the age of fifteen he played the part of Father Dolan, the priest who patriotically sheltered a Fenian rebel. From 1926, when O'Casey was awarded the Hawthornden Prize for *Juno and the Paycock*, he chose to live in England; principal reasons were the Dublin riot over his play *The Plough and the Stars* and the rejection of his new play, *The Silver Tassie*, by the Abbey Theatre directors. O'Casey was in his forty-seventh year before he earned sufficient money to marry.

The dramatist was proud of his origins and social affiliations, and was therefore out of sympathy with directors of the Abbey Theatre, with the exception of Lady Gregory, who encouraged his talent, and welcomed him as an equal at Coole Park. She and Yeats freely acknowledged that *The Shadow of a Gunman* filled the Abbey Theatre to capacity for the first time, that *Juno and the Paycock* not only proved the outstanding success of that theatre, but even rehabilitated the finances at a time when it was near bankruptcy. O'Casey was, however, alienated by the growing antagonism of a public that hated his outspoken realism, especially when he chastised or satirised Irish inconstancy, as well as the irresponsibility of the people. Throughout his life, the dramatist possessed a capacity for the grotesque as a source of tragedy; but Irish critics persisted in claiming that the plays of his middle and last periods were formless.

O'Casey's asceticism and fiery imagination were seen at

their highest potential when he handled Irish scenes, in which the motivations were understood perfectly. When he chose voluntary exile, he carried his Irish pugnacity of mind with him. In *The Flying Wasp* (1937) he fell foul of the English stage and its critics; but the battle here was on aesthetic, rather than national and religious grounds, for this suited him better. This book and the correspondence show that he could be perverse and obstinate in critical attitudes, but was seldom arrogant. Wilfulness of judgement is, indeed, a comic feature of the Hogarthian characters in his Dublin plays, where he revealed himself as a brilliant manipulator of the language the Irish proletariat used.

In England O'Casey wrote ten full-length plays and several shorter ones of the morality type; their inspiration came partly from Shakespeare's final romances, and partly from the Bible or the Gaelic past. He was at his best only when the experiences of four decades in Dublin moved him. He saw the half-literate city-dweller as the unconscious victim of exploit-ation by powerful groups, including the church. Sympathy and anger were spontaneous reactions to the historical events that overtook his people between 1913 and 1923. How could the class war be won by men of known improvidence, yet rife with materialistic self-interest? The redeeming feature, for O'Casey, was the loyalty and devotion of Dublin's hard-working mothers and wives, whom he modelled on his own mother. The positive actions of the men in the Abbey Theatre plays are few, and full of the irony of social tragedy.

Being of western stock from the county of Limerick, O'Casey enjoyed the use of forceful language, as a means of dramatic tension in tragicomedy; his comic effects are Aristophanic, rather than Boucicaultian. The reader needs to skim the crudities, in order to enjoy the rich and vital energy of O'Casey's imagery. The garrulous fantasists of his plays seem devoid of political commonsense or social respon-sibility; the belly-laughter and frequent invocations of the Deity and the Virgin Mary mask the innate gloom of their vacuous existence. Iterative verbalisms, which critics have deprecated, were symbols of O'Casey's stock types, to be seen all over Dublin; they do not disturb one's appreciation of the poetry that invariably colours O'Casey's dialogue. His control of language is a delight to those who value, as he did, the creative power of words; he risks much to keep the spirit of his plays alive. When in 1957 the BBC broadcast a selection from his plays, this is what he wrote:

> I have always aimed at bringing emotion and imagination on to the stage, in the shapes of song, dance, dialogue, and scene; each mingling with the other, as life does, for life is never rigid. . . . The intellectual has to live through the commoner nature of man, has to move through the seasons, has to sweat in the sun, shiver in the frost, has to work while it is yet day. . . . Imagination is a far geater power in the drama than intellect of the highest. . . . Intellect can never banish emotion from the theatre, for emotion is deep within us and round us everywhere. . . . We shouldn't be afraid of the fanciful, for it is a gay part of life, and, after all, even the poorest play is fancy-bred.
>
> (*Blasts and Benedictions*, pp. 83-4)

O'Casey's dramatic experiments were as important as those of Synge and Shaw for the future of British and Irish theatre; he was seemingly undaunted by the critics' accusations of rhetoric or melodrama. Life was to him as incongruous as the contrasts depicted in his plays. Testimony is to be found in the *Autobiographies*, the first four titles of which appeared half a century after the events they record. With Moore's *Hail and Farewell*, and Joyce's *Portrait of the Artist as a Young Man*, these volumes provide the liveliest and most readable picture of the times.

The dramatist who closely resembles O'Casey in technique and construction is the American playwright, Eugene O'Neill, who was of Irish extraction. Varied as the body of O'Casey's work is, his methods are not as heretical as those of Chekhov and Shaw. Competent judges of theatre were agreed that O'Casey's strong suit was characterisation. He stoutly defended his writings against the accusations of documentary realism and naturalism, which he said were either false or illusory. Though O'Casey often gave precedence to his later plays, e.g. *The Silver Tassie, Within the Gates* and *Cock-a-Doodle Dandy*, the summit of his achievement was the three plays he wrote for the Abbey Theatre from 1923 to 1925, namely *The Shadow of a Gunman, Juno and the Paycock* and *The Plough and the Stars*. They were all concerned with the disturbances and Civil War in Ireland between 1916 and 1923. On these plays Raymond Williams based his comment that O'Casey's concept of his task was a degenerate art, consisting mainly of materialistic caricature (see *Drama from Ibsen to Eliot*, pp. 187-92).

Williams grounded his charge of naturalism on the fictional device of describing settings and personal characteristics in the stage-directions — a procedure he seems to have learnt from Bernard Shaw. The critic also alleges the caricaturist's trick of using stock phrases to stamp the eccentricities of a comic personality, such as that of Fluther in *The Plough and the Stars* or Captain Boyle in *Juno and the Paycock*; this he suggests is derived from Strindberg's *Miss Julie*, and he holds that it dissipates the genuine impact made by the use of dialect. In general, Williams deplores the play upon words as one of O'Casey's music-hall mannerisms, perhaps an outdated attempt to mimic the fun of Elizabethan stage clowns. There is also the more serious charge of 'adjectival drunkenness', though this is not well substantiated. Synge, says Williams, has a finer sensibility in the use of dialect, because the dignity and vitality of his language are 'directly based on an organic living process'. This is unfair, since O'Casey deals with a more sophisticated stratum of society, whose speech was certainly not 'colourless and drab', or guilty of the routine 'language of the novelette'. Williams's critique concludes with the conviction that O'Casey developed mechanical habits, in which 'words and rhythms of popular sentiment are accumulated in an attempt to overlay a dramatic substance . . . limited and essentially inarticulate'.

The vigour and rhythm of O'Casey's city talk is recognisably different from that of Synge's peasantry; but it would be perverse to deny Dublin English the same place in literature as is accorded to the Cockney dialogue of Dickens. O'Casey's Dublin English is not only rich in malapropisms and catch-phrases; it reflects quirks of invention of many other kinds. The writer is especially adroit in conveying a sense of disorganisation through novel captions such as 'Ireland's in a state of *chassis*'.

One theme of *The Shadow of a Gunman* is the folly of hero-worship, especially when the hero is unworthy of the cause. O'Casey assured Ronald Rollins that there was something of himself in all his plays; although they were not biographical, nearly all the characters in the Irish plays were persons he had actually known, or composite portraits. In *The Shadow of a Gunman* the character with whom the author is identified was Donal Davoren, a sardonic pragmatist and a dreamer, whose lyrical fantasies were fostered by reading Shelley. This is as far as verisimilitude in O'Casey goes. In 1960 O'Casey told Rollins: 'I never consciously adopted "expressionism" which I don't understand and never did. To me there are no "impressionistic", "expressionistic", "realistic" (social or otherwise) plays: there are very good plays and bad ones' (*Sean O'Casey's Drama*, p. 107).

The Shadow of a Gunman concerns the Black and Tan era of the struggle that dominated events in 1920. The chaos of guerilla warfare undermined civilised social values, especially among neighbours with divided loyalties. Davoren, the author's mouthpiece and commentator, is interested only in 'the life that he creates for himself'. The different viewpoints of Davoren and the pedlar, Seumas Shields, are intended to make the audience think as well as feel. The tone is unlike that of comic fiction, because it is suffused with ironic counterplay of a unique kind.

SEUMAS: I don't know much about the pearly glint of the morning dew, or the damask sweetness of the rare wild rose, or the subtle greenness of the serpent's eye — but I think a poet's claim to greatness depends upon his power to put passion in the common people.

DAVOREN: Ay, passion to howl for his destruction. The People! Damn the people! They live in the abyss, the poet lives on the mountain-top; for the people there is no mystery of colour: it is simply the scarlet coat of the soldier; the purple vestments of a priest; the green banner of a party; the brown or blue overalls of industry. To them the might of a design is a three-roomed house or a capacious bed. To them beauty is for sale in a butcher's shop.

(*Collected Plays*, vol. I, p. 127)

One of the ironies of situation in O'Casey's first Abbey Theatre play was the mistaking of a pacifist and poet for a rebel gunman of the IRA. The anti-heroic note is evident when Davoren, the man of peace, is shown by the hypocritical Shields actually to relish the adulation lauded upon an imagined figure of war; but Davoren takes no steps to save the woman he vainly believes he loves from sacrificing herself for the cause. In *The Irish Drama* A. E. Malone classified this play as 'the parody of tragedy called melodrama' (p. 213); but it is really a polemical drama on political disorder, by a writer who valued people more than causes, and who had himself survived the chaos. As a genuine lover of poetry, O'Casey knew well enough that the enthusiasm of Davoren was posturing rather than idealism.

June and the Paycock (1924) was a play of less political complexity than its predecessor, but of greater artistic unity, for there is a better balance between the comic and tragic elements. Its theme is the Civil War that followed the treaty of independence between Britain and the Irish provinces, excluding Ulster. The tragicomedy depicts the disintegration of family life through poverty and wilful disregard of economic commonsense. Juno, with a headstrong daughter, a crippled son, and a wastrel husband, represents the sterling qualities of O'Casey's mother. Indigence strips the Boyle family of any shred of security a tenement household might expect; the illusion of inherited wealth serves merely to accentuate its improvidence.

O'Casey handles the problem with tremendous verve, intimate knowledge, and a remarkable sense of its comic potentialities. The middle-class Englishman, Charles Bentham, who fabricates the existence of the phoney will, is an instrument for bringing to a head the triple crises of the play's ending. National politics has no hand in the denouement, and this gives the play a universal quality it might not otherwise have possessed. O'Casey maintained that Irish diehards quarrelled over minor issues that had no connection with the real problems of democratic life; mothers invariably bear the brunt of the fathers' futile blathering. The dramatist extracts grim laughter from the inanity of political slogans.

The irrepressible comic figures, Jack Boyle and Joxer Daly, make this ironical play what it is, the one flamboyant, the other amusingly platitudinous. They are not the only examples of O'Casey's Falstaffian humour, in which no attempt is made to minimise the character's discredit to humanity. They serve as a comic foil to Juno's matter-of-factness and harassed anxiety. O'Casey confided to Rollins that Jack Boyle was a composite of two characters he had known; he continued as follows:

> *Juno* is a tragedy of vanity and of relinquishment to vanity. There are many Captain Boyles in this world — in love with their own images. Most of us have minor vanities but they do not cripple our ability to act sensibly. But the Captain and his parasitic companion have let their egos ruin their lives — and the lives of others. The Captain, intent on his personal glory, ignores his duties and disaster ensues; he is an Irish Narcissus.

(op. cit., p. 105)

O'Casey felt that *The Plough and the Stars* was the best constructed of the Dublin plays, though its theme, the Easter rebellion of 1916, was the most explosive, and caused noisy objections in the Abbey Theatre, only a decade after the historical events. The actual words of Padraic Pearse's bellicose harangue are quoted in Act II. O'Casey described Pearse elsewhere as a charming and gentle person; the mesmeric effect of his address upon tenement drinkers in the bar is intended to emphasise the hollowness of patriotic rhetoric. The call to arms was less meaningful to such persons than the vanity of rank, and the prestige of a colourful uniform. The episodic development of a play so remarkable for stage-worthiness reflects the ironic nature of its action.

The flimsy reasons for the Dublin protest against this drama — the bringing of a prostitute on the stage, and the appearance of the national flag in an Irish bar — need not detain us. The real purpose of *The Plough and the Stars* was to draw attention to the disruption of human relations caused by inopportune rebellion in times of war; the sufferers were those already victimised by the miserable conditions of their existence. The principal instance of this is the break between Jack Clitheroe, a commandant in the citizen's army, and Nora, his recently married wife, who is expecting her first child. Their tragedy is exacerbated by the tense drama of street fighting, and the impossibility of communication that it entails. Here O'Casey's producer introduced sound effects with terrifying realism.

The dramatist's running commentator is a carpenter, Fluther Good, who is argumentative and abrasive towards his tormentor, young Covey, who happens to be Clitheroe's cousin. Fluther's part was created for Barry Fitzgerald, the theatre's principal comic actor. The scene in which Nora, crazed by the loss of her child, recreates the part of Ophelia in *Hamlet* has often been noted; but the likeness of Bessie Burgess's death to that of Mercutio seems to have been overlooked.

O'Casey, like Shakespeare, had a flair for crowd scenes and mass psychology. Few scenes are more characteristic of this gift than the looting episodes in Act III, which followed the shelling of the General Post Office, where the dissident leaders were housed. The unleashing of predatory passions, in a series of comic and tragic contrasts, shows O'Casey's dramatic art at its best, and acquisitive society at its lowest ebb of hypocrisy. As anti-heroic war dramas, *The Plough and the Stars* and *The Silver Tassie* were two of the most successful plays of the nineteen-twenties.

O'Casey was right in disclaiming relationship with documentary naturalists of the theatre, such as Galsworthy, or with chroniclers who expose evils for the sake of satire. He offers pulsating life, in which human virtues and vices are more significant than the abstract issues that men choose to argue about. The dialectical skill that O'Casey does muster is, like Shaw's, part of the theatrical heritage, which has always favoured characters with shrewdness in the handling of words. The real discovery of the modern stage is that contending ideas are just as stimulating to attentive audiences as opposing actions.

Raymond Williams has not been the only critic to fault O'Casey's dramatic style; the latest contribution comes from G. J. Watson, in *Irish Identity and the Literary Revival* (1979). He writes:

One feels that either O'Casey is too aware of the English audiences who had greeted his earlier plays with enthusiasm, or that — as frequently happens in the Irish psyche — he has actually come to believe in the myth of the 'Elizabethan' richness of Irish speech. Either way, the language of *The Plough and the Stars* trades too easily on the indulgence of the audience for an expected 'comic' blather. Its colour and 'energy' are too frequently factitious — ironically, too 'literary', not earned by observation but created by a few devices such as alliteration, heaped-up epithets, and heaped-up clauses. . . . His 'powers of enjoyment' are convincingly mediated through a successful and enormously funny rhetoric, but the whole conception is of a man locked inside his own world, and quite happy with it, and anxious to keep the world of positive action at bay. And then, finally, as regards the 'energy' of much of the language of O'Casey's other men and women, it simply is not there; it is either self-deceiving blather that we are to criticise for its evasions, or merely a product of O'Casey's collusion with a received view of Irish eloquence.

(p. 286)

This is impressionistic criticism, which is difficult to counter in a brief space; but the 'Elizabethan richness of Irish speech' is less mythical than Watson supposes. O'Casey knew the plays of Shakespeare better than any book but the King James Bible, which belongs to the same age. He was also aware that the Anglo-Irish dialects were the result of mating Augustan English speech with the musical mode of medieval bardic language. *English as We Speak it in Ireland*, by P. W. Joyce (1910) is still of permanent value, especially the chapters on the origins of Anglo-Irish dialects; and the appearance of this book when O'Casey was thirty is not without significance.

O'Casey did more than most writers to demonstrate the vigour and artistic potentialities of Irish colloquial speech, without employing it for sentimental quaintness. His ear for living speech sought rather to preserve the rugged, blunt and picturesque proclivities of Irish, which possess rhythmical subtlety of another kind. He perceived that, not only the images, but the archaisms, portmanteau words and circumlocutions, are substantial relics of the Gaelic spirit. His style of adaptation was not unlike that of James Joyce in *Dubliners* and *Finnegans Wake*, exploiting the knowledge that Anglo-Irish, and the Dublin dialect in particular, was a hybrid language. Maria Edgeworth, Walter Scott and Dickens set the fashion in the nineteenth century of using class and regional dialects to enliven dialogue; their methods included word-minting, malapropisms, colloquial contractions and approximate spellings, which were not always consistently employed. A brief list is appended of O'Casey specimens from the Dublin plays just discussed:

1. *Word-minting: argufyin', fairity. cleverality, particularated, Christianable, upperosity* (snobbishness), *compromisation.* Most of the words are polysyllables, and there is some overlapping between this class and the next.

2. *Malapropisms: burgeons* (burdens), as good a letter as was *decomposed* by a scholar, *primary fashy* (prima facie), *parrotox* (paradox), you will be *supernally* positive (always), *attackey* case, *formularies* (formalities), nothing *derogatory* wrong, *scarifyin'* people (scaring), *vice versa* (opposite), *conspishuous.*

3. *Anglo-Irish cant and familiar words and phrases: I'm all of a tremble, I'm to sing dumb* (remain silent), *have you me?* (do you follow?), don't be acting as if you couldn't *pull a wing out of a dead bee, chiselurs* (children), *collogin'* (gossiping), *press* (cupboard), *riz* (raised), right as the *mail, ball o' malt* (tot of whiskey), *banjax* (mess), *yous* (dialect plural of second personal pronoun).

4. *Words from Gaelic sources: gostherin'* (talking idly, from *gastaire,* chatterer), *traneen* (grass stalk, from *tráithnin,* a straw), *allana* (my child, from *leanbh*), *blather* (foolish talk, from *bladar* flattery).

5. *Colloquial contractions: ud* (would), *oul'* (old), *d'ye* (do you), *me* (my), *da* (father), *ou'* (out), *han'* (hand), *y'are* (Jacobean usage), *t'England* (to), *amn't I?, looka* here

(Elizabethan usage), *y'ass* (you ask), making fun *o'th'* costume (Jacobean usage), *ha'* (have, Elizabethan usage), *fr'*instance, *t'*other (the), up *th'* pole (elision before consonants, Jacobean usage).

6. *Ad hoc phonetic spellings: selt* (Celt), *beyant* (beyond), *wanst* (once), *g'win* (go in), *twiced* (twice), *wan* (one), *gradle* (great deal), *boorzwazee* (bourgeoisie).

The phonology of spoken Irish changed considerably from the twelfth to the sixteenth centuries, with the result that the old spelling of the bards was largely at odds with eighteenth-century pronunciation. The spirants *dh* [ð] and *th* [θ] were lost, and many Anglo-Irish speakers had difficulty in pronouncing words that contained the English dentals *t* and *d* especially in the neighbourhood of *r*. O'Casey's way of reflecting such difficulties is shown in the following spellings:

dh'other, twart (thwart), *dhribble, titther, consthruction, clatther, thick* (tick) and *ordher.*

VIII

Celtic Strands in Anglo-Irish Fiction

Irish fiction of the nineteenth and twentieth centuries has an abundance and diversity that needs must limit discussion to those novelists who have made a considerable impact upon the neo-Celtic way of life. The earlier of these, Maria Edgeworth (1767-1849), anticipated O'Casey in her transparent honesty and her power to observe the idosyncracies of the Irish country folk amongst whom she lived in County Longford. *Castle Rackrent* (1800) and *The Absentee* (1812) are instances of historical fiction that owe as much to sympathetic observation as to book-learning.

Miss Edgeworth is valued as a realist who seldom forgot the Augustan principles of her art. A voluminous author, she began with the mundane task of writing her father's domestic and business letters. No better training could have been devised for the exercise of tact, and getting to know the motives behind the thinking of Irish rural society. She became the unwitting founder of a sociological school of novel-writing that had its roots in the Protestant Ascendancy and materially diverted the mainstream of English and European fiction. Compared with the practice of Sean O'Casey, her use of dialect in *Castle Rackrent* is sparing and judicious, one reason being that she wrote for much the same English audience as Jane Austen did. This one learns from the postscript to her first novel:

He [the Editor] lays it before the English reader as a specimen of manners and characters, which are perhaps unknown in England. Indeed the domestic habits of no nation in Europe were less known to the English than those of their sister country, till within these few years. . . .

All the features in the foregoing sketch were taken from the life, and they are characteristic of that mixture of quickness, simplicity, cunning, carelessness, dissipation, disinterestedness, shrewdness and blunder, which in different forms, and with various success, has been brought upon the stage or delineated in novels.

(Castle Rackrent, pp. 96-7)

This short novel, written between 1797 and 1799, marked the Union of Ireland with England, Scotland and Wales in 1800. The author's mouthpiece, Thady Quirk, was in real life her father's steward, John Langan; but this was her only authentic portrait. Thady had loyally served four generations of land-owners, and his bland response to their eccentricities shows that Irish class distinction were as *de rigueur* as English ones. Miss Edgeworth explained in a letter to Mrs Stark, dated September 1834:

I began to write a family history as Thady would tell it, he seemed to stand beside me and dictate; and I wrote as fast as my pen could go, the characters all imaginary.

(ibid., p. xi)

Castle Rackrent breaks new ground in several respects. Watson in his Introduction calls it a 'memoir novel', like *Robinson Crusoe*, because it purports to be the autobiography of Thady, edited by the author. Secondly, *Rackrent* is the earliest socio-historical novel in English, forecasting decline of the paternalistic landlord that ruled the roost during the Irish Independency; but it is not documentary fiction. Thirdly, though the novel depicts the immediate past, the narration is based on personal experience, and tends to be ironic, but with a kind of subtlety distinct from Fielding's. Fourthly, *Rackrent* was the only regional novel in English so far to utilise the syntactical peculiarities of Anglo-Irish dialect. The novel has yet another claim to priority in its special bearing upon Irish social history; for it contains an inimitable account of Big House dominance in agrarian economy during the English Ascendancy. The concept of the Big House was grounded in feudal principles in a somewhat attenuated form. *Castle Rackrent* mirrors the demise of this system from 1782, under the government of Grattan's Parliament.

Big House economy depended largely on the wealth and organisation of the owner; some managements were viable, but many were not, especially where the estate belonged to an absentee landlord. The army of servants and tenants in such a household played an inevitable role in its destiny, in which the capacity of the head for good human relationships was tested to the limit.. There is evidence enough that Richard Lovell of Edgeworth's manor was progressive and morally responsible; nevertheless, English acquisitive practices led to the disastrous famine of the eighteen-forties, through which Maria Edgeworth lived. That there had been, and still were, corruption and hypocrisy, Maria Edgeworth leaves us in no doubt.

The Edgeworths, father and daughter, had most of their Protestant education in England, at a time when social ideas were under the influence of literature from France. We are not, however, told in the novel to what religion the Rackrent family actually belonged. Maria seems to have handled the Freudian problem of her father's didactical influence with masculine courage and some independence, yet did not escape the suspicion of writing moral tales. Her father married four times and produced nineteen children. What Maria saw of the domestic situation did not induce her to marry, although three of her father's marriages had been happy. Edgeworth was uncritically a devotee of Rousseau's educational theories, and endeavoured to put them into practice in his large family. His posthumous *Memoirs*, edited by Maria in 1820, show that he was the friend of Thomas Day, author of the three-volume *History of Sandford and Merton* (1783-9), a humourless exposition of Rousseau's doctrines. Edgeworth not only affected his daughter's thinking, but he collaborated with her in the writing of such purposive works as *Practical Education* (1798); she was always extremely proud of her share in this. She believed, with her father, that schooling the heart through good habits created a sound personality, and had more to commend it than training the rational faculties.

Thady Quirk, the landlord's steward in the novel, is unique in Irish literature as a member of the obsequious class that used exaggeratedly deferential means of pursuing its own ends. His mixture of servility and loyalty enabled the author to treat Thady's manoeuvres and opinions with superb irony. She was aware that rambling garrulity concealed his artfulness; but what was pardonable in the divided loyalty displayed by the father became legalistic unscrupulousness in Jason, his son. The second part of the book dealing with the downfall of the last owner, Sir Condy Rackrent, was written two years after the first part, when Maria's changed attitude seems to have been influenced by her father's vote against the Union in the Irish Parliament of 1800. She was herself unsure whether British manufacturers would benefit Ireland, but noticed the increased consumption of beer instead of whisky. Irish intemperance among all classes had a marked effect upon those who appear in *Castle Rackrent*.

Maria writes in no spirit of malice or passion, but always with the same vivacity, forbearance and dignity. Her humour is genteel, but infectious, for she enjoyed the intuitive gift of evaluating traits, without the taint of romantic sentiment, even when she perceived them through the minds of associates. The account of Sir Murtagh's end illustrates her amusing knack of vernacular digression, with all its asides and amplifications, while avoiding the risk of crudity and vulgarity:

He was a great speaker, with a powerful voice; but his last speech was not in the courts at all. He and my lady, though both of the same way of thinking in some things, and though she was as good a wife and great economist as you could see, and he the best of husbands, as to looking into his affairs, and making money for his family; yet I don't know how it was, they had a great deal of sparring and jarring between them. — My lady had her privy purse — and she had her weed ashes, and her sealing money upon the signing of all the leases, with something to buy gloves besides; and besides again often took money from the tenants, if offered properly, to speak for them to Sir Murtagh about abatements and renewals. Now the weed ashes and the glove money he allowed her clear perquisites; though once when he saw her in a new gown saved out of the weed ashes, he told her to my face, (for he could say a sharp thing) that she should not put on her weeds before her husband's death. But it grew more serious when they came to the renewal businesses. At last, in a dispute about an abatement, my lady would have the last word, and Sir Murtagh grew mad; I was within hearing of the door, and now wish I had made bold to step in. He spoke so loud, the whole kitchen was out on the stairs — All on a sudden he stopped, and my lady too. Something had surely happened, thought I — and so it was, for Sir Murtagh in his passion broke a blood-vessel, and all the law in the land could do nothing in that case. My lady sent for five physicians, but Sir Murtagh died, and was buried. She had a fine jointure settled upon her, and took herself away to the great joy of the tenantry. I never said any thing, one way or the other, whilst she was part of the family, but got up to see her go at three o'clock in the morning — 'It's a fine morning, honest Thady, says she; good bye to ye' — and into the carriage she stept, without a word more, good or bad, or even half-a-crown; but I made my bow, and stood to see her safe out of sight for the sake of the family.

(op. cit., pp. 17-19)

The irony of many passages is illuminated by the notes which Maria appended in her 'Glossary'. Ash from the burning of weeds contained alkaline properties, which were used for bleaching fabric; while 'sealing-money' was the tribute (sometimes as much as fifty guineas) due to the landlord's wife, on the signing of a tenant's lease.

The Glossary is sometimes used to assure the reader of the author's acquaintance with the full flavour of dialect, as in the note on 'fairy mounts' on pages 105-6. Here the leavening of dialectal idioms and phrases does not obscure the principal feature of the Irish way with English — a shapeless sequence of paratactic clauses.

Some peculiarities of Maria Edgeworth's language are recorded below.

1. *Spelling:* (a) Authorial: *sirname, growse, tythes, replevying, chearful, skreen, chuse, tantarums, coloring, incumbrance.* (b) Dialectal pronunciation (see P. W. Joyce, ch. VII): *cratur* (creature), *larning* (learning), *sacret* (secret), *shister* (sister), *sartain* (certain), *fader* (father), *prefarred, plase* (please).

2. *Vocabulary: herriots* (dues in kind on the death of a tenant), *flam* (torch), *vails* (tips), *gossoon* (small boy, Irish *garsún* from Fr. *garçon*), *gripers* (extortioners), *gauger* (exciseman), *tester* (sixpence, from Fr. *tête*, head); *shebean-house* (alehouse).

3. *Regional Illiteracy:* the master *was sailed* for England; the *thick coming* of the master's drafts; she was a *Jewish*; *ashamed like* (as though ashamed); one out of *their* right mind; at daggers *drawing; aims-ace* (*ambs-ace*, meaning 'double ace'); cross-examined by *them* lawyers; I *seed* my poor master chaired; so it was all done very *proper*; *tings* (things); *tink* (think); wanted to know where you *was*; relation to my *own's*; *kilt* (injured); *ungratitude*; *womens* (plural).

4. *Popular phrases: he looked to me no more like himself than nothing at all; at the cant* (at auction); she found *I understood the weather-cock* (knew how the land lay); *childher* (plural, children); he got *a* horseback; he was *at a terrible nonplus*; to drink whiskey *out of the egg-shell*; she had a *quality toss* with her; a *raking pot of tea* (women's gossip party); I was sent ... *to put him up* (i.e. in gaol); still *cutting* his joke; *Sarrah* (sorrow, i.e. 'the Devil'); would *go to Cork* to serve him; can't he be wakened? *and I standing* at the door (as I am standing); I'll consider *of* it; *out of the face* (from beginning to end); she kicked *me* a new car (dative of advantage).

Thady's sly exposure of corruption in relations between land-owner and tenant is magnified in chapters X to XII of *The Absentee*, which was originally written as a play. Lord Clonbrony and his spendthrift wife, a social climber living in London, employ agents to manage extensive estates in Ireland. One of these is a model of responsibility; the other a scoundrel, residing in Dublin, who uses his brother as a sub-agent. This man demands payment of rent in guineas, the securing of which involves the tenants in preposterous rates of commission. The evil is disclosed by the absentee owner's son, Lord Colambre, in the following terms:

> The agent would take nothing but gold. The same guineas were bought and sold several times over, to the great profit of the agent and loss of the poor tenants; for as the rents were paid, the guineas were resold to another set, and the remittances made through bankers to the landlord; who, as the poor man that explained the transaction to Lord Colambre expressed it, 'gained nothing by the business, bad or good, but the ill-will of the tenantry.'
>
> The higgling for the price of the gold: the time lost in disputing about the goodness of the notes, among some poor tenants, who could not read or write, and who were at the mercy of the man with the bag in his hand: the vexation, the useless harassing of all who were obliged to submit ultimately — Lord Colambre saw: and all this time he endured the smell of tobacco and whiskey, and the sound of various brogues, the din of men wrangling, brawling, threatening, whining, drawling, cajoling, cursing, and every variety of wretchedness.
>
> 'And is this my father's town of Clonbrony?' thought Lord Colambre. 'Is this Ireland? No, it is not Ireland. Let me not, like most of those who forsake their native country, traduce it. Let me not, even to my own mind, commit the injustice of taking a speck for the whole. What I have just seen is the picture only of that to which an Irish estate and Irish tenantry may be degraded in the absence of those whose duty and interest it is to reside in Ireland to uphold justice by example and authority; but who, neglecting this duty, commit power to bad hands and bad hearts — abandon their tenantry to oppression, and their property to ruin.'

(The Absentee, pp. 241-2)

The visit of Lord Colambre, incognito, to his father's estates provides the most agonising revelation of the book; but it also pinpoints the novel's didactic purpose, where good and evil are opposed with blatant clarity.

The novels of Maria Edgeworth have certain qualities in common with Jane Austen's — class consciousness, the social graces and proprieties, doweries as marriage portions, and heroes or heroines that tend to be measured by a code of cultural behaviour scarcely human, because oversimplified. But the social novel of Ireland before 1850 revealed another characteristic that set it apart — a nascent desire for nationality that bore a perceptible relation to puritanical Catholicism. One reason for this was that the land-owners were Protestants who were protected by laws that the exploited peasantry did not respect.

This period in Ireland's history was therefore marked by violence and a large-scale disregard for the rule of law, which undermined the authority of the class to which writers like Maria Edgeworth belonged. A tradition of lawlessness grew out of one agitation after another, even when the Penal Laws were abolished in the eighteen-twenties. The Great Famine, preceded by lesser famines, produced the culminating crisis, inexorably changing the face of Ireland. Its inevitability lurks in the background of most novels of the time. Before this crisis Maria Edgeworth had already abandoned the writing of novels in order to devote her energies to the amelioration of social conditions. Her final verdict on the Irish situation is contained in a letter to her brother, Pakenham:

> It is impossible to draw Ireland as she now is in the book of fiction — realities are too strong, party passions too violent, to bear to see, or care to look at their faces in a looking glass. The people would only break the glass, and curse the fool who held the mirror up to nature — distorted nature, in a fever. We are in too perilous a case to laugh, humor would be out of season, worse than bad taste.

(*Life and Letters*, ed. Augustus Hare, vol. II, p. 550)

What is vaguely termed the Anglo-Irish novel was thus born in a period of unrest, which left indelible traces, not only in the tone of the writing, but in the character of fictional dialogue. There were recognisable regional dialects, northern, western and southern, which left their mark on the

English then being used, but these were less significant than sociological factors. In *English as We Speak it in Ireland*, P. W. Joyce relies largely on the evidence of novelists such as Banim, Griffin and Carleton, for his citations. Of those writers, Carleton was the sole representative of the northern or Scots-Gaelic influence.

The Banim brothers, John and Michael, who came from Kilkenny, collaborated in the writing of *Tales by the O'Hara Family*, the first and third series, which they published in 1825 and 1827. John alone was responsible for the second series, containing his ablest novel, *The Nowlans*, a work that discreetly handles the thorny problem of proselytism in Ireland. When the brothers wrote in partnership, John was invariably the innovator; he had been a promising student at the prestigious Kilkenny College, a Protestant foundation of the sixteenth century, under the patronage of the Ormondes. John's initial success had actually been in dramatic form, a tragedy entitled *Damon and Pythias*, produced by Macready at Covent Garden in 1821. This induced Banim to join the school of young Irish writers in London, of whom William Maginn and Crofton Croker were the principals. Interest in the theatre enabled him to find employment as an assistant at the English Opera House; but his income from this source had to be augmented by journalism.

It is doubtful whether John Banim knew Irish peasants more intimately than Maria Edgeworth; but he saw their foibles from a different point of view, and presented the tragic and comic aspects with sympathetic insight. His task was not, like hers, to uplift them through utilitarian education. The peasantry presented him with a number of realistic portraits, executed with considerable skill, but the gentry that appear in *The Nowlans* are mere puppets.

Frustrated in his attempts to become a London dramatist, John Banim returned to Ireland and applied his energies to the writing of historical fiction. Much research went into the compilation of *The Boyne Water*, which handles the conflict between James II and William of Orange; models for this were, of course, Walter Scott's popular *Waverley* series. Most distressing evils of his country Banim traced to the mistakes that were made in the Jacobite struggle. The implications of it were that royalism was already out of date, and that the burden of such an anachronism went beyond Ireland; the political future of western Europe was clearly in the balance. Banim was cautious, however, in identifying Ireland's conflict with contentious religious affiliations; yet the great event for his country had been the displacement of the Protestant nationalist, Grattan, by the Catholic prophet of emancipation, Daniel O'Connell.

Gerald Griffin (1803-40) is now regarded as a more accomplished novelist than Banim, even if more parochial. Griffin's strength lies in his ability to project the spirit of place faithfully, and this was valuable, because changes of considerable importance took place in the physical likeness of Ireland during his lifetime. He managed, too, to evoke a Gaelic tradition that was disappearing under economic and political pressures. His principal concern, as a novelist, was to create an atmosphere suitably adapted to the nature of his characters and the spirit of the scene.

Griffin was born and educated in Limerick; but when he was only seventeen, his father and most of the family emigrated to Pennsylvania. Only the three sons, who were on the threshold of their careers, remained in Ireland, and one of them became a Limerick physician. Gerald then tried to make a name for himself as a dramatist in London, where he was welcomed and introduced to the Irish fraternity by his friend, John Banim. But being of an introspective and religious nature, Griffin became depressed by the city environment and disillusioned with London's theatrical taste. He dutifully shouldered the manifold tasks of translator, reporter and reviewer for *The Literary Gazette* and other journals, while working on a book of sketches, called *Holland-Tide*, which was published in London in 1826. Not surprisingly, the style was awkward, though in good taste, the gaucherie being particularly noticeable in the dialogue.

After three years, a decline in health compelled Griffin to return to Ireland, where he determined to become a regional novelist. He paved the way by publishing *Tales of the Munster Festivals* in 1827, a book in which the Irishman's cynical contempt for the law is the main concern. This fault was not confined to offenders below the gentry class. A mature work, *The Collegians*, appeared two years later, which proved to be the most durable fiction since Maria Edgeworth. Some twenty years later, Dion Boucicault founded on it his romantic drama, *Colleen Bawn*. The appeal of Griffin's novel was partly its involvement of all strata of Irish society. The plot was based on a murder which took place near the Shannon estuary in 1819; Daniel O'Connell was briefed to defend the murderer. Griffin took the liberty of antedating the events, to bring them within the scope of the Penal Laws.

Most of *The Collegians* was written in London, and this may explain the impact upon Griffin's style of Goldsmith and Dickens, especially in the dramatic episodes. Lowry Looby and Poll Naughton, two of the peasant characters, speak the language of the south. The Daly family represents the Irish middle-class, to which Griffin himself belonged. Pretentiousness in the midst of chaos is an apt designation of the society the author depicts before the Famine. Indeed, the considerable merit of *The Collegians* is Griffin's astute analysis of social attitudes. The deference shown by the gentry towards good breeding seems to have survived in English fiction of the Victorian age as late as Thomas Hardy's *Tess of the d'Urbervilles*, a book that Griffin's novel resembles in some respects. At the heart of Hardress Cregan's dilemma, when he contracts a secret marriage beneath his class, is the description of Eily O'Connor's table manners:

> Nothing however could exceed the bashfulness, the awkwardness, and the homeliness of speech and accent, with which the ropemaker's daughter received their compliments; and to complete the climax of his chagrin, on happening to look round upon her during dinner, he saw her in the act of peeling a potato with her fingers! This phantom haunted him for half the night. He dreamed, moreover, that, when he reasoned with her on this subject, she answered him with a degree of pert vulgarity and impatience which was in 'discordant harmony' with her shyness before strangers, and which made him angry at heart, and miserable in mind.
>
> (*The Collegians*, vol. II, pp. 100-1)

Griffin continued his analysis of the contemporary Irish

scene in two short studies, *The Rivals* and *Tracy's Ambition*, published in 1830. The first is an incoherent account of the violent aftermath of the Tithe War; but a secondary theme deals with the proselytising practised by an evangelical group, which was ably abetted by the writings of the young journalist, William Carleton. Sinister aspects of *The Rivals* are lightened by a comic interlude, in which Griffin pictures the procedure in a hedge school, which Flanagan suggests was modelled on McEligot's celebrated academy; but more likely the novelist drew upon his experiences in the Limerick school, where Donovan, a teacher of Latin and classical Irish, had a memorable influence on his education. Griffin describes in what follows a lesson on the Dido interlude of Vergil's *Aeneid*:

> Observe, boys, he no longer calls him, as of old, the *pius Aenaes*, only *dux Trojanus*, the Throjan leader, in condemnation of his crime. That's where Virgil took the crust out o' Homer's mouth, in the neatness of his language, that you'd gather a part o' the feelin' from the very shape o' the line an' the turn o' the prosody. . . . The same way, when Juno is vexed in talkin' o' the Throjans, he makes her spake bad Latin to show how mad she is. . . . He laves you to guess what a passion she's in, when he makes her lave an infinitive mood without anything to govern it. You can't attribute it to ignorance, for it would be a dhroll thing in airnest, if Juno, the queen of all the gods, didn't know a common rule in syntax, so that you have nothing for it but to say that she must be in the very moral of a fury. Such, boys, is the art o' poets, and the genius of languages.

(The Rivals, pp. 54-5)

Like Banim, Griffin wished also to become an historical novelist, and wrote two works, *The Invasion* (1835) and the more ambitious *Duke of Monmouth* (1837), the research for which took him to England during several seasons. In 1838, however, he became dissatisfied with the usefulness of the work he was doing, and being a man of impulse, he destroyed all his manuscripts. Griffin then became a teacher of the poor for the newly founded Christian Brothers Order; but two years later died from an outbreak of typhus.

William Carleton (1794-1869) became the favourite Irish novelist of W. B. Yeats, whose publisher suggested that he should make a selection of this writer's stories in 1889. Carleton was the youngest son of a large Tyrone family, the offspring of a tenant farmer, whose wife was a well-known Irish folk-singer. The education of young William was typically unorthodox, as is clear from references to hedge schools in *Traits and Stories of the Irish Peasantry* (5 vols, 1830-33). In a story entitled 'The Hedge School', Carleton gives a spirited but ironical account of the methods of his *alma mater*:

> I know not whether the Commissioners of Education found the monitorial system of instruction in such of the old hedge schools as maintained an obstinate resistance to the innovations of modern plans. . . . I think it is a mistake to suppose that silence, among a number of children in school, is conducive to the improvement either of health or intellect. That the chest and the lungs are benefited by giving full play to the voice, I think will not be disputed; and that a child is capable of more intense study and abstraction in the din of a school-room, than in partial silence . . . There is something cheering and cheerful in the noise of friendly voices about us − it is a restraint taken off the mind, and it will run the lighter for it − it produces more excitement, and puts the intellect in a better frame for study. The obligation to silence, though it may give the master more ease, imposes a new moral duty upon the child, the sense of which must necessarily weaken his application. Let the boy speak aloud, if he pleases − that is, to a certain pitch; let his blood circulate; let the natural secretions take place, and the physical effluvia be thrown off by a free exercise of voice and limbs: but do not keep him dumb and motionless as a statue − his blood and his intellect both in a state of stagnation, and his spirit below zero. Do not send him in quest of knowledge alone, but let him have cheerful companionship on his way; for, depend upon it, that the man who expects too much either in discipline or morals from a

boy, is not, in my opinion, acquainted with human nature. If an urchin titter at his own joke, or that of another — if he give him a jagg of a pin under the desk, imagine not that it will do him an injury, whatever phrenologists may say concerning the organ of destructiveness. It is an exercise of the mind, and he will return to his business with greater vigour and effect. Children are not men, nor influenced by the same motives — they do not reflect, because their capacity for reflection is imperfect; so is their reason: whereas, on the contrary, their faculties for education (excepting judgment, which strengthens my argument) are in greater vigour in youth than in manhood. The general neglect of this distinction is, I am convinced, a stumbling-block in the way of youthful instruction, though it charac-terises all our modern systems. We should never forget that they are children; nor should we bind them by a system, whose standard is taken from the maturity of human intellect. We may bend our reason to theirs, but we cannot elevate their capacity to our own. We may produce an external appearance, sufficiently satisfactory to ourselves; but, in the mean time, it is probable that the child may be growing in hypocrisy, and settling down into the habitual practice of a fictitious character.

(pp. 162-3)

The school system that Carleton here pretends to fancy was in vogue at Findramore, the picturesque setting of this story. The mentor he had in mind was Pat Frayne, one skilled in mathematics, grammar and Christian doctrine, who possessed a travelling library. Probably this man introduced him to Le Sage's *Gil Blas*. Carleton's writings are peopled with eccentric scholars, spoiled priests and witty rogues.

Carleton's parents spoke Gaelic, and intended him for the priesthood; he actually went on a pilgrimage to Lough Derg, possibly with a view to entering Maynooth College; but the discipline proved too unnerving for a spirited young man who had even once been a Whiteboy. In the Ulster of Carleton's teens rebellious individualism was not incon-sistent with competent scholarship, and this William undoubtedly possessed. In the autobiographical novel *Going to Maynooth* Denis O'Shaugnessy's self-assurance as a classic-ist encourages the youth to give himself airs before his father:

'Pay attention, therefore to my words, for I expect that they will be duly observed: — buy me a knife and fork; and when I get them, it's not to lay them past to rust, you consave. The beef and mutton must follow; and in future I'm resolved to have my *tay* breakfast. There are geese, and turkeys, and pullets enough about the yard, and I am bent on accomplishing myself in the art of carrying them. I'm not the man now to be placed among the other riff-raff of the family over a basket of potatoes, wid a black clerical coat upon me, and a noggin of milk under my arm! I tell you the system must be changed: the schoolmaster is abroad, and I'll tolerate such vulgarity no longer. Now saddle the horse till I ride across the bog to Pether Rafferth's Station, where I'm to serve mass: plase heaven, I'll soon be able to say one myself, and give you all alift in spirituals — ehem!'

'Throth, Dinny, I b'lieve you'r right, avick; and —'

'*Vick* me no longer, father —that's another thing I forgot. It's full time that I should be *sirred*; and if my own relations won't call me *Sir* instead of Dinny, it's hardly to be expected that strangers will do it. I wish to goodness you had never stigmatised me wid so vulgar an epithet as Dinny. The proper word is Dionysius; and, in future, I'll expect to be called Misther Dionysius.'

'Sure, I or your mother needn't be *sirrin'* you, Dinny?'

'I haven't made up my mind as to whether I'll demand that proof of my respectability from you and my mother, or not; but on this I'm immovable, that instead of Dinny, you must, as I said, designate me Dionysius.'

'Well, well, avourneen, I suppose only it's right you wouldn't be axin' us; but I'm sure your poor mother will never be able to get her tongue about Dionnisis, it's so long and larned a word.'

'It *is* a larned word, no doubt; but she must persevere until she's able to master it. I wouldn't for three ten-pennies that the priest would hear one of you call me Dinny; it would degradate me very much in his estimation. At all events, if my mother cannot manage the orthography of Dionysius, let it be Denis, or anything but that signature of vulgarity Dinny. Now father, you won't neglect to revale what I've ordered to the family?'

'No, indeed I will not, avick — I mean Dionnisis, avourneen — I'll tell them everything as you ordhered; but as to Dionnisis, I'm cock sure that poor Mave will never be able to get her ould tongue about so new-fangled a piece of larnin' as that is. Well, well, this knowledge bates the world!'

(Traits and Stories, pp. 114-15)

Even by Victorian standards, the sentiment of this tale rings false, especially in the love motive with which it ends.

When Carleton first came to Dublin he worked for the Protestant Erasmus Smith Schools; on the strength of his growing reputation as a journalist, he married the niece of one of the schoolmasters. Unfortunately, his talents were exploited by Caesar Otway, the evangelical reformer who edited *The Christian Examiner*. Carleton's opposition to Catholicism then became clear; for he made no bones about accommodating his views on religion to those of his employer. But he soon became the indispensable recorder of Irish life in the decades immediately preceding the Great Famine — a writer of compelling exuberance and rhetorical power. The long narrative, *Larry M'Farland's Wake* is unique in the social annals of his country; nowhere else are the oddities of Irish peasants made more vivid, or the evils and brutalities of the period so forcibly displayed. The truthfulness of Carleton's observations earned him immense popularity or disfavour, depending on the reader's point of view. In 1845 he was hailed by Thomas Davis as a true peasant's son, possessing an intelligence as wise as his passions were intense.

Carleton understood clearly the influence which the Irish priesthood exerted upon education, as well as on the private lives of country people. What he principally exposed, however, were the evil results of sectarian hatred, of which, as an Ulsterman, he had much experience. As he wrote mainly to enlighten the English public, he supplied an abundance of explanatory detail. There is a splendid instance of this kind of enlargement in 'The Geography of an Irish Oath', in which the irony is palpable:

> But Paddy! Put *him* forward to prove an *alibi* for his four-teenth or fifteenth cousin, and you will be gratified by the pomp, pride, and circumstance of true swearing. Every oath with him *is* an epic — pure poetry, abounding with humour, pathos, and the highest order of invention and talent. He is not at ease, it is true, under *facts*; there is something too commonplace in dealing with them, which his genius scorns. But his flights — his flights are beautiful; and his episodes admirable and happy. In fact, he is an *improvisatore* at oath-taking; with this difference, that his *extempore* oaths possess all the ease and correctness of labour and design. . . .
>
> 'Tis true, there is nothing perfect under the sun; but if there were, it would certainly be Paddy at an *alibi*. Some flaws, no doubt, occur; some slight inaccuracies may be noticed by a critical eye; an occasional anachronism stands out, and a mistake or so in geography; but let it be recollected that Paddy's *alibi* is but a human production; let us not judge him by harsher rules than those which we apply to Homer, Virgil, or Shakespeare.
>
> 'Aliquando bonus dormitat Homerus,' is allowed on all hands. Virgil made Dido and Æneas contemporary, though they were not so; and Shakespeare, by the creative power of his genius, changed an inland town into a sea-port. Come, come, have bowels. Let epic swearing be treated with the same courtesy shown to epic poetry, that is, if both are the production of a rare genius. I maintain, that when Paddy commits a blemish he is too harshly admonished for it. . . . Some persons, who display their own egregious ignorance of morality, may be disposed to think that it tends to lessen the obligation of an oath, by inducing a habit among the people of swearing to what is not true. We look upon such persons as very dangerous to Ireland and to the repeal of the Union; and we request them not to push their principles too far in the disturbed parts of the country. Could society hold together a single day, if nothing but truth were *spoken*? Would not law and

lawyers soon become obsolete, if nothing but truth were *sworn*? What would become of parliament if truth alone were uttered there? Its annual proceedings might be dispatched in a month. Fiction is the basis of society, the bond of commercial prosperity, the channel of communication between nation and nation, and not infrequently the interpreter between a man and his own conscience.

(*Traits and Stories*, pp. 2-3)

Carleton's story of the Famine, *The Black Prophet* (1847), has claims to be regarded as a genuine novel, rather than a record of the times; yet the element of propaganda in it is unmistakable. The object seems to have been to remind the Westminster government of its maladministration, worsened by callous neglect of human rights. The novel at the same time brings to a head the problem of Carleton's dialogue, which Frank O'Connor regards in *The Backward Look* as a deafness to living speech, producing what is sometimes 'stilted nonsense'. This critic probably had in mind Carleton's frequent descent to comic extravagance, rather than hollow rhetoric. Carleton did have the habit of incorporating Gaelic words and linguistic mannerisms to give colour to the intensity of his writing; but all are elucidated by footnotes and are to most readers a help rather than hindrance.

Samuel Lover (1797-1868) was the son of a Dublin stockbroker, who wanted him to enter the world of business; but the lad, revealing a flair for music and painting, chose to become a portrait painter, who specialised in miniatures. He rose in this profession to become Secretary of the Royal Hibernian Society of Arts (1818) and exhibited at the London Royal Academy for twelve years. A taste for literature was acquired through friendship with the poet Moore, and with writers associated with the *Dublin University Magazine*.

Lover's much neglected prose work *Legends and Stories of Ireland* (1831) was preceded by a collection of ballads entitled *Rory O'More*, which appeared in 1826. He used the title poem eleven years later as the theme of a romantic novel as well as a play. By this time Lover had taken up residence in London, where he wrote ephemeral musicals and comedies for the Haymarket Theatre. He toured America in 1846 as a raconteur and popular entertainer in a programme which he called 'Irish Evenings'. Parts of his amusing novel, *Handy Andy* (1842) appeared serially in *Bentley's Miscellany*.

In an Address to the Reader, Lover described the hero of *Handy Andy* as 'a blundering servant', a figure of 'fun and whimsicality', but quite as important to the author as the gentleman and the patriot. Lover was a purveyor of grotesque characters, but his gift for portraying the comic ranks with those of Banim and Carleton. The very ease of his craftmanship sometimes made for carlessness. With Lever, he belonged to the group of burlesque writers who were held responsible for the ludicrous stage Irishman of Victorian times; but his caricatures now seem flattering when compared with those of his contemporaries.

That Lover is not all 'fun and whimsicality' is shown by the disarming directness of his style, when he chooses to give point to a thumb-nail sketch, as in the following instance:

The Rev. Dominick Dowling was austere and long-winded; *his* mass had an oppressive effect on his congregation, and from the kneeling multitude might be seen eyes fearfully looking up from under bent brows; and low breathings and subdued groans often rose above the silence of his congregation, who felt like sinners, and whose imaginations were filled with the thoughts of Heaven's anger; while the good-humoured face of the light-hearted Father Phil produced a corresponding brightness on the looks of his hearers, who turned up their whole faces in trustfulness to the mercy of that Heaven, whose propitiatory offering their pastor was making for them in cheerful tones, which associated well with thoughts of pardon and salvation.

Father Dominick poured fourth his spiritual influence like a strong dark stream, that swept down the hearer resistlessly, who struggled to keep his head above the torrent, and dreaded to be overwhelmed at the next word. Father Phil's religion bubbled out like a mountain rill, — bright, musical and refreshing; — Father Dominick's people had decidedly need of cork jackets: — Father Phil's might drink and be refreshed.

(*Handy Andy*, ch. XXVIII, p. 299)

For Charles Lever (1806-72) novel-writing became a delightful avocation, but one that he could only indulge freely when living abroad. He was only half Irish, on the mother's side, his father being an English architect-builder who settled in Dublin. He was privately educated until ready to enter Trinity College, from which he graduated in 1827. He then proceeded to Göttingen to qualify in medicine, but came back to complete the degree at Trinity in 1831. For six years he practised as a doctor in different parts of Ireland, until he was convinced that literature was his forte, a discovery made when he published parts of *The Confessions of Harry Lorrequer* in the *Dublin University Magazine*. The book itself appeared in 1839, and proved an immense success. *Charles O'Malley* followed in 1840, and Lever returned from an army practice in Brussels, when he was offered the editorship of the *Magazine* to which he had been a contributor. For three years he held this office, amidst constant unpleasantness and endless discussion; but he was able to produce *Tom Burke of Ours* and two other novels before tendering his resignation.

Lever then left for Florence to make fiction his career, writing prolifically until he was appointed British Consul at Spezzia in 1857, and at Trieste a decade later. There he died, after penning novel after novel, without much care for construction or form. The Ireland of which he continued to be the narrator was the country of his youth, convivial, sporting and full of the high-spirited creations for which he became famous. In the Preface to the Routledge edition of *Harry Lorrequer*, written just before his death, Lever disclaimed any prospect of permanence for his writings; for there was, he admitted, a 'prodigal waste of material' (p. vii). Parts of the novel were autobiographical, and Father Malachi Brennan was drawn, he said, from life, without any attempt at caricature.

Flanagan says aptly that Lever presented Ireland to the reading public as 'an enchanting and dowdy land of *dolce far niente*, in which dashing dragoons and impoverished fox hunters held genial sway over a mob of feckless rustics' (*The Irish Novelists*, p. 39). Lever's Irish inspiration was mainly that sporting parson William Hamilton Maxwell, a fellow graduate of Trinity College and a contributor to the *Dublin University Magazine*; this author wrote military fiction, such as *Stories of Waterloo*, and a more readable book entitled *Wild Sports of the West of Ireland*. Lever's lesser debt is to Thackeray, especially for the cynical circumspections on life in Dublin.

Daniel O'Connell denounced Lever in Phoenix Park, accusing him of ridiculing the Irish in caricatures of both peasant and priest. Charles O'Malley's servant, Mickey Free, was quickly repudiated by the Irish press. Yet *Charles O'Malley, the Irish Dragoon* (1841) was one of Lever's best novels; the sketches of the battles in the Peninsular campaign are graphic and truthful. In the Irish novels, the portraits of the pleasure-loving and foolish gentry are just as biting as those of the peasantry. Indeed, Sean O'Casey justly likened Lever's prodigious output to a 'sprawling, chaotic cartoon of life (*Blasts and Benedictions*, p. 228). His novels abound in incidents like the bogus medical examination for leave of absence from Lorrequer's regiment:

'A sick certificate,' said I, in some surprise.

'The only thing for you,' said Fitzgerald, taking a long pinch of snuff; 'and I grieve to say you have a most villanous look of good health about you.'

'I must acknowledge I have seldom felt better.'

'So much the worse — so much the worse,' said Fitzgerald, despondingly. 'Is there no family complaint; no respectable heirloom of infirmity you can lay claim to from your kindred?'

'None that I know of, unless a very active performance on the several occasions of breakfast, dinner, and supper, with a tendency towards port, and an inclination to sleep ten in every twenty-four hours, be a sign of sickness. These symptoms I have known many of the family suffer for years without the slightest alleviation, though, strange as it may appear, they occasionally had medical advice.'

Fitz took no notice of my sneer at the faculty, but proceeded to strike my chest several times with his finger tips. 'Try a short cough, now,' said he. 'Ah, that will never do! Do you ever flush — before dinner, I mean?'

'Occasionally, when I meet with a luncheon.'

'I'm fairly puzzled,' said poor Fitz, throwing himself into a chair. 'Gout is a very good thing; but then you see you are only a sub., and it is clearly against the articles of war to have it before being a field officer at least. Apoplexy is the best I can do for you; and, to say the truth, any one who witnesses your performance at mess may put faith in the likelihood of it. Do you think you could get up a fit for the medical board?' said Fitz gravely.

'Why, if absolutely indispensable,' said I, 'and with good instruction — something this way. Eh, is it not?'

'Nothing of the kind — you are quite wrong.'

'Is there not always a little laughing and crying?' said I.

'Oh no, no; take the cue from the paymaster any evening after mess, and you'll make no mistake — very florid about the cheeks; rather a lazy look in one eye, the other closed up entirely; snore a little from time to time, and don't be too much disposed to talk.'

'And you think I may pass muster in this way?'

'Indeed you may, if old Camie, the inspector, happen to be (what he is not often) in a good humour. But I confess I'd rather you were really ill, for we've passed a great number of counterfeits latterly, and we may be all pulled up ere long.'

(*Harry Lorrequer*, ch. VIII, pp. 87-8)

The aftermath of the Famine left Ireland a smouldering land of disaffection, for which patriots were often prepared to die; thus Irish fiction was at a low ebb for the next quarter of a century. For part of this time both Samuel Lover and Charles Lever were alive and active; but they lived abroad, and like most authors born and educated in Dublin, wrote for the English-speaking world. Irish politics was, for them, largely irrelevant to the contemporary cultural scene. The indifference of England to Ireland could only have resulted from ignorance of colonial conditions. Lover's desire, at least, was to ameliorate this situation by showing Irish life (as he once knew it) in a more amiable and tolerant light. But both novelists touched life at the surface only. Their aim was to reach as wide an audience as possible; and they wrote in English in the conviction that it was bound to be the future language, not only of Ireland, but of the United States and the British colonies.

George Augustus Moore (1852-1933) became by sheer industry one of Ireland's most distinguished men of letters; he was the author of sixteen novels and four volumes of short stories. He began as a writer of verse and plays, and later produced four volumes of criticism and five autobiographical works, besides a translation of *Daphnis and Chloe*. Because of his Irish birth, he cared for Ireland's destiny, and the best of his fiction was the result of intermittent contact with his native land. Moore owed very little to English predecessors, although the longest part of his working life was spent in London. Inspiration came mainly from Zola, Balzac, Flaubert and Dujardin in France, Turgenev and Chekov in Russia. This was a superficial indication of his preference for realism. H. E. Bates has even described him as the father of the modern short story.

Moore's birthplace was the family estate in County Mayo, on the shores of Lake Carra. His forebears had both Catholic and Protestant affiliations; he seems to have profited little from a Catholic education at Oscott boarding school, near Birmingham. The principal passion of adolescence was the family tradition of horse-breeding and racing, interests that figure largely in his best esteemed novel, *Esther Waters* (1894). When he came of age he lived for seven years in Paris, hoping to become a painter. In the café-life of the time, he mixed with painters, poets and novelists, who left a lasting impression on his thinking and bohemian way of life. Finding he had no talent for the plastic arts, Moore sought ineffectually to become a poet, in the manner of Baudelaire, Mallarmé and Swinburne. In 1880 he was compelled to return to London to augment his income, fully determined to become a novelist. He took humble lodgings in the Strand, and strove tirelessly to master the English language, while most of his thinking was in French. All the novels were later conscientiously revised and, where necessary, curtailed. He matured slowly and he was over thirty before his first novel appeared. It was 1886 before he made use of his Irish experience in *A Drama in Muslin*, re-issued in 1915 under the more modest title *Muslin*.

The fiction of George Moore is invariably classed as naturalistic, but reservations are necessary, because there were variable stages in his development. The early style was marred by alien mannerisms, particularly Zolaesque rhetoric of description, which he later sought to eliminate. He chose the profession of novelist because fascinated by the difficulty of inventing a story. The compositional, rather than auditory, complexities first appealed to him; but priorities were reversed in the mature novels. English prose, he found, was an unresponsive medium; not surprisingly, since Pater's *Marius the Epicurean* and Landor's *Imaginary Conversations* were his chosen models. After the publication of his earliest successful novel, *A Mummer's Wife* (1884), he realised that art meant sacrificing brash enthusiasms and expansiveness; a rhythmical style then became a *sine qua non*; but the desired firmness and balance were not achieved until *Esther Waters* in 1894.

By the time Moore returned to live in Ireland, he had acquired remarkable control over his medium. His forte was undoubtedly social fiction, in which narrative rejected the picaresque; he preferred not to handle heroes or heroines. *A Drama in Muslin* portrayed Alice Barton as a free-thinking, yet dutiful daughter of land-owning parentage, sensitive to the entrenched position of her class. The privileged gentry were in the process of being reduced to impotence by the Land League of Michael Davitt, as Moore realised to his own cost. This unnatural hierarchy, with many social misfits, Moore sought to depict in a number of experimental styles, intended to differentiate, as well as to deflate, interesting characters and temperaments. A principal aim was to demonstrate, through dialogue, that the artificial life of marriageable young women often had deep spiritual and moral consequences. The stream-of-consciousness technique was familiar to Moore from Continental sources, and his use in this novel was to blend it with authorial comment and such lyrical prose as might be evoked by a particular mood or situation. Here is an example from the presentation of debutantes at Dublin Castle:

> ... veils of silver tissue softened the edges of the train, silver stars gleamed in the corn-coloured hair, the long hands, gloved with white undressed kid, carried a silver fan; she was adorably beautiful and adorably pale, and she floated through the red glare, along the scarlet line, to the weary-looking man in maroon breeches, like some wonderful white bird of downy plumage. He kissed her on both cheeks; and she passed away to the farther door, where her train was caught up and handed to her by two aides-de-camp. He had seemed to salute her with deference and warmth; his kiss was more than ceremonial, and eager looks passed between the ladies-of-honour standing on the *estrade*; the great bouquet of red-coats placed in the middle of the floor, animated by one desire, turned its sixteen heads to gaze after the wonderful vision of blonde beauty that had come — that had gone.
>
> (*Muslin*, ch. XIX, p. 145)

This passage should be compared with one where Alice's state of mind is clearly 'dramatised' through comment:

> The drama in muslin was again unfolded, and she could read each act; and there was a 'curtain' at the end of each. The first was made of young, hopeful faces, the second of arid solicitation, the third of the bitter, malignant tongues of Bertha Duffy and her friend. She had begun to experience the worst horrors of a Castle ball. She was sick of pity for those around her, and her lofty spirit resented the insult that was being offered to her sex. . . . There are psychological reasons that to-day more than ever impel women to shrink from the intellectual monotony of their sex, and to view with increasing admiration the male mind; for as the gates of the harem are being broken down, and the gloom of the female mind clears, it becomes certain that woman brings a loftier reverence to the shrine of man than she has done in any past age, seeing, as she now does,

in him the incarnation of the freedom of which she is vaguely conscious and which she is perceptibly acquiring. So sets the main current that is bearing civilisation along; but beneath the great feminine tide there is an undercurrent of hatred and revolt.

(ibid., pp. 162-3)

Moore's part in the Irish Literary Renaissance from 1901 was not as undistinguished as detractors pretend. He left London under a cloud, because of sympathies with W. T. Stead and the pro-Boer agitation. His playwright-cousin, Edward Martyn, and W. B. Yeats prevailed upon him to come to their assistance in Dublin, where he already knew AE (George Russell). He soon learnt to admire Synge, but literary relations with Yeats and Lady Gregory were never very cordial. Yeats certainly respected Moore's gifts, but thought his French mannerisms and erratic independence egocentric. Like most Irish contemporaries, Moore made no effort to learn Irish, and after an initial wave of enthusiasm looked upon the zeal of the Gaelic League with mild disapproval. In Dublin he lived intimately with other writers, held soirées at his home in Ely Place, and emulated AE in remaining a father-figure and adviser to the new movement; he declined to have any share in the running of the Literary Theatre.

Of the ten years Moore spent in Ireland, most were occupied in composing the autobiographical books *Ave, Salve* and *Vale*, afterwards revised and amalgamated under the title *Hail and Farewell*. This sceptical work, in fictional style, is unique in Irish or English writing; it is indispensable to a study of the pitfalls of national literature. Despite some unreliability as an historical record, there is hardly a livelier account of social and political life in Dublin at the turn of the nineteenth century. It also explains Moore's change of heart regarding the value of the language movement. There were party issues at stake, which justified scepticism. Shaw and Joyce, prominent figures in the later stage of the revival, sympathised with Moore by withdrawing from the abrasive effect of Irish politics; they believed, too, that creative instincts would be denied their full scope.

Moore's comparative neglect by literary critics was remedied towards the end of his career by two studies, John Freeman's *Portrait of George Moore* (1922) and Humbert Wolfe's *George Moore*, which was written with the novelist's conniv- ance in 1931, and revised in 1933. These were the result of personal acquaintance with Moore, during his long residence at 121 Ebury Street. Moore, they show, pretended not to care whether the reading public liked him or not after reading *Hail and Farewell*, providing the work was admired.

In a Preface to *The Untilled Field* (1903) Moore opined that this series of stories contained his most important contribution to the Anglo-Irish revival, in which rural con- versation is supposed to have imitated the dialects of Wicklow, Munster and Connacht. Soon after the novelist made Dublin his home, Yeats brought Synge from Paris, and encouraged him to fabricate in English what he picked up in Wicklow and the Aran Islands. In bantering mood, Moore enjoyed parodying what he considered was a phoney representation of peasant chatter:

> Wasn't he dreaming, too, he could be writing like a French fellow of the name of Loti, that knew the trick with a couple of twists of the pen of turning every country in the wide world into a sweet-shop? But 'tis little of the taste of sugar-candy he got into his articles, and his book about the Aran Islands has more of the tang of old leather, like as if he'd be chewing the big brogues he did be always wearing on his feet. And, morebetoken, his language in the same book is as bald as the coat of a mangy dog, and trapsed along over a page of print like the clatter of a horse that was gone in the legs. It's many a heart scald this same must have given to my bold Yeats, for it's the grand judge entirely he is of the shape and the colour and the sound of words.
>
> (*The Untilled Field*, p. vii)

It was even more preposterous in Moore's mind that Gaelic should be regarded an essential part of the Irishman's identity (see *Hail and Farewell*, ed. R. A. Cave, Intro. p. 14). If that were indispensable, why were sincere protagonists of the Literary Renaissance writing in the language of the conqueror? He could not resolve the Gaelic movement's incongruities, and openly doubted the utility of reverting to ancient mythology as Yeats was doing. In Ireland's unhappy situation, the immediacy of Russian fiction-writers, such as Turgenev and Chekhov, who were concerned with their own times, would have had more point. Disillusioned, Moore returned to London in 1911, muttering his sardonic judgement: 'an Irishman must fly from Ireland, if he would be himself' (ibid., p. 56).

The short stories in *The Untilled Field* were therefore modelled on Turgenev's *Sketches of a Sportsman*, and written to comply with an educational suggestion of Father Tom Finlay, editor of the *New Ireland Review*; the plan was that a translator, Taidhg O'Donoghue, should turn them into the vernacular for use in schools. But the initial results unnerved the Catholic sensibilities of the Gaelic League, since one of Moore's aims was to expose the narrow puritanism of the priest class. What should have been a reconstruction of rural Ireland of his youth was further jeopardised by Moore's public renunciation of Catholicism and declaration that he had joined the Anglican Church of Ireland. The prickly novelist, it was concluded, had come to Ireland, less to contribute to the Literary Renaissance, than to unburden his wit at the expense of what he disapproved of. *The Untilled Field* served to affirm that Moore supported Protestantism, because it offered a religious atmosphere in which art could breathe. Most tales show the baneful relationship between authoritarian priests and browbeaten peasants. Exceptions are, however, the humorous 'Letter from Rome' and the simple homily 'So on he fares'; for as Moore pointed out, 'it is the telling that makes a story true or false' (*Muslin*, Preface, p. viii). Moore, the ironist, undertook only themes that were thoroughly in accord with his temperament. *The Untilled Field* was almost certainly read by Joyce before he attempted *Dubliners*; and 'The Wild Goose' must have been intended as a contrast to the theme of *The Lake* (1905).

The Lake had two principal sources, Turgenev's *A Month in the Country* and Wagner's *Lohengrin*. Moore and his cousin Edward Martyn were Wagner enthusiasts, and had made a pilgrimage to Bayreuth on several occasions. Though this tale was intended to form part of *The Untilled Field*, the publisher wisely wanted it printed separately, on account of its length. A prefatory dedication to another Wagnerite, Edouard Dujardin of Paris, explains that Moore appropriated his title 'The Source of the Christian River', because it was apposite to the conversion of Father Oliver Gogarty.

Moore's love of music, according to Humbert Wolfe, was due to deferential regard for a 'strict integrity of form' (op. cit., p. 31); but why, he asks, did he choose so undisciplined a composer as Wagner? Perhaps because he defined art as 'a lyrical sequence of events described with rhythmical sequence of phrase' (see Walter Allen, *The English Novel*, p. 297). This criterion of excellence finds almost perfect expression in Moore's mature novels, *The Lake* and *The Brook Kerith* (1916). An article with the curious title 'The Nineness in the Oneness', contributed to the *Century Magazine* (No. 99, Nov. 1919, p. 63) assures the reader that 'the writing of *The Lake* would not be as it is if I had not listened to *Lohengrin* many times'. Moore's particular fondness was, however, for *Tannhäuser*, *Rheingold* and *Siegfried*; his novel *Evelyn Innes* (1898) is concerned with Wagnerian opera and its performers.

The technique of interior dialogue which *The Lake* incorporates so effectively is combined with an epistolary self-revelation, characteristic of Richardson, Fanny Burney and Dujardin. Ever-present is the background of Lake Carra and its islands, especially the one on which lived the devotional poet Marban, the hermit. Under the spell of his youthful environment, Moore ceased to be a petulant critic of the church; there is a distinct note of sympathy with religious attitudes of a certain type of mind. Fathers Gogarty and Moran have to grapple with the emotional difficulty of loneliness in different ways; and against these he sets the balanced figure of Father Michael O'Grady of London, whose urban experience left him without a trace of rancour towards sceptics. Moran remarked pointedly that 'religion in Ireland was another form of love of country. . . . If Catholics were intolerant to every form of heresy, it was because they instinctively felt that the questioning of any dogma would mean some slight subsidence from the idea of nationality that held the people together' (*The Lake*, p. 52). Gogarty comes finally to the realisation that 'an intellectual influence is always more dangerous than a sensual influence, and the sins of the faith are worse than the sins of the flesh' (ibid., p. 92). Antiquarianism in retrospect makes a valuable contribution to Gogarty's historical philosophy, for instance on p. 109:

> Religion in Ireland in the seventh and eighth centuries was clearly a homely thing, full of tender joy and hope, and the inspiration not only of poems, but of many churches and much ornament of all kinds, illuminated missals, carven porches. If Ireland had been left to herself — if it had not been for the invasion of the Danes, and the still worse invasion of the English — there is no saying what high place she might not have taken in the history of the world. But I am afraid the halcyon light that passed and passed on in those centuries will never return.

Moore convinced himself that emigration of Irish Catholics to America before and during his lifetime was symptomatic of an anti-clerical movement, actuated by the church's ownership of property and higher standard of living among the priest class. Anti-clericalism in Ireland was more disturbing to Rome than the feared invasion of English Protestantism, which Home Rule was certain to promote. Oliver Gogarty thus questioned restrictions upon social life imposed by his training at Maynooth. One was grounded on the illusion that sexual interest between men and women was fundamentally evil. Nora Glynn was able to convince Gogarty because she demonstrated the worth of natural intelligence, and insisted on the right of her sex to educate itself by enquiring into the true nature of religion. Moore suggests that the medieval Christian of Ireland was in a better relation with his faith, enjoying as he did a closer contact with nature, which taught him that the flesh could sometimes redeem the spirit.

Edith Somerville (1858-1949) and Martin Ross (the pen-name of Violet Martin) (1862-1915) were contemporaries of Moore, but had the advantage of constantly living in Ireland, after the Famine years, when significant social changes were taking place. The mass emigration of disillusion-ed Irish people to America began in 1846; and the objective and sensitive reporting in the novels of Somerville and Ross provides ample explanation of it. Both writers were at school when the Protestant Irish Church was disestablished in 1869, and Gladstone's Land Act saw the demise of the feudal era in 1870. The next decade brought a period of crop failures and economic crises.

Somerville and Ross were second cousins, who met for the first time in 1886; they belonged to the Irish Protestant Ascendancy and were daughters of land-owners, who held large estates in the south and west, not far from Cork and Galway. In Violet Martin's family sons were outnumbered by daughters, who felt their inferior social status acutely. Edith Somerville wrote:

> In 1884 those who were spoken of as Elders and Betters, the first always pre-supposing the second, were untram-melled by doctrines of self-determination for their young — especially for their female young. A girl did what she was told, and, as to clothes, wore what her mother wished her to wear, and there was no more about it.
>
> (*French Leave*, p. 2)

Both writers became militant feminists and neither married. Their novels and short stories are a mirror of rural domestic life at many levels, presented with frankness and veracity, but with a limited social outlook. The treatment is not unlike Maria Edgeworth's in *Castle Rackrent*, though less subtle, the characterisation being of lesser depth. Their rebellion against 'quality' manners was notable for its blood-snobbery and upper-class ethics. Somerville characterised the Big House mentality succinctly in *Irish Memories* (1912):

> Ireland was, in those days, a forcing bed for individuality. Men and women, of the upper classes, were what is usually described as 'a law unto themselves,' which is another way of saying that they broke those of all other authorities. . . . Each estate was a kingdom, and, in the impossibility of locomotion, each neighbouring potentate acquired a relative importance quite out of proportion to his merits,

for to love your neighbour — or, at all events, to marry her — was almost inevitable when matches were a matter of mileage, and marriages might be said to have been made by the map. Enormous families were the rule in all classes, such being reputed to be the will of God, and the olive branches about the paternal table often became of so dense a growth as to exclude from it all other fruits of the earth, save, possibly, the potato.

(p. 68)

The best account of their methods of collaboration is contained in the same book, written by Edith Somerville to commemorate the death of her colleague during the First World War. Together they wrote five novels, four volumes of short stories and four travel books, in a period of less than thirty years. Both firmly maintained that their work could not be dissected with the object of discerning the individual contributions. As kindred spirits, they enjoyed exceptional unanimity in both character and plot. Submerging their different personalities, they created by conversational agreement; it was therefore immaterial which writer actually held the pen; first thoughts were jotted down, and afterwards critically and meticulously revised. If one examines the first two chapters of *Irish Memories*, containing Violet Martin's memoir of her brother Robert, as well as her letters in the final chapter, a lively perspective of vivacity and discipline emerges; these were the paradoxical qualities of her mind. Here, for instance, is a political opinion, expressed to Stephen Gwynn, M.P. in February 1912:

By 'snakes' in Ireland, I mean a set of new circumstances, motives, influences, and possibilities acting on people's lives and characters, and causing disturbance. My chief reason for this fear that I have is that Irish Nationalism is not one good solid piece of homespun. It is a patch work. There are some extremely dangerous factors in it, one of the worst being the Irish-American revolutionary. The older Fenianism lives there, plus all that is least favourable in American republicanism. . . . [These] will look on Ireland as the depot and jumping-off place for their animosity to England, dormant and theoretical, innate and inherited. . . .

A Roman Catholic ascendancy and government will bring Socialism, because now-a-days Socialism is the complementary colour of R.C. government or ascendancy. . . . A Vatican policy for Ireland it will have to be, under Home Rule, or else the Priesthood is shouldered aside, and that is an ugly and demoralising thing. The religious question is deep below all others. . . .

The people that I am most afraid of are the town politicians. I am not fond of anything about towns; they are full of second-hand thinking; they know nothing of raw material and the natural philosophy of the country people. As to caste, it is in the towns that the *vulgar* idea of caste is created. The country people believe in it strongly; they cling to a belief in what it should stand for of truth and honour — and there the best classes touch the peasant closely, and understand each other. . . . Social ambition is vulgarity, of course, and even a republican spirit does not cure it — witness America. It is not Ireland alone that is 'sicklied o'er with the pale thought of caste!'

(ibid., pp. 319-33)

This is highly competent writing, colourful and precise. Similar refinement and perspicacity are noticeable in the life-story of Robert, and recur in the collaborated fiction. The writers knew well their limitations, and refused to draw upon imagination for love scenes; such as occur in the novels are brief, and without sexual interest. After Martin Ross's death in 1915 Edith continued to use her partner's pseudonym on the title-page.

Strong family ties and resolute loyalties persisted in the isolated pockets of Irish Ascendency culture. Blood was a symbol of caste, and to override the tradition was to invite social censure. Religious tolerance was, however, indispensable, because family servants were invariably of the opposite faith, and very superstitious, though not wanting in courtesy and respect. Living in the country, Somerville was not as well acquainted with the urban class as was Ross, who had lived in Dublin for sixteen impressionable years of her education. Among Ascendancy families, it was unthinkable to lower one's cultural standards through marriage; excess of women

over men in Protestant communities therefore made spinster-
hood fairly common. Unmarried daughters often inherited
domestic responsibilities and educational duties, as both
writers discovered. Not surprisingly, they became defenders
of women's rights somewhat earlier than the active suffra-
gette movement in England. Art, humour and common sense
alone prevented family life from becoming unendurable.
Consequently Somerville and Ross soon became inveterate
travellers.

Edith was a budding artist, who trained first at Düsseldorf
and subsequently in Paris. Her observation and perception of
idiosyncracy were the sources of an admirable sense of
humour. Both writers were bohemian in taste, Edith in
particular, because of her association with Latin Quarter
studios. A disregard for convention and superficial appearances is displayed in the first joint novel, *An Irish Cousin*
(1889), though this is far from being a humorous book.
Robust hilarity was reserved for the short stories, which are
mostly hunting sketches. The original intention of *An Irish
Cousin* was to produce a 'shilling shocker'; but the mood of
writing for fun was speedily dissolved. Ideas of the collaborators were always well aired; and a twofold approach to art
obviously required self-discipline. Martin Ross told her
colleague: 'Writing together is one of the greatest pleasures
I have . . . [it] doubles the triumph and enjoyment, having
first halved the trouble and anxiety' (*Irish Memories*, p. 134).

Somerville subsequently regarded *An Irish Cousin* as a
poorly constructed novel; but the air of mystery was well
sustained until the twentieth chapter. Then the plot declined
to inferior Brontëan melodrama, though without emotional
vulgarity. No novel the partnership undertook foregoes the
frenzied exhilaration of fox-hunting, or the division of classes
by the character of their speech. The lowest stratification is
the illiteracy of peasants, such as Mrs Sweeney in chapter
fifteen; less commonplace is the brogue of the *nouveau-
riche* middle-class, which no device of spelling can adequately
capture; and last comes the affected public-school manner
of persons who received their education in England. The
unconscious Irishness of the gentry is marked by occasional
lapses of syntax, and their resorting to indigenous expressions.

The distinguished pedigree of Madam O'Neill is merely signified by the affectation of her snobbery '. . . we are quite in the backwoods here — all the *nice* people live at the other end of the county — and you mustn't take these as specimens of Irish society' (*An Irish Cousin*, p. 169). The custom of keening at funerals belonged to the lower orders, and was regarded by 'the quality' as barbaric and savage.

Nowhere is distinction of manners more palpable than in *The Real Charlotte* (1894), regarded by the partners as their best novel. It is also the longest, because their original intention had been to provide a mature three-volume work. The model was to be Maria Edgeworth; but the fiction of Balzac, Thackeray and Trollope had intervened. The ambitious trilogy was inevitably in the school of realism; but the skilled character delineation was concentrated on an unpleasant, unscrupulous woman, rather than a man. Lady Dysart, on the other hand, was candidly a version of Edith Somerville's mother, and a *réchauffé* of eighteenth-century 'humours'; the original is reported to have disliked the fiction her daughter wrote, because of the economy of love-making, and the avoidance of happy endings (see p. 90). Thackeray's influence upon the novel is to be seen principally in the personality of Francie Fitzpatrick, founded on the Dublin experiences of Ross. The abundant scriptural references look back to the young pupil's meritorious Sunday school days.

Fifty chapters afforded ample scope for a variety of characters, and a considerable diversity in the employment of regional dialogue; but little attempt was made to distinguish the brogues of Cork, Dublin and Galway. As usual, chapters are short, and look like impressionistic sketches, designed to end at a climactic point. Each seems to represent the work of a single session, perhaps curtailed in the making of a fair copy. The point of view of the novelists was invariably that of Francie Fitzpatrick, rather than of Charlotte Mullen.

Care must have been taken, especially by Martin Ross, in camouflaging the real-life personality of this odious middle-class adventuress, unsoftened by a classical education. There may also be some recollection of Ross's Dublin sojourn in Francie, the sincere adolescent who is unhappy in her choice of adult lovers. Francie could even be a spinster's warning against the danger of unchaperoned flirtation. In a society preoccupied with the indolent pursuits of riding, dancing and tennis parties, one is led to assume that love-making was rather superficial.

The Real Charlotte is unusually long in establishing plot and *raison d'être*, but its cross-sections of aristocratic and plebian society are illuminating. The social discomfiture of Francie is due less to instability of character than to a deplorable Dublin accent. Most middle-class characters in this novel are differentiated by speech or subtle gradations of Irish vulgarity. The moral issues of a complicated domestic tragedy are typical of Victorian fiction, and resemble those of George Eliot.

Some Experiences of an Irish R.M. (1899) represented the comic debut of the partnership, and was their most popular success. The twelve short stories were written to comply with a request from the editor of the *Badminton Magazine*, and were begun while the authors were on holiday at Étaples, on the northern French coast. Major Sinclair Yeats and Flurry Knox, the central figures, were obviously conceived in holiday spirit. These humorous sketches, devoted to the chase and the ludicrous situations the sport encourages, had two sequels, *Further Experiences* (1908) and *In Mr Knox's Country* (1915). The comic exuberance equals or surpasses that of Robert Surtees in *Handley Cross*. Martin Ross was a splendid mimic of the intonations of the Galway dialects, and the language the authors evolved for their amusing characters deserved some observations:

Phonetic spelling in matters of dialect is a delusive thing, to be used with the utmost restraint. It is superfluous for those who know, boring for those who do not. Of what avail is spelling when confronted with the problem of indicating the pronunciation of, for example, 'Papa'; the slurring and softening of the consonant, the flattening of the vowel sound — how can these be even indicated? And, spelling or no, can any tongue, save an Irish one, pronounce the words 'being' and 'ideal,' as though they owned but one syllable? Long ago Martin and I debated the point, and the conclusion that we then arrived at was that the root of the matter in questions of dialect was in the idiomatic phrase and the mental attitude.

(*Irish Memories*, p. 175)

The regional vocabulary was largely derived from conversations with 'Rickeen', one of Violet Martin's tenants, who believed in the Evil Eye, leprechauns and other supernatural spirits of the Irish peasantry.

Soon after returning from France, Violet Martin was injured in a riding accident, and was for months in pain from a back injury; Edith Somerville, moreover, had contracted to provide the illustrations. The amusing tales were thus produced under trying physical circumstances, yet three thousand copies were sold in the first month. This unlooked-for success was due partly to the incongruity of class encounters, which hunting undoubtedly occasioned; an international reputation was built upon comic misadventures, farcical situations and Irish extravagance of speech. The Resident Magistrate here describes in bantering tone the arrival of his old college friend, Leigh Kelway:

The stout young friend of my youth had changed considerably. His important nose and slightly prominent teeth remained, but his wavy hair had withdrawn intellectually from his temples; his eyes had acquired a statesmanlike absence of expression, and his neck had grown long and birdlike. . . .

During the next few days I did my best for Leigh Kelway. I turned him loose on Father Scanlan; I showed him Mohona, our champion village, that boasts fifteen public-houses out of twenty buildings of sorts and a railway station; I took him to hear the prosecution of a publican for selling drink on a Sunday, which gave him an opportunity of studying perjury as a fine art, and of hearing a lady, on whom police suspicion justly rested, profoundly summed up by the sergeant as 'a woman who had th' appairance of having knocked at a back door.'. . .

For my own part, I had at the end of three days arrived at the conclusion that his society, when combined with a note-book and a thirst for statistics, was not what I used to find it at Oxford.

(*Some Experiences of an Irish R.M.*, pp. 98-9)

After Violet Martin's death in 1915, Edith wrote five more novels, the most impressive being *The Big House of Inver* (1925). She had for some years taken an interest in spiritualism and automatic writing, and believed that she was able to communicate with her erstwhile collaborator. *The Big House* and *Mount Music* were planned while Ross was still alive. *Castle Rackrent* made a considerable impact upon the former; but the historical setting owed a good deal to Thackeray's *Henry Esmond*. Martin had been visiting Lady Gregory at Coole Park, and was taken to see Tyrone House in Galway; she met there the last descendent of the St George family. This unmarried figure inspired Shibby Pindy of *The Big House*. In the novel she was the illegitimate daughter of Jas Prendeville, a retired army officer, whose acknowledged heir was a feckless but handsome son, Kit. Somerville here depicted the sinister fate of many Irish gentry, who forfeited their estates through riot, quarrelling and gambling. But more important was the loss of caste by marriage or intercourse with peasant tenants. For the Irish aristocrat, purity of blood was held to be the final criterion of superior status.

The Big House pointedly suggests that the temptations open to gentlemen of quality living in the country were due to the friendliness and conviviality of the Irish character; there was an expected informality in the land-owner's way of life. Captain Prendeville is thus the scion of loose-living ancestors, who leave all estate business to a trustworthy bailiff. John Weldon is Prendeville's agent and proves more honest than his scheming and perfidious son, married to an English wife. Kit Prendeville, the captain's legitimate heir, is a masterful horseman, with vacillating moral principles, and little education. The theme of the book may have been suggested by Exodus XX, 5: the iniquity of the fathers shall be visited upon the children, unto the third and fourth generation.

Edith Somerville's handling here reveals a strong grasp of character, and a sense of fitness in conducting a well-regulated household; she is especially well informed on relationships with servants. Her eye for landscape and personal idiosyncracy was superior to her sense of structural form. Like other women of her class, she admired physical courage, and approved the socially acceptable pleasures. She had an appreciative ear for 'the gentle western voice' of Ireland, 'with the sing-song rise and fall [and] an unwonted spring in it'. But she was fully aware of servility in the lower orders of her countrymen. Here is her analysis of Nesta, a typical member of the servant class:

> She was of those whose inveterate unselfishness can only be explained by the theory of a heredity of slave ancestresses. Creatures so submissive as to have no independent existence, so unselfish as to become the centre of a vortex of practically enforced selfishness; born slaves, perpetual servers of the domestic altar, whose single redeeming vice is their self-indulgent virtue, who can only urge in self-defence that they do not often transmit their infirmity to their male offspring.
>
> (*The Big House*, pp. 55-6)

Perhaps the main virtues of Edith's partner were sincerity of conviction, a keen sense of fun, and a fine command of language.

A single comedy, *French Leave* (1925), came from Edith Somerville in later years. It is partly autobiographical and looks back to the nineteen-eighties, when the artist was a headstrong young woman, fired with the ambition to make her own career. Entertainingly, she displays the paternalistic life of an Ascendancy land-owner, who is well-to-do, but not affluent. The master of the household, Sir Ingram Kirwen, is a coarse-grained patriarch, whose domestic domination is such that a woman of spirit, like Edith Somerville, could not endure it. She was outraged at the thought that education was 'unnecessary for wives, and ruinous for servants' (p. 45).

In this novel the new stream-of-consciousness technique was employed with effect in some of the reflective narrative; but there is an evident decline in the quality of writing. Thackeray in the *Book of Snobs* (ch. XVII), said that he had 'met as many descendants from Irish kings as would form a brigade'; but his satire was mild when compared with Sir Ingram's disparagement of his tenant, Holy George, a nonconformist 'hymn-singing scoundrel':

> George had inherited something of the iron Irish Protestant backbone that had come to him and his father by direct descent from one of those Cromwellian soldiers whose stock, prosperous, upright, bigoted, and contentious, has penetrated most of Ireland, contributing with potency to her welfare and to her rebellions, if not to her pacification.
>
> (*French Leave*, p. 133)

James Stephens (1880-1950), already briefly considered as a poet, was one of Ireland's most distinguished writers of prose. His youth was clouded in poverty, to which he constantly alludes, claiming that he did not even know the date of his birth. Nevertheless, he received a moderate education in ten years at the Meath Protestant Industrial School, to which he was admitted when found begging on the Dublin streets. While he was at this school for underprivileged children, and later as a solicitor's clerk, a love of reading was prompted by the borrowing of books from the YMCA library. Stephens's novels and short stories live as first-hand chronicles of the conditions of life that existed in the back streets of Dublin, during the last two decades of the nineteenth century.

After his schooling Stephens became a clerk-typist in a legal office, and was there sought out by George Russell after he had seen some of his poems. The influence of AE on his literary career was as lasting as their friendship. At twenty-five Stephens saw his first prose work published, and then became a contributor to *Sinn Féin*, a nationalist journal edited by Arthur Griffith. It was Russell who introduced him to Dublin's literary circles. In spite of an initial dislike of James Joyce's work, Stephens established a friendship with that writer, later to be renewed in Paris, which after 1913 Stephens regarded as his second home. Some of his best writing was done in French boulevard cafés, or in an apartment permanently maintained, after the publication of his second novel, *The Crock of Gold* (1912).

From 1909 to 1920 Stephens acted in a number of Dublin

theatres, including the Abbey, and for some years he served on the executive of the Dublin Drama League. He found time also to become an expert gymnast. While co-editor of the *Irish Review* (1911-14), he published his first novel, *The Charwoman's Daughter*, now deservedly regarded as his best. W. B. Yeats presented him with the Polignac Prize for *The Crock of Gold* in 1913. In order to afford more time for writing, a post was found for him as Registrar of the National Gallery of Ireland (1915-24). But from 1925 Stephens settled in London, from which he soon embarked on a number of successful lecture tours of America. His popularity as a speaker was probably due to a natural gift of humour and a fine command of expression. He became a much-loved broadcaster on the BBC from 1928 until the year of his death.

Dr Johnson's epitaph on Goldsmith, 'everything he touched he adorned', may be appropriated with fitness to James Stephens. He was far from being a major novelist, but it was not in his nature to be dull. He shared with AE an innate courtesy and *bonhomie*, to which was added a Gallic whimsicality regarding the life he saw around him. Public distinction forbade that he should become a recluse, like James Joyce. Whether he was writing of nature or the gods, the pictures are vivid and detailed, the language figurative in the use of epithets. Here is an instance from a sketch that appeared in *Here are Ladies* (1913):

> He liked to think of his first French conversation. He wanted something to read in English, but was timid of asking for it. He walked past all the newspaper kiosks on the Boulevard, anxiously scanning the vendors inside — they were usually very stalwart, very competent females, who looked as though they had outgrown their sins but remembered them with pleasure. They had the dully-polished, slightly-battered look of a modern antique. The words 'M'sieu, Madame' ran from them as from bells. They were very alert, sitting as it were, on tiptoe, and their eyes hit one as one approached. They were like spiders squatting in their little houses waiting for their daily flies.
>
> ('A Glass of Beer', *James Stephens, a Selction*, pp. 113-14)

From nearly everything Stephens wrote there emerges a unique gift of humour and fantasy; the reader must bring to this writer's treatment of the supernatural the same suspension of disbelief that he grants to *Alice in Wonderland*. With this difference, however: Stephens is the kind of visionary who writes for adults, displaying unusual tenderness and generosity of mind. He went to France to broaden his outlook; but in his four novels the Irishness is unmistakeable. Naturalism in Stephens is associated with a rhythm of phrase characteristic of the Celtic spirit; the talkativeness is far from encouraging volubility. Moreover, the translucency of the writing forbids superfluity of sentiment. Stephens maintained that the prose writer needs to love his craft with the same zeal for the *mot juste* as the poet. His letters and critical utterances were invariably tolerant, undogmatic and practical.

Stephens saw Britain and France as nations which complemented each other in the development of style, as Rome complemented Athens. The philosophical aura of his brief novels is copious, but ostensibly intended at wisdom for living, because pronouncements invariably arise from a situation that is interesting. Stephens believed that the qualities which seem unique in his work should be attributed to a knack of lively perceptiveness:

The parts of my books which I read with pleasure, and upon which I have expended all the writing and art and craft that is in me, are precisely those parts which other people treat with something of disdain: i.e. the hinging-on parts. The scrap of writing which lies between two pieces of action, the beginnings of chapters where one is only preparing for the story, the ends of chapters where one is wiping up the mess which the action has made, into these I put all the energy I have got, much more than in the *important* places. . . . It is in response to a feeling of 'life' my best writing comes, and even with thinking I use somewhat the same method, seeking to hand it out to the reader hot or visible or savoury.

(*Letters*, p. 203)

When he commenced *The Charwoman's Daughter*, Stephens remembered the advice of Sidney: 'look in your heart and write'; his wife Cynthia was the model for Mary Makebelieve. In the presentation of character, he revealed a distinctly Dickensian turn of thought. A wealth of detail accompanies the domestic settings, and the vocabulary is astonishingly appropriate to the social ambience and the quaintness of manners. Mrs Makebelieve's maternal care exacts a high standard of morality and discipline, despite the meagreness of her means. Stephens was determined to show that the poor are seldom without their innocent domestic joys, though these are largely wishes fulfilled in imagination. Fantasy was essential to this novelist's concept of plot; and his major achievement was to match it with the realism of commonplace circumstance. Editor L. Frankenberg did readers of Stephens's novel a considerable service in bringing to light an unpublished preface, which was intended for the French translation of *The Charwoman's Daughter*:

> Poetry is created in the whole phrase; is even, when the gods are benevolent, created in the entire verse. But prose must be invented from comma to comma. . . .
>
> The ear must be unflaggingly active and watchful, and inquisitive. It must serve even as an eye, surveying whole swathes and pastures of sense and action and passion, which poetry needs only to indicate, but which prose must wholly fabricate and complete to the last possible verb and noun and adjective. For the matter of poesy comes eagerly to its statement, but that which prose can serve is loath and reluctant; is without any spring or readiness; is void of good-will or good-humour. . . .
>
> In verse, even before the work is begun, the ear is marvellously, is prophetically, attuned to an unknown key and its permissive harmonies; but prose is chromatic and accidental, and the ear dealing with it must cover strange and continuously-changing intervals, and must seek harmonic values in unexpected places and at great and greatly-varying distances. . . . The key changes after every full stop. . . .
>
> Between the artist and his own most intimate compre-

hensions there is a screen of words which have wide general significances, but no precise meanings. . . . The values of these words fluctuate so violently — their meanings are at every moment so great and so small, as to render them purely personal to the user. . . .

(*James Stephens, a Selection*, pp. 401-7)

The Crock of Gold, published in the same year as *The Charwoman's Daughter*, wholly supports Stephens's declaration of faith; inconsistencies of character and the lack of an orderly plan are its principal defects. Moreover, Irish folklore and French fabliaux do not seem to go well in double harness. The Greek demigod Pan, who represents the sensual life, is at odds with Angus Óg, Stephens's god of love and creative imagination, and their clash tends to be theatrical. The extravagance of the proper names, the reference to the talking salmon that lies in the pool of Glyn Cagny, both remind us that *The Crock of Gold* is a fairy-tale whose worldly wisdom can be taken *cum grano salis*. The loquacious, thick-skinned Philosopher who lives in the pine forest, Coilla Doraca, has curious resemblances to St Patrick and the Hebrew prophets, and to Stephens himself, his guiding principle being that 'hunger, love and curiosity are the great impelling forces of life' (p. 9). The Philosopher's wife, the Thin Woman of Inis Magrath, is a grotesque humour, with supernatural blood, designed to explain her shrewishness and contrariness. The Thin Woman's former home had been the Shee (Irish *sidhe*) of Croghan Conghaile; she was a fairy woman who belonged to the 'little people' referred to as leprechauns (see ch. IV, pp. 105-6). A *shee* was usually depicted as a round, green elf-mound, beneath which was concealed a fairy palace. By the eighteenth century, leprechauns, like policemen, had become figures of fun in representing Irish legend; Swift's Lilliputians were recollections of the 'little people', as the Brobdignagians were of Celtic giants.

Stephens's Philosopher is clearly a pseudo-scientist, with a fixation on definition, classification and generalised functions. This makes him an amusing bore to the pragmatists. The Philosopher's gnomic utterances contain paradoxes and *bons mots* of bland precision, for example:

> A woman should be seen seldom but never heard. Quiet-
> ness is the beginning of virtue. To be silent is to be
> beautiful. Stars do not make a noise. Children should
> always be in bed. These are serious truths, which cannot
> be controverted.
>
> (ch. IV, p. 35)

This oracular style, with comic purpose, is a favourite technique of Stephens. But in poetic mood, the language flows
in rhythms of profounder amplitude, in which antithesis
and parallelism play a major role. Here is a passage describing
Caitilin, the innocent shepherd girl:

> A thought is a real thing and words are only its raiment,
> but a thought is as shy as a virgin; unless it is fittingly
> apparelled we may not look on its shadowy nakedness: it
> will fly from us and only return again in the darkness
> crying in a thin, childish voice which we may not com-
> prehend until, with aching minds, listening and divining,
> we at last fashion for it those symbols which are its
> protection and its banner.... The standard of either
> language or experience was not here; she could listen but
> not think, she could feel but not know, her eyes looked
> forward and did not see, her hands groped in the sunlight
> and felt nothing. It was like the edge of a little wind which
> stirred her tresses but could not lift them, or the first
> white peep of the dawn which is neither light nor darkness.
> But she listened, not with her ears but with her blood. The
> fingers of her soul stretched out to clasp a stranger's hand,
> and her disquietude was quickened through with an eager-
> ness which was neither physical nor mental.
>
> (ch. VI, pp. 51-2)

One of the special attractions of *The Crock of Gold* is
the diversity of styles. Stephens used the book as a workshop
for fruitful experiment, not only in fictional theory, but in
the art of writing. He suited the tone of his talk not only to
social classes and grades of occupation, but to age groups,
sexes and imaginary demigods. The chatter of the police in
Book V is maked by officialese and stereotyped attitudes

of mind. In the same book he conjures up the psychological effects upon a man's thoughts of finding himself in gaol for the first time; he even makes this scene the occasion for practising techniques of the short story. In one account he recaptures the conversation of his landlady's young daughter as follows:

> Her talk was as involved as her actions: she always seemed to be sliding down mental bannisters; she thought in kinks and spoke in spasms, hopped mentally from one subject to another without the slightest difficulty, and could use a lot of language in saying nothing at all. . . . Under her scampering tongue I began to learn something of humanity. . . .
>
> (*The Crock of Gold*, pp. 256, 258)

Stephens must have possessed an attentive ear for the nuances of Irish speech. In Book II, ch. XI, the travelling Philosopher encounters an aged peasant widow, muttering to herself about recollections that alone made life tolerable:

> Ah, the kind man, with his soft eyes, with his nice voice, and his jokes and laughing, and *him thinking* the world and all of me — ay, indeed. . . . And the neighbours to be coming in and sitting round the fire in the night time, *putting the world through each other.* . . . I wish to God I had a cup of tea and a bit of meat . . . or, maybe, an egg. A nice fresh egg laid by the *speckeldy* hen that used to be giving me all the trouble, *the thing!* Sixteen hens I had, and they *were the ones for laying, surely.* . . . It's *the* queer world, so it is, the queer world — and the things that do happen for no reason at all. . . . Ah, God be with me! I wish there weren't stones in my boots, *so I do,* and I wish to God I had a cup of tea and a fresh egg. Ah, *glory be,* my old legs are getting tireder every day.
>
> (ibid., pp. 120-21)

This monologue has the ring of authenticity, secured with the minimum of verbal expenditure. It employs a quaint idiomatic phrase *putting the world through each other.* The confused thinking of the gammer is aptly conveyed by circumlocutory syntax, repetitive clichés, and folk coinages, such as *speckeldy. The Crock of Gold* became a much-loved

Book because its attitude to life is inconsequential and amusing; whimsical irrationality constitutes its charm. It has an Irish uniqueness, comparable to that of *Gulliver's Travels, The Playboy of the Western World, Ulysses* and *Waiting for Godot*.

Somewhat similar in style, but tighter in structure, is *The Demi-Gods*, which Stephens wrote in a Paris café in seven weeks and published in 1914, as a gesture to Theosophical and Hermetic Society interests, shared with AE. The tale is about a wandering tinker and his good-looking daughter, unexpectedly joined in the west country by three guardian angels, whose habits are as unfamiliar as their disguise. The wanderers show, by the easiness of their fellowship, a surprising compatibility with the amoral strangers, who show no signs of Christian influence. Situations are rendered more amusing by the spoken thoughts of an anthropomorphosised donkey, an object of callous neglect as well as of incongruous affection. This is the ideal context for Stephens's comedy, and makes for extremely sensitive writing, without resort to leprechauns and their kind. In a letter to Lewis Chase in January 1917, Stephens said that the opening of chapter VI of *Demi-Gods* might be regarded as characteristic of the personal quality to which his writing aspired. A further aspect, that of the moral philosopher, strikes other critics as the more enduring, because it reveals the novelist as an analyst of character. For example:

> If the denominations of virtue or vice must be affixed to his innocent existence, then these terms would have to be re-defined, for they had no meaning in his case; he [Patsy MacCann] stood outside these as he did outside of the social structure. But, indeed, he was not outside of the social structure at all; he was so far inside of it that he could never get out; he was at the very heart of it; he was held in it like a deer in an ornamental park, or a cork that bobs peacefully in a bucket, and in the immense, neglected pastures of civilisation he found his own quietude and his own wisdom. . . .
> It is to be remarked that the angels were strangely like Patsy MacCann. Their ideas of right and wrong almost

. entirely coincided with his. They had no property and so they had no prejudices. . . .

Civilisation, having built itself at hazard upon the Rights of Property, has sought on many occasions to unbuild itself again in sheer desperation of any advance, but from the great Ethic of Possession there never had been any escape, and there never will be until the solidarity of man has been really created, and until each man ceases to see the wolf in his neighbour. . . .

(James Stephens, A Selection, pp. 165-7)

These splendidly rounded paragraphs demonstrate the rhythmical completion at which Stephens excelled. His work was a durable link between the leisurely life of Victorian fiction and the modern novel, of which Joyce was one of the innovators. In Stephens's own words, he had learned to adapt the Irish mode of speech to the English tongue (*Letters*, p. 197); and he actually credited Yeats, Russell, Synge and Lady Gregory with making this development possible. He understood the need for new techniques in prose as in poetry; but he foresaw that the action-packed novel, encouraged by the cinema, would produce a clever, but lazy, style of writing (see Preface to the *Collected Poems*, 1926). There remained for the fiction writer, as Stephens realised, the ever-present imperative that description and narrative should be kept alive, and to this end there is no alternative but to cultivate the garden of imaginative prose.

IX

A Trio of Innovators, Joyce, Beckett and Flann O'Brien

James Joyce (1882-1941) left Ireland for the Continent before he attained his majority, yet no Irish novelist wrote more knowingly about his native city, Dublin, at a critical stage in its history. His creative talent found an outlet in naturalistic language, which is central to any genuine understanding of his work. Though his novels were few in number, the range of experimentation, and the time devoted to their improvement, give the writings a unique importance. Everything Joyce created is symbolic of some aspect of his life. The work bears no resemblance to that of D. H. Lawrence, but Joyce's attitude to the land of his birth was remarkably similar to that of the English novelist. To both viewers the realities of history were a nightmare, and independence of judgement could be preserved only through exile. Formative influences in Joyce's career were undoubtedly the works of Flaubert and Ibsen, but the psychology of his human creations would hardly have been feasible without the study of Sigmund Freud and Carl Jung. There was a contemporary and similar development in Stravinsky, Picasso and Salvador Dali.

When Joyce decided to live and work as a teacher of English in Trieste, he deprived himself of English-speaking society and the literary sources of its inspiration, and became largely dependent upon memory and his personal inventiveness. In human relationships, Joyce was the soul of courtesy; he shied away from any unpleasantness with people he knew quite well, and was surprised to learn that friends did not understand what he thought he wrote quite naturally. The Rabelaisian coarseness of his writing is reported to have been largely imaginary. Other careers had been open to him. At the Jesuit College of Belvedere, his tutor tried to persuade him to become a priest; he was also a singer with a fine tenor voice. But Joyce lived for little else than his writing, and believed it inevitable that a modern writer should elect to intellectualise himself. Burlesque and parody were his strong meat; but his primary interest was to explore the complexities of individual consciences.

Joyce, in his youth, was profoundly religious, as well as an avowed aesthete. He kept a small notebook in his waist-coat pocket on which to jot down words or sentences, often those overheard in the course of the day. Most of his academic learning was acquired in Dublin before the age of twenty; but defective eyesight probably prevented him from reading much modern literature. Joyce spoke Italian, French and German fluently, and in 1907 delivered three lectures on Ireland in Trieste, keeping in touch with Irish life by reading the leading Dublin newspapers.

It is worth recalling some of the paragraphs Joyce wrote in the first of these lectures:

> Even a superficial consideration will show us that the Irish nation's insistence on developing its own culture by itself is not so much the demand of a young nation that wants to make good in the European concert as the demand of a very old nation to renew under new forms the glories of a past civilization. . . . A new Celtic race was arising, compounded of the old Celtic stock and the Scandinavian, Anglo-Saxon, and Norman races. Another national temperament rose on the foundation of the old one, with the various elements mingling and renewing the ancient body. . . .
>
> Ireland prides itself on being faithful body and soul to its national tradition as well as to the Holy See. The majority of the Irish consider fidelity to these two traditions their cardinal article of faith. But the fact is that the English came to Ireland at the repeated requests of a native king, without, needless to say, any great desire on their part, and without the consent of their own king, but armed with the papal bull of Adrian IV and a papal

letter of Alexander. .... In addition, there is the fact that parliamentary union was not legislated at Westminster but at Dublin, by a parliament elected by the vote of the people of Ireland, a parliament corrupted and undermined with the greatest ingenuity by the agents of the English prime minster, but an Irish parliament nevertheless. ....

Although the present race in Ireland is backward and inferior, it is worth taking into account the fact that it is the only race of the entire Celtic family that has not been willing to sell its birthright for a mess of pottage. ....

I confess that I do not see what good it does to fulminate against the English tyranny while the Roman tyranny occupies the palace of the soul. ....

Ancient Ireland is dead just as ancient Egypt is dead. .... The old national soul that spoke during the centuries through the mouths of fabulous seers, wandering minstrels, and Jacobite poets disappeared from the world with the death of James Clarence Mangan.

(*The Critical Writings of James Joyce*, 'Ireland, Island of Saints and Sages', pp. 157-74)

It would be mistaken, however, to imagine that Joyce was alienated from his homeland; he actually visited it again several times, helped to establish the first cinema in Dublin, and at one stage thought of applying for a university post there. He lived abroad for reasons of domestic privacy, and to avoid involvement in public controversy. An artist, he was convinced, could not preserve his integrity in the social, religious and literary atmosphere of Dublin. He wanted, in particular, to dissociate himself from the sentimental attitude to Ireland's past, and the *hemiplegia* (his word — 'paralysis') of its present.

Joyce took into exile a quantity of fictional material, which he had not yet decided how to handle in a way consonant with his aesthetic principles. There was much trouble, and therefore correspondence, with publishers in regard to his collection of short stories entitled *Dubliners*; this was not satisfactorily settled until the appearance of the book in London in 1914.

Different as *Dubliners* is from the rest of Joyce's fiction, there were nascent indications of the attitude to life, as well as to expression, that distinguished his later work. The stories in this collection begin with the death scene of The Sisters, depicting a group of typical Irish Catholic mourners, and end with a tale entitled 'The Dead', paradoxically describing festive pleasures among the city's living. Though the latter tale was an afterthought that occurred to Joyce in Rome, it is technically the best story in *Dubliners*. Joyce set out to celebrate Irish hospitality, but developed a situation that was thoroughly Chekhovian in its frustration, not alone for the central figure. This frustration arose from the living death of the city's hide-bound Victorian population, who were seemingly unaware of the paralysis of spirit that had overtaken them. Characters in *The Dead* are portrayed by Joyce with consummate detachment, as though he perceived them in a mood of unemotional neutrality. The language, even when the sense is lively, has a clinical meanness of tone; an astonishingly realistic cross-section of urban life is thus presented.

Joyce maintained more than once that his art was in 'the classical tradition' (see *Letters*, no. 60); and the harmony of parts in the final tale of *Dubliners* affirms that belief. The manner of the unfolding is reminiscent both of Gissing and of Katherine Mansfield. Gabriel Conroy, a respected businessman from Bray, has a rather routine and egotistical relationship with his wife Gretta. Stanislaus Joyce was able to show that 'The Dead' had an autobiographical background, Gabriel representing Joyce's father, as well as himself, while Gretta resembled the author's wife, Nora Barnacle, who was a native of Galway. The song that moved Gretta deeply ('The Lass of Aughrim') was one Joyce learnt from Nora, though his personal favourite from Moore's *Irish Melodies* was 'O ye Dead'. The combination of frankness and reticence in the tale is disarming, when compared with the thwarted vacuity of life depicted elsewhere. For the short-story genre, *Dubliners* was an innovation for English readers, who were unaccustomed to comparative absence of plot, and unemotive writing that gives the impression of distance, as well as flatness.

A close analysis of the dialogue in most of *Dubliners* reveals a lively acquaintance with the speech of the lower middle-class; for the people with whom Joyce associated at the National University, Dublin, were largely of bourgeois origin, however fanciful their private aspirations may have been. Characters as varied as Lenehan in 'The Two Gallants' and McCoy in 'Grace' afford a wealth of slang expressions, which are by no means confined to speakers of Dublin origin. It is surprising to find that many English catch-phrases may have originated in Ireland. The following examples of slang and colloquial language are culled both from stories in which Joyce himself was the narrator (e.g. the first three), and the dozen stories in *Dubliners* presumably reported by other persons:

The Sisters
one of them new-fangled carriages that makes no noise
. . . them with the *rheumatic* wheels (malapropism)

An Encounter
I asked him why he had brought it [a catapult], and he told me he had brought it to *have some gas* with the birds
Mahony said it would be *right skit* to run away to sea
Mahony mentioned lightly that he had three *totties* (girl friends)

Two Gallants
She doesn't know my name. I was too *hairy* to tell her that (wily)
Whenever any job was vacant a friend was always ready to give him the *hard* word

Counterparts
he thought of Terry Kelly's pawn-office in Fleet Street. That was the *dart*. Why didn't he think of it sooner? (bright idea)
O'Halloran stood *tailors* of malt, hot, all round (cant phrase)
At the corner of Duke Street Higgins and Nosey Flynn *bevelled* off to the left (veered, turned at a slight angle)
Pony up, boys. We'll have just one little *smahan* more and then we'll be off (drink)

Ivy Day in the Committee Room
   I wish he'd turn up with the *spondulicks* (cash)
   They won't suspect you. Do you *twig*? (follow, under-
   stand)
   Ah, poor Joe is a decent *skin*
   And how does he *knock it out* (make a living)
   he was leaning on the counter in his shirt-sleeves having
   a deep *goster* with Alderman Cowley (confab, cf p. 247)

The dynamism of Joyce's dialogue conceals the subjectivity of his approach to character, and shows how sensitive
he was to the common speech of his time. Yet he shunned
the notion that environment is a significant factor in the
sociological development of class speech.

The problem uppermost in Joyce's mind was how to do
things arrestingly with words, whether in emotive, rational
or moralistic utterances. In relating art to history, for
instance, he sought to implant a personal validity that would
convert the dull metal of statement into a viable new coinage.
In English fictional prose, Joyce is master of the stream-of-
consciousness technique, and the related uses of interior
monologue. He repudiated the customary employment of
inverted commas to indicate dialogue. He seems to have disliked performative utterance, and his single drama, *Exiles*,
is consequently of slender merit; he admired Elizabethan
lyrical verse, but abandoned an early ambition to become
a poet. But he possessed, *in excelsis*, a sense of the psychological resources of language, serious and sportive; even a
melancholy story like 'The Sisters' found occasion for the
malapropism above quoted. Language, for Joyce, was the
source of many intellectual subtleties, besides magic and
evocation. Words in context could be made to provide
textures and overtones that would add important
secondary effects to primary meanings. Dialogue that is
representational is like photography set beside plastic art.
In whatever form his novel took, Joyce knew that the
fictional must be no less truthful than that which has
historical foundation.

Dubliners anticipated most of the effects that Joyce was
later to perpetuate through symbolism. The impact of these

effects upon the development of English prose was similar to that made by Ezra Pound and T. S. Eliot in verse. The Joycean symbol, it is said, had its origin in the Catholic ritual inherent in Jesuit training; but this may be an over-simplification. When Joyce absolved himself from the restrictive influence of the Church, he had already devised a framework of aesthetic theories, grounded on those of leading epic poets, such as Homer and Dante. All his later work tends to be epical in scope, form and content, even when mock-heroic. The *Odyssey* and the *Divina Commedia* were both composed by exiles in quest of a remote symbolic purpose. The naturalism that Joyce gleaned from Dante would have come principally from the *Inferno*, with which the narrow, restrictive life of Dublin is overtly compared.

During World Wars I and II, Joyce took refuge in Zurich, and some effects of his varied contacts there are recorded by Frank Budgen in *James Joyce and the Making of Ulysses*. A cosmopolitan like Joyce living abroad so long would hardly have been able to expand his personal acquaintance with countrymen in Ireland. Consequently the treatment of Irish characters ignores equally the semi-literate peasant class and the remnants of Anglo-Irish aristocracy who figure prominently in the novels of George Moore, and Somerville and Ross. When the Catholic training college at Maynooth was established in the mid-nineteenth century, the provincially minded Irish priesthood forfeited much of the humanistic culture that was inculcated at similar institutions in Italy, Spain and France. Joyce consistently deplored the association of the Irish Catholic Church, after emancipation, with the nationalist movement, which was financially supported by expatriate Irishmen in America. The Joyces, father and son, resented the Catholic treatment of Parnell, as shown in the opening chapter of *A Portrait of the Artist as a Young Man*, and it was this event, primarily, that led the novelist to revile the current state of Irish politics.

A Portrait of the Artist is autobiographical, and occupied Joyce's leisure for ten years. When published in 1916, it proved to be no more a work of fiction than George Moore's *Hail and Farewell*. One of the diverse preoccupations was to account for Joyce's early rejection of the Jesuit philosophy that underpinned his Catholic-school education. He never desired to rid himself of the scholastic method of reasoning acquired from Aquinas, nor did he lose the Dublin brogue, which is so pleasant a feature of his recorded rendering of *Anna Livia Plurabelle*. *A Portrait* first appeared in Harriet Weaver's journal *The Egoist*, between February 1914, and September, 1915.

During the decade when Joyce had settled in Trieste as a teacher of English for the Berlitz School, he was involved with several publishers concerning the printing of his work. In a letter dated February 1906, addressed to Grant Richards, Joyce stated: 'I have written nearly a thousand pages of a novel, but I have little leisure, comfort or prospects for continuing it.' Four months later he confided to the same publisher: 'The Irish are the most spiritual race on the face of the earth. . . . It is not my fault that the odour of ash-pits and old weeds and offal hangs round my stories. I seriously believe that you will retard the course of civilization in Ireland by preventing the Irish people from having one good look at themselves in my nicely polished looking-glass.'

The novel here referred to could only have been the original manuscript of *Stephen Hero*, the remaining pages of which (519-902) were edited by Theodore Spencer and published in 1944. This was probably the portion that Mrs Joyce rescued from the flames to which her despairing husband had consigned the manuscript. Sylvia Beach, who first published *Ulysses*, said in 1935 that *Stephen Hero* was returned to its author by no less than twenty publishers. Years later in Zürich, when Joyce found a patron in Miss Harriet Weaver, the novel came to be re-written as *A Portrait of the Artist as a Young Man*. The revision ended abruptly, with Joyce's final departure from Ireland in 1904, the reason apparently being that much of the remaining material was being incorporated in *Ulysses*. It is noteworthy that 'Bloomsday' in that great Freudian novel took place in the same year.

Several studies have been published to explain the textual relationship between the two texts, and the steps taken by Joyce in the last section of *A Portrait* to compress the 383 pages of *Stephen Hero* into a single chapter. The effect has been to show that Stephen Dedalus (the name is spelt 'Daedalus' in the earlier MS) is an ambiguous figure, whose portrait was distorted by two endemic influences of Irish history, nationalism and religion. Joyce was in the habit of keeping notes on his conversations with friends, teachers and members of his family; he must have used this diary freely in the troubled conception of *Stephen Hero*. His real strength lay in the subtlety of character analysis, and profound understanding of the psychology of personal relationships. *Stephen Hero* provides the fullest account of Joyce's purpose in the concept of 'epiphany':

> By an epiphany he meant a sudden spiritual manifestation, whether in the vulgarity of speech or of gesture or in a memorable phase of the mind itself. He believed that it was for the man of letters to record these epiphanies with extreme care, seeing that they themselves are the most delicate and evanescent of moments.
>
> (*Stephen Hero*, p. 216)

One of the most vigorously sustained discourses in this novel is Stephen's defence of his paper on Ibsen with the President of his university (chapter XIX). A perusal of *Stephen Hero* enables one better to appreciate Joyce's distinction between 'kinetic' and 'static' art. Kinetic experience, which appeals especially to the young, finds its principal outlet in narrative. Aesthetic emotion, or the lyrical impulse, Stephen regarded as the typical condition of *stasis*.

One merit of *Stephen Hero* is that it depicts the character of the principal figure more objectively than the later book does. We are told, for instance, that 'he read Skeat's Etymological Dictionary by the hour'; and he was 'hypnotised by the most commonplace conversation'; and he concluded that most people were 'strangely ignorant of the value of the words they used so glibly' (p. 32). These were the same people who cared little 'what banality a man expresses so long as he expressed it in Irish' (p. 58).

The subjective handling of Stephen Dedalus in *A Portrait of the Artist as a Young Man*, on the other hand, gives the revised novel a better symmetry of parts; this is therefore a maturer work of art, in the style of Samuel Butler's *The*

Way of All Flesh. In 1916, however, the British public was not ripe for Joyce's introspective candour. London reviewers saw a streak of vulgarity in Irish bourgeois manners masquerading as shabby gentility. What impressed the discerning American critic, Ezra Pound, was Joyce's vivid use of words, 'clear-cut and definite sentences' and 'thwarted desire for beauty' (see *The Future*, May 1918).

Pound was, like Joyce, a hypercritical exile, and expressed his regard for an original voice in fiction. In *Stephen Hero*, Joyce had argued that 'isolation is the first principle of artistic economy' (p. 37). Teaching English to foreign students in Trieste, Joyce soon became fascinated by the association of words, as well as their derivation. A rebellious self-education (for he seldom attended lectures at his university), taught him to weave words into novel patterns. An invigorating stratum of his style is the exploitation of sounds and rhythms, and the exploration of secondary meanings. The dialectology pursued was, however, isolative, not gregarious. Joyce became eccentrically suspicious of all close human ties, other than those of his own family.

In the *Portrait* Joyce often substituted interior monologue for narrative. There is little natural description to be found in his novels. In order to further 'consonance' or symmetry, he altered the relationship between Stephen, the fictional character, and the author presenting him. His plan was to transmute autobiography into plausible fiction; and in making this change he ensured the desired continuity between the *Portrait* and his epical mythology, *Ulysses*. Stephen of the *Portrait* is not to be viewed as a Byronic figure; he is essentially the nostalgic Dubliner; his creator, only, had elected to live abroad. But this Stephen is, to modern eyes, a fallen rebel of ambition, one who was not unaware of his own arrogance; hence the surname Dedalus.

Joyce's flight from Ireland seems to have been made less for soul-searching than from pride and his burning desire to be self-sufficient. Paradoxically, he became a literary nomad with no other territory to explore than the city in Ireland from which he came. His reviling of Dubliners provoked alienation; but, like Lucifer, he seems to have been driven by a masochistic wish to be damned. In disciplining his art, he sought to emulate the great classical writers, but was unable to bridle his own extravagant temperament. Because of the antipathetic nationalism of his instructor, Joyce made only a half-hearted attempt to learn Irish; yet those who knew accounted him an exceptional linguist.

Stephen Dedalus's impression of society was invariably that of a scientific analyst; he lacked the milk of human kindness that makes a novelist loved rather than esteemed. It would be a mistake, however, to identify Stephen of the *Portrait*, with more than one aspect of Joyce, namely, his self-love. When he undertook to re-write *Stephen Hero*, during war-time seclusion in Zürich, he was thirty-two years of age — a mature, rather than a young man. He realised that his neo-platonic aesthetic doctrine needed re-thinking, perhaps because he no longer believed in it. In the *Portrait*, humourless discussions, or the sermons deemed necessary to the plan of the book, are penned with greater economy. A reader feels, none the less, a disquieting sense that the self-inflicted unhappiness of Stephen is fathomless:

> All the leisure which his school life left him was passed in the company of subversive writers whose jibes and violence of speech set up a ferment in his brain before they passed out of it into his crude writings. . . . Nothing moved him or spoke to him from the real world unless he heard in it an echo of the infuriated cries within him. . . .
>
> He would create proudly out of the freedom and power of his soul, as the great artificer whose name he bore, a living thing, new and soaring and beautiful, impalpable, imperishable. . . . There was a lust of wandering in his feet that burned to set out for the ends of the earth.

(*A Portrait of the Artist as a Young Man*, pp. 80, 95, 174)

One should not, therefore, take Stephen as seriously as he takes himself.

Joyce's brother, Stanislaus, expressed the view that the epithet 'hero' in the incomplete novel was ironic. Stephen's contempt for most of his associates is seldom concealed, and his unwillingness to go along with other men's ideas often required considerable moral courage. It would be difficult to find another instance in Irish literature that affords so searching a critique of Catholic education at the turn of the nineteenth century. That class snobbery affected the different systems of the Jesuit fathers and the Christian Brothers, Joyce had learnt from personal experience of both; but he seems to have acquired intellectual pride from the Jesuit school to which his élitist father sent him.

A Portrait of the Artist as a Young Man is a necessary preliminary to the understanding of *Ulysses*, as A. Walton Litz shows in *The Art of James Joyce* (OUP 1961); this is a detailed study of the genesis of the novel, which was first published in 1922. *Ulysses* took five years to complete, and was printed in Paris for Shakespeare and Company, through the initiative of the American, Sylvia Beach. From 1918, parts of the book had been serialised in *The Little Review*, New York; then, in October 1920, legal action to suppress them was taken against the editors. Litz's interest lay in the workshop techniques of composition, and he made the unexpected suggestion that *Ulysses* was inspired (as were the temptations of Leopold Bloom) by Joyce's early reading of Charles Lamb's mystical version of the *Adventures* of Homer's hero, published in 1808. This was substantially an abridgement of Chapman's Homer.

Ulysses was apparently first conceived as a short story for *Dubliners*, then as a sequel to *A Portrait*, exemplifying Joyce's favourite artistic theory. Litz showed that Joyce planned carefully in advance, and wrote the final sections of *Ulysses* first. His major difficulty was to fuse the various episodes distinguished by their Homeric titles; and this was overcome by writing two or three simultaneously. He spent some two hundred hours on the third draft of what he called *Telemachia*, viz. the three opening episodes. Only in 1920 did Joyce commence his monumental revision, which was completely to transform the style of the novel. The most exacting of all the episodes, *Circe*, was written no less than nine times. Five proofs were called for, and each received substantial author improvements.

Though Joyce was an artist in words in the plastic sense, according to Litz his herculean labours were occasioned by his strange obsession for an accumulation of realistic detail. He determined to be wholly naturalistic in speech rhythms,

296 Language and Society in Anglo-Irish Literature

as well as characters. He was possessed of an irrepressible urge to experiment in every possible form and direction with English in its prose usage. Full appreciation of the book is therefore not possible, except after several readings. Those who have made the effort have found it desirable to follow step by step the different stages of the artist's handling of his materials. There is no plot development at all to be distinguished in Joyce's last two works of fiction.

There had been nothing remotely resembling Joyce's latest novel, unless one considered Laurence Sterne's *Tristram Shandy*. But the psychological exploration of the three chief characters, Stephen Dedalus, Leopold Bloom and his wife Marian (Molly), was clearly influenced by Joyce's reading of *Hamlet*; this he saw as the tragedy of a broken filial relationship. In *Ulysses*, Stephen, enacting the role of Telemachus, represents a son in search of a father-figure; Stephen, indeed, expressly finds an analogy — 'the son consubstantial with the father' — in Jesus of Nazareth, as revealed in the synoptic gospels. Stephen obviously supported the then fashionable belief in the 'mythical sorrows of Shakespeare', which biographers derived from the four great tragedies and the final romances (see *Ulysses*, ch. 9 'Scylla and Charybdis'). Joyce did not, however, add anything important to the contemporary investigation of Shakespeare's domestic relations.

One of the principal novelties of *Ulysses* was the time-scheme; its plan was to record the experiences during a single day of a commonplace Dublin salesman, in the person of Bloom, who, in the fourth chapter, became the cynosure of fictional concern, largely replacing the intellectual Stephen. This was an astute step, because Joyce was enabled to indulge his best claim to success — the art of parody; it presented infinite possibilities for varying the tone and the rhythm. He was not content to parody the prose of well-known authors only; he often mimicked, with delightful distortions, the conversation of acquaintances, some distinguished fellow-citizens. The dramatis personae of *Ulysses* consist almost entirely of friends, relations and literary or business colleagues. They are recollected in travail, rather than tranquillity.

The complexity of the novel results largely from unheralded switches in the execution of Joyce's experimental technique, and from sometimes abrupt transitions of thought in the interior monologue. There are incredibly sudden alterations of scepticism, bathos and humour in the eighteen chapters, which fall into three distinct parts. As first written, the chapters of the novel were given Homeric titles, but these were withdrawn on the book's publication. Joyce firmly declined to provide either notes or preface.

In the following passage from chapter 12 ('The Cyclops') Joyce parodies archaic narrative and transmutes it, without perceptibly changing the style, into pseudo-scientific writing, which indulges a facility for categories:

> In Inisfail the fair there lies a land, the land of holy Michan. There rises a watchtower beheld of men afar. There sleep the mighty dead as in life they slept, warriors and princes of high renown. A pleasant land it is in sooth of murmuring waters, fishful streams where sport the gunnard, the plaice, the roach, the halibut, the gibbed haddock, the grilse, the dab, the brill, the flounder, the mixed coarse fish generally and other denizens of the aqueous kingdom too numerous to be enumerated.
>
> (pp. 378-9)

In chapter 14 ('Oxen of the Sun') Joyce's resourcefulness is taxed in mimicking the style of some two dozen English prose masters from Mandeville to Carlyle. In chapter 7 ('Aeolus') he incorporates ninety-five examples of rhetorical forms, and a number of topical headlines, to illustrate the meanderings of journalese. Yet it cannot be said that Joyce's linguistic virtuosity seriously vitiates his art.

Each episode of *Ulysses* is planned to display a rhythmical movement independent of others, but characteristic of its particular *leitmotif*; and all have an interlocking function in the grand design. In chapter 4 ('Calypso') Joyce extracts philological humour from the word *metempsychosis* (transmigration of souls); having AE in mind, he treated theosophy and re-incarnation with a certain equivocal levity. The episodes in chapter 14 ('Oxen of the Sun') take place in a maternity hospital, enabling Bloom to trace the development of an embryo, and speculate on the evolution of the *élan vital* (Bergson's life force). As the turn of events shows, it was not eccentric to cast Jewish Bloom in the role of Ulysses, and his wife Molly as Penelope. Incidents untold are bizarre; but much more unusual is the stylised arrogance of the language.

Joyce is a verbal manipulator deliberately setting out to shock, and employing all his visual and auditory cunning to do so. Swift's *Polite Conversation* is mock-pedantry beside this audacity; it exploits the gamut of Dublin speech, as Joyce had known it. Speakers are drawn from every class of Irish urban society, as it had been influenced by two centuries of English education, using a medium of instruction that had changed very little since the eighteenth century. For instance, Joyce twice alludes to Lindley Murray's *New English Grammar* (1798, 1824), namely, in *Ulysses* (p. 760) and *Finnegans Wake* (p. 269). The dialogue of the novel abounds in ellipses and fragmentary utterances, hard to classify except as a sort of ideographic slang; this design extends to curtailment of commonplace words, such as *ha'* for *hat*. Grammatical completeness in speech is hardly to be expected, except from intellectuals, such as Stephen Dedalus, J. J. Molloy and 'Professor' McHugh, a teacher of Latin, whose academic status is ironical.

Punning was one of the comic devices Joyce found it hard to resist; another was a penchant for outlandish verbal combinations, studiously avoiding hyphens, e.g. *panthersahib* (55), *roguewords* (59), *manshape* (60), *pickmeup* (61), *peacocktwittering* (61), Davy Byrne *smiledyawnednodded* all in one (226), *Yogeybogeybox* (245), *beautifulinsadness* (262). Some coinages are etymologically amusing, such as *abstrusiosities* (57); his mouth moulded issuing breath, *unspeeched* (60); *weggebobbles* (210, vegetables). Rhyme and assonance Joyce employed with expertise, as in: They [the waves] serpented towards his feet, *curling, unfurling* (58); *click* does the *trick* (61).

Joyce's concern for the ironic possibilities of everyday language was not unlike that of Homer. E. V. Rieu, in the Introduction to his Penguin translation of the *Odyssey*, has some acute observations on the poet's care for, and emphasis on clichés, recurring epithets and stock phrases, again and again used with ironic effect. The description of Gerty MacDowell in *Ulysses* (chapter 13, 'Nausicaa', pp. 452-4) is full of the clichés of fashion magazines, Joyce's purpose being to deflate sentiment by aping the language of cheap Victorian novelettes. A kind of telegraphese often proved effective when Joyce resorted to interior monologue, as in chapter 8 ('The Lestrygonians'):

> Poor Mrs Purefoy! Methodist husband. Method in his madness. Saffron bun and milk and soda lunch in the educational dairy. Eating with a stopwatch, thirtytwo chews to the minute. Still his muttonchap whiskers grew. Supposed to be well connected. Theodore's cousin in Dublin Castle. One tony relative in every family. Hardy annuals he presents her with. Saw him out at the Three Jolly Topers marching along bareheaded and his eldest boy carrying one in a marketnet. The squallers. Poor thing! Then having to give the breast year after year all hours of the night. Selfish those t.t's are. Dog in the manger. Only one lump of sugar in my tea, if you please.
>
> (pp. 203-4)

Here the adjective *tony* and the cliché *hardy annuals* (for 'offspring') illustrate the light-hearted sarcasm Rieu had in mind.

Joyce did not, of course, attempt a complete and accurate explication of the mind of his characters. When they speak they are expressive types, rather than veracious portrayals of personal consciousness. There is, for instance, a morbidity akin to disharmony in Stephen's mental make-up, and the interior monologue of chapter 3 ('Proteus') is designed to establish this.

Though curiously dehumanised, as art, *Ulysses* was auto-biographical in concept, like its predecessor; Joyce himself observed that it was an epic of the Jewish people, as well as the Irish; the travails of both nations seemed to him similar. The subjectivity of the book's cultic styles evoked much adverse criticism from reviewers, and obscurity has been an obstacle to better informed interpretation. The novel is as likely to be neglected by posterity as the poetry of

Pound and Eliot, to which *Ulysses* has many affinities. Few critics have noticed how rhetorical, in the pejorative sense, the writing of Joyce can be. Modern readers are disinclined to digest a novel that is so encyclopaedic in content and fragmentary in execution.

A similar method was used in *Finnegans Wake*, which was begun in March 1923, and published by Faber and Faber in 1939. (There is no apostrophe before *s* in the proper name.) *Finnegan* (a diminutive) represents Everyman, especially if Irish and of small account, like the principal figure, H. C. Earwicker. Under the provisional title of *Work in Progress*, several parts of this book appeared between 1924 and 1938 in T. S. Eliot's *Criterion*, as well as *The Transatlantic Review* and the *avant garde* Parisian journal *transition*, edited by E. Jolas. Between 1930 and 1932 Faber and Faber undertook the publication in the 'Criterion Miscellany' series of three self-contained sections of the novel, under the titles of *Anna Livia Plurabelle* (F. W. 196-216), *Haveth Childers Everywhere* (F. W. 532-54) and *Two Tales of Shem and Shaun* (F. W. 152-9 and 414-19). By the centenary year of Joyce's birth (1982) these had already become collectors' items. Ten years after Joyce's death, his benefactor, Harriet Shaw Weaver, presented to the British Museum the manuscript collection of *Finnegans Wake*; this included notes, drafts, typescripts and galley proofs. It then became possible to trace the entire order of composition of the four books.

The apparently complex pattern of the *Wake* was suggested to Joyce while reading *La scienza nuovo* of Giambattista Vico, the Neapolitan social historian and critic of Homer; this work was published as early as 1725. Vico's cyclical theory of history which was partly supported by Spengler and Toynbee, but not by other historians, was admirably suited to Joyce's conception of *Finnegans Wake*. The cycle had four ages, the divine, the heroic, the human and the disintegrating, the last leading inevitably to a renewal of the cycle. Whether Joyce himself believed this to be true is open to question; he once told Cyril Connolly that he was more interested in 'Dublin street names than in the riddle of the universe' (*New Statesman and Nation*, XXI, Jan. 18, 1941, 59).

Enjoyment of *Finnegans Wake*'s 'funnominal world' depends on one's ability to grasp simultaneously the significance of language on two levels, the comic as well as the historical. At the aesthetic level Joyce's new writing sought to evoke the auditory imagination, and to aspire, like Eliot's *Four Quartets*, to the condition of music. The author himself described the art as 'verbivocovisual presentment', implying that the effect he intended was to counterpoint word and theme. Throughout there is evidence of the impact of Wagner's operas, and especially the Tristan and Iseult mythology.

Joyce regarded *Anna Livia Plurabelle* as the most satisfying of his experiments; significantly, he began it in the year Eliot published *The Wasteland*. The first draft of ALP was penned in the traditional manner of *Ulysses*. By 1930, however, Joyce had translated this prose-poem, suggested by the opening of the *Odyssey*, into the new idiom that obsessed him. Litz's above-mentioned investigation throws valuable light on its textual evolution, the process of aesthetic revision, and the improver's resourcefulness in handling difficulties, whether carried to a natural or supernatural conclusion. Litz argues that Joyce's technique, lacking proper perspective, led to distortion and burlesque. It would seem that in *Finnegans Wake*, as *Ulysses*, the author had written so much that revision became a gargantuan undertaking. Frank Budgen and Joyce's letters show that literary friends and *avant garde* admirers rallied to Joyce's assistance, so that order might be made out of chaos.

The *Wake* is, among other things, a burlesque of Freudian dream analysis, using Vico's theories as a springboard. Autobiographical material predominates in what is less a novel than a fantasy, like *Through the Looking-Glass*, from which it borrows, though extends, the Jabberwocky language. The readability of this fantasy results chiefly from its extraordinary magniloquence and Joyce's virtuosity of verbal invention; it goes far beyond the proverbial Irishman's 'gift of the gab'. Besides Carroll's work, Joyce made deliberate use of Freud's *Interpretation of Dreams* and *Psychopathology of Everyday Life*, as well as Sir James Frazer's *The Golden Bough*.

The portmanteau words in *Finnegans Wake* are more com-

302 *Language and Society in Anglo-Irish Literature*

plex in intention than those of Lewis Carroll. They are often
formed by telescoping syllables from two or more other
words, that may have entered the author's mind by association,
or even adventitiously. Irrelevance is here seen to have some
comic advantages. The enormity will become more engaging
if the coarse-grained humour or mockery happens to be in
the spirit of the context; it has no other creative function. A
similar gaff is malapropism, which is funniest when the guilty
speaker is the user of an Irish brogue. The outcome of this
many-sided sleight-of-hand is nonsense literature, with a
distinct leaning towards Anglo-Irish 'pidgin'. A surprising
number of modern readers respond to Joyce's eccentricities
and extravagances, as they do to 'Goon' comedians. Joyce's
description of Shem the Penman is one of many examples:

> Shem was a sham and a low sham and his lowness creeped
> out first via foodstuffs. So low was he that he preferred
> Gibsen's tea-time salmon tinned, as inexpensive as pleasing,
> to the plumpest roeheavy lax or the frickiest parr or smolt
> troutlet that ever was gaffed between Leixlip and Island
> Bridge . . . Rosbif of Old Zealand! he could not attouch
> it. . . . He even ran away with hunself and became a
> farsoonerite, saying he would far sooner muddle through
> the hash of lentils in Europe than meddle with Irrland's
> split little pea.
>
> (*Finnegans Wake*, 170-71)

Though Joyce never wrote for a livelihood, Harry Levin
believes that his last years were clouded by the public's
neglect of his experiments. In an essay 'The Language of the
Outlaw', this writer regrets the 'appalling frankness and the
labored obscurity' with which *Finnegans Wake* introduces
'the hieratic tones of the liturgy'. Levin notices, in particular,
a lack of compulsion to economise, especially in 'raucous
chamber music and prefabricated repartee'. Many faults here
described the critic attributes to the use of the dream convention, which permitted Joyce 'free association of ideas and
a systematic distortion of language' (see Chace, *Joyce: A
Collection of Critical Essays*, pp. 116-22).

Another important critical judgement of Joyce's language
comes from Anthony Burgess in *Joysprick*, the chapter on

'Oneiroparonomastics'. This coinage seems to mean 'wordplay in the dream situation'. Burgess holds that the term *pun* is inappropriate for the kind of wordplay that haunts *Finnegans Wake*; that *portmanteau words* hardly fits the transpositions and alphabetical substitutions which one finds in *Shapesphere* and *'muddlecrass* pupils' (p. 152). The 'real problems of *Finnegans Wake'*, says Burgess, 'are not semantic but referential' (p. 138). Biographical information and a good encyclopaedia are often more helpful than linguistic scholarship. We are reminded that a good deal of *Finnegans Wake* is actually verse, though it may look like prose. Much of the auditory satisfaction derived from *Anna Livia Plurabelle* results from the subtle employment of known and loved rhythms of English poetry.

There are several parallels between the attitudes to their craft adopted by Joyce and Eliot; for instance, the cultivation of recondite significance, concern with the difficulties of using a language, and a desire to enlarge literary speech by adapting it to musical or mathematical principles, this last to increase its powers of association. The musical desideratum became mechanical in Joyce, and it seems that he had constant recourse to reference libraries. He attempted so much that his linguistic virtuosity tended to become contrived. Joyce soon abandoned respect for the *mot juste*, preferring to play with extravagances, such as *alphybettyformed verbage; once current puns, quashed quotations, messes of mottage* (*Finnegans Wake*, p. 183).

It is sometimes held that Joyce remained a nominal Catholic until his death; but in what sense can this be true? From his twentieth year he believed in neither Catholicism nor Protestantism. His refusal to pray for his mother on her deathbed, his unwillingness to embark on a formal marriage with Nora until late in life, and his injunction that no religious rites should be offered at his funeral, do not support the view that he remained within the church. The fact remains that there was no actual severance; his allegiance was simply left to go by default. But it is probable that he never escaped the effects of his Jesuit education. Joyce certainly imagined himself a sincere scholastic reasoner; but Catholic churchmen maintain that his aesthetic theories, and such moral views as he held, owed little to Thomas Aquinas. At the root of Stephen Dedalus's unqualified convictions was pride, rather than a capacity for ratiocination.

Joyce's dislike of the institution of marriage bore some relation to his disapproval of parliamentary democracy. Ireland's treatment of Parnell convinced him that the homeland was no place for a writer who was unable to stomach bourgeois nationalism. In Zürich, Trieste and Paris, Joyce lived in an atmosphere of libertarianism and nascent socialist politics, though he was not actively involved in it. His correspondence with brother Stanislaus is enlightening on the subject of secular liberty for the Irish people. Among other things, he disapproved of the adoption of Irish as an official language, and admitted that he was a socialist (Letter of 12 Aug. 1906). The language question was a part of Arthur Griffith's racial policy, which Joyce opposed, because he thought it educationally more urgent to advance the living standards of the proletariat (Letters dated 12 Aug. and 25 Sept. 1906). After the banning of *Ulysses* in the nineteen-twenties, Joyce's importance as a literary figure was discredited by the Irish, largely on moral and religious grounds, but chiefly because of his supposed subversive opinions.

The adulation lavished on Joyce after his death by many devotees was not shared by critics during the author's lifetime. Joyce's friend, James Stephens, to whom he actually contemplated handing *Finnegans Wake* for completion, was among those whose attitude was tempered by the apprehension of sameness:

> A world that is teeming with interest and newness and originality is there for him to fathom if he can. . . . This is the crime of Joyce, that he is incapable of any current impression, and that, at the age of about twenty five, he ceased to live either as a man or an artist. He has written, say, three books in prose — they are all the same book, and the man that he is at forty five or six is only and merely the boy that he was at nineteen and twenty five.

> (Letter to John Quinn, 15 Aug., 1922, p. 283)

When Joyce appealed to H. G. Wells, whom he had just met, for assistance in publicising *Finnegans Wake*, he was rebuffed by a polite, though curt, refusal:

> Your mental existence is obsessed by a monstrous system of contradictions. . . . Your crowded composition reveals a mighty genius for expression. . . . But I don't think it gets anywhere. You have turned your back on common men, on their elementary needs and their restricted time and intelligence.
>
> (R. Ellmann, *James Joyce*, pp. 620-21)

Outspoken critics, who practised the craft of fiction, doubted the value of Joyce's brand of realism, and some preferred to think of it as disillusion. The vagabond rebel, an uncommitted Sinn Féiner, took no offence; his avowed purpose was to subvert the old traditions, which he rebutted as irrational. He pictured himself in a similar role to Blake, Nietzsche or Ibsen, rather than Shaw, Wilde or D'Annunzio. By the nineteen-thirties the free-thinking rebel had become the literary Socrates of the market-place; and the cities most congenial to eccentricity seemed to be Paris and Dublin. Joyce's principal contribution to the Dublin scene was his unique version of Irish humour, with not a little covert political bias. That Joyce conceived the shabby life of *Finnegans Wake* in the spirit of comic epic is confirmed by his unconventional preference for a Dublin advertising agent, H. C. Earwicker, as the leading human figure in his final novel.

Samuel Beckett, born in 1906, seems at first to be the natural heir of Joyce; but closer acquaintance reveals that he is akin rather to Proust, Sartre and Kafka. Beckett's long essay on *Proust* is, indeed, fundamental to understanding Beckett's artistic principles. His cosmopolitanism was of the astringent kind that only Paris between the wars could have afforded. Though he claimed to have understood few philosophers, Beckett's introspective world was linked with those of Descartes and Kierkegaard. His impact upon Irish literature since the third decade of this century has been even slighter than that of Wilde and Shaw. But it was strong on the Continent, and he was therefore awarded the Nobel Prize for Literature in 1969.

Beckett's father practised as a quantity surveyor and belonged to the Irish Protestant middle-class. He sent his son to an exclusive public school in northern Ireland, and to Trinity College, Dublin, where he turned out to be an accomplished scholar and cricketer, graduating in French, English and Italian. He was then appointed exchange lecturer in Paris (1928), and taught French on his return to Trinity for four terms. He broke with the academic world before the death in 1933 of his father, who left him a modest income, on which he travelled abroad, until settling permanently in France. There he wrote first in English, but since World War II almost entirely in French; indeed, most of his creative writing has emanated from Paris.

Beckett's ambition, while at Trinity, seems to have been to become a poet, and he said that his main interest in Italian was to read Dante, whose Belacqua Shua figures in his collection of short stories, entitled *More Pricks than Kicks* (1934). Several of Beckett's Poems in *Echo's Bones and other Precipitates* (1935) have an Irish setting, and so have his novel *Watt* (1953) and play *All that Fall* (1957); but the style of Beckett's narrative and the dialogue of his characters have nothing really Gaelic about them. In Paris he became the friend of Joyce, at a time when the latter's eyesight was failing, and the author of *Work in Progress* received aid from his friends in completing its revision. Beckett then began, but did not complete, a French translation of *Anna Livia Plurabelle*, and wrote, apparently at the suggestion of Joyce, his involved essay 'Dante . . . Bruno. Vico . . . Joyce.'

Beckett was comparatively unknown as an author until in 1952 he wrote (in French), the epoch-making play *Waiting for Godot*; it has since been translated into over twenty languages. When this work was staged in Paris a year later, it gave a new significance to the French and English Theatre of the Absurd. The tramps Vladimir (Didi) and Estragon (Gogo), wearing Chaplinesque bowlers (Anglo-Irish 'block-hats') became symbols of shabby unemployed intellectuals, who drift and are chronically indolent. In *Theatre of the Absurd* (p. 18) Martin Esslin says that the tendency of *Godot* is 'toward a radical devaluation of language', Beckett's intentions being 'anti-literary'. Audience intelligibility is not, in fact, a primary asset, because Beckett felt that spectator response had become passive to the point of decadence. The enigmatic success of *Waiting for Godot* was due precisely to the play's plotless and undramatic conception. The author, in particular, sought to avoid the logic of language, and to concentrate on what a literary language usually conceals, 'the uncertain, the contradictory, the unthinkable' (Claude Mauriac, *L'Alittérature Contemporaine*, 1958, p. 83). The Theatre of the Absurd tends to accentuate the importance of static drama.

The uncertainty of *Godot* invariably turns on the identity of the figure who does not appear on the stage at all; futility is suggested by routine and the passing of time. The change that everyone on the stage anxiously anticipates never comes to pass. Seeds of uncertainty are sown about the whimsical dispensation of divine grace. Beckett hints that those who stand and wait do so from no Miltonic motive of service; their expectations are, on the contrary, irrational. Those who prefer action and wealth to passivity sacrifice the calm that comes from unselfconsciousness. If *Waiting for Godot* has a message, it may well be that life is boring and pointless, because all habit deadens.

Whatever he wrote in English or French Beckett himself translated into the other medium, taking the liberty of small changes to secure the response of a different audience or reading public. French he considered to be the better language for the fictional prose he wrote; he said that, as an Irishman, he wrote with less facility in the acquired tongue, and therefore with greater structural care. This decision was connected, in some measure, with Beckett's perpetual identity crises. Psychology, he said, had two principal entities, mind which is capable of limited rationality, and the self, or *ego*, which is complex and virtually impotent, because of its frequent bewilderment. His view of life in the novel is filtered through the flickering despair of his strangely recondite personality. Beckett, a modest, reserved and retiring person, is sure that he found himself as a writer by intentional isolation from literary cliques, movements and publicity.

His earliest novel, *Murphy*, made little impression on its

first appearance in 1938 — which may have been due to the formal tone of the dialogue, and the unfamiliar blend of sardonic humour and pessimism. Comic irony centres on a sequence of epiphanies that take place in a Kensington mews, Hyde Park or a mental asylum, and some of its effect is missed by a reader who fails to perceive that Beckett is parodying, inter alia, authors who work in specialised fields, such as medicine and clinical psychology. In its polysyllabic inventiveness, the style occasionally resembles that of Joyce. Some of Beckett's more characteristic examples follow:

> Mr Kelly's face was narrow and profoundly seamed with a lifetime of *dingy, stingy* repose. Just as all hope seemed lost it burst into a fine *bulb of skull*, unobscured by hair. Yet a little while and his *brain-body ratio* would have sunk to that of a small bird.

> When she came full circle she found, as she had fully expected, the eyes of Murphy still open and upon her. But almost at once they closed as for a supreme exertion, the jaws clenched, the chin jutted, the knees sagged, the *hypogastrium* came forward, the mouth opened, the head tilted slowly back. Murphy was returning to the brightness of the firmament.

> Murphy had been too absorbed in this touching little *argonautic.* and above all in the ecstatic demeanour of the sheep, to pay any attention to Nelly. He now discovered that she had eaten all the biscuits with the exception of the Ginger, which cannot have remained in her mouth for more than a couple of seconds. She was seated after her meal, to judge by the infinitesimal angle that her back was now making with the horizon. There is this to be said for Dachshunds of such length and lowness as Nelly, that it makes very little difference to their appearance whether they stand, sit or lie. If *Parmigianino* had gone in for painting dogs, he would have painted them like Nelly.

> The skill is really extraordinary with which *analphabetes*, especially those of Irish education, circumvent their dread of verbal commitments. Now Cooper's face, though it did not seem to move a muscle, brought together and threw

off in a single grimace the finest shades of irresolution, revulsion, doglike devotion, catlike discretion, fatigue, hunger, thirst and reserves of strength, in a very small fraction of the time that the finest oratory would require for a greatly inferior evasion, and without exposing its proprietor to misquotation.

                                                (*Murphy*, pp. 11, 12, 59, 115)

These passages have the dexterity of an accomplished figure-skater, who seems conscious of his originality in combining taut with ornate styles.

Murphy and Celia, his down-to-earth girl-friend, are nominally Dublin characters, and so are the Jonsonian grotesques with whom they associate. While he lived in London, Beckett's interest in Freudian clinical techniques was aroused through a Trinity friend, who was studying psychiatry at St Mary's of Bethlehem, the institution popularly known as Bedlam. Murphy, the tragi-comic, footloose, disaffected Irish intellectual, has all the characteristics of a solipsist, and obviously represents Beckett himself. He is also a cosmic figure, not unlike the prophet Ezekiel, soured by his poverty-stricken exile in Babylon; for he describes everything with misanthropic particularity — Celia's vital statistics, consultations of his horoscope, and forty-three moves in a game of chess, which Murphy plays against one of Bedlam's schizophrenic inmates. It is typical of Murphy's zany comicality that he finds greater solace and at-one-ment with the patients than with Celia, and the malcontents of his own nation.

The mature works of Beckett, *Molloy*, *Malone Dies* and *The Unnamable*, were published in English between 1955 and 1958, and are bound in one volume, as a related trilogy. The last two are of Jamesian *novella* class, rather than true novels. They are conceived without plot, and it is difficult to determine where the inner compulsion of the principal character begins or ends. Absurdity in such writing has a terrifying actuality, of whose presence the reader is confusedly aware. Beckett confided to an interviewer: 'All I am is feeling. Molloy and the others came to me the day I became aware of my own folly. Only then did I begin to write the things I feel' (1961; see Mercier, *Beckett*, p. 36).

Molloy, which Beckett was busy on by 1947, abounds in

abstract writing, sensitive rhythms and contrived cadences that please the ear, but leave the reader none the surer for the aesthetic experience. For the writer's mollifying neutrality denies logical analysis. But the difficulties are of a different order of perplexity from those inherent in the language of *Godot*, where optimum use is made of short, staccato sentences. In Molloy, so far from removing the dubiety of suspense by narration, Beckett actually increases it; the lapse of time serves only to augment the character's disibilities. The method is not unlike Proust's, where the transmutations effected by time are a compelling factor in the fiction. The events in Molloy's life are of minor importance, because he is self-enclosed, regarding relations with other persons in the fable. With those who live in different worlds there is little prospect of meaningful communication.

Molloy is in two parts: the sustained monologue of the first reflects the *persona* of a well-bred member of the Irish bourgeoisie; the second, with Moran as narrator, presents Molloy's French *alter ego*, a small-holder whose sole affection is for his garden, his poultry and his bees. In Moran, Beckett finds occasion for some attractive pastoral prose, in the spirit of Vergil's *Georgics*:

> All during this long journey home, when I racked my mind for a little joy in store, the thought of my bees and their dance was the nearest thing to comfort. For I was still eager for my little joy, from time to time! And I admitted with good grace the possibility that this dance was after all no better than the dances of the people of the West, frivolous and meaningless. But for me, sitting near my sun-drenched hives, it would always be a noble thing to contemplate, too noble ever to be sullied by the cogitations of a man like me, exiled in his manhood. And I would never do my bees the wrong I had done my God, to whom I had been taught to ascribe my angers, fears, desires, and even my body.
>
> (*Molloy*, p. 170)

It would be wrong to suppose that the dual-personality rôle, suggested by the Molloy/Moran masks, was intended as an allegory; allegorists are not usually writers whose work consists of sustained self-exploration. Both personae are depicted as cyclists, destined to end as frustrated cripples, dependent on crutches for their wretched mobility. It is more likely Beckett planned *Molloy* as an existentialist novel, with a subtly concealed theological motive.

The negative introspections of Beckett do not make him an existentialist whose artistic imperatives are altogether nihilistic. *Malone Dies*, which complements the preceding story, is a *novella* seemingly undertaken to try out a theory of style that explodes the dogmas of classical rhetoric. Malone is an octogenarian who is bent on recording his impressions, even on the point of death; there is no reason, in the circumstances, to disguise the truth; what he writes with the stub of a pencil is couched in dispassionate and clear-sighted terms. There is no trace of Murphy's ostentatious pedantry in the writing, because Beckett is occasionally roused to eloquent observation:

> I tremble a little, but only a little. The groaning of the bedstead is part of my life, I would not like it to cease, I mean I would not like it to decrease. It is on my back, that is to say prostrate, no, supine, that I feel best, *bony*. I lie on my back, but my cheek is on the pillow. I have only to open my eyes to have them begin again, the sky and smoke of mankind. My sight and hearing are very bad, on the vast main no light but reflected gleams. All my senses are trained full on me, me. Dark and silent and stale, I am no prey for them. I am far from the sounds of blood and breath, *immured*. I shall not speak of my sufferings. Cowering deep down among them I feel nothing. It is there I die, unbeknown to my stupid flesh. That which is seen, that which cries and writhes, my witless remains. Somewhere in this turmoil thought struggles on, is too wide of the mark. . . . It too cannot be quiet. On others let it wreak its dying rage, and leave me in peace.
>
> (*Malone Dies*, pp. 186-7)

The appeal of this passage lies in its sensitive manipulation of sentence length, rhythm and cadence. One instance of the last is the syntactical effect secured by placing *bony* and *immured* at the end of sentences.

It has been suggested that Beckett had been reading Blaise

Pascal's *Pensées*, when he wrote *Malone Dies*; but this would apply only to several passages, such as the above. The *raison-d'être* of the *Molloy* trilogy was alienation, the result of a sense of estrangement to which exiles are prone. *Malone Dies* therefore reads like a prose-poem with Swiftian overtones, noticeable in the characterization of Mr and Mrs Saposcat, the victims of sweated labour, and their parrotlike acceptance of man as a departmentalised social animal. Like *Piers Plowman* and other medieval complaints, the book is concerned with the deterioration of life in modern society, and with the gradual atrophy of man's bodily functions. It is surely significant that so many of the author's aliases are depicted as maimed or crippled. The novel's autobiographical elements are intimately connected with Beckett's early life in Ireland. Though the holder of a neutral passport, he preferred to remain in France after 1940, when he might have been repatriated; and he even joined the underground movement, while employed as a farm-hand in the Vaucluse countryside.

The last work in the trilogy, *The Unnamable*, is a sequel to the two novels that preceded it; it is introduced by a fulsome pretence that the inarticulate author has an urgent compulsion to speak, whatever his limitations. His solitariness is a disadvantageous ground from which to do this. The inarticulacy is a false modesty, because he at once uses words like *aporia* (a rhetorical term for 'scepticism') and *ephectic* ('tending to suspend judgement'). The least surprising feature of this introduction is that Beckett professes dissatisfaction with his earlier creations, Murphy, Watt, Molloy and Malone. Being a recluse, he has written of mankind merely from report, and he admits that the point has been reached when he cannot continue without repeating himself. There are times when he feels like a mythological figure visiting the underworld:

> It seems impossible to speak and yet say nothing; you think you have succeeded, but you always overlook something, a little yes, a little no, enough to exterminate a regiment of dragoons. And yet I do not despair, this time, while saying who I am, where I am, of not losing me, of

not going from here, of ending here. What prevents the
miracle is the spirit of method to which I have perhaps
been a little too addicted. The fact that Prometheus was
delivered twenty-nine thousand nine hundred and seventy
years after having purged his offence leaves me naturally
as cold as camphor. For between me and that miscreant
who mocked the gods, invented fire, denatured clay and
domesticated the horse, in a word obliged humanity, I
trust there is nothing in common. But the thing is worth
mentioning. In a word, shall I be able to speak of me and
of this place without putting an end to us, shall I ever be
able to go silent. . . .

(The Unnamable, p. 305)

Who are the delegates upon whom the speaker of this
monologue relies for his knowledge of men and women in
their pursuit of illusory happiness? In their order of appearance, these fictitious agents are Basil, Mahood and Worm, the
last a death-denoting mask of dissolution. These aliases,
Mahood in particular, are as meaningless to the reader as
Godot was to the playgoer. No author could possibly be
drawn on the function of their supposed existence. (*Waiting
for Godot* was, in fact, written between the composition of
Malone Dies and *The Unnamable*). By his own admission,
Beckett in *The Unnamable* had given up the pretence that
he was not his own narrator. The trilogy ends with a pro-
tracted monologue of one hundred and twelve pages, in
which there is no paragraphing whatever.

Richard N. Coe writes of this novel as follows:

The Unnamable is one of the profoundest explorations of
the problem of self-knowledge ever attempted; and if it
fails, it is because it must necessarily fail. Knowledge,
which is the province of the 'I', of consciousness, is positive
and finite; the Self, in Beckett's view, is infinite and void.
Therefore the one can never grasp the other, save in the
act of its own annihilation.

(Beckett, p. 69)

The metaphysical problems here posed are too complex for
any reader who has not some kind of Buddhist faith; it is

difficult for anyone who is not a mystic to accept the Self as infinite. To existentialists such concepts are nevertheless valid, because they involve certain aspects of language — Coe mentions, for instance, the separate identity of the personal pronouns and the shades of differentiation implied by the tenses of verbs. Beckett actually argues that the Self can only be free, if it is immune to the laws of physical causation. Because this is not feasible in life as we know it, the Self exists in a state of anxiety — Beckett's condition of Negation. An individual's much-sought-after 'identity' is therefore an illusion, initiated by the remembrance of things past. Coe's valued line of reasoning suggests that Beckett's Worm symbolises this Negation, and that Mahood is its antithesis — another of our pseudo-selves. The implications of the argument for semantics are equally significant; for, as Beckett points out, the words we use are all acquired from the speech and thinking of others.

Beckett was so diffident about submitting a trilogy of over four hundred pages for publication, that he left the touting to his French wife, a teacher of music. The real difficulty was that he refused to allow the three novels to appear separately; and in this his judgement was sound. When the trilogy finally appeared in a single volume in 1948, its effect upon young writers like Harold Pinter was immediate. But Beckett's own vein of introspective novel-making was virtually exhausted.

The last of the experimental novelists here considered is Brian O'Nolan (1911-66), who was born in County Tyrone, took a degree at University College, Dublin, and entered the Civil Service. In his leisure time he wrote fiction under the pseudonym of Flann O'Brien, and contributed his 'Cruiskeen Lawn' column to the *Irish Times*. For the latter he took the pen-name of Myles na Gopaleen, borrowed from Gerald Griffin's *The Collegians*, na Gopaleen meaning 'of the little horses or ponies'. This popular column was published on alternate days in English and Irish. Though the themes of 'Cruiskeen Lawn' are characteristically Irish, there are hints of the impact of Stephen Leacock and Ogden Nash.

O'Brien's stylistic originality is not, however, without more enduring fictional influences, for example, the fantasy of Lewis Carroll and the satire of Swift; but this satire had a less vindictive tone. The lively aggressiveness O'Brien does display is undisguisedly to debunk what has bored him in the modern realistic novel. Whenever he re-creates the Irish hero- or fairy-tale, as he did with *At Swim-Two-Birds*, the satirical directive is rather towards the formulaic treatment. Here is an example:

> Quickly they repaired to a small room adjoining Miss Lamont's bedroom where the good lady was lying-in, and deftly stacked the papered wall steads with the colourful wealth of their offerings and their fine gifts — their golden sheaves of ripened barley, firkins of curdy cheese, berries and acorns and crimson yams, melons and marrows and mellowed mast, variholed sponges of crisp-edged honey and oaten breads, earthenware jars of whey-thick sack and porcelain pots of lathery lager, sorrels and short-bread and coarse-grained cake, cucumbers cold and downy, straw-laced cradles of elderberry wine poured out in sea-green egg-cups and urn-shaped tubs of molasses crushed and crucibled with the lush brown-heavy scum of pulped mellifluous mushrooms, an exhaustive harvesting of the teeming earth, by God.
>
> (pp. 196-7)

The final expletive amply conveys the author's critical intention.

O'Brien, indeed, seldom treats the heroic past with dutiful reverence; he was too busy exposing the irrational behaviour of the present. His link with Joyce was the obvious enjoyment he took in parody, and his determination to by-pass sentimentality. As he lost no opportunity in laughing at farcical pretensions of the heroic era, he was equally in character when he mocked the modern Irishman's deplorable urban life, particularly his inconsistent servitude to religion.

In the critical survey of his own time, O'Brien showed a repeated aversion to Jesuit casuistry, to the inadequacy of classics-grounded education, and to the morbid sense of doom so often expressed in his country's literature. The remedy he adopted for immature escapism was salutary laughter, and he tried to give a less sardonic turn to it through an amusing expertise in the vernacular. As soon appears in the dialogue, O'Brien possessed an unrivalled command of Dublin and provincial slang. He was able to dramatise whatever his discerning eye lighted upon, in language that rejected the trained writer's academic enslavement to English of the Home Counties.

O'Nolan, the private man, is reported to have been blessed with an aristocratic mind and genuine scholarship; he was also convinced that chapters in topical fiction should be brief and incisive. The inutility of classical education by no means implied a preference in his work for juvenile loutishness, drunkenness and a lack of personal hygiene. He perceived, however, that the indolent Dubliner's moral delinquency and aggressiveness in political matters presented a novelist with many comic possibilities; and these he brought to light with a surprising fecundity of invention. O'Brien's Irish types possess a caustic alertness of speech similar to that of Dickens's Cockney creations, and they have the characteristically Irish propensity to magnify social evils.

At Swim-Two-Birds (written at the age of twenty-eight) has a curious title explained (p. 95) in the story which Finn the giant tells concerning the madness of King Sweeney. In the king's flight through the length of Erin, one of his resting places was the church of Snámh-da-en (Swim-Two-Birds) by the side of the River Shannon, where a woman was about to give birth to a child. The fable was penned at a likely age for a young rebel to complain that the modern novel is a 'self-evident sham' (p. 33) and to argue, tongue in cheek, that it might be bettered by becoming a work of reference. The book from which O'Brien himself drew his satirical gobbets of encyclopaedic learning was entitled *A Conspectus of the Arts and Natural Sciences*. O'Brien's running commentary on his own 'Work in Progress' was far from random; the comic obliquity well serves his cyncial purpose. *At Swim-Two-Birds* is, indeed, comparable to *Finnegans Wake*, part of the plan being to liberate the self-righteous Irish Catholic from the constricting influences of his dogmas, by using the inconsequential tactics of Lewis Carroll and even Edward Lear. But O'Brien's sportive intellect differs markedly from theirs in the derisiveness with which

Victorian restraints are shed, especially in his concessions to verbiage and vulgarity. The Irishman's intuitive earthiness is underlined, and happily married to his Gaelic fantasy. The best instance of this is the riotous journey undertaken by the Pooka MacPhellimey and the Good Fairy.

One section of the novel is devoted to reminiscences, which O'Brien pretends are autobiography. Here he hints at the 'primacy of Irish and American authors', and suggests that 'true dialogue is dependent on the conflict rather than the confluence' (p. 230). This claim is well substantiated in his successful play *Faustus Kelly*, presented at the Abbey Theatre in January, 1943. The outspokenness with which he conveys the sinister aspects of nationalistic electioneering and political hypocrisy must have been a sensitive area in a comedy remarkable for the grossness of its manners.

In the stricter form of novel-writing, O'Brien's first critic-ally acclaimed venture was *The Hard Life*, published in 1961 and dedicated to Graham Greene 'whose own forms of gloom' he professed to admire. This heartless tale, described in the epigraph as an 'exegesis of squalor', is told with astonishing wit and economy; it moves with the rollicking ease of an Elizabethan comedy. The story concerns two orphans, of uncertain parentage, brought up and educated by a maternal half-brother, Mr Collopy, one of whose eccen-tricities is to send the boys to different schools. Collopy proves a disputatious but well-informed foster-parent, of somewhat vague philanthropic occupation. His milieu is the canal area of south Dublin in 1890, just two decades before O'Nolan himself was born. Nonetheless the author justly proclaims that his novel was based on personal experience. A good deal of fun is extracted from orthographic malapropisms in spelling familiar names, e.g. the musicians Mose Art and Pagan Neeny, which reflects only the ephemeral writing of a newspaper columnist. The compensating factor is an extraordinarily wide range of colloquial slang, to be examined in due course. Collopy's talk abounds in the Dublinesque aphorisms of worldly persons, for instance, 'Only people of no experience have theories' (p. 35); 'We have too much law in this country' (p. 43); 'you are for ever double-thinking and double-talking. You slither everywhere like quicksilver' (p. 76); 'Where would we be if we couldn't produce our certified statistics?' (p. 97). The rhetoric which O'Brien here favours tingles with vitality. Chapters 7 and 10, in which Collopy discusses the Jesuit Society with his German friend, Father Fahrt, are telling examples of the well-informed Irishman's capacity for pugnacious debate.

The principal characters in *The Hard Life* are drawn with Dickensian verve and eccentricity; the writing is so adroit that a casual reader may miss its artistry. The metier is not so much novelty as surprise, achieved through challenging statement, *ad hoc* coining of words, and the use of vigorous secondary senses of those words which the reader already knows. This last incorporates many terms of technical significance, gleaned from popular science. O'Brien's interest in etymology lay at the heart of his expertise as a practising linguist; and he often drew on this word-hoard when he intended to be funny. The elder of the orphans, Manus, becomes indefatigable in his egocentric desire to live on a grand scale, and the grotesque shadiness of his dealings is only made palatable by an accompanying flamboyance and generosity. By the nineteen-sixties O'Brien's name was undoubtedly associated with the novel of the absurd, and a Texan tendency to exaggeration. The unfinished novel, *Slattery's Sago Saga*, typifies, in Ned Hoolihan and Crawford MacPherson, the probable exhaustion of this vein.

Among the moderns O'Brien spoke with respect of the novels of Aldous Huxley, perhaps with a view to such specimens as *Brave New World* and *After Many a Summer*. His debt to science fiction is contained in *The Dalkey Archive* (1964), in which he freely drew upon the verbal prodigality of *Finnegans Wake*. He also returned to his *bête noire*, Jesuit philosophy (see p. 38 and passim) undermining it with glib comment from biblical and patristic learning. Two loosely related themes activate the plot, one dominated by De Selby, a phoney experimentalist posing as a 'pneumatic' chemist, the other by James Joyce, *redivivus*; both are anti-climactic figures whom the narrator, Michael Shaughnessy, manipulates as puppets. His plans go awry when he assumes the role of a footloose idealist, planning to join a Trappist Brotherhood. O'Brien's surprise-ending, like those of

O. Henry, is clearly pre-ordained. There is no characterisation worthy of the name; De Selby, Sargeant Fottrell, Father Cobble and Joyce himself are mere caricatures.

A farce of such inordinate dimensions cannot be put across without histrionic exuberance, and this O'Brien possessed abundantly. De Selby plans to exterminate life by depleting the atmosphere of oxygen, and he claims ability to suspend time, and so to communicate with dead celebrities, such as John the Baptist and St Augustine of Hippo. He arranges a controversial interview with the latter in a submarine cave, using equipment similar to that of the Frenchman J. Y. Cousteau.

The specious Joyce plot is no less fantastic, being based on the assumption that the novelist did not die in Zürich, as reported in the press, but secretly returned to Ireland, where he lived as a barman in Skerries, north of Dublin, blandly unaware of the absurdities being written about him in America. Shaughnessy finds and interviews Joyce, only to find that he has the pious intention of joining the Jesuit order. Joyce denied that he had ever written or seen that 'dirty book' *Ulysses*; he acknowledged only one fiction, *Dubliners*, and a number of tracts written for the Catholic Truth Society of Ireland. *Ulysses* he could only explain as a practical joke, engineered by Sylvia Beach, because she was in love with him, and undertook to make him famous.

Joyce's object in seeking to be a Jesuit Father was to reform the order from within, and to 'clear the Holy Ghost out of the Godhead and out of the Catholic Church' (*Dalkey Archive*, p. 201). There is a lively discussion with his interviewer on the relative meanings of Hebrew *ruach*, Greek *pneuma* and Latin *spiritus*, in which Joyce asserts that 'there is not a word about the Holy Ghost or the Trinity in the New Testament' (p. 198). This is altogether unfounded; the phrase occurs in the Synoptic Gospels in Matthew XII, 32; Luke XI, 13; John XIV, 26, as well as Acts II, 23 (Peter's Pentecostal sermon); and in all of these citations the Greek couples *hagion* with *pneuma*, which English translations, including the Catholic Rheims Bible, agree in translating 'Holy Ghost'. What *is* true, however, is O'Brien's statement that the third hypostasis was added to the Nicene Creed by the Council of

Constantinople in AD 381; to the effect that the Holy Ghost proceeded from the Son Incarnate, *as well as* the Father; and that this caused a schism between the Eastern and Roman Catholic Churches.

The temptation to introduce Joyce as a fictional character in this novel was altogether consistent with O'Brien's judgement of him in *A Bash in the Tunnel*:

> Joyce spent a lifetime establishing himself as a character in fiction. . . . Beginning with importing real characters into his books, he achieves the magnificent inversion of making them legendary and fictional. It is quite preposterous. . . . He could not see the tree for the woods.
>
> Perhaps the true fascination of Joyce lies in his secretiveness, his ambiguity (his polyguity, perhaps?), his leg-pulling, his dishonesties, his technical skill, his attraction for Americans. . . . But at the end, Joyce will still be in his tunnel, unabashed.
>
> (*Stories and Plays*, pp. 206-8)

The Dalkey Archive has its semi-literate Dogberry in Sargeant Fottrell, with his bicycle as a symbol of office; but he is a more sophisticated exponent of malapropism. The polysyllabic humour that emerges from this official's 'cycle liturgy' is a little overdone; for instance:

> Our work is walking work if you understand my *portent* (51)
> Let us make our way *sedulously* to the shop (52)
> Here is the elixir of youth *innocuously* in its mundane perfection (53)
> Yesterday he met a missionary father, a *Redemptiorist* (56)
> His soft yearning for *parturitional* land *phlegmatically*, with its full *deposits* of milk and honeysuckle (70)
> O'Scariot was a man of *deciduous* character *inferentially* (70)

This penchant for resonant misfits, like Myles's 'Catechism of Cliché' in *The Irish Times*, is a reminder of O'Brien's constant preoccupation with the propriety of words.

Resourcefulness of vocabulary comes over less vigorously in the work written in Gaelic, for instance, in *The Poor Mouth*

(*An Béal Bocht*) a bizarre fantasy at the expense of Irish writers of the Synge era who attempted to glamorise the Irish peasantry. Translated by Patrick C. Power and published in 1941, the novelette was supposed to emanate from Bonaparte O'Coonassa of Corkadoragha on the south-west coast, the area most in demand among earnest researchers in the *Gaeltacht*. The phrasing is idisoyncratic to a degree, but naturally loses some of its force in English. The following exemplifies the irony with which Gaelic enthusiasts were regarded by the peasants:

> That is how the group, called the Gaeligores nowadays, came to Corkadoragha for the first time. They rambled about the countryside with little black notebooks for a long time before the people noticed that they were not *peelers* but gentle-folk endeavouring to learn the Gaelic of our ancestors and ancients. As each year went by, these folk became more numerous. Before long the place was dotted with them. With the passage of time, the advent of spring was no longer judged by the flight of the first swallow but by the first Gaeligore seen on the roads. . . .
>
> They carried away much of our good Gaelic when they departed from us each night but they left few pennies as recompense to the paupers who waited for them and had kept the Gaelic tongue alive for such as them a thousand years. People found this difficult to understand; it had always been said that accuracy of Gaelic (as well as holiness of spirit) grew in proportion to one's lack of worldly goods and since we had the choicest poverty and calamity, we did not understand why the scholars were interested in any half-awkward, perverse Gaelic which was audible in other parts.
>
> (*The Poor Mouth*, pp. 48-9)

One of O'Brien's jests was to ensure literal significance for Gaelic clichés, such as 'a child among the ashes', as well as to parody nostalgic utterances of idolators who revered the past, despite the squalid conditions. The influential book *Séadna*, compiled by Father Peter O'Leary (Peadar O'Laoghaire) in 1904, (*The Poor Mouth*, p. 49) did much to enhance the status of the Gaelic language in modern use.

Brian O'Nolan used different pseudonyms for his dual role as journalist and novelist. Though confusing to cataloguers, this did not mean that he was afflicted with any Freudian malady. The style is characteristic whatever form his composition took. He never wrote down to his readers, and there are those who hold that journalism broadened his experience, and strengthened his Elizabethan taste for the well-turned line. Narrative, plain statement or description, came alive when he chose to present it as anecdote; for he was a born raconteur, and pre-eminently a craftsman in words.

The Irish Times, which was edited by Robert Smyllie when Myles undertook his column in 1939, was a highly conservative journal; but O'Nolan enlivened his column with parody, pun, bogus and fanciful erudition, clichés and ironical dissections of phrases. Eventually he secured as immense a following in America as in Ireland and England. Here is an instance of his verbal fooling:

> The Irish lexicographer Dinneen, considered *in vacuo* is, heaven knows, funny enough. He just keeps standing on his head, denying stoutly that *piléar* means bullet and asserting that it means 'an inert thing or person'. Nothing stumps him. He will promise the sun moon and stars to anybody who will catch him out. And well he may. Just *take* the sun, moon and stars for a moment. Sun, you say, is *grian*. Not at all. Dinneen shouts that *grian* means 'the bottom (of a lake, well)'. . . . Most remarkable man. Eclectic I think is the word.
>
> That, of course, is why I no longer write Irish. No damn fear. I didn't come down in the last shower. Call me a bit fastidious if you like but I like to have some idea of what I'm writing. . . .
>
> There is scarcely a single word in the Irish (barring, possibly, *Sasanach*) that is simple and explicit. Apart from words with endless shades of cognate meaning, there are many with so complete a spectrum of graduated ambiguity that each of them can be made to express two directly contrary meanings, as well as a plethora of intermediate concepts that have no bearing on either. And all this strictly within the linguistic field.
>
> (*The Best of Myles*, pp. 276-8)

Only a writer thoroughly disciplined in both of Ireland's media could have contrived so many subtleties as O'Nolan has done in a vocabulary colloquial, vibrant and flexible. Appended is a word-list intended to illustrate the writer's resourcefulness; the categories are not watertight. The following abbreviations have been used:

ASTB   *At Swim-Two-Birds*
HL   *The Hard Life*
DA   *The Dalkey Archive*
SP   *Stories and Plays*
PM   *The Poor Mouth*

1. *Colloquialisms, probably of Gaelic or other dialectal derivation*

ASTB	24	Finn ... could carry an armed host in the *craw* of his gut-hung knickers (stomach)
	184	duidins (pipes for smoking)
	221	The man with a *bowsy* (lout, low fellow)
	267	The Pooka had put the entirety of the *farl* deep down in the pit of his stomach (Scots, round cake)
HL	21	bosthoon (Ir. bastún, senseless fellow, softic); smahan (drink)
	22	cogging (cheating, cribbing)
	41	great tact and *plawmaus*
	61	pills and drugs and *falthalals*
	62	ignorant *guff* (nonsense, empty talk)
	74	the torture had him *banjaxed* (broken)
	75	*rawmaish* and pseudo-theology
	83	You are only trying to *grig* me (make fun of)
	89	She was what was known as a good *hoult*; a horrible limp, lank *streel* of a creature
	91	The *banatee* up at six in the morning (Ir. *bean a'tí*, woman of the house)
HL	92	country *rozzers* (policeman); 93 pinkeens
	93	had to be *lurried* into hospital (dragged, carried)
	96	It's a bit *hash* this evening
	100	Annie quietly crying into her *prashkeen*

HL 103 spondulics (money)

110 Mulloy with two other *butties* (Eng. buddies)

DA 13 I know you will not refuse a *taiscaun*

17 the dry *gawks* (ungainly persons)

28 I'll buy a *glawsheen* all round (tot of whisky)

51 a fastidious little wade for the good of my *spawgs* (legs)

77 He disobeyed God's orders because, *muryaa*, he knew better

87 twenty *punky leprahauns* (miserable brownies)

97 he had the people driven *loopy* (mad)

120 was the priest, in a sort of way, *mitching*? (playing truant)

159 a hard *chaw* (Dublin slang for 'yokel')

166 cruiskeens (jars); 183 ling (fish of the cod family)

219 we've decided to take the jump and be *fluthered* ever afterwards (also SP 42 *floothered*)

SP 84 *Gorawars!* Mr. Toole said (expletive)

122 Yerrah, now you're *coddin* me surely (chaffing)

123 having a few *rossiners* down the way (stiff drinks)

125 *bogman's* back-chat

128 He was not a smart *maneen* from Cork

138 Hold on to the wire now, *avic*!

161 a good feed of Cork *crubeens*

191 no decent man would be such an *omadaun*

2. *Terms of abuse or disapprobation*

HL 18 put a name the like of that on the poor *bookul* (Ir. buachaill, boy)

19 thullabawns (also SP 194 thollabawns); looderamawns

36 gougers (swindlers); 38 gurrier; 39 thoolermawns

60 crawthumpers (Roman Catholics)

71 there is a bold *rossie* for you

83 that Corporation *ownshucks*

HL	91	*gobhawks* from the down country; That's the sort of *cods* we have looking after law and order (fools). Cf 150 it may have been all *cod* (tomfoolery)
	92	This is the work of some *pultogue* that doesn't like me
	93	give the young *pogue-mahones* an education
DA	10	gawms (same as *gorms*, low-class persons); gobshites (fools or dupes)
	40	blatherskite (Scots, 'speaker of voluble nonsense')
	159	you long-faced *sleeveen*; 160 gobdaw
SP	128	thumbawns

3. *Catch-Phrases*

ASTB	31	That was the pigs whiskers
HL	18	I'll go bail (I'm certain); Dug with the other foot (Protestant)
	30	cornerboy (street loafer)
	34	the dear ∧ knows (name of the Deity omitted)
	39	By the *jappers* (Eng. *jabers*)
	67	Faith and that would *take me to the fair*
	91	Perjury. They'd *swear a hole in an iron bucket*
	122	fixed up with a *monkey suit* (tight-fitting, with short jacket)
	133	It put the heart across me
DA	24	Those mask affairs are bothersome to *horse about*
SP	85	the house of a *great skin* in Cumann
	87	Jakers (expletive)
	121	that fellow *has me worn* with his politics
	122	a western brogue on which *seaweed could be hung*
	124	he's *half-Cork* on the da's side
	126	*Hould yer whisht* for pity's sake
	137	This is some class of a *ready-up*
	151	We'll have to *bate the lard* out of that Protestant (bate = beat)
	151	that's *all me eye for a yarn*

SP 161 skidaddle (slang 'leave, go')
    174 I'm nearly home and *dried*
    177 'Tisn't worth a *fiddler's* curse
    189 that's a different *pair of sleeves*
    193 I tink (sic) I'll *mosey off* (depart quickly)
PM   13 we'll get a dirty tempestuous night of it will *knock a shake* out of us
     13 you've told *nary* a lie (never)

4. *Unusual words, some probably coined*
HL   46 *colloquing* with Mrs Crotty
     74 Catesby and a crowd of his *segocias* (DA 11 segotia)
    100 Panpendarism
DA   11 theopneust; 12 astrognosy; 22 christophobe; 42 formulist (from formula)
     42 cognoscible (from Scottish legal *cognosce* 'to examine')

5. *Ad hoc witticisms* (coined)
DA   36 heterosexual? *heterononsense*
     36 gymnastiness
     37 saintliness was next to *bedliness*
     38 He often *encorpifies* himself (assumes bodily form)
     42 a corpus of patristic *paddeology*
    108 Fottrell's *bicyclosis*

6. *Malapropisms*
HL   17 Annie here had everything *infastatiously* in order (Mrs Crotty)
HL   84 what *rodomondario* is this you are giving us (Mr Collopy)
SP 185 emanciated with exertions ... and *strenualities* (Westerner Shawn of the Urban Council)

7. *Archaisms* (perhaps dialectal)
HL   18 the river Lee, down *fornenst* Queenstown
         Amn't I nearly crippled?

8. *Dialogue in phonetic spelling*
HL   107   that good man is *day tros* (Fr. *de trop*)
SP   151   I left word for them to *folly* me here

9. *Syntax*
HL   17   *The* brother and myself (Definite article for
                1st personal possessive *my*)
        118   Isn't this *the* nice state of affairs?
        139   I asked him what the subject of Mr Collopy's
                representations *were* (subjunctive = 'might
                be')

10. *Solecisms*
ASTB 143   leaving their half-*took* drinks behind them
DA   113   had many times since made a *daily* trip to
                revisit the scene (day trip)

X

Irish Shorter Fiction since the Civil War

Flann O'Brien made an important observation when he said in 'John Duffy's Brother' that modern writing had passed the stage 'when simple events are stated . . . without any clue as to the psychological and hereditary forces working in the background' (*Stories and Plays*, pp. 93-4). Such forces were active also among Irish writers who did not live in the homeland, or visited it only at rare intervals. When the Irish Republic, liberated from the yoke of Anglo-Saxon imperialism, returned to its 'natural' sources of inspiration, writers like AE in *The Inner and Outer Ireland* reluctantly discovered that the sources of nature had been much undermined by the social effects of urbanisation upon the indigenous arts. Most Irish writers earned their livelihood by working in Dublin, Cork or Belfast. Moreover, the pure Celtic strain had sometimes been mingled with the blood of other hereditary streams. Materialism and industrialisation, centred in the cities, may have had their roots in nineteenth-century imperialism; but unquestionably they modified, if they did not imperil, AE's ideal of cultural independence. As Yeats maintained in *The Living Torch* (p. 134) a nation is no more than 'a collective imagination held with intensity'.

For reasons such as these the criteria for distinguishing an Anglo-Irish writer from an Englishman writing about Ireland are hard to define, except in vague terms such as the author's personality. In the symposium *Place, Personality and the Irish Writer*, Andrew Carpenter found a difference in the *tone* of the writing, reflected in 'the plurality of Irish attitudes and the uncertainties of Irish life' (p. 188). I propose in the present chapter to test this by reference to modern writers of fiction who, since George Moore's *The Untilled Field*, have developed the art of the short story.

Liam O'Flaherty (born 1896) fought both in World War I and in the Irish civil struggle of the nineteen-twenties; the horror of his experiences affected not only his career, but the texture and quality of his writing. Though he lived largely abroad until 1932, he became one of Ireland's leading short-story writers, a genre to which Anglo-Irish literature made a conspicuous contribution. By 1950 O'Flaherty had published five volumes of short stories, and fifteen novels, the most important of the latter being *The Informer* (1925) and *Famine* (1937). During World War II O'Flaherty roamed in the Caribbean and South America, the roving life being characteristic of his unsettled state of mind. He then returned to Dublin to become a popular broadcaster of his own fiction; for he was a fluent speaker in both media. Several critics have likened O'Flaherty to D. H. Lawrence; but though he was acquainted with Lawrence, there was much difference between their realism and their attitude to life. The Irishman was a prolific writer, but impelled more by what he saw and felt, than by what he thought.

In the period between the world wars O'Flaherty found it hard to endure the captivity of urban life, and his career took a similar course to that of Henry Williamson, author of *Tarka the Otter*. As a lover of nature he wrote much about animals, for instance in the short-story collections *Spring Sowing* (1924) and *The Tent* (1926). O'Flaherty despised mediocrity, and destroyed much of his early writing that failed to meet his standards of self-discipline. One disadvantage of the animal tales was the comparative absence of dialogue; yet stories like 'The Conger Eel' and 'The Wild Sow' contain some of his most vivid narrative and descriptive writing. Another tale, 'Fairy Goose', is more ironical, and illustrates the attraction of violence for O'Flaherty. He used to say that had it not been for his war experience he would never have become a thoroughly fulfilled person.

O'Flaherty admired in animals the ease and grace of their movements, their robust acceptance of the predatory necessities of existence. With Darwinian powers of observation, he found similar instincts in men and women, whom he depicted with a clear perception of their emotional responses in tense situations. Such situations might arise from economic conditions, or from the vagaries of Ireland's depressing weather. Here is a passage from 'The Tent' in the volume of that title:

> The stranger accepted the cigarette, lit it, and then looked at them. . . . The tinker was sitting on a box opposite him, leaning languidly backwards from his hips, a slim, tall, graceful man, with a beautiful head poised gracefully on a brown neck, and great black lashes falling down over his half-closed eyes, just like a woman. A womanish-looking fellow, with that sensuous grace in the languid pose of his body which is found only among aristocrats and people who belong to a very small workless class, cut off from the mass of society, yet living at their expense. A young fellow . . . blowing out cigarette smoke through his nostrils and gazing dreamily into the blaze of the wood fire. The two women were just like him in texture, both of them slatterns, dirty and unkempt, but with the same proud arrogant, contemptuous look in their beautiful brown faces. . . .
> 'Tinkers,' he said to himself. 'Awful bloody people.'
> (*Penguin Book of Irish Short Stories*, pp. 132-3)

The stories about humans are mostly brief and humourless, resembling character sketches, bearing such titles as 'Beauty', 'Blood Lust' and 'Struggle', all found in *Spring Sowing*. The passions are elemental, stark and powerful; but whatever the feelings involved, the treatment is usually compassionate and lyrical. Words that glow and irradiate the scene had a particular fascination for O'Flaherty. The stratum of society he handled discountenanced a reflective mode of presentation; he disapproved of writers who did not present life as they found it, but sought to mould it to their ideal of what life ought to be. For precipitate action and poetic language, there is no better example than his pagan fable, 'The Mermaid', which requires a narrator.

For O'Flaherty, economy of means was essential to the concept of the short story, for he was motivated by the conviction of Katherine Mansfield that 'life can be made to appear anything by presenting only one aspect of it.' The stories about city life, and those that treat of war, are different in tone, containing not only more dialogue, but those shades of irony and satire that are peculiar to embittered Irishmen. This is not therefore a singular aspect by which to distinguish O'Flaherty as an Irish writer. Indeed, he resisted any conscious attempts at style, as he told Edward Garnett, on the ground that it was 'artificial and vulgar' (Letter of 2 April 1924). But in this correspondence he acknowledged a deliberate coldness of language, which he sometimes adopted to offset the abandoned and poetical passages.

This appreciation of the value of contrast was dominant in the mood of tragic-farce to which O'Flaherty was often addicted. A distinctly Irish idiosyncracy was, however, his love of Gaelic repetition of phrase, one of the formulaic oral practices associated with the folk-tale. His writing is strong through the dynamism it gathers perpetually from Gaelic speech. His brand of it is steeped in the pantheism he substituted for orthodox religion, and he made the emotions more complex through the interest he showed in minds that are plagued with obsessions. There is a degree of pantheism evident in the affection he showed for his birthplace: 'The island [Inishmore in the Aran group] has the character and personality of a mute God. One is awed by its presence, breathing its air. Over it broods an overwhelming sense of great, noble tragedy. The Greeks would have liked it.' (Letter to Garnett, June 1927). The letters of O'Flaherty are preserved in the Academic Centre Library, Austin, Texas. Quotations are from Kelly, *O'Flaherty*.

Frank O'Connor (1903-66) was the only son of poor parents, the mother being the dominant partner. He grew up in Cork, where his education was indifferent, but it improved when he met Corkery and Sean O'Faolain before he was twenty. Describing himself as an 'auto-didact', he claimed that he owed little to Irish education, except politics and religion, and both were disadvantageous. For him, creative experience 'came through the study of the 19th century novel', and young people of his generation were indeed fortunate, because that literature was 'incomparably the greatest of the modern arts' (*Towards an Appreciation of Literature*, pp. 13-14). O'Connor taught himself German in order to read Goethe in the original, and French to acquaint himself with the language of Flaubert and de Maupassant. The Russian novelists Tolstoy and Dostoevsky he studied in English translation. The novel, he said, is essentially an expression of the needs and aspirations of the middle classes; its characteristic note is a 'deep human feeling'. The study of Classics declined when new professions and Protestant attitudes began to be taken seriously. But, said O'Connor, in an interview with *Paris Review*:

> ... I am old fashioned! It's the only old-fashionedness you can come back to. You've got to come back eventually to humanism, and that's humanism in the old sense of the word, what the Latins and Greeks thought about human beings, not the American sense of the word, that everybody is conditioned ... people are as you see them, and no psychiatrist is going to tell you anything fundamentally different.

> (*Writers at Work*, Series I, p. 178)

O'Connor himself wrote only two novels, *The Saint and Mary Kate* (1932) and *Dutch Interior* (1940); neither was entirely successful. But he produced nearly a hundred short stories, and it is on these that his reputation largely rests. He was determined in his humanity and breadth of outlook to become a sensitive mirror of Ireland in his time; and it is important to notice the principles of short-story writing he favoured, because he regarded it as a distinct art. Gogol conceived it, he said, but Turgenev, Chekhov and de Maupassant brought it to perfection. O'Connor remained undecided on the merits of the maverick Kipling, but lauded the craftmanship of Sherwood Anderson, Hemingway and J. D. Salinger in America. Moore's *The Untilled Field* was unquestionably the forbear of the short story in Ireland, and the prime influence on Joyce's *Dubliners*.

While O'Connor's critical pronouncements are always challenging, some of his evaluations are too self-assured for acceptance. But *The Lonely Voice* (1963), a series of lectures delivered at Stanford University, may well prove to the short story what E. M. Forster's *Aspects of the Novel* has become to the longer forms of fiction. It is difficult to fault O'Connor on his expertise as a practitioner of the short story; and he is equally sound on distinctions between allied forms, such as the *conte* and the *nouvelle*, in which French influence predominates. He believed, for instance, that the long short story should supply sufficient information for 'the moral imagination to function' (op. cit., p. 25). His metier, the short story proper, he defined comprehensively as 'an ideal action worked out in terms of verisimilitude' (ibid., p. 13); it is 'a private art intended to satisfy the standards of the individual, solitary, critical reader.' It need not, like the novel, contain a character with whom the reader should personally identify himself, because it cannot afford the novelist's expansiveness.

The controversial element in O'Connor's opinions remains his contention that the short story should centre upon the interests of 'a submerged population group' (ibid., p. 18). O'Connor was undoubtedly thinking of the outlawed groups in nineteenth-century Russia, France, America, and Ireland in particular. The revival of interest in folklore had brought to the fore the fate of the depressed Gaelic peasantry, which was not unlike that of the proletariat under the Tsars, or the last French kings. To allay the suspicion of untenable generalisation, O'Connor continues: 'The submerged population is not submerged entirely by material considerations; it can also be submerged by the absence of spiritual ones' (p. 18); and he concludes that a characteristic short story is the better for containing 'an intense awareness of human loneliness'. Among his own stories, one finds this demonstrated in 'My First Protestant' from *Travellers' Samples* (1951):

I had now drifted into another spell of loneliness, but loneliness with a new and disturbing feeling of alienation; and Cork is a bad place for a man who feels like that. It was as if I couldn't communicate with anybody. On Sundays, instead of going to Mass, I walked down the quays and along the river. It was pleasant there, and I sat on a bench under the trees and watched the reflection of the big painted houses and the cliffs behind them in the water, or read some book. A long, leisurely book — it looked as though I should have a lifetime to read it in.

I had been doing it for months when, one day, I noticed a man who turned up each Sunday about the same time. I knew him; he was a teacher from the South Side. We chatted, and the following Sunday when we met again he said quizzically:

'You seem to be very fond of ships.'

'Mr Reilly,' I said, 'those that go down to the sea in ships are to me the greatest wonder of the Lord.'

(*The Mad Lomasneys and Other Stories*, pp. 142-3)

Length is not, for O'Connor, a major criterion for the form of a short story; the story gains in appeal and liveliness only if the narrator captures the tones of an actual speaking voice. O'Connor had already discovered this when he published his first volume of stories, *Guests of the Nation*, which arose out of oddities of behaviour observed in the Irish Civil War of 1922. As a result of equivocal motives attributed to patriots on either side, he wrote an adulatory biography of Michael Collins, whose cause on behalf of the Free State he had opposed by force of arms. From the tragic tone of the opening tale 'Guests of the Nation', from which the volume is named, it is safe to conclude that O'Connor never again made himself an instrument of warring factions.

O'Connor was as sceptical about the activities of the Church, and in many stories saw through the hypocrisy or unwisdom of its social procedures. He attributed these to the Jansenist narrowness of the priesthood trained by Maynooth College; he held it responsible for the rigid control exercised over Irish family life. He was less concerned with Maynooth's political implications, which angered Moore, Joyce and O'Flaherty. It is worth noting that O'Connor's attitude was not dogmatic, but often generous, perhaps in deference to his mother's piety. The fallible priest in 'My First Confession', regarded as an opportunity for humour rather than spleen, is not to be compared with the ineffectual one in 'News for the Church'. One can see from the attitude of the father confessor in the latter story that O'Connor reacted to the introspective and fatalistic turn that Irish

Catholicism had taken; he thought it largely responsible for mass emigration, long after the initial impetus of the Great Famine.

O'Connor did not adopt the role of the apostle of freedom; but he believed he understood the ethos of the Irish tradition, and made clear its racial pride, mysticism and superstition in *A Short History of Irish Literature* (1968), a series of lectures delivered at Trinity College, Dublin, shortly before his death. The short stories dwell on the pertinacity of these influences, but also on the conflict he experienced between his mother's faith and his own belief in human compassion. He could see the evil effects of the harsh discipline exacted by priests who meddled in secular affairs, even sport, as exemplified by Father Crowley in 'Peasants', a story remarkable for the rusticity of its language. A priest wielding power as tyrannically as he does, had not the right to expect exemption from criticism from members of his own parish.

O'Connor also believed that the vanity of the priest class was partly the outcome of enforced celibacy. An immediate result was the disinclination to marry among the young lay population. This was not only due to economic problems, such as property succession, or disagreement over marriage settlements for prospective brides. A primary cause was sexual repression in the young, induced by the watchful eye of the church over the courting habits of adolescents. They were the victims of the dual effects of ignorance and curiosity, which the conviction of sin did nothing to redress. The church's pressure on private morality occupies a considerable place in O'Connor's stories. So do mother-complexed sons, and daughters whose duty it has traditionally been to support widowed parents. The problem is skilfully handled in such stories as 'Judas' and 'The Impossible Marriage'.

O'Connor sometimes resembled O'Casey in his power to present a case, and in the knowledge that dramatic power comes from concreteness as well as characterisation. There is very little abstraction in the imagination of both writers; they treat illiberal fantasies with natural disdain. It was this that led to O'Connor's disillusionment with Corkery's romantic nationalism. Whether living in Cork or Dublin, he did not react to his environment from any feeling of spiritual claustrophobia. Long before he went to lecture in the United States, O'Connor had learnt to slough off the insular hatreds disclosed in stories of Irish feuds, such as 'The Luceys'.

Occasionally O'Connor experimented with the long short story. 'The Mad Lomasneys' is in six episodes, giving him sufficient room to dramatise the leading characters and expand the dialogue. The youngest daughter, Rita, is depicted as unstable, but erotically adventurous, the feminine equivalent of the 'wild Irishman'. Her first affair is with an aspirant priest, made comic by Rita's clash with the Mother Superior of her school, which ends with dismissal from her teaching post. During a spell of depressing wet weather, Rita again displays eccentricity by quixotically accepting in marriage a man twice her age:

> There was I, sure that my life was over and that it was marriage or the river. 'Women!' she cried, shaking her head in a frenzy. 'Good God. The idiots we make of ourselves about men!'
>
> (*The Mad Lomasneys and Other Stories*, p. 69)

O'Connor lavished the utmost attention on the construction of his stories, re-writing some of them a dozen times. His other major care was lucidity and inevitability in the management of his workaday language. Even when parsimonious with words, he sought to engross the reader's attention, and never allowed himself the luxury of elaborate picture-making. 'Peasants' is an attractive story, not only for the powerful clash of wills and ironical results for the unhappy offender, but for its realistic representation of the peasant language. Here are examples from *The Stories of Frank O'Connor* (1953) in which the author re-casts with care the version that first appeared in *Bones of Contention*; by replacing, for instance, *easy* for *aisy* (156), and *angashores* for *aindeiseoirs* (159), the latter a southern Irish word for a 'poor, miserable creature':

1. *Idiomatic expletives, words and phrases*
   p. 154 Divil's cure to him! 'Tis the price of him! Kind father for him! . . . The Heavens be his bed!
   155 till he had the *blood lighting* in the Cronin eyes

p. 155 he might have *danced a jig* on their backs (originally *hornpipe*)

156 *True for you* (you are quite right)

157 all my life I'm fighting the *long-tailed* families
(those with lengthy genealogies)

158 you'd better keep the *soft* word for the judge
(placating)

159 We'll *leave* the matter drop for good and all (let)

160 Is it *the way* you want me to perjure myself
(because)

161 We don't ask you to go *next, nigh or near* the court
(legalistic tautology)

163 *Only* for him, people say, Michael John would be
in America (But)

2. *Unusual use of adverbs and prepositions*

p. 155 anyone that had a grudge *in* for one of them

159 'twon't be forgotten *for* you

A story similar in tone and atmosphere is 'The Long Road
to Ummera', in which O'Connor uses several notably Irish
expressions:

p. 130 You did, *amossa*, you did (the usual form is *mossa*,
from Irish *ma' seadh*, usually found, like *wisha*, at
the beginning of a sentence, in the sense of 'indeed')

132 you must stand up *overright* the neighbours (opposite). This usage is said by P. W. Joyce (op. cit.,
p. 299) to be an erroneous translation of Irish
ós cómhair (over + opposite)

134 Ach, you old *oinseach*, your mind is wandering
(This is an Irish word for 'foolish woman', the male
equivalent being *omadaun*).

Versatile Sean O'Faolain, born in Cork in 1900, has to his
credit three novels, half-a-dozen volumes of short stories,
four biographical studies (besides his autobiography *Vive
Moi!*), three travel books, and several volumes of critical and
miscellaneous prose. His prolonged residence in, and deep
regard for, Ireland explains the esteem in which O'Faolain's
reputation is now held. His father was enrolled in the Royal
Irish Constabulary and bore the anglicised surname of

'Whelan'; but when his youngest son had learnt Irish, he adopted the Gaelic form of the name which is pronounced O'Fay-lawn. In 1918 Sean began to attend the University College of Cork, joined the IRA and was subsequently to become its underground Publicity Director — a traumatic experience. During the Civil War O'Faolain served in the Republican cause, then became a commercial traveller and taught at a country school. In 1926 he was awarded a Commonwealth Fellowship at Harvard University, where he stayed for three years taking a Master's degree in English. For the following four years he lectured at Strawberry Hill Teachers' Training College on the outskirts of London, and while there he published his first book of stories *Midsummer Night's Madness* in 1932. Both this and his novel *Bird Alone* (1936) were banned in Ireland, as respectively provocative and obscene. Nevertheless, O'Faolain returned to live in Ireland from 1933, and to become his country's most unbiased spokesman.

O'Faolain's treatise on *The Short Story* is a sensitive instrument for measuring his achievement, and a means of comparing his approach with that of O'Connor. He writes:

> The things I like to find in a story are punch and poetry. . . .
> 'technique' is the least part of the business. . . . Irish writers are far less interested in the technique of writing than in the conditions of writing, though inclined to think exclusively in terms of their own local conditions and to imagine them unique.
>
> (op. cit., pp. 11 and 23)

He approved of neither the French realistic convention, nor the discursiveness of Henry James. What a reader needs to know, even the names and background of principal characters, is seldom to be vouchsafed in the opening paragraphs. Nor is suspense a matter of events alone. The attractive short story invariably unfolds itself by suggestion and implication. The short story writer's obligation, he says, is to convey personality through speech, without sacrificing the necessary compression. To contain the story within its artistic limits, situation and construction need to merge; a hint of drama is feasible, but hardly ever a plot.

In the foreword to *The Heat of the Sun* (1966), O'Faolain distinguishes short stories from tales. The latter he finds more relaxing, because the ampler tale roves further and carries more weight. It affords 'time and space for more complex characterisation, more changes of mood, more incidents and scenes' (op. cit., p. 6). He does not consider length in itself a satisfactory criterion; his own tales vary from fifteen to forty pages, in examples such as 'In the Bosom of the Country' (30), 'Lovers of the Lake' (28) and 'A Dead Cert' (18). Exemplary specimens of the short story proper are his 'The Man who Invented Sin' (12 pages) and 'Childybawn' (11). 'Lady Lucifer' (16 pages), contains a short story within a tale, and may be regarded as an intermediate type.

'The Man who Invented Sin' from *Teresa and Other Stories* (1947) is in the spirit of Flann O'Brien's *The Poor Mouth*. With delightful humour, O'Faolain relates his experiences at a Summer School in south-western Ireland, at the height of the Gaelic language revival. Prospective teachers from many walks of life multiplied, until available accommodation was severely strained; the participators tended to turn study groups into light-hearted picnic parties. In 1920 he found lodgings at a private house on the shores of a Munster lake, where he was joined by two monks and two nuns, who came from the slum schools. Isolation from the main body brought the five closely together after hours; whenever rain spoilt the long summer evenings, they foregathered in the drawing-room, where the lay student entertained the others at the piano. By amusing themselves with talk and folk-song, reserve was quickly broken down.

Discussions often began with the difficulties of Irish pronunciation; for like German, Gaelic tends to be a guttural language, as one of the monks explained to a nun: 'You make a great big shpit inside your mouth and gurgle it' (*Collected Stories* I, p. 339). A word commonly used in the Cork area was *rath* (pronounced rá) 'a circular hill-fort', whose origin is attributed to the Danes. In light-hearted chaffing, one of the monks called his colleague a *gom*, the reduced form of Irish *gamal*, meaning a 'half-wit'.

In the fraternal atmosphere thus created brothers and

nuns exchanged confidences about birthplaces and youthful experiences, and were already on Christian-name terms. When the weather was propitious, they might play at pitch-and-toss in the garden; when it was not, they learnt Irish folk-songs, and even practised waltzing. The religious were obviously letting their hair down, when one evening the frivolity was halted by the arrival of a kill-joy curate. 'If Martin Luther could only see this!' he exclaimed, and protested that the Serpent had again returned to the garden. One of the nuns shed a few tears, but her colleague said that the curate was no gentleman, and his rebuke was soon forgotten.

The last fling took the form of a boat-party on the lake the evening before departure; singing reached their persecutor across the water, and he was waiting to take names when the culprits stepped ashore at midnight. The monks wore caps instead of black hats, and the nuns, with skirts pinned up, had discarded guimps, coifs and cowls. The *guimp* (English 'wimple') is a starched neckerchief, and the *coif* a close-fitting cap, fastened under the chin; both words were of French origin. One nun dropped her guimp in her embarrassment, but the evidence was promptly retrieved by stealth from the curate's study.

The story is no more than an amusing anecdote to illustrate that church discipline is often needlessly inflexible, especially for the young in heart. But time changes everything; and when one of the brothers recalled the incidents twenty-three years later, humanity had seemingly passed from his life. Humourlessly, he said, 'You mightn't understand it, now! But it's not good to take people out of their rut. I didn't enjoy that summer' (ibid., p. 348).

A familiar topic of the longer tales, especially in O'Faolain's maturity, is marital infidelity. He suggests that the fundamental cause is Catholic disapproval of divorce, subsidiary ones being a childless marriage, a husband's pre-occupation with his work, and the boredom with which many women face middle-age. Alcoholism is the alleged cause of Anna Mohan's escapade in 'In the Bosom of the Country'. Anna had married young, when her emotional responses were undeveloped; she managed to keep her affair with an English Protestant, Major Keene, secret for ten years, though the Major had a trustworthy confidant. He had come to live in Ireland from Kenya, when he had inherited property from his late uncle. Facts are subtly disclosed by means of reminiscential epigrams, such as 'Love lies in sealed bottles of regret', 'the Irish have a great gift for death, wakes and funerals' (*The Heat of the Sun*, p. 11).

The lovers were together when Anna's husband died in hospital; their relationship could now be regularised by marriage. As a Catholic, Anna insists on a wedding in her church, for reasons of social propriety; among her friends mixed marriages caused raised eye-brows. Reluctantly, the Major consults a Monsignor, who is also a man of intellectual distinction; he is the third character of the tale. (O'Faolain's practice is not to exceed that number.) The two men establish a firm, but rather convivial, friendship. Six months after her husband's passing, Anna marries her Catholic husband.

The irony is, however, that a convert to the faith, whose convictions are rationally grounded, often turns out to be more zealous in practice than those who inherit their religion as a family tradition. There are frequent disputes about the interpretation of dogma, and the upshot is that the Major goes regularly to early-morning Mass by himself, leaving his wife at home in bed. She proves to be a woman who has been thoroughly spoilt, and absolutely refuses to confess her sins of the flesh; she even denies that her liaison had been adultery. Her religion is obviously a cloak to put on or off as she pleases. According to the Monsignor, thousands of her like have been active in Ireland since the nineteen-twenties.

'Lovers of the Lake', a better constructed tale, has a similarly frank theme, but there is more poetry in the telling. Jenny, the childless, deceiving wife of a well-to-do husband, is entering her forties, and decides to make peace with her conscience by going on a pilgrimage and fast to the island retreat of Lough Derg. Her lover, Bobby, a Dublin surgeon and non-practising Catholic, is querulous concerning her motives, but drives her to her destination and agrees to await her return in the neighbourhood. After their parting, however, Bobby unselfishly determines to take part in the three-day pilgrimage himself, though quite unenthusiastic about the fasting. Some two thousand pilgrims have assembled in miserable weather, and respond very differently to proceeding barefoot from station to station. O'Faolain, seeing the pilgrimage as a religious craze, does not disguise pampered Jenny's feelings:

> She soon found that the island floated on kindness. Everything and everybody about her seemed to say, 'We are all sinners here, wretched creatures barely worthy of mercy.' She felt the abasement of the doomed. She was among people who had surrendered all personal identity, all pride. It was like being in a concentration camp.
>
> (*Penguin Book of Irish Short Stories*, p. 151)

Bobby is better able to discern the psychotherapy of the mission, where hunger, repetitious prayer and confession play a major part in transformation. When Jenny encounters him, she soon realises her inability to give him up; besides, her husband is rich, and she admits that she enjoys the physical pleasures. When the ordeal is over, the two do not return to Dublin, but drive to the Galway coast, knowing that their fasting still has twelve hours to run. True to this commitment, neither partakes of the trout that Bobby catches and cooks; they also reject buttered toast served with black tea at a restaurant. A few hours are beguiled by going to a cinema, and at midnight, they enjoy the epicurean delights of a dinner that Bobby had had the foresight to order. They dance until three in the morning, and then retire to separate hotel rooms. Self-denial had thus done both parties some good, and Bobby suggests that they might even visit the island again next year. O'Faolain in this tale shows that many women (and men) perform the offices of the church perfunctorily; that most take Catholicism in their stride, as do many religious folk in France, Italy and Portugal.

In 'A Dead Cert' from *The Talking Trees* (1968), Jenny Rosse is mated with an indulgent husband, who does not realise that she is troubled with the seven-year itch. He is a prosperous barrister in Cork, who does not pry into visits to her home-town, Dublin, for shopping-sprees or re-union with members of the Hunt and Yacht Clubs. Jenny is thirty-four, has two children, a comfortable home and a private car; but her sporting temperament hankers after the active life. In

Dublin she prefers the Shelbourne Hotel to staying with relations; and here she flirts outrageously after dinner with an old flame, Oweny Flynn, one of her husband's former colleagues. She had reputedly chosen her partner by a draw of the cards, but now finds that her gambling nature retains an obstinate attachment to her dobbinish husband.

O'Faolain is invariably shrewd in depicting domestic situations like this one; he is certainly the most experienced interpreter of the freedoms women assumed in Ireland after World War II. Among her temptations, Jenny's holidays with friends abroad arouse the reflection that, when single, she had been too naïve to risk a romantic attachment. Now, when it comes to the crunch, she flees compulsively to the arms of her husband. Yet she continues to live dangerously by inviting Oweny to make up a foursome on a skiing trip to Gstaad. The problem of the amoral wife is handled with equal tact, humour and irony in O'Faolain's tale 'I Remember, I Remember'.

In the foreword to *Finest Stories*, a selection made by O'Faolain himself for Bantam Books in 1959, the author acknowledged the inadequacy of his immature romanticism, in passages like the following:

> There was silence for a few minutes, with only the noise of the rain *cat-pattering* against the window.... Leaving Henn to himself we drove the rest of the herd before us from the hall, into the darkness, so *rain-arrowy* and cold. From the great front door I watched them go tramping down the avenue....
>
> ('Midsummer Night Madness', p. 42)

Most young patriots, he confessed, tended to use words rhetorically, or with the spirit of pure poetry in mind. It took twenty years to subdue his own idealistic fervour, and to discover that 'half the art of writing is re-writing' (p. xi). He was chary about the legend of Balzac's sending unrevised sheets to the printer. But a powerful story like 'No Country for Old Men' (from *I Remember, I Remember*) bears the hall-mark of a seasoned writer; for instance in an observation like the following: 'It is a terrible and lovely thing to look at the face of Death when you are young, but it unfits a man for the long humiliation of life' (op. cit., p. 179). This story is an angry *exposé* of two calculating Irish businessmen, trying in vain to escape from the cynicism of their corrupt past, while cool-headedly implicating themselves in an IRA raid on Northern Ireland, for which both are sentenced.

The peak of romantic essentialism is perhaps to be found in O'Faolain's *Bird Alone* (1936), a novel comparable in poetry and pathos to George Moore's *The Lake*. Edward Garnett, Jonathan Cape's formidable literary adviser, objected to the story's pathetic element; on the ground of extreme subjectivity, he wanted it re-written in the manner of Balzac. But the author declined and published his book as he conceived it (see *Vive Moi!* pp. 254-6). The sin-complex of an unmarried mother ends inevitably in tragedy, which O'Faolain handles with tact and sympathy. By way of ironic contrast, the chapters that concern the shabby-genteel life of the Crone family are drawn with verve and tense satirical clarity. The crafty old grandfather, Philip Crone, is a relict of the grotesque humour that one finds in the two-dimensional characters of Victorian fiction. A precocious craftsmanship enabled O'Faolain to use Grander Crone with choric effect, in order to animadvert upon the rigidity of Catholicism in Ireland, and its tragic results for the domestic morals of adolescents.

O'Faolain's use of the vernacular is not extensive, but his pages teem with slang locutions and expressive terms from the less cultured strata of society. In the random selection below, the following are the title abbreviations to indicate the stories cited: BA, *Bird Alone*; KW, 'Kitty the Wren'; F, 'Fugue'; T, 'Teresa', ULHD, 'Unholy Living and Half Dying'; LL, 'Lovers of the Lake'; H, Hymeneal; BW, 'A Broken World'; UBS, 'Up the Bare Stairs'; FC, 'The Fur Coat'; YG, 'The Younger Generation'; LYD, 'Love's Young Dream'; NCOM, 'No Country for Old Men'; VM, *Vive Moi!*

BA   within two years of her marriage she was *streeling* around the house in her petticoat (lazing untidily). de yeh think I'd pay as much as a *lop* for an English pig's *crubeen*? (*lop*, dialect 'small coin'; *crubeen*, pig's foot, trotter, from Irish *crúb*)

BA   Not a bloody *make*. Not a *lop* or *tosser*. No! Not
a pin's fee, as Shakespeare says (*make* = halfpenny)
Look at me with my *ponthers* and my peraphernalia
on
that will be the *cockawalla* of a pantomine then if
she's in it

KW   She drew from a *clevvy* in the wall, a book with
black shamrocks (open dresser)

F   I had heard a noise before us in the *lag*

T   what right have you to be going on with these
andrewmartins off your own bat (eccentricities)

ULHD These bloody *kips* are neither private nor hotels
(boarding-houses)
the sort of frown he would have turned on a junior
in the bank who had not been *soapy* enough
(obsequious, complaisant)
The usual Irish *miserere*. All based on hellfire and
damnation
With Easter coming on now I suppose we'll have to
get the ould *skillet* cleaned again (metonymic
use of 'frying pan' for 'conscience')
Now, Jacky, there's no earthly use your *beefing*
about religion (complaining)
Nor, mind you . . . that I'm going to hand myself
over to some *bogtrot* from the County Meath
(disparaging name for Irishman)

LL   starve for days and sit up all night *ologroaning* and
ologoaning (a pun with onomatopoeic purpose:
ologoaning seems to be derived from Ir. *olagón*, a
wail or lament)

H   The blind boshtoon! The total botch! The braying
polthacawn (ass)

BW   The *jarvey*, who was waiting for him, bowed as he
received the bags (cabman)

UBS   He had a marvellous trick of flinging his *cappa* over
one shoulder

FC   If you have a *scunner* against fur coats, why not
buy something else? (dislike, used chiefly in Armagh
area)

YG   we'll have a little *gosther* about old times (gossip, from Irish *gastaire*, a chatterer)

LYD   apart from a few grey streaks of hair . . . she was getting 'right *loguey*' too (lethargic, slow moving) the fierce love of a woman for her *by-child*

NCOM   I'm going to do Lough Derg if I get safe out of this bloody *kip-o'-the-reel* (*kip* means 'stake', and *reel* 'whirl' or 'dance')

VM   went out into the mountains to learn Gaelic among the *cottiers* of the west (Irish tenant farmers)

O'Faolain unconsciously developed certain mannerisms of style, notably in the use of emotive verbs to indicate speakers' attitudes, e.g. he *snorted* or *guffawed*. *Slew* (turn) is another verb to which he was curiously addicted. In 'Lovers of the Lake', for instance, he wrote:

She *slewed* her head swiftly away from his angry eyes. . . .
    'It was never routine. It's the one thing I have to hang on to in an otherwise meaningless existence. No children. A husband I'm not in love with. And I can't marry you.'
    She *slewed* back to him. He *slewed* away to look up the long empty road before them. He *slewed* back; he made as if to speak; he *slewed* away impatiently again.
    'No?' she interpreted. 'It isn't any use, is it? It's my problem, not yours.'
                    (*Penguin Book of Irish Short Stories*, p. 147)

The indebtedness of Irish fiction to Turgenev, Chekhov, Tolstoy and Dostoevsky is apparent in the writing of Mary Lavin, who was born in Massachusetts in 1912. While still a child, she returned with her parents to Ireland, where she was educated at a Convent School. She then took a bachelor's degree at University College, Dublin, and presented an MA dissertation on Jane Austen, following this with research on the novels of Virginia Woolf. Of these two authors she made perceptive use in her stories. Her two novels, she said, would have been better, had they been published as collections of short stories. For a while she went back to the United States to teach, and has revisited that country several times. The greater part of her life has, however, been spent on a farm in County Meath, or in Dublin. She has been twice married, the second time to an ex-Jesuit. Two volumes of her collected short stories were published in 1964 and 1974 by Constable. In 1943 she was awarded the James Tait Black Memorial Book Prize for *Tales from Bective Bridge*, which contains ten stories.

Like her Russian prototypes, Miss Lavin is a realist, and a somewhat disillusioned interpreter of the social scene she has observed so well. The stories are distillations of her personal experience, meticulously designed and economically worded. The shorter ones, such as 'A Cup of Tea' are just sketches, without plot; but however brief, they are entirely feminine in outlook, with a discernible antipathy towards the domineering Irish matriarch. The younger women in Lavin's domestic scene often crave for the freedom that their sex enjoys in the United States, and lament that it is denied them in Catholic Ireland. They have by no means overcome an instinct for the celibate life, even in families whose fathers regard this as unnatural, for instance in 'The Nun's Mother'. This is one of Miss Lavin's most compelling monologues; it is an account of the soul-searching of Mrs Latimer, through whose mind the situation is presented:

> Men had such an irrational horror of the cloister. Their views on the religious life were positively medieval. Luke himself until quite recently always spoke of convents as nunneries! Such a word!
>
> He could hardly have been more upset if Angela had got into trouble — yes, yes — even that kind of trouble! If anything like that had happened, Luke would have been shocked, grieved, worried, but deep down he would have been able to understand that such things could happen even to a well-brought-up girl. . . . What his daughter had, in fact, done, however, was something absolutely incomprehensible to him. His nature rebelled against it. He'd found it unnatural, abnormal — abhorrent.
>
> (*The Stories of Mary Lavin* II, p. 44)

Lavin's middle-aged mothers are invariably tiresome and voluble when they justify themselves. In 'The Nun's Mother' there is a note of cynicism, as well as irony in the psychology of Mrs Latimer's equivocations. One observes this in the nuance which words, phrases and sentences are given; they are skilfully matched or varied to take every advantage of the stream-of-consciousness narrative. Indeed, when the story was revised for the edition of 1974, thirty years after it had been written, many changes in the wording took place that critics have not bothered to collate. The changes reveal a persistent vigilance to clarify the subtleties of introspection, and to make the naturalness of Mrs Latimer's ramblings more circumspect. But it seems from the impressive writing of the following passage that the original version is stronger than the diluted one that succeeds it:

> It was so hard for women to be frank with each other. With men it was easy. With each other impossible. Or so she had found. Always. At school even. Women were so covert and sly when they were alone, so prudish, so guarded. All that awful, lumpy, shuffling and protruding of elbows that went on under slips and nightdresses in order to dress or undress. No simplicity, no grace. And that was what it was to be a modest woman, to shuffle and clutch at straps and buttons.
>
> She must singe the edges of the past and its dear delight with a religious remorse. She must seal the memories of her love into a casket of stern taciturnity. She must let her fate fall into its natural folds, and she must act and think like a nun's mother. . . . Yes. That was the way she should feel. She would discipline herself to feel so. She would make her brazen soul seek shame in the joys of its past.
>
> (*The Long Ago*, 1944, pp. 200 and 203)

The truth is that Miss Lavin's gift of lyrical expression is better adapted to some themes than to others. Monologue is again favoured in 'The Inspector's Wife'; but her introduction describes the official's 'dilapidated two-seater' arriving at the farm in the following pretentious images: 'It came around the corner *like a terrier in hysteria,* and out from under it came the dust, *curling in cornucopias.*' Much of Lavin's girlhood was spent on a farm which her father managed on the banks of the River Boyne; hence the technical knowledge she exploits in 'The Haymaking' when she refers to *timothy* and *tremblegrass*, and a litter of *bonhams*. The following passage in this story is of particular language interest:

> My father is the same. He is as nervous as a cat from the time the first *swarth* is brought down to the time the last rope is tied on the top of the last cock, and the last dray loaded and gone rattling into the *haggard*. Men are all the same. If the sun was splitting the cobbles, they'd say that it was only a *pet-day*, and that you'd see torrents of rain before the night.
>
> (*The Long Ago*, p. 91)

Swarth is here a strip in a corn- or grass-field covered by a sweep of the mower's scythe. *Haggard* (O. Norse *hay-garth*) is the stack-yard in which mown hay is deposited. A *pet-day* is one which the gloomy farmer thinks 'too good to last'.

Four longer stories published in *The Becker Wives* (1946) are nearly like novelettes, of which the title story is the most intriguing. Lavin's picture of domestic life among the prosperous middle and commercial classes of Dublin is not flattering. The second generation of Beckers act like educated philistines, all except the youngest son, who is an unimaginably tactless snob. He marries superciliously, but is overshadowed by his psychic wife, a slim young woman with a remarkable talent for impersonating all her acquaintances. This mimicry leads finally to a fixation, of which I can find no parallel in Freud or Jung. She seems to have become subconsciously jealous of her pregnant sister-in-law, and insists on being called by her name, though she herself is physically unable to bear a child. The aphasia of her personality is presumably caused by a perverted empathy with that of the character she enacts.

Uxoriousness in marital relations, and its effect upon the fantasy of young children, as in 'Loving Memory' is a problem that troubles Mary Lavin as much as indifference and intemperance. She is even more concerned with the Irishman's reluctance to marry, and with unsatisfactory relations between the sexes when approaching middle-age, themes which she handles in 'Love is for Lovers' and 'A Memory'. Religious convictions do not create difficulties to the distressful extent that they do in the stories of Sean O'Faolain. But they do lead to unfortunate misunderstandings and suspicions, as in such stories as 'The Convert' and 'Limbo', where a young Protestant child (non-sectarian) is not allowed to participate in Catholic prayers by the monitress of the Catholic school she has to attend.

Miss Lavin's imagination is suitably and spontaneously engaged when she pursues the innocent, but often amoral, spirit of children still at school, as in 'The Bunch of Grape', 'The Living' and 'A Likely Story'. The impersonal realism of the first of this trio does not even require that the persons be given names; the two girls are called simply Red Dress and Blue Dress, and their dialogue is like a medieval morality, in which temptation gradually undermines prohibition. Red Dress has the role of a dare-devil, Blue Dress that of a 'scare-cat', the latter being cajoled by every device of duplicity to part with some of her mother's shopping. 'The Living' is a story in similar vein, but the adventurers are boys, aged seven and eight, whose macabre curiosity about the dead and the wake ritual craves to be satisfied. The brazen initiator of the enterprise is the first to run when he is faced with the grim reality. Again this story was critically overhauled for inclusion in the collected *Stories of Mary Lavin*, second volume. 'A Likely Story' is the most delightfully written in this group, because it neatly emulates the James Stephens blend of mythology and humanism. The touch is lighter than in the *Crock of Gold*; for the other-worldliness implied in the mention of Tuatha de Danaan is never allowed to overshadow the lyrical significance of the Bective environment:

> He [Packy] was a fine stump of a lad. He was as strong as a bush, and his eyes were as bright as the track of a snail. As for his cheeks, they were ruddy as the haws. And his hair had the same gloss as the gloss on the wing of a black-bird.
>
> (*The Stories of Mary Lavin* II, p. 365)

Not content with imitating the folk-tale of James Stephens, Miss Lavin also reproduced the style of Synge's *Riders to the Sea* in 'The Green Grave and the Black Grave'. The text of this story in *Tales from Bective Bridge* (1943) differs, particularly in its Irish names, from the revised version in the second volume of *The Stories of Mary Lavin* (1974). The fisherman drowned at sea in this tragedy was married not to an islander, but to a more sophisticated woman of the mainland; her alienation regarding customs of death and burial are the principal theme of the story:

'It's a great thing that he was not dragged down to the green grave, and that is a thing will lighten the nights of the one-year wife,' said Tadg Mor.

'It isn't many are saved out of the green grave,' said Tadg Og.

Mairtin Mor wasn't got', said Tadg Mor.

'It was a good thing, this man to be got,' said Tadg Og, 'and his eyes bright in his head.'

'Like he was looking up at the sky!'

'Like he was thinking to smile next thing he'd do.'

'He was a great man to smile, this man,' said Tadg Mor. 'He was ever and always smiling.'

'He was a great man to laugh too,' said Tadg Og. 'He was ever and always laughing.'

'Times he was laughing and times he was not laughing.' said Tadg Mor.

'Times all men stop from laughing,' said Tadg Og. . . .

'An island man should take an island wife,' said Tadg Og.

'An inland woman should take an inland man.'

'The inland woman that took this man had a dreadful dread on her of the sea and of the boats that put out in it.'. . .

'Times I saw her wetting her feet in the sea and wetting her fingers in it and you'd see she was a kind of lovering the waves so they'd bring him back to her.' . . . She said, 'There's no sorrow in death when two go down together into the one grave. Clay binds close as love,' she said, 'but the green grave binds nothing.'

(*The Stories of Mary Lavin* II, pp. 3-4)

The dilemma of the alien bride's grief in her deprivation is handled again in 'The Bridal Sheets'.

The language of 'The Green Grave and the Black Grave' is notable for its vivid imagery and poetic rhythm. There is a sinister, yet evocative, presence in phrases such as *the scaly, scurvy sea, his silver-dripping oar, the shivering silver-belly boat*, and *the scabby back of the sea*. In spite of her academic background, Lavin's vocabulary is not a learned one; she distrusted any style that degenerated into 'a great hunk of abstraction' (*Penguin Book of Irish Short Stories*, p. 208), and she belies the view of Myra in 'A Memory' that verbal exactitude is not a quality one usually finds in a woman (ibid., p. 204). Here are a few of the idisoyncracies peculiar to her short and longer stories; the titles are abbreviated as follows: M, A Memory; VFD, A Voice from the Dead; SCLB, Say Could that Lad be I; L, The Living; BW, The Becker Wives; LS, A Likely Story:

M	he'd encouraged her to get it over and done with; not *to put it on the long finger* (procrastinate)
VFD	He hated the sight of that shroud . . . he went *on a batter* every time she took it out to air it (berserk, into a rage) when I picked them all up — as I thought — *unbeknownst* I left Lottie's card behind (the form, with final *-st*, is colloquial and probably dialectal; in fiction it occurs as late as Kipling)
SCLB	Take *would* you think of bringing that blaggard of a dog into the village (conditional clause, using *would* without *if*; probably dialectal) that was the one thing I made sure she couldn't do: let him out and *stray him on me* (stray after me — dialectal) Fast *and all* as I had run I hadn't lost the money (colloquial)
L	Mind *would you* fall (= be careful not to, probably dialectal) He was *a class of* delicate (= sort of, colloquial) Those boyos have *a few jars in them* (been drinking, slang)
BW	Anna had chuckled and nodded her head towards the big *ormolu* sideboard (alloy of copper, zinc and tin, used to decorate furniture)
LS	every branch was *crotched* over with grey lichen (this past participle is now confined to the USA; it

LS
normally means 'forked', as of branches or saplings)

He'd have to *stoup* his finger in hot water (not in use as a verb in English; the substantive meaning is 'bucket' or 'drinking vessel', from O. Norse *staup*)

I was just wondering if it is *a thing* that you are a foreigner (possible)

my finger is beginning to *beal* (suppurate — dialectal, from O. Norse *beyla*, a 'boil' or 'pustule'. Still used in Scotland)

Irish short stories of the twentieth century offer us a valuable view of their society and illustrate the growth of Anglo-Irish speech in the same period. The English employed incorporates modified gaelicisms. Norse borrowings, slang and colloquialisms, the study of which makes a good Anglo-Irish dictionary a necessity; a book on the problems of Irish dialectology is also called for. Archaisms abound in the local customs and humour of Irish comedy, and many quaint modes of expression are peculiar to people struggling with both the languages to be heard in Ireland.

After the intitial enthusiasm for the revival of Gaelic as a spoken language, there followed an unexpected decline in the use of that speech, except in isolated pockets, mainly on the west coast. O'Connor attributed this to a remarkable flowering of English literature during the same period. The decline does not imply that the Gaelic-speaking movement had been ineffectual in preserving Irish culture; it means rather that Irishmen had discovered an equally patriotic ethos in idiomatic modifications of English by their own speakers, especially since the turn of the nineteenth century. Writers and debaters in this medium became vehement in reaction to the nationalist government's notion that Irish literature in English should be restrained and, since 1940, severely censored.

It is clear from the writers discussed in the foregoing chapters, that their Irishness was not peripheral, but genuine, sometimes even obsessive. But the desire for identity through every nuance of expression became less and less dependent

on traditional mythology. Novelists, dramatists and biographers perceived that, since the founding of the Land
League in 1879, when the peasant became a tenant farmer,
a positive amalgam of politics and religion became deeply
ingrained in the national character, and this was regarded as
a topic of perennial interest. The countryman's inferiority
and political impotence was not, indeed, lessened for another
half century, owing largely to the tradition that farming
land should be inherited by the eldest son, which compelled
the rest of the family to emigrate or drift into towns as
domestic servants. Thomas Kinsella called urbanised peasants
'the shamrock lumpenproletariat' (Yeats and Kinsella, *Davis,
Mangan, Ferguson?* p. 64).

By the time of Yeats, the Anglo-Irish included many
Catholics whose status had been enhanced by education,
and Brendan Behan's gibe that an Anglo-Irishman was 'a
Protestant with a horse' became socially irrelevant. Reputable
Irish literature continued to be published in English for
commerical reasons; there was a greater demand for it in
England, Scotland, the United States and the British
Commonwealth. Irish descendants in America were numerous,
but few had taken the trouble to learn Gaelic, or had
occasion to use it there. In Ireland the desirability of retain-
ing Gaelic educationally was obvious, as Flann O'Brien
observed:

> It provides through its literature and dialects a great field
> for the pursuit of problems philological, historical and
> ethnological, an activity agreeable to all men of education
> and good-will. Moreover, the language itself is ingratiating
> by reason of its remoteness from European tongues and
> moulds of thought, its precision, elegance and capacity for
> the subtler literary nuances; it attracts even by its sur-
> passing difficulty, for scarcely anybody living today can
> write or speak Irish correctly and exactly in the fashion of
> 300 years ago. . . .
>
> (*The Best of Myles*, p. 282)

In a paper on 'The Irish Writer' read to the Modern Language Association of America in 1966, Thomas Kinsella
explained that, when contact was lost between authors and

their language tradition, they were compelled to write about personal experience; and they acknowledged that successful authorship was 'a matter of people and places', not merely of technique. O'Connor and O'Faolain have left no doubt that they suffered emotionally from polarisation of political and psychological stances. Misguided nationalism gave rise to divided personalities among those who remained to write in Ireland, and it sometimes led to unwarranted suspicion and harshness of tongue. O'Connor said that a book would be necessary to describe the irrationalities of the Civil War, yet movingly told his tale in the last two chapters of *An Only Child*:

> It was clear to me that we were all going mad, and yet I could see no way out ... I could not detach myself from the political attitudes that gave rise to it. I was too completely identified with them, and to have abandoned them would have meant abandoning faith in myself. ...
>
> In spite of all the sentimental high-mindedness, I felt it went side by side with an extraordinary inhumanity. ...
>
> Living in the presence of God was one thing; living in the presence of Ireland was more than I could tolerate. ... I said bitterly that it was a great pity God hadn't made mothers with the durability of principles. ... I cursed the inhumanity of the two factions with their forms and scruples. ... Mass martyrdom was only another example of the Shelleyan fantasy, though there were plenty on our side to whom it wasn't even a fantasy but a vulgar expedient to break the stalemate caused by De Valera's Ceasefire Order. ... It took me some time to realize what Mother had seen in that first glimpse of me, that I had crossed another shadow line, and make me wonder if I should ever again be completely at ease with the people I loved, their introverted religion and introverted patriotism.

(pp. 240-75)

O'Connor and O'Faolain were deeply influenced by Corkery to support the Republican (Fenian) cause against the Free State and Michael Collins, head of the Provisional Government. De Valera, the leading Republican, enjoyed wide support among Irishmen whom he had lobbied for funds in the United States. He and the other elected Fenians at first refused to sit in Parliament, on the ground of disloyalty to Pearse and the martyrs of 1916, who had sacrificed their lives for the Republican principle. Fenian rebels in Cork were denied the sacraments by their church, and this led to embarrassing situations, as described by O'Faolain in *Bird Alone*, when burial rights were refused in Catholic cemeteries. When the ceasefire was proclaimed, Republican prisoners, among them O'Connor, were kept in custody unless they signed an undertaking to refrain from subversive activity; the result was an ineffective hunger-strike, and renewed disaffection among the recent rebels.

O'Connor and O'Faolain thus became disillusioned critics, not merely of Irish politics, but of the religion which neither wanted to give up. O'Connor wrote 'It may, I hope, be accepted as common ground that no Irishman is of much interest until he has lost his faith' (*The Backward Look*, p. 163). The mediocrity of the de Valera government was denounced, and political martyrdom described as folly. Both writers sought refuge in humanism and dedicated the remainder of their lives to literature; but there were obvious heart-burnings over their compromise with first principles. They understood how Joyce, the champion of the middle classes, and Yeats, who abhorred them, achieved eminence by keeping aloof from internecine politics. O'Connor and O'Faolain admitted freely that they supported the wrong cause; their subsequent relationship is described in O'Faolain's autobiography:

> For years we stimulated one another. . . . Our quarrels were the quarrels of colleagues; our arguments were the arguments of friends; we supported one another in our public controversies; we chose to imagine that the responsibility for the future of Irish literature was on our two backs.
>
> (*Vive Moi!*, p. 285)

The most sinister debacle that resulted from complete independence for Éire has been the problem of Northern Ireland, and the turmoil that continues under the British connection. Yeats, the senator, in 1925 delivered a searching address against the introduction of a bill to make divorce impossible in Ireland. Of relations between north and south, he said:

> It is perhaps the deepest political passion with this nation that North and South be united into one nation. If it ever comes that North and South unite, the North will not give up any liberty which she already possesses under her constitution. You will then have to grant to another people what you refuse to grant to those within your borders. If you show that this country, Southern Ireland, is going to be governed by Catholic ideas and by Catholic ideas alone, you will never get the North. You will create an impassable barrier between South and North, and you will pass more and more Catholic laws, while the North will gradually assimilate its divorce and other laws to those of England.
>
> (*The Senate Speeches of W. B. Yeats* (ed. D. R. Pearce), 1961, p. 92)

Northern Ireland is locked in what appears to be an irreconcilable civil war, which began in 1964 with the Divis Street Riots in Belfast. The issues at stake are *inter alia* civil rights for the Catholic minority, the gerrymandering of constituencies, and political corruption. The illegal IRA purports to protect the Catholic cause against the sectarian constabulary; and the unhappy situation is aggravated by unemployment, which creates poverty among the industrial working class.

No solution is likely to appeal to the underprivileged, as long as Ulster is regarded as an English colony, administered from Westminster. If this were not so, the insurgents argue, conservative majorities would not be returned to Parliament, because Ulster people are preponderantly of the working class. Protestants continue to be favoured in the major industries, such as ship-building, and are invariably Unionists.

The Ulster problem is an instance of Irish obstinacy and religious confusion, and the responsibility for resolving it has been the British government's since 1921, when the unwise separation of Ulster from the rest of Ireland took place. The guarantee then given to the Unionists of Northern Ireland, renewed in 1949, was a political indiscretion, which surrendered to passions that should have been resisted. There now appear to be only two options; to retain Northern Ireland as part of the United Kingdom and continue the perennial sources of friction; or to grant the province republican independence, as part of the political entity to which it originally belonged. Both courses would be difficult, but the latter is the only one likely to succeed. If an equitable solution has to be *imposed*, it should be by a force that is not English. The Irish insurgents, like other terrorists, are being sustained by financial assistance from the western world, thereby prolonging an impasse that calls for United Nations intervention. The case of Northern Ireland is as important to world peace as that of Israel.

There is a good reason why the 1973 referendum in Northern Ireland was heavily in favour of the British connection. The Catholic losers, it is said, were not freely permitted to put their case. It is argued by some competent Irishmen that the Ulster Catholics do not want to be taken over by the Republic of Ireland, because they would lose the benefits of the English Welfare State. From Éire's point of view, the incorporation of belligerent Ulster people might produce economic and other rivalries; for Unionists' business methods are known to be more competitive than those of the rest of Ireland. But these are partisan issues, and should not stand in the way of national progress, at a time when economic pressures are multiplying. Northern Ireland carries the heavy past on its back; and this will continue as long as the burden is one of fear, not of patience and forbearance.

George Orwell maintained that a disquieting feature of nationalism is its tendency to label people 'good' or 'bad' *en masse*. 'All nationalists,' he said, 'have the power of not seeing resemblances between similar sets of facts' (*England my England*, 1953, pp. 41-67). Orwell accepted the doubtful dichotomy that patriotism is *defensive*, nationalism *aggressive*; and he therefore supposed that English neo-Toryism was preferable to Celtic 'anglophobia.' A more sympathetic attitude, and one consonant with Irish mythology, was voiced in Lady Augusta Gregory's 'Sorrowful Lament for Ireland':

> I do not know anything under the sky
> That is friendly or favourable to the Gael,
> But only the sea that our need brings us to, . . .
> The ship that is bearing us away from Ireland.

It would be mistaken, however, to end on a fateful note. Despite many set-backs, Irish creative writing since the latest revival has been impressive. Its future may depend on the viability of agriculture in the Gaeltacht area, which is not large. Educationally, Irish has advanced since the Gaelic script was abandoned for the Roman in the nineteen-fifties; this concession to modern technology is surely significant. Conor Cruise O'Brien, a Republican Minister, has reminded his country that insistence on Irish as 'the first official language' is likely to minimise the chances of a worthy national culture. Irish speakers in the Republic, as well as Northern Ireland, are predominantly Catholics; but so much that is fruitful in Irish life and literature was made possible by the Protestant intervention in their history that it should not be jeopardised by extremists on either side — the Sinn Féin movement on the one hand, and the Orange Order on the other.

Bibliography

Where an older and a modern edition of a book are both given, page references in the text are to the modern one.

CHAPTER I
(pages 1-21)
Chauviri, R., *A Short History of Ireland*, New York, Davin-Adair, 1956
Curtis, E., *A History of Medieval Ireland*, Methuen, 1938
——, *A History of Ireland*, Methuen, 1936; reprint 1961
Deanesly, M., *A History of Early Medieval Europe 476-911*, Methuen, 1969
Greene, D., *The Irish Language*, Cork, Mercier Press, 1972
Jackson, K. H., *Language and History in Early Britain*, Edinburgh U.P., 1953
——, *The Oldest Irish Tradition, A Window on the Iron Age*, Cambridge U.P., 1964
Kee, R., *A History of Ireland*, Weidenfeld and Nicolson, 1980
O'Rahilly, T. F., *Early Irish History and Mythology*, Dublin, 1946
Powell, T. G. E., *The Early Cultures of North-Western Europe*, Cambridge U.P., 1950
——, *The Celts*, Thames and Hudson, 1958
Rafferty, J., *The Celts*, Cork, Mercier Press, 1964
Sweeney, J. J., *Irish Illuminated Manuscripts*, Collins and Unesco, 1965
Thomas, C., *Britain and Ireland in Early Christian Times*, Thames and Hudson, 1971

CHAPTER II
(pages 22-53)
Arnold, M., *On the Study of Celtic Literature*, Dent, 1910
Carney, J. (ed.), *Studies in Irish Literature and History*, Dublin, 1955
——, *Early Irish Poetry*, Cork, Mercier Press, 1965; reprint 1969
Dillon, M., *The Cycles of the Kings*, Oxford U.P., 1946
——, *Early Irish Literature*, Chicago, University Press, 1948
——, *Irish Sagas*, Cork, Mercier Press, 1968
Faber Book of Irish Verse, The, see under Montague

Flower, R., *The Irish Tradition*, Oxford, Clarendon, 1970

Green, A. S., *History of the Irish State to 1014*, Macmillan, 1925

Gregory, Augusta (trans.), *Cuchulain of Muirthemne*, Murray, 1902; fifth edition, Colin Smythe, Gerards Cross, 1970

Hughes, K., *The Church in Early Irish Society*, London, 1966

Hull, E., *A Textbook of Irish Literature*, 2 vols., Dublin, M. H. Hill, 1906

Hyde, D., *A Literary History of Ireland*, Fisher Unwin, 1899

Jackson, K. H., *A Celtic Miscellany*, Routledge and Kegan Paul, 1951

Kinsella, T. (trans.), *The Tain*, Oxford U.P. and Dolmen Press, Dublin, 1970

Knott, E., *Irish Classical Poetry*, Dublin, 1957

——, *Irish Syllabic Poetry*, Cook, 1928

MacCullogh, J. A., *The Celtic and Scandinavian Religions*, Hutchinson, 1948

MacDonagh, D. and Robinson, L. (eds.), *The Oxford Book of Irish Verse*, Oxford U.P., 1958

Mercier, V., *The Irish Comic Tradition*, Oxford, Clarendon, 1962

Meyer, K. (ed.), *Imram Brain, The Voyage of Bran*, 2 vols., David Nutt, 1897. Volume II contains *The Celtic Doctrine of Re-birth* by A. Nutt

Meyer, K., *Selection from Ancient Irish Poetry*, Constable, 1911; reprint 1928

Montague, J., *The Faber Book of Irish Verse*, Faber, 1974

Murphy, G., *Saga and Myth in Ancient Ireland*, Dublin, 1955

——, *The Ossianic Lore and Romantic Tales of Medieval Ireland*, Dublin, 1961

O'Grady, S. J., *History of Ireland*, 2 vols., Sampson Low, Searle, Marston and Rivington, 1878; reprint, Lemma, New York, 1970

Oskamp, H. P. A., *The Voyage of Mael Duin*, Groningen, Wolters-Noordhoff, 1970

Oxford Book of Irish Verse, The, see under MacDonagh and Robinson

Sharp, W., *Lyra Celtica*, Edinburgh, Grant, 1924

Tolkien, J. R. R., *Tree and Leaf* etc., Unwin, 1975

CHAPTER III
(pages 54-86)

Beckett, J. C., *A Short History of Ireland*, Hutchinson, 1952; fifth edition, 1973

Canny, N. P., *The Formation of the Old English Elite in Ireland*, Dublin, National Univ., 1975

——, *The Elizabethan Conquest of Ireland*, Harvester Press, 1976

Edwards, R. D., *An Atlas of Irish History*, Methuen, 1973

——, *Ireland in the Age of the Tudors*, London, Croom Helm, 1977

Hawthorne, J. (ed.), *Two Centuries of Irish History*, BBC, 1966

Johnston, E. M., *Ireland in the Eighteenth Century*, Dublin, Gill and Macmillan, 1974

Nicholls, K., *Gaelic and Gaelicised Ireland in the Middle Ages*, Dublin, Gill and Macmillan, 1972

O'Connor, F. (ed.), *A Book of Ireland*, Collins, 1964

Spenser, E., *A View of the Present State of Ireland* (ed. J. Ware), Dublin, 1633; Clarendon, 1970

Swift, J., *The Prose Works* (ed. Temple Scott), 12 vols., Bell, 1897-1908

——, *The Drapiers' Letters to the People of Ireland* (ed. H. Davis), Oxford U.P., 1935

——, *Selected Prose* (ed. J. Hayward), Crescent Press, 1949

CHAPTER IV
(pages 87-119)

Brooke, Charlotte, *Reliques of Irish Poetry* (1789) and *A Memoir of Miss Brooke* (1816) by A. C. H. Seymour (facsimile) ed. L. R. N. Ashley, Gainesville, Florida, 1970

Campion, E., *A Historie of Ireland* (1571). Intro. R. B. Gottfried, New York, Scholars, Facsimiles and Reprints, 1940

Collier, J. P. (ed.), *The Poems of Jonathan Swift*, 3 vols., Bell, 1833

Ehrenpreis, I., *Swift: The Man, His Works and the Age*, Methuen, 1961

Goldsmith, O., *Poems*, (ed. A. Dobson), Oxford U.P., 1907; reprinted 1912, 1928

——, *The Bee and Other Essays*, Oxford U.P., 1914

Greene, D. H., *An Anthology of Irish Literature*, 2 vols., New York U.P., 1954; reprinted 1971, 1974

Kennelly, B., *The Penguin Book of Irish Verse*, Penguin Books, 1970; reprinted 1971

Kenney, J. F., *The Sources for the Early History of Ireland*, New York, 1929

Lynam, E. W., 'The Irish Character in Print', *The Library*, Fourth Series, Vol. IV, 1924

MacDonagh, T., *Literature in Ireland and Studies in Irish and Anglo-Irish*, Fisher Unwin, 1916

Murphy, G. (ed.), *Early Irish Lyrics*, with translation, Oxford, Clarendon, 1956

Penguin Book of Irish Verse, The, see under Kennelly

Quintana, R., *The Mind and Art of Jonathan Swift*, Oxford U.P., 1936; reprint, Methuen, 1953

——, *Swift, an Introduction*, Oxford U.P., 1955

Renwick, W. L. (ed.), *Edmund Spenser, A View of the Present State of Ireland*, Oxford, Clarendon, 1970

Swift, J., *The Poems* (ed. H. Williams), Oxford U.P., 1967

CHAPTER V
(pages 120-156)

Boyd, E., *Ireland's Literary Renaissance*, New York, Barnes & Noble, 1916

Brown, M., *The Politics of Irish Literature*, Allen and Unwin, 1972

Churchill, W. S., *The World Crisis: The Aftermath*, Odhams Press, 1929
Corkery, D., *The Hidden Ireland*, Dublin, Gill, 1929
Duffy, C. G. (ed.), *The Ballad Poetry of Ireland*, facsimile of 40th edition (1869), intro. L. R. N. Ashley, Scholars' Facsimiles and Reprints, Delmar, New York, 1973
Fitzgibbon, C., *Red Hand: The Ulster Colony*, Michael Joseph, 1971
Moore, G., *Parnell and his Island*, 1887, London, Ebury edition, 20 vols., 1937
O'Faolain, S., *The Irish*, Penguin, 1947
Orwell, G., *Collected Essays, Journalism and Letters* (ed. S. Orwell and I. Angus), Vol. III, Secker and Warburg, 1968
O'Sullivan, M., *Twenty Years A-Growing*, Chatto and Windus, 1933
Rundle, S., *Language as a Social and Political Factor in Europe*, Faber, 1946
Sayers, Peig, *Autobiography* (trans. Bryan MacMahon), Dublin, Talbot Press, 1974
Shaw, G. B., *The Matter with Ireland* (ed. D. H. Greeve and D. H. Laurence), Hart-Davis, 1962
Sheehy, M. (ed.), *Michael/Frank: Studies on Frank O'Connor*, Dublin, Gill and Macmillan, 1969
Synge, J. M., *Four Plays and the Aran Islands* (ed. R. Skelton), Oxford U.P., 1962
Taylor, G. (ed.), *Irish Poets of the Nineteenth Century*, Routledge and Kegan Paul, 1951
Yeats, W. B., *The Celtic Twilight*, Macmillan, 1893; enlarged 1902
Yeats, W. B., and Kinsella, T., *Davis, Mangan, Ferguson? — Tradition and the Irish*, Dublin, Dolmen Press, 1970

CHAPTER VI
(pages 156-193)
Boyd, E., *Ireland's Literary Renaissance*, New York, A. A. Knopf, 1916; revised 1922, Barnes and Noble, 1968
Brown, M., *The Politics of Irish Literature: From Thomas Davis to W. B. Yeats*, Allen and Unwin, 1972
Carpenter, A. (ed.), *Place, Personality and the Irish Writer*, Gerards Cross, C. Smythe, 1977
Clarke, A., *Selected Poems* (ed. T. Kinsella), Dublin, Dolmen Press, and Wake Forest U.P., North Carolina 1976
Corkery, D., *Synge and Anglo-Irish Literature*, Cork, Mercier Press, 1966; original edition 1931
——, *The Fortunes of the Irish Language*, Dublin, Fallon, 1954
Davis, T., *Literary and Historical Essays* (ed. C. G. Duffy), Dublin, Duffy, 1845; edition 1883
Eddins, D., *Yeats, The Nineteenth Century Matrix*, Alabama U.P., 1971
Eglington, J., *Irish Literary Portraits*, Macmillan, 1935
Eliot, T. S., *After Strange Gods*, Faber and Faber, 1934
Fallis, R., *The Irish Renaissance*, Syracuse U.P., 1977

Gregory, Augusta, *Ideals in Ireland*, Unicorn Press, 1901
Halpern, S., *Austin Clarke, his Life and Works*, Dublin, Dolmen Press, 1974
Henn, T. R., *Last Essays*, New York, Barnes and Noble, 1976
Kain, R. M., *Dublin in the Age of William Butler Yeats and James Joyce*, Oklahoma U.P., 1962; Newton Abbot, David and Charles, 1972
Kelly, A. A., *Liam O'Flaherty the Storyteller*, Macmillan, 1976
Moore, T., *Irish Melodies*, Longman, Green and Roberts, 1865
——, *Poetical Works*, Oxford U.P., 1929
O'Brien, C. C., *States of Ireland*, Hutchinson, 1972
Rodgers, W. R., *Irish Literary Portraits*, BBC, 1972
Stephens, J., *Collected Poems*, Macmillan, 1926; reprint 1931
——, *A Selection* (ed. L. Frankenberg), Macmillan, 1962
——, *Letters* (ed. R. J. Finneran), Macmillan, 1974
Ure, P., *Yeats and Anglo-Irish Literature* (ed. C. J. Rawson), Liverpool U.P., 1974
Watson, G. J., *Irish Identity and the Literary Revival*, Croom Helm, 1979
Yeats, W. B., *Collected Poems*, Macmillan, 1952
——, *Autobiographies*, Macmillan, 1956
——, *Essays and Introductions*, Macmillan, 1961
——, *Poems* (ed. A. N. Jeffares), Macmillan, 1962
——, *A Critical Anthology* (ed. W. H. Pritchard), Penguin, 1972

CHAPTER VII
(pages 194-235)
Adams, H., *Lady Gregory*, Lewisburg, Bucknell U.P., 1973
Ayling, R., *Sean O'Casey: Modern Judgements*, Macmillan, 1969
Coxhead, E., *Lady Gregory*, Macmillan, 1961
Ellis-Fermor, U., *The Irish Dramatic Movement*, Methuen, 1939; 2nd edition, 1954
Fay, G., *The Abbey Theatre*, New York, Macmillan, 1958
Fay, W. G. and Carswell, C., *The Fays of the Abbey Theatre*, Richard and Cowan, 1935
Fraser, G. S., *The Modern Writer and his World*, Penguin, 1953; rev. 1964
Greene, D. H. and Stephens, E. M., *J. M. Synge 1871-1909*, Macmillan, 1959; New York, Collier, 1961
Gregory, Lady I. Augusta, *Journals* 1916-30 (ed. L. Robinson), Putnam, 1946
——, *Seven Short Plays*, Putnam, 1909
——, *Our Irish Theatre*, Putnam, 1913
——, *Seventy Years, 1852-1922*, Gerards Cross, C. Smythe, 1974
——, *Collected Plays*, 4 vols. (ed. A. Saddlemyer, Coole Ed.), Gerards Cross, C. Smythe, 1970
Hogan, R., *The Experiments of Sean O'Casey*, New York, St Martin's Press, 1960

Joyce, P. W., *English as We Speak it in Ireland*, Dublin, Gill, 1910; reissued Dublin, Wolfhound, 1979; (page references are to the earlier edition)

Kilroy, T. (ed.), *Sean O'Casey: A Collection of Critical Essays*, New Jersey, Prentice Hall, 1975

Knight, G. Wilson, *The Christian Renaissance*, Methuen, 1933; rev. 1962

——, *The Golden Labyrinth*, Phoenix House, 1962

Krause, D., *Sean O'Casey, The Man and His Work*, MacGibbon and Kee, 1960

Malone, A. E., *The Irish Drama*, Constable, 1929

Mickhail, E. H., *Lady Gregory, Interviews and Recollections*, Macmillan, 1977

O'Casey, S., *Autobiographies*, 2 vols., Macmillan, 1963

——, *Blasts and Benedictions* (ed. R. Ayling), Macmillan, 1967

——, *Collected Plays*, 4 vols., Macmillan, 1949-58

——, *The Flying Wasp*, Macmillan, 1937

Ó Cuív, Brian, *A View of the Irish Language*, Dublin Stationery Office, 1969

Robinson, Lennox, *The Irish Theatre*, Macmillan, 1939

——, *Curtain Up*, Joseph, 1942

Rollins, R. G., *Sean O'Casey's Drama*, Alabama U.P., 1979

Ryan, W. P., *The Pope's Green Island*, Nisbet, 1912

Skelton, R., *The Writings of J. M. Synge*, Thames and Hudson, 1971

Styan, J. L., *The Development of Modern Comic Tragedy*, Cambridge U.P., 1962

Synge, J. M., *Four Plays and the Aran Islands* (ed. R. Skelton), Oxford U.P., 1962

——, *Plays and Poems* (ed. T. R. Henn), Methuen, 1963

——, *Collected Works*, 4 vols. (ed. R. Skelton), Oxford U.P., 1961-8

Usher, A., *Three Great Irishmen*, Gollancz, 1952

Williams, R., *Drama from Ibsen to Eliot*, Chatto and Windus, 1952; rev. 1964

Yeats, W. B., *Responsibilities*, Dublin, Cuala Press, 1914

——, *Plays and Controversies*, Macmillan, 1923

——, *Dramatis Personae*, Dublin, Cuala Press, 1935

——, *Collected Plays*, Macmillan, 1952

——, *Letters* (ed. A. Wade), Macmillan 1954

CHAPTER VIII
(pages 236-283)

Allen, W., *The English Novel*, Phoenix House, 1954; Penguin, 1958

Banim, J. and M., *Tales by the O'Hara Family*, 3 series, London, 1825-27

Butler, M., *Maria Edgeworth: A Literary Biography*, Oxford U.P., 1972

Carleton, W., *The Black Prophet*, 1847; (ed. T. Webb), Irish U.P., 1973

Carleton, W., *Traits and Stories of the Irish Peasantry* (2 Series), Dublin, 1830-33
——, *Traits and Stories of the Irish Peasantry*, 10 vols., Ward, Lock and Co., N.D.
——, *Autobiography*, Fitzroy ed., 1968
Cave, R., *A Study of the Novels of George Moore*, Gerard's Cross, C. Smythe, 1978
Cronin, J., *Gerald Griffin 1803-1840*, Cambridge U.P., 1978
——, *The Anglo-Irish Novel*, Vol. I, The Nineteenth Century, Belfast, Appletree Press, 1980
Edgeworth, M., *Castle Rackrent* (ed. G. Watson), Oxford U.P., 1964
——, *Castle Rackrent and The Absentee* (intro. B. Matthews), Dent, 1910
Flanagan, T., *The Irish Novelists, 1800-1850*, New York, Columbia U.P., 1959
Freeman, J., *A Portrait of George Moore in a Study of his Work*, T. W. Laurie, 1922
Griffin, G., *Holland-Tide*, London, 1826; reprinted 1842
——, *Tales of the Munster Festivals*, 3 vols., London, 1827
——, *The Collegians*, 3 vols., Simpkin and Marshall, 1829; Dublin, 1847
——, *The Rivals* and *Tracy's Ambition*, 3 vols., London, 1830
Hone, J., *The Life of George Moore*, Gollancz, 1936
Hughes, D. (ed.), *The Man of Wax*, New York U.P., 1971
Lever, C., *Harry Lorrequer*, Routledge, 1872
Lover, S., *Handy Andy*, Dent, 1907; reprint 1954
Moore, G. A., *Muslin*, Heinemann, 1936
——, *The Untilled Field*, New York, Freeport; reprint, 1970
——, *Hail and Farewell* (ed. R. Cave), Gerard's Cross, Colin Smythe, 1976
——, *The Lake*, Heinemann, 1932
O'Faolain, S., *The Short Story*, Collins, 1948
Powell, V., *The Irish Cousins*, Heinemann, 1970
Pritchett, V. S., *The Living Novel*, Chatto and Windus, 1946
Raleigh, W., *The English Novel*, Murray, 1919
Somerville, E. and Ross, M., *An Irish Cousin*, Bentley, 1889; reprint Nelson, N.D.
——, *Irish Memories*, Longmans, Green, 1917
——, *The Real Charlotte*, Ward and Downey, 1894; reprint Zodiac Press, 1972
——, *Some Experiences of an Irish R.M.*, Longmans, Green, 1899; reprint 1906
——, *The Irish R. M. Complete*, Faber and Faber, 1937
——, *The Big House of Inver*, Heinemann, 1925; reprint Zodiac Press, 1973
——, *French Leave*, Heinemann, 1928; reprint Tom Stacey, 1973
Stephens, J., *The Crock of Gold*, Macmillan, 1912; reprint 1934
——, *A Selection* (ed. L. Frankenberg), Macmillan, 1962

Stephens, J., *Letters* (ed. R. J. Finneran), Macmillan, 1974
Wolfe, Humbert, *George Moore*, Butterworth, 1931; rev. 1933

CHAPTER IX
(pages 284-327)
Alvarez, A., *Beckett*, Woburn Press, 1974
Beck, Warren, *Joyce's Dubliners*, Durham N.C., Duke U.P., 1969
Beckett, S., *Waiting for Godot*, Faber and Faber, 1956
——, *Endgame*, Faber and Faber, 1958
——, *Murphy*, John Calder, 1973
——, *Molloy, Malone Dies, The Unnamable*, John Calder, 1959
Beja, M., *James Joyce, Dubliners and A Portrait of the Artist as a Young Man*, Macmillan, 1973
Budgen, F., *James Joyce and the Making of 'Ulysses' and other Writings*, Oxford U.P., 1972
Burgess, A., *Joysprick*, Deutsch, 1973
Chace, W. M. (ed.), *Joyce, a Collection of Critical Essays*, Englewood Cliffs N.J., Prentice-Hall, 1974
Coe, R. N., *Beckett*, Edinburgh, Oliver and Boyd, 1964
Cohn, R., *Samuel Beckett: The Comic Gamut*, New Brunswick, N.J., Rutgers U.P., 1964
Connolly, T. E. (ed.), *Scribbledehobble: The Ur-Workbook for Finnegans Wake*, Northwestern University, 1961
——, *Joyce's Portrait, Criticisms and Critiques*, New York, Appleton Century-Crofts, 1962
Eliot, T. S., *Introducing James Joyce, a Selection*, Faber and Faber, 1943
Ellman, R., *James Joyce*, Oxford U.P., 1966
Esslin, M. (ed.), *Samuel Beckett*, Englewood Cliffs, N.J., Prentice Hall, 1965
——, *Theatre of the Absurd*, Eyre and Spottiswoode, 1962
Fletcher, J., *The Novels of Samuel Beckett*, Chatto and Windus, 1964
Friedman, M. J. (ed.), *Samuel Beckett Now*, Chicago U.P., 1970
Gilbert, Stuart, *James Joyce's Ulysses, a Study*, Faber and Faber, 1930
—— (ed.), *Letters of James Joyce*, Faber and Faber, 1957
Goldberg, S. L., *The Classical Temper: A Study of James Joyce's 'Ulysses'*, Chatto and Windus, 1963
Goldman, A., *The Joyce Paradox*, Routledge and Kegan Paul, 1966
Hayman, R., *Samuel Beckett*, Heinemann, 1968
Hodgart, M., *James Joyce, a Students' Guide*, Routledge and Kegan Paul, 1978
Joyce, James, *A Portrait of the Artist as a Young Man*, Cape, 1916; reprint 1956
——, *Stephen Hero* (ed. Theodore Spencer), Cape, 1944
——, *Dubliners*, Penguin, 1956; *Text, Criticism and Notes* (ed. Scholes, R. and Litz, A. W.), New York, Viking Press, 1969
——, *Ulysses*, Paris, Shakespeare and Co., 1922; Lane, Bodley Head, 1960

Joyce, James, *Finnegans Wake*, Faber and Faber, 1939; reprint 1975
——, *Critical Writings* (ed. Mason, E. and Ellman, R.), Faber and Faber, 1959
——, *Letters*, see under Gilbert (ed.)
Joyce, S., *My Brother's Keeper*, Faber and Faber, 1958
——, *Complete Dublin Diary* (ed. Healey, G.H.), Ithaca, Cornell U.P., 1962
Kenner, H., *A Reader's Guide to Samuel Beckett*, Thames and Hudson, 1973
Lirz, A. W., *The Art of James Joyce*, Oxford U.P., 1961
MacCabe, C., *James Joyce and the Revolution of the Word*, Macmillan, 1978
Magalaner, M. and Kain, R.M., *Joyce: The Man, the Work, the Reputation*, Calder, 1957
Manganiello, D., *Joyce's Politics*, Routledge and Kegan Paul, 1980
Mercier, V., *Beckett*, New York, Oxford U.P., 1977
Morris, W. E. and Nault, C. A. (eds.), *Portraits of an Artist, a Casebook on James Joyce's A Portrait of the Artist as a Young Man*, New York, Odyssey Press, 1962
O'Brien, Flann (O'Nolan, Brian), *At Swim-Two-Birds*, Frome, Somerset, MacGibbon and Kee, 1939; third impression 1966
——, *The Hard Life*, MacGibbon and Kee, 1961
——, *The Dalkey Archive*, MacGibbon and Kee, 1964; reprint 1968
——, *The Poor Mouth (An Béal Bocht)*, Hart-Davis, MacGibbon, 1973
——, (Myles na Gopaleen), *The Best of Myles*, MacGibbon and Kee, 1968
Scholes, T. and Kain, R.M. (eds.), *The Workshop of Daedalus: James Joyce and the Raw Materials for A Portrait of the Artist as a Young Man*, North-western University, 1965
Senn, F. (ed.), *New Light on Joyce from the Dublin Symposium*, Indiana U.P., 1972
Smidt, K., *James Joyce and the Cultic Use of Fiction*, Oslo U.P., 1959
Smith, P. J., *A Key to the Ulysses of James Joyce*, New York, Covici-Friede, 1927
Tindall, W. Y., *A Reader's Guide to James Joyce*, Thames and Hudson, 1959

CHAPTER X
(pages 328-359)
Bowen, Z., *Mary Lavin*, Lewisburg, Pa., Bucknell, 1975
Cowley, M. (ed.), *Paris Review*, Writers at Work, Series I, Viking Press, 1959
Fallon, P. and Golden, S., *Soft Day*, Dublin, Wolfhound Press, 1980
Gibbon, Monk (ed.), *The Living Torch*, Macmillan, 1937
Kiely, B. (ed.), *Irish Short Stories*, Penguin, 1981
Lavin, M., *Tales from Bective Bridge*, Joseph, 1943
——, *The Long Ago*, Joseph, 1944

Lavin, M., *The Becker Wives*, Joseph, 1946
——, *Stories*, Constable, Vol. I, 1964, Vol. II, 1974
O'Connor, F. (Michael O'Donovan), *Guests of the Nation*, Macmillan, 1931
——, *Towards an Appreciation of Literature*, Dublin, Metropolitan Publishing, 1945
——, *Stories of*, Hamish Hamilton, 1953
——, *Collection Two* and *Collection Three*, Macmillan, 1964, 1969
——, *Modern Irish Short Stories*, Oxford U.P., 1957
——, *An Only Child*, Macmillan, 1959
——, *The Mirror in the Roadway*, Hamish Hamilton, 1957
——, *Kings, Lords and Commons*, Macmillan, 1961
——, *The Lonely Voice*, Macmillan, 1963
——, *The Backward Look*, Macmillan, 1967
——, *A Short History of Irish Literature*, New York, Capricorn, 1968
O'Faolain, S., *Bird Alone*, New York, Viking, 1936
——, *The Short Story*, Collins, 1948
——, *The Finest Stories*, New York, Bantam Books, 1957
——, *I Remember, I Remember*, Hart-Davis, 1959
——, *Vive Moi!*, Hart-Davis, 1965
——, *The Heat of the Sun*, Hart-Davis, 1966
——, *The Talking Trees*, Cape, 1971
——, *Collected Short Stories*, Vols. I and II, Constable, 1980, 1981
O'Flaherty, L., *Spring Sowing*, Cape, 1924
——, *The Informer*, Cape, 1925
——, *The Tent*, Cape, 1926
——, *Short Stories*, Cape, 1937
——, *Famine*, Gollancz, 1937
Penguin Book of Irish Short Stories, The, see under Kiely
Sheehy, M. (ed.), *Studies on Frank O'Connor*, Dublin, Gill and Macmillan, 1969
Wohlgelernter, M., *Frank O'Connor*, New York, Columbia U.P., 1977
Yeats, W. B., *The Senate Speeches* (ed. D. R. Pearce), Bloomington, Indiana U.P., 1961
Yeats, W. B. and Kinsella, T., *Davis, Mangan, Ferguson? Tradition and the Irish Writer* (ed. R. McHugh), Dolmen (Ireland), 1970

Index

Abbey Theatre, 157, 187, 199-201, 203-5, 207, 211, 213, 222, 225, 227, 230, 276, 317

Adamnán, Abbot of Iona, *Vita Columbae*, 12, 13, 29

Adventurers Act, 73

AE, see Russell, George William

Aedh (the sun-god), 38

Allingham, William, 171; *Diary* 172; *Laurence Bloomfield* 172

Amergin (Milesian poet), 46

Anglo-Irish war (1920-21), 129

Annals of the Four Masters, 32, 39, 43, 92, 106-7, 134

Ard Ri (High King), 17, 18, 56

Armagh, Book of, 19

Arnold, Matthew, *The Study of Celtic Literature*, 52, 180

Arthurian Cycle, 26, 31; 'Tristan and Iseult', 41

Asquith, Herbert Henry, Earl of Oxford, 127

Athenry, Battle of, 60

Ayling, R., ed. O'Casey's *Blasts and Benedictions*, 227

Badminton Magazine, 271

Bagenal, Sir Henry, 69, 70

Bagenal, Sir Nicholas, 67

Ballymote, The Book of, 23, 48

Banim, John, 245, 247, 254; *Boyne Water*, 244; *Damon and Pythias*, 244; *The Nowlans*, 244; *Tales by the O'Hara Family*, 244

Banim, Michael, *Tales of the O'Hara Family* (1st and 3rd Series), 244

Beach, Sylvia, 291, 295, 319

Beckett, Samuel, xii, 305-14; *All that Fall*, 306; *Echo's Bones and other Precipitates*, 306; *Malone Dies*, 309, 311-13; *Molloy*, 309-312; *More Pricks than Kicks*, 306; *Murphy*, 307-9; *Proust*, 305; *The Unnamable*, 309, 312-13; *Waiting for Godot*, 282, 306-7, 310, 313; *Watt*, 306

Bede, Venerable, *The Ecclesiastical History of the English Nation*, 4, 8, 45

Bedell, Bishop William, 89

Behan, Brendan, 184

Beltine, 2, 3

Benedictines, 28, 59

Benson, Frank, 198

Bentley's Miscellany, 254

Berkeley, Bishop George, 79

betaghs ('food providers' or serfs), 58, 65

Binchy, D. A., 'Patrick and His Biographers', 9

Black and Tans (military police), 129, 229

Blackwood's Magazine, 138

Bolgic P-Celts, 5

Borlase, Sir John, 73

Boucicault, Dion, 194-5, 225-6; *Arrah-na-Pogue*, 195; *Colleen Bawn*, 195, 246; *London Assurance*, 195; *The Shaughraun*, 195

Boucicault, Dion, the younger, 195

Boulter, Hugh (Archbishop of Armagh), 79

Boycott, Capt. Charles Cunningham, 125

Boyle, Richard, Earl of Cork, 72

Boyle, Robert, 89

Boyle, William, 201

Boyne, Battle of the, 76, 118, 126, 209

Bran, see Brendan

241-2; *Castle Rackrent*, 121, 236-40, 266, 273
Edgeworth, Richard Lovell, *Memoirs*, 238; *Practical Education*, 238
Eglington, John, 182
Eliot, T. S., 191, 222, 290, 300; *After Strange Gods*, 178; *Four Quartets*, 301; *Murder in the Cathedral*, 204
Emain Macha (royal palace), 33-4
Emmet, Robert, 111, 122, 163
Encumbered Estates Act (1849), 123
Eóganachta, 6
Erainn invaders (Firbolg), 5
Erasmus Smith Schools, 251
Erse (Scots Gaelic), ix, 19
Essex, Robert Devereux, earl of (Lord Deputy), 70
'Exile of the Sons of Uisliu, The', 7, 34

Famine, the Great, x, 120, 123, 193, 243, 251, 253, 257, 265
Farr, Florence, 196
Fay, Frank 198
Fay, Gerard, *The Abbey Theatre*, 201
Fay, W. G., 195, 198; *The Fays of the Abbey Theatre*, 201
Fenian (or Ossianic) Cycle, 8, 26, 38-40; 'The Colloquy of Ancient men', 40; 'The Pursuit of Diarmaid and Grainne', 40
Fenian militia, 101
Fenian movement (1858), 124-5, 193
Fergus Mor, 11, 31, 107
Ferguson, Samuel, 51, 136-40; 'The Burial of King Cormac', 138; 'Conary', 139; *Congal*, 139-40; 'Deirdre's Lament for the Sons of Uisnach', 50, 130; 'Lament for the Death of Thomas Davis', 140; *Lays of the Western Gael*, 140
Fermoy, The Book of, 23
Fiana (warrior-band), 8, 38, 40
Fianna Fáil, 129-30
file (bard), 8, 17, 46
filid (seers), 3, 10, 27-8, 48
Fine Gael, 129
Finlay, Father Tom, 263
Finn mac Cumaill, 8, 38-41, 43
Firbolg, 4, 5
Fitzgerald, Barry (actor), 232
FitzGerald, Edward, 111, 122

FitzGerald family, 55, 57, 61, 63
FitzGerald, Maurice, 55, 57
FitsGerald, Nesta, 55, 58; 'race of Nesta', 57
FitzGerald, Garret More (Gerald the Great, Lord Lieutenant), 63-4, 67
FitzGerald, Garret Oge (Gerald the Younger), 66
FitzGerald, Thomas, baron Offaly, earl of Kildare, 63-4, 67
FitzGerald, Thomas, Lord of Offaly ('Silken Thomas'), 65
FitzGilbert family, 55, 57
FitzHenry, Meiler, Justiciar, 59
FitzMaurice, Patrick, lord Kerry, 69
FitzStephen, Robert, 55, 58
Fleetwood, Charles, 75
Flood, Henry, 79
Folk-drama, 196
Fomorians, 24
Fomoiri (giants), 7
Frankenberg, Lloyd, *James Stephens: A Selection*, 187, 276, 278-9, 283
Frayne, Pat, 249
Froissart, Jean, *Chronicles*, 62

Gaelic League (1893), 90, 127, 133, 175, 193, 195-6, 224, 261, 263
Gaelic literature, 132, 145
Gaeltacht, 193, 196, 321, 359
Gaeity Theatre, Dublin, 194, 198
Galioin, 4, 5
Gall-Gaels (foreign Irish), 15, 55
Gallo-Celts, 25
gallowglass (mailed mercenary), 60, 82
Gardiner's Second Relief Act, 80
Gaura, Battle of, 40
Geraldine family, 55, 68, 70
Gilbert, Sir Humphrey, 68
Giraldus Cambrensis, 103; *Conquest of Ireland*, 56-7; *Expugnatio*, 56
Gladstone, William, 125; Land Act (1870), 126
Gogarty, Oliver St John, 183-5, 265; *As I was Going down Sackville Street*, 184; *Collected Poems*, 184; *An Offering of Two Swans*, 184-5; *Start from Somewhere Else*, 184
Goidels (*Feni*, Q-Celts), 3-5, 17, 31
Goldsmith, Oliver, xii, 145, 194, 246, 276; *The Bee and Other Essays*, 98; 'The Deserted Village', 98
Goll mac Morna, 40